THE COMPLETE RHODES AROUND BRITAIN

The Complete Rhodes Around Britain

Published by BBC Worldwide Limited,
Woodlands, 80 Wood Lane,
London W12 0TT

First published 2001
Reprinted 2001, (three times), 2002, 2003
Copyright © Gary Rhodes, 2001
The moral right of the author has
been asserted.

ISBN 0 563 53711 6

All recipes in this book first published in *Rhodes
Around Britain*, *More Rhodes Around Britain*
and *Open Rhodes Around Britain*.

Commisioning Editor: Nicky Copeland
Project Editor: Khadija Manjlai
Copy-editor: Deborah Savage
Art Editor: Lisa Pettibone
Designer: Paul Welti

Set in Helvetica light
Printed and bound in Britain by
Butler & Tanner Ltd, Frome and London
Cover printed by Belmont Press, Northampton

About the author

Gary Rhodes first started cooking at 14 when his mother returned to work. After winning awards as Student and Chef of the Year at college, he worked at the Amsterdam Hilton, the Reform Club, and Capital Hotel in Knightsbridge. At just 26 years old, he was appointed Head Chef at the Castle Hotel in Somerset, where he won a Michelin Star. Three other Michelin Stars have since followed: at The Greenhouse Restaurant in Mayfair, city rhodes near Fleet Street and Rhodes in the Square in Dolphin Square, all in London. Gary also runs two Rhodes & Co. brasseries, in Manchester and Edinburgh.

Three television series and books, *Rhodes Around Britain*, *More Rhodes Around Britain* and *Open Rhodes Around Britain*, appeared in successive years from 1994, confirming his reputation as champion of great British food. He has since written three other books, including his bestseller *New British Classics*.

In addition to the four Michelin Stars, Gary has won other awards and accolades, including the Special Award at the Hotel and Caterer Magazine Awards (the catering industry's equivalent of the Oscars) for his contribution to the British food industry, and he most recently won the Michael Smith Award from the Guild of Food Writers.

In partnership with his hero Sir Alex Ferguson, Gary has lately launched www.toptable.co.uk, an online restaurant booking service, and is currently working on his next television series and book.

He lives in Kent with his wife Jenny and his two boys Samuel and George. His other passions include cars, fashion and music.

Contents

Introduction

Following the success of my first three *Rhodes Around Britain* books, it was almost inevitable that this volume would happen: the range and sheer number of recipes offer the home-cook an easy solution when it comes to choosing good, traditional and inspired food. The recipes have been grouped not only into chapters for each course but also into sections within them to provide you with a selection of recipes for a main ingredient in one go. So, for instance, if you look up the Meat Main Courses chapter, you'll find the recipes for lamb together, or pork, or offal, which makes it easier to select the appropriate one for the occasion.

While this book gives you over 450 recipes to choose from, it has the potential to offer you more than that. I want to break the pattern of strict rules and regulations when it comes to cooking, and I hope you will read this book differently from other cookery books. After all, every recipe has room for movement and improvement. You can follow the recipes, you can change them, use them as guidelines, or follow the alternatives – the point is it's up to you.

If, for instance, you read a recipe and think that it sounds tasty but you haven't got the time to make a fresh custard or fruit *coulis*, don't be put off. Just look at the alternative simple method: use ready-made custard mix with tinned fruits or ready-made preserves, add a dot of fresh cream and you have a delicious ice-cream mix. You might not have an ice-cream machine, but don't let that stop you either. Simply follow the alternative method for churning the mix. And the results? Nothing but the best of course.

While I'd love it if you are able to try some of the traditional methods – it might even surprise you how straightforward they are – I understand that not everyone has as much time to spend in the kitchen as they'd like, which is why I hope you will experiment with the recipes and adapt them to suit your own style.

Supermarkets and grocers nowadays stock a range of exciting ingredients, which can give a new twist to a dish. I'm all for discovering new tastes and flavours but also believe that you first have to learn about the flavour itself before you can think of using it. Soy sauce, for example, has been around for a long time and has a very powerful flavour. I wonder how many times an ingredient like that is misused and the real fullness of a dish is not achieved.

As the great chef Auguste Escoffier once wrote, '*Faites simple*', and what that means is we should avoid unnecessary complication and elaboration. To prove the point, try simplifying a recipe that calls for rather a lot of ingredients down to its barest essentials. You might well find that the dish is more pleasing in its primitive form, and then you'll know that your original recipe was too fanciful. If, on the other hand, the simplified recipe seems to lack flavour, start building it up again. By the end of this process you'll have discovered what is essential to that dish, what are the extras which enhance it and at what point it's spoilt by over-elaboration. You can also use this system to judge an existing recipe rather than following it blindly from a cookery book.

While much of my cookery is British, I have included styles from different cuisines simply because I feel they have become a strong part of British eating. The ones included are simple to prepare and of course very tasty to eat.

Whichever recipes you decide to try out, I hope you enjoy the process – and the results. Happy cooking.

Soups

Tomato Soup

This soup stands up as both a starter or a main course. It has a chunky texture and draws on all the flavours of the ingredients. The real beauty, of course, is how simple it is to make. I always like to serve it with bread croûtons cut from a loaf of crusty or olive bread and then fried or baked in olive oil. Also, fresh Parmesan flakes (done with a potato peeler) sprinkled over the soup are really delicious, but of course all these extras are really up to you. This soup can make a great vegetarian dish – simply leave out the bacon and replace the chicken stock with a vegetable stock.

SERVES 6–8

3 onions, chopped

3 carrots, cut into 5 mm (^{1}/4 in) dice

3 celery sticks, cut into 5 mm (^{1}/4 in) dice

50 ml (2 fl oz) olive oil

25 g (1 oz) unsalted butter

^{1}/2 bunch of fresh basil, chopped

^{1}/2 bunch of tarragon, chopped

1 bay leaf

1 large garlic clove, crushed

6 smoked back bacon rashers, rinded and chopped

900 g (2 lb) ripe tomatoes, preferably plum

600–900 ml (1–1^1/2 pints) Chicken Stock (see p. 399)

Salt and freshly ground white pepper

Tomato purée (optional, to taste)

Sweat the chopped onions, carrots and celery in the olive oil and butter for a few minutes, then add the herbs, bay leaf and garlic and cook for a few more minutes. Add the bacon and continue to cook for about 5 minutes until the vegetables are slightly softened.

Cut the tomatoes into quarters and then cut again into eight pieces. Add them to the vegetables, cover the pan and cook gently for about 15 minutes. The cooking will create its own steam and slowly cook the tomatoes. The mixture must be stirred occasionally, which will help the tomatoes to break down and start to create the soup.

When the tomatoes have softened, start to add the chicken stock, just a ladle at a time, until you have a looser consistency. This brings us to personal choice. The soup can be as thick or as thin as you like. Leave it to cook for a further 20 minutes. Check for seasoning, and you may find that a little tomato purée will help the strength of taste. The soup is now ready to serve.

Chilled Tomato Soup

This is almost like a puréed gazpacho. It's a lovely soup for a hot summer day when you've got the whole family to feed. Just some good bread and this soup will do for lunch. This recipe gives you a good quantity and keeps very well, chilled. If the tomatoes are not quite as ripe as you would like, adding 2 teaspoons of caster sugar to them will add a little sweetness to the flavour.

**MAKES 1.5 litres (2¹/2 pints) to
serve 6–8**
4 tablespoons red wine vinegar
1 garlic clove
150 ml (5 fl oz) olive oil
1 teaspoon caster sugar (optional)
Salt and freshly ground black pepper

FOR THE STOCK
675 g (I¹/2 lb) plum or salad tomatoes,
blanched, skinned and seeded

400 g (14 oz) tinned red pimentos
¹/2 Ogen or Charentais melon, skinned
and seeds removed
¹/2 cucumber, peeled and seeded
10–12 fresh basil leaves
250 ml (8 fl oz) Vegetable Stock
(see p. 400)
100 g (4 oz) good-quality fresh white
breadcrumbs

First blitz the stock ingredients to a purée in a food processor or liquidizer. Now blitz the wine vinegar, garlic, olive oil and sugar, then mix the two together and push through a sieve. The soup is now made and should be checked for seasoning with salt and pepper, before eating and enjoying.

Gazpacho

This is a wonderful summer soup that has so many variations. My version has plenty of flavours and textures. Gazpacho can be served chunky-style or can be blitzed in a liquidizer and served smooth. It is traditionally served with everything raw but, if you want to make a winter Gazpacho, then just cook the ingredients in the olive oil first, then add the tomatoes and the rest of the ingredients to give you a spicy tomato and sweet pepper soup. To make the soup totally vegetarian, and retain the depth of flavour, you could make the Tomato Coulis with vegetable stock and replace the chicken stock with the vegetable version. Alternatively, you could use tomato juice for these two ingredients.

SERVES 4
450 g (1 lb) ripe plum or salad
tomatoes
1 red pepper
2 green peppers
1 yellow pepper
1 cucumber, peeled and seeded
1 garlic clove
1 onion
2 teaspoons tomato purée

2 tablespoons red wine vinegar
75 ml (3 fl oz) olive oil
300ml (10 fl oz) Tomato Coulis
(see p. 375)
300 ml (10 fl oz) Chicken Stock
(see p. 399)
Salt and freshly ground black
pepper
6–8 fresh basil leaves
12–16 fresh tarragon leaves

Remove the eyes from the tomatoes, then plunge them into boiling water for 8–10 seconds. Transfer to cold water and slide off the skins. This is called blanching. Once the tomatoes have been blanched, halve and seed them. Remove the stalks and seeds from the peppers. The tomatoes, peppers, cucumber, garlic and onion can now be minced through a medium cutter, finely diced or blitzed in a liquidizer until almost puréed.

Mix together the tomato purée and red wine vinegar. Whisk the olive oil slowly into the purée. Now add three-quarters of the tomato coulis and chicken stock. Stir in the minced ingredients and check the seasoning with salt and pepper. Lightly cut the basil and tarragon leaves and add them to the soup.

The soup can be as thick or thin as you wish. If you want to make it thinner, then add the remaining tomato coulis and stock.

VARIATIONS

A slice of white bread can be blitzed with the vegetables to give a thicker texture.

The flavour of the soup can be made hotter and more spicy by adding a few drops of Tabasco or Worcestershire sauce or even both.

Cream of Onion Soup

This is a very simple soup to make, using just a few basic ingredients. It's delicious served with thick slices of toasted French stick, finished with melting Cheddar or Parmesan. I like to serve it with Parmesan croûtons. Make these by slicing the crusts off a loaf of bread – any type you like: white, wholemeal, olive or anything else – and cutting it into 1cm ($^1/_2$in) dice. Cook the bread in a roasting pan with just enough olive oil to cover the pan in a pre-heated oven at 200°C/400°F/gas 6. As the croûtons are heating they will become golden and crispy. Every 1–2 minutes, turn the bread croûtons over to give an all-round colour. Once the croûtons are totally golden and hot they can be sprinkled with finely grated Parmesan and mixed to give an overall cheesy taste. A small loaf makes a good quantity of croûtons, but you can freeze them, so they are to hand whenever you need them.

SERVES 4
50 g (2 oz) unsalted butter
675 g (1$^1/_2$lb) onions, diced
2–3 celery sticks, diced
1 small potato, diced (optional)
1 leek (white only), diced

1 small garlic clove, chopped
900 ml (1$^1/_2$ pints) Chicken Stock
(see p. 399) or Vegetable Stock
(see p. 400)
2 tablespoons double cream or milk
(optional)

Melt the butter in a pan. When the butter begins to bubble, add all the vegetables and cook for 8–10 minutes over a medium heat without colouring. Add the stock and bring to a simmer. Continue to cook for 20–30 minutes. The soup can now be blitzed in a liquidizer until totally puréed, then pushed through a sieve. If the soup is very thick, thin it with a little extra stock.

As an added extra, stir in the double cream or milk to help the consistency and make a good cream of onion soup.

Green Lentil Soup

This soup is a good cold winter dish. I personally like to eat it any time of the year but, on a cold winter evening, a large bowl of this soup served with plenty of crusty bread in front of the fire (are you getting hungry?) is absolutely delicious. I also like to add some smoked bacon to this soup to lift the flavour and almost make it a main course dish. It can, of course, be a vegetarian soup by simply omitting the bacon and replacing the chicken stock with vegetable stock.

SERVES 4

25 g unsalted butter
1 tablespoon olive or vegetable oil
2 large carrots, diced
2 onions, diced
2 celery sticks, diced
4 smoked streaky bacon rashers, cut
   into strips

175 g (6 oz) green dried lentils
900 ml–1.2 litres (1 1/2–2 pints) Chicken
   Stock (see p. 399) or Vegetable
   Stock (see p. 400)
Salt and freshly ground black pepper
150 ml (5 fl oz) milk or double cream
   (optional)

Melt the butter with the oil. When the butter begins to bubble, add the diced vegetables and bacon and cook for 2–3 minutes without colouring. Add the lentils and continue to cook for a few minutes. Add 900 ml (1 1/2 pints) of the stock and bring to a simmer. The soup can now be left to cook slowly, just ticking over for 45–60 minutes.

The lentils must be cooked all the way through, becoming tender and thickening the soup. If the soup is a little too thick, slowly add the remaining stock. This is now a lentil broth.

To help the lentils become more evenly spread through the soup, blitz gently with a hand blender or in a liquidizer to give a thick broth consistency with the bacon and vegetables not totally broken. Alternatively, the soup can be totally blended to a purée, in which case you'll need a lot more stock. Season to taste.

To finish either of the soups, you can add the milk or double cream to give a slightly creamy texture.

Six Oyster and Leek Soup

Oyster soup is a lovely way to eat oysters. Each portion of the soup is finished by adding six fresh oysters and all their juices. I normally make the soup with an oyster fish stock. This is made by adding some defrosted frozen oysters (12 oysters to 600 ml /1 pint of stock) to a home-made or ready-made basic fish stock to give a good oyster taste. After the stock has been made, the remaining ingredients for the soup are very simple: shallots, leeks and, of course, fresh oysters. An added bonus is that with stock to hand you can make this soup very quickly.

MAKES 1.2 litres (2 pints) to serve 4
2 teaspoons olive oil
50 g (2 oz) unsalted butter
4 large shallots or 2 onions,
    sliced
1–2 glasses of Champagne or sparkling
    wine, about 150–300 ml (5–10 fl oz)
    (optional)

900 ml (1½ pints) Fish Stock
    (see p. 399) or oyster stock
    (see recipe introduction)
2 leeks, thinly sliced
24 fresh oysters, opened and kept in
    oyster juices
1 teaspoon chopped fresh tarragon
Salt and freshly ground black pepper

Warm the olive oil and 15 g (½ oz) of the butter in a pan, add the sliced shallots or onions and cook without colouring until they begin to soften. It's also good to add 1 or 2 glasses of Champagne as an extra and then boil to reduce until almost dry. We all know how well oysters and Champagne taste together. Add the stock and bring to a simmer. The soup only needs to simmer for 10 minutes before being ready to finish.

To finish, bring the soup to the boil and add the sliced leeks. The leeks will only take 1–2 minutes to become tender. The remaining butter can now be added and stirred in. Add the chopped tarragon and the fresh oysters with any remaining juices. Check for seasoning with salt and pepper and the soup is ready. Once the soup is complete and the oysters have been added, do not re-boil as this will overcook them. The soup should only be brought back to soft simmer, then removed from the heat.

To serve, divide the oysters into bowls, then finish with the remaining soup and garnish.

HOW TO OPEN OYSTERS

Keep the fresh oysters chilled until you are ready to finish the soup. Protect your hand with a cloth and lay the oyster, rounded-side down, in your hand, so that you catch the juices as you open it. Insert an oyster knife between the shells near the hinge and lever the shells apart. Pour any juices into a bowl through a fine sieve and add to the soup as described above. Gently loosen the oyster from the bottom shell with a sharp knife. It is now ready to use.

Mulligatawny Soup

This is a wonderful winter soup. When it's freezing cold outside, just sit and eat a bowl of this to warm you through and through. This recipe has two varieties: chicken or vegetarian. Both work equally well.

The list of ingredients does look a bit daunting, but all these flavours work and give you a very tasty soup. However, not all are essential, in particular the soy, teriyaki and Worcestershire sauces. These are flavours that I have added that I've found help release other tastes. The soup can be garnished with plain boiled rice and, if it's not vegetarian, poached strips of chicken just before serving. Plenty of choice and even more taste.

MAKES 1.2 litres (2 pints) to serve 4–6

A knob of unsalted butter

1 potato, cut into 1 cm ($1/2$ in) dice

1 large carrot, cut into 1 cm ($1/2$ in) dice

1 large onion, cut into 1 cm ($1/2$ in) dice

1 leek, cut into 1 cm ($1/2$ in) dice

2 celery sticks, cut into 1 cm ($1/2$ in) dice

1 garlic clove, crushed

1 teaspoon crushed fresh ginger root

$1/2$ teaspoon chopped fresh thyme

1 teaspoon ground turmeric

1 teaspoon cayenne pepper

1 teaspoon paprika

$1/4$ teaspoon chopped dried chillies

$1/4$ teaspoon cumin seeds

1 star anise

1 bay leaf

$1/2$ teaspoon ground mixed spice

2 tomatoes, quartered

3 tablespoons soy sauce (optional)

3 tablespoons teriyaki sauce (optional)

1 tablespoon Worcestershire sauce (optional)

1.2 litres (2 pints) Chicken Stock (see p. 399) or Vegetable Stock (see p. 400)

Salt

Melt the butter in a pan, stir in the chopped vegetables, then add all the other ingredients except the stock. Stir and cook over a moderate heat for a few minutes. Cover with a lid and allow the vegetables to soften, stirring occasionally. Add the stock and bring to a simmer. The soup should now cook for 45 minutes.

Once cooked, blitz in a food processor or liquidizer, then push through a sieve. This will give you a good, thick, curried soup. Season with salt, if necessary.

VARIATIONS

Another flavour that can be added is a squeeze of fresh lemon juice, which enhances all the tastes. Or, if you would like it slightly sweeter, then add a tablespoon of honey. Chopped apple can also be cooked in the soup, for a fruity taste.

Mussel and Macaroni Soup

This soup is very wholesome, and I like to eat it as a supper dish with toasted French bread in the bowl – this soaks up all the juices and is lovely to eat.

SERVES 4

FOR THE MUSSELS

450 g (1 lb) fresh mussels

225 g (8 oz) mixed vegetables (carrot, onion, celery and leek), cut into 5 mm ($1/4$ in) dice

1 sprig of fresh thyme

1 bay leaf

6 black peppercorns

1 star anise (optional)

50 g (2 oz) unsalted butter

300 ml (10 fl oz) dry white wine

1.2 litres (2 pints) Fish Stock (see p. 399)

FOR THE SOUP

2 carrots, cut into 5 mm ($1/4$ in) dice

2 onions, cut into 5 mm ($1/4$ in) dice

4 celery sticks, cut into 5 mm ($1/4$ in) dice

1 garlic clove, crushed

50 ml (2 fl oz) olive oil

100 g (4 oz) unsalted butter

1 bouquet garni (1 bay leaf, 1 star
anise, a few fresh basil leaves,
1 sprig each of fresh thyme and
tarragon, tied in a square of muslin)
or bouquet garni sachet
300 ml (10 fl oz) dry white wine
100 g (4 oz) dried or fresh macaroni,
cooked

6 tomatoes, skinned, seeded and
diced
1¹/2 tablespoons Pesto Sauce
(see p. 374)
A few knobs of unsalted butter
Salt and freshly ground white
pepper

Scrape and wash the mussels well. Remove the beards (the threads that hang out of the shells). Discard any mussels that gape and do not close when tapped sharply with a knife.

To cook the mussels, sweat all the diced vegetables, herbs and spices in the butter for a few minutes, then add the white wine and boil to reduce until almost dry. Add the fish stock, bring to the simmer and cook for 10 minutes. Bring the liquor back to the boil and add the mussels. Cover with a lid and shake carefully. The mussels will start to open after a few minutes. Drain the mussels and pass the stock through a fine sieve. Discard the vegetables and spices. Remove the mussels from their shells and keep them moist in a little of the stock. Discard any that have remained closed.

To make the soup, sweat the diced vegetables and garlic in the olive oil and butter for a few minutes. Add the bouquet garni and continue to cook for about 4–5 minutes until the vegetables have softened. Add the white wine and boil to reduce until almost dry. Pour in the mussel stock and simmer for 15–20 minutes.

To finish the soup, add the cooked macaroni, tomatoes and shelled mussels. Stir in the pesto sauce and a few knobs of butter, remove the bouquet garni and taste for seasoning before serving.

Mussel Chowder

Chowder is an old dish that was (and still is) a complete meal made with mussels, onions, potatoes and pork all cooked together. It was originally made with cider or white wine but, over the years, milk and/or cream were added instead. This recipe has two stages: the first one tells you how to cook the mussels and the second is for the finished soup. Mussels, of course, can be bought already cooked. The vegetables and white wine are optional extras which will give more flavour to the stock; you can just cook the mussels in the hot fish stock. If you are just using water, increase the quantity of mussels to 675 g (1¹/2 lb).

SERVES 4

FOR THE MUSSELS
1 carrot, roughly chopped
1 onion, roughly chopped

1 celery stick, roughly chopped
¹/2 leek, roughly chopped
1 bay leaf
25 g (1 oz) unsalted butter

1 glass white wine

750 ml (1¼ pints) Fish Stock (see
    p. 399) or water

450 g (1 lb) fresh mussels, washed and
    bearded (see p. 17)

FOR THE CHOWDER

50 g (2 oz) butter

4–6 rashers streaky bacon, cut into
    2.5 cm (1 in) pieces

2 large potatoes, cut into 2 cm (³/₄ in)
    dice

3–4 large onions, cut into 2 cm (³/₄ in)
    dice

2 celery sticks, cut into 2 cm (³/₄ in)
    dice

600 ml (1 pint) mussel stock, Fish
    Stock (see p. 399) or water

300 ml (10 fl oz) hot milk

150 ml (5 fl oz) single cream

Salt and freshly ground black
    pepper

To cook the mussels, cook the vegetables with the bay leaf in a little butter without colour until just beginning to soften. Add the white wine and boil to reduce until almost dry. Add the stock and bring the liquor to the boil. Add the mussels to the boiling cooking liquor and cook for a few minutes until the shells open. Discard any that do not open. Drain the mussels, reserving the strained cooking liquor.

Melt the butter in a hot pan and add the streaky bacon pieces immediately. The pan must be kept hot to fry the bacon, allowing it to become golden; this will bring out the flavour of the bacon. There may be some bacon residue sticking to the base of the pan. Don't worry about this; it will give a good flavour to the soup. Once the bacon is coloured, add the diced potatoes, onions and celery and cook, without colouring, for a few minutes, reducing the heat under the pan. Add the mussel or fish stock or water and bring to the simmer. Continue to simmer for about 20 minutes or until the potato is cooked but not breaking too much. The stock will have reduced a little, increasing the flavour. Add the hot milk and single cream and bring back to the simmer. Check the seasoning and add salt and pepper if necessary. Add the mussels and warm for 1–2 minutes before serving.

Red Mullet Soup

I love all fish soups but I find red mullet gives the best taste. For this soup, fresh or frozen red mullet fillets can be used. Garlic toasts with Rouille (see p. 378) are a delicious accompaniment. Cut a French stick into 1 cm (¹/₂ in) slices and spread with some garlic butter (simply mix crushed garlic to taste into softened butter). Toast the slices then top with Rouille.

SERVES 8–10

225 g (8 oz) tomatoes, chopped

1 fennel bulb, chopped

1 large onion, chopped

2 carrots, chopped

1 leek, chopped

2 celery sticks, chopped

1 garlic clove, crushed

¹/₂ bunch of fresh basil

¹/₂ bunch of fresh tarragon

A pinch of saffron

25 ml (1 fl oz) olive oil

50 g (2 oz) unsalted butter
450 g (1 lb) red mullet fillets, scaled
  and sliced into pieces
300 ml (10 fl oz) Noilly Prat or dry white
  vermouth

300 ml (10 fl oz) dry white wine
1.2 litres (2 pints) Fish Stock
  (see p. 399)
2 teaspoons tomato purée
Salt and freshly ground white pepper

Sweat all the chopped vegetables, garlic, herbs and saffron in the olive oil and butter for a few minutes. Add the red mullet fillets, the Noilly Prat and white wine and allow to cook and reduce for 5–6 minutes. Pour on the fish stock and tomato purée. Bring the soup to the simmer and cook for 40 minutes.

Purée the soup in a food processor or liquidizer and push through a sieve. Season with salt and pepper. The soup should be a rich, orangey-red colour with a powerful depth of flavour and eats beautifully with the Rouille toasts.

Red Mullet Broth

This soup has a bisque-like consistency, in contrast to the thick, puréed broth in Red Mullet Soup (see p. 18). This one has a totally different taste and texture. It's just a question of making a good stock and then garnishing it. I've also included, as an optional extra, some slices of crispy Bayonne or Parma ham. I like the edge they give the dish. A good quality streaky or back bacon can also be crisped and served for a bit of extra taste.

MAKES 1.2 litres (2 pints) to serve 4

FOR THE STOCK
350 g (12 oz) red mullet, fresh or frozen
I onion, cut into rough 1 cm (1/2 in) dice
I carrot, cut into rough 1 cm (1/2 in)
  dice
1 leek, cut into rough 1 cm (1/2 in) dice
2–3 celery sticks, cut into rough 1 cm
  (1/2 in) dice
1 fennel bulb, cut into rough 1 cm
  (1/2 in) dice
1 garlic clove, crushed
1/2 bunch of fresh tarragon or a few
  dried tarragon leaves
A pinch of saffron (optional)
1 star anise (optional)
A knob of unsalted butter
4 tomatoes, quartered
2 glasses of white wine, about 300 ml
  (10 fl oz)
1.2 litres (2 pints) Fish Stock

(see p. 399) or water with extra
  100 g (4 oz) of red mullet to improve
  the finished taste

FOR THE FISH AND SOUP
4 small red mullet fillets (1 per portion)
1 tablespoon olive oil
I large carrot, cut into 5 mm (1/4 in)
  dice
I large onion, cut into 5 mm (1/4 in) dice
2 celery sticks, cut into 5 mm (1/4 in)
  dice
1 small fennel, cut into 5 mm (1/4 in)
  dice (optional)
Red mullet stock from above
Salt and freshly ground black pepper
12–16 × 1 cm (1/2 in) strips of Bayonne
  or Parma ham
2 tomatoes, skinned and diced
25 g (1 oz) unsalted butter
A few fresh tarragon leaves,
  chopped

To make the stock, cook the vegetables with the garlic, herbs, saffron and star anise, if using, in the knob of butter for a few minutes, until beginning to soften. Add the tomatoes and continue to cook for another 2–3 minutes. If you are using water rather than fish stock, add the additional fish as well. Now add the white wine, bring to the boil and leave to reduce by three-quarters. Add the fish stock or water and bring to a simmer. This can now be cooked for 20–30 minutes, allowing the stock to reduce a little as it cooks to increase the flavour. The stock can now be strained through a sieve. You will have a loose red mullet stock ready to make into soup.

Pre-heat the grill.

To make the soup, warm the olive oil in a pan and add the diced vegetables. Cook without colouring for 6–8 minutes until softened. Add the red mullet stock, bring to a simmer and cook for 10 minutes. While the soup is cooking, butter a tray and sit the seasoned red mullet fillets on top. These can now be cooked under the grill and will only take between 3– 4 minutes. Grill the Bayonne or Parma ham until golden and crispy.

Add the tomato dice and butter to the soup and season with salt and pepper. Add the tarragon. The soup can now be served in soup plates with a grilled red mullet fillet sitting on top. The broth is now ready to eat and enjoy.

VARIATION

If you are including bacon or ham, you can use sage leaves instead of tarragon. Then it's best to flour them lightly and fry in a deep-fat fryer at 180°C/350°F or in hot oil at least 1 cm (1/2 in) deep, for I–2 minutes until crispy.

Lobster Bisque

Lobster bisque is regarded as the king of all soups and I don't think I can or want to argue with that. It is so rich in flavour and texture that it is really worth every effort in making it. If you make this quantity, you can freeze what you don't need.

Like all recipes, other flavours can be used. Crab, prawns or shrimp will all give you a full flavour. I use the same recipe to make a crab bisque to go with Crab Risotto (see p. 59)

This recipe also holds lots of little extras – saffron, brandy, fennel – which all help to make this a better soup but can be left out for a basic bisque.

MAKES about 2.25 litres (4 pints)
1 × 450 g (1 lb) lobster
1.75–2.25 litres (3–4 pints) Fish Stock
  (see p. 399)
50–75 g (2–3 oz) unsalted butter
1 tablespoon olive oil
2 large carrots, diced

4 shallots or 2 large onions, diced
2 celery sticks, diced
1 leek, diced
1 fennel bulb, diced
1 garlic clove, crushed
A few fresh basil leaves
A few fresh tarragon leaves

A pinch of saffron

6 ripe tomatoes, quartered

50 ml (2 fl oz) brandy

1/2 bottle of white wine

50 g (2 oz) long-grain rice

Salt and freshly ground black pepper

A pinch of cayenne pepper

150 ml (5 fl oz) single cream (optional)

A few drops of lemon juice or brandy

(optional)

If you are using a live lobster, bring the fish stock to the boil and drop in the lobster. Cook for about 5–6 minutes, then remove from the heat. The best way now is to leave the lobster in the stock until completely cooled. This will help flavour the stock and keep the lobster meat moist. If you are going to remove the lobster from the stock immediately, cook for 6–8 minutes, remove the lobster from the pan, then allow it to cool slightly before breaking the shell. Make sure you keep the cooking liquor to use in the soup.

Break off the claws and crack them with the back of a heavy knife to remove the lobster meat. Split the body and tail through the middle lengthways and remove the tail meat. Reserve the meat to garnish the soup. The lobster shells are used to flavour the soup itself. I prefer to crack the lobsters down (with a rolling pin) in a large saucepan as finely as possible, making sure I get the maximum taste. It's also possible just to break the shells down without finely crushing them.

Melt the butter with the olive oil. Add the roughly chopped carrots, shallots or onions, celery, leek and fennel with the crushed garlic, basil and tarragon leaves. Add the pinch of saffron and the tomatoes and cook for a few minutes. Add the crushed lobster shells and cook for a further few minutes. Add the brandy and boil to reduce until almost dry. Add the white wine and continue to reduce. Add 1.75 litres (3 pints) of stock, bring to the simmer and continue to simmer for 20 minutes.

Add the rice and bring back to the simmer for 20–25 minutes. The rice should cook until overcooked to create a starch and thicken the soup. Check the soup for seasoning with salt, pepper and a pinch of cayenne pepper. The bisque can now be blitzed in a liquidizer, with the lobster shells, to cream the soup, then pushed through a fine sieve. You now have a good, rich lobster bisque. The soup should be reasonably thick, well coating the back of a spoon. If it's very thick, add some more stock until you have the right consistency.

Always when making soups taste for seasoning once finished. Add the cream, and a few drops of lemon juice or extra brandy will always lift the taste.

VARIATION

This recipe works well with prawns or shrimps. If you want to make a shrimp bisque, use either 450 g (1 lb) of good quality shrimps or 450 g (1 lb) of shrimp shells. The same applies to prawns.

Crab Bisque

Try this with my Crab Dumplings (see p. 58) – the flavours obviously work so well together, it's delicious. This soup, which also works as a sauce, can take on some garnishes: perhaps add some chopped tomatoes, leeks and basil to finish it or even the whitemeat from the crab? You can also keep the white meat for a good crab salad.

MAKES 900 ml (1 1/2 pints) to serve 4

1 cooked crab shell, broken into small pieces

2 tablespoons cooking oil

1 medium carrot, cut into 1 cm (1/2 in) dice

1 onion, cut into 1 cm (1/2 in) dice

1/2 leek, cut into 1 cm (1/2 in) dice

1–2 celery sticks, cut into 1 cm (1/2 in) dice

1 garlic clove, crushed

1 small fennel bulb, chopped, or 1 star anise (optional)

A few fresh tarragon leaves

A few strands of saffron (optional)

4–6 tomatoes, quartered

1 glass of brandy, about 50 ml (2 fl oz)

1 glass of dry white wine, about 150 ml (5 fl oz)

2 teaspoons tomato purée

900 ml (1 1/2 pints) Fish Stock (see p. 399), crab cooking liquor or water

40 g (1 1/2 oz) unsalted butter (optional)

Heat the oil in a large pan and add the chopped vegetables, garlic, fennel or star anise, tarragon and saffron. Add the crab shell, cover with a lid and cook for 10–15 minutes to soften the vegetables. Add the tomatoes and continue to cook for a further 5–6 minutes. Add the brandy and boil to reduce by two-thirds, then add the white wine and boil to reduce by two-thirds again. Add the tomato purée and stock and bring to a simmer. Leave to simmer gently for 30 minutes. Blitz the soup in a food processor or liquidizer, then push through a sieve to give a thicker consistency. The bisque will now be packed with crab flavour. If it's too thick, then simply loosen with more stock or water.

NOTE

The crab cooking liquor listed in the ingredients can be made simply by cooking the crab shells in fish stock or water first. This will give you a good crab stock, maximizing the taste. The bisque can be used as a sauce, which eats very well if finished with a dot of cream and a squeeze of lemon.

Cabbage Soup with Dumplings

Good food does not have to be made with fancy, unusual ingredients. Everyday produce will cook easily and taste just as delicious. This recipe is easy to prepare, simple to cook and cheap to make – and it can be served as a starter or a complete meal. The dish itself came together purely by accident. I was braising some cabbage for one dish and making dumplings for a beef stew. The cabbage and dumplings became an instant success, as it has plenty of textures, tastes and flavours from just a few ingredients.

Both the cabbage soup and dumpling recipes are very basic and can, of course, be varied – a little garlic in the soup, or different herbs and spices in the dumplings. Even the Spinach Dumplings on page 209 could be rolled smaller and used as a garnish.

SERVES 4–6

1 Savoy cabbage, finely shredded

50 g (2 oz) unsalted butter

1.2 litres (2 pints) Chicken Stock (see p. 399) or Vegetable Stock (see p. 400)

2 onions, finely shredded

6 smoked bacon rashers, rinded and cut into thin strips

Salt and freshly ground white pepper

FOR THE DUMPLINGS

225 g (8 oz) plain flour

15 g (1/2 oz) baking powder

100 g (4 oz) dried shredded suet

1/2 teaspoon chopped fresh thyme

1 teaspoon chopped fresh basil

About 50 ml (5 fl oz) water

450 ml (15 fl oz) Chicken Stock (see p. 399) or Vegetable Stock (see p. 400), warmed

If you intend to bake the dumplings (see below), pre-heat the oven to 200°C/400°F/gas 6.

To make the dumplings, mix together the flour, baking powder, suet and herbs and season with salt and pepper. Gradually add just enough water until the mixture forms a dough. Leave to rest for 20 minutes then roll into 2 cm (3/4 in) balls. These can be placed in the warm stock and either cooked in the pre-heated oven or on top of the stove, allowing them to bake or simmer slowly for about 20 minutes.

While the dumplings are cooking, cook the cabbage. Place the butter in a warm pan, add the onions and cook for 5 minutes without allowing them to colour. Add the bacon and cook for a further 5 minutes. Pour in the stock, bring to the simmer and simmer for 5–10 minutes. Bring to the boil, add the cabbage and simmer for about 4–5 minutes until tender. Check the seasoning and add the dumplings. The dish is now complete.

Ham and Vegetable Soup

To achieve the maximum taste from this soup it is best to buy some fresh ham or bacon, to soak it in cold water for 24 hours to remove any saltiness, and then cook it in some stock. This will create a good ham stock, and you can make a vegetable broth and I would suggest you add some diced smoked ham to give a more pronounced flavour. Anyway, here is my recipe for the original idea.

The soup can be served as a starter, main course or a supper dish. It looks lovely in a bowl with all the colours and tastes there. You can make it with your own favourite vegetables and serve it with garlic toasts and Parmesan, fried croûtons or just good old-fashioned bread and butter.

SERVES 8 as a starter,
4–6 as a supper or main course

FOR THE HAM OR BACON
900 g raw bacon or ham collar, soaked
   in cold water for 24 hours
1 onion
2 carrots
1 leek
2 celery sticks
25 g (1 oz) unsalted butter
1 sprig of fresh thyme
1 bay leaf
2.25 litres (4 pints) Chicken Stock
   (see p. 399) or water

FOR THE SOUP
450 g (1 lb) carrots
2 onions
6 celery sticks
450 g (1 lb) swede
450 g (1 lb) parsnips
100 g (4 oz) unsalted butter
50 ml (2 fl oz) olive oil
1 large garlic clove, crushed
50 g (2 oz) pearl barley (optional)
Salt and freshly ground white pepper

To cook the ham or bacon, roughly chop all the vegetables into 1 cm (1/2 in) dice and cook in the butter for about 5 minutes without allowing them to colour. Add the herbs, cover and continue to cook until slightly softened. Keeping a lid on the vegetables will create steam within the pan; this prevents them from colouring and cooks them at the same time.

Pour on the chicken stock and bring to the simmer. Add the bacon or ham and bring back to the simmer. Cover the pan and cook for about 45 minutes. Leave the meat to stand in its own cooking liquor until cold. This part of the job can be done the day before or in the morning. It keeps the meat moist and helps the stock take on the maximum taste.

Remove the bacon or ham from the stock and cut it into 1 cm (1/2 in) cubes. Strain the stock through a sieve.

To prepare the soup, roughly chop all the vegetables into 1 cm (1/2 in) dice, keeping the swede and parsnip separate from the others. Melt the butter in a large pan with the olive oil. Add the carrots, onions, celery and garlic, cover and cook for 2–3 minutes. Add the pearl barley, if using, and cook for a further 2–3 minutes, stirring from time to time. Pour on the reserved stock and bring to the simmer. Allow the soup to simmer gently until the diced carrots are softened, about 20 minutes.

Add the diced swede and parsnips and continue to cook for a further 10 minutes until all the vegetables are cooked. Add the diced bacon or ham and season with salt and pepper.

Starters and Light Meals

Potato and Parsnip Crisps

We all like crisps with lots of different flavours (although some of them I'm not so sure about), but you can't beat home-made salted crisps with no other tastes to spoil. If you're having a dinner party and want something to go with pre-dinner drinks, then try these. The parsnip crisps are brilliant, just deep-fried slices of parsnip, as easy as that. They eat well dipped in Cranberry Sauce with Orange (p. 371).

SERVES 4
2 large potatoes, peeled
2–3 large parsnips, peeled
Oil, for deep-frying
Salt

Pre-heat a deep-fat frying pan to 180°C/350°F.

Shape the potatoes into neat cylinders, then slice them very, very thinly. Dry the slices on a cloth and fry a handful at a time until crisp and golden all the way through. Lift out and shake off any excess oil, sprinkle with salt and serve. The crisps will stay fresh and crisp for a few hours, or longer if kept in a sealed container. Always make sure you eat them within 24 hours.

For the parsnips, just slice very thinly lengthways and cook as for the potato crisps until golden all the way through. Lightly salt and serve.

Grilled Aubergines with Tomatoes and Cheddar

This dish is very good as a starter, or it can be served with a salad for a vegetarian main course.

SERVES 4
2 aubergines
300 ml (10 fl oz) Tomato Coulis
  (see p. 375)
A few drops of Spicing Essence
  (see p. 371)
Salt and freshly ground white pepper
2 onions, finely chopped

1 garlic clove, crushed
10 fresh basil leaves, chopped
2 tablespoons olive oil
25 g (1 oz) unsalted butter
150 ml (5 fl oz) dry white wine
4 tomatoes, skinned, seeded and
  diced
175 g (6 oz) Cheddar, thinly sliced

Slice the aubergines into 5 mm (1/4 in) rounds, allowing three to four per portion. Lightly salt the slices and place in a colander for about 30 minutes to drain out all the bitterness. Pat dry.

Heat the tomato coulis gently and add a few drops of the spicing essence to give the coulis a slightly spicy taste. Season with salt and pepper.

Sweat the chopped onions, garlic and basil in the olive oil and butter for a few minutes, then add the white wine and boil to reduce until almost dry. Add the spiced tomato coulis and simmer for 15 minutes.

Pre-heat the grill. Grill the aubergines for 5 minutes each side (or they can be pan-fried in some extra butter). Lay the grilled or fried aubergines slices on flame-proof plates. Add the diced tomato to the coulis and spoon it on to each portion of aubergines. Cover the sauce with the Cheddar and brown quickly under the grill.

Chick Pea Patties

Chickpeas are a dried pulse that, once soaked to become tender, are eaten raw or cooked. They are used in many national dishes: falafel from Israel and hummus from the Middle East are two classics.

This recipe is similar to a falafel. It's basically seasoned and flavoured minced chick peas that are then rolled or moulded before being deep-fried until golden and crispy. Chick peas are also often part of couscous dishes, so to go with this dish I am serving a parsley couscous relish.

Couscous is made from fine semolina that has been rolled in flour. Most couscous available in Britain has previously been cooked, so when soaked or warmed becomes immediately edible. Couscous originally comes from northern Africa and contains the same ingredients as most pastas: semolina and flour.

The chick peas will need to be soaked for a minimum eight hours so it's best to soak them the day before; 24 hours soaking will guarantee a tender finish. It's also important to make sure they are not too old, preferably no more than 12 months. This dish needs to be eaten immediately, so simply fry and serve. These eat very well on their own with just a squeeze of lime. But to eat them at their best serve them with the couscous relish.

MAKES 16 patties
450 g (1 lb) chick peas, soaked for
    24 hours
6 spring onions
1/4 bunch of fresh flatleaf parsley,
    including stalks
1 garlic clove
1–2 red chillies, seeded and very finely
    chopped

A bunch of fresh coriander
40 g (1 1/2 oz) fresh root ginger
Salt and freshly ground black pepper
Oil for deep-frying

FOR THE PARSLEY AND
COUSCOUS RELISH
2 tablespoons couscous, soaked
    overnight

1 bunch of fresh flatleaf parsley, finely shredded

2 plum or salad tomatoes, skinned, seeded and diced

4 spring onions, finely diced

Juice of 1 lemon or lime

6 fresh mint leaves, chopped

4–6 tablespoons olive oil

Once the chick peas have been soaked, rinse and strain off. Now it's time to mince the chick peas with all the other ingredients through a fine mincer. Check for seasoning with salt and pepper. Shape the patties between 2 tablespoons.

To make the relish, mix together all the ingredients and season with salt and pepper, adding enough olive oil to give a moist consistency. You will have about 300 ml (10 fl oz).

When ready to fry, the temperature of the oil should be about 150°C/300°F. The patties will take between 4–6 minutes to deep-fry and become golden brown.

To serve the complete dish, spoon some of the relish on to plates, making a flat disc in the centre. Now simply sit the patties on top.

Stuffed Mushrooms

Stuffed mushrooms can be made so many different ways, with a range of fillings, toppings and textures. They work very well as vegetarian starters or main courses, or you can use prawns, mussels, bacon or other fish or meat ingredients. Rather than give you a basic recipe, I thought I would just share a few ideas.

I like to use large, flat mushrooms which have a good meaty texture and taste. It's best to half-cook them before adding any filling. They can then be stuffed, topped and baked. I always half-cook the mushrooms on a seasoned and buttered tray under the grill, with a trickle of olive oil.

My favourite filling is cooked spinach. You can flavour this with garlic, leeks or even crispy smoked bacon pieces, then top the spinach with either a herb crust (see p. 188) or thick slices of grated Cheddar or Gruyère. Bake the mushrooms in a pre-heated oven at 200°C/400°F/gas 6, then finish under the grill. These eat very well as a starter.

Other good fillings are a small, diced ratatouille finished with Parmesan or Stilton and spinach or just Stilton and breadcrumbs, leeks with mustard and Cheddar, or sliced tomatoes topped with Welsh Rarebit mix (see p. 40).

Red Pepper and Anchovy Salad

The only way to serve this is to use the marinated and oiled anchovy fillets. These can be obtained from a delicatessen, usually sold loose over the counter. If the only ones available are tinned, then it would be best just to serve a red pepper salad. Serve with Spanish Omelette (see p. 36).

SERVES 4–6
2 red peppers
12 anchovy fillets (not tinned)
2–3 tablespoons Vierge Dressing (see p. 380)

Pre-heat the grill to hot. Put the whole red pepper under the hot grill and wait until the skin begins to colour and bubble. Turn the pepper until this has happened all round. While the peppers are still warm, peel off all the skin and leave to cool. When cold, halve the peppers and remove all the seeds. Cut the peppers into thin strips and cover with vierge dressing. It is now best to leave them for 1–2 hours to marinate.

Just before serving, split the anchovy fillets in half lengthways and mix them with the peppers.

Caesar Salad

This salad was a great invention. Caesar Cardini, from Caesar's Palace in Los Angeles, found himself with some unexpected dinner guests and quickly came up with this dish. I'm not sure if this is the absolute original. I think plenty has been added and taken away, but it always stays similar and very tasty.

You'll notice that the egg should only be boiled for $1^1/2$ minutes. This helps the binding of the dressing without the whites being totally raw. If you are still worried about this, then simply use the yolk from one or two hard-boiled eggs; the dressing will still work. Tabasco sauce is very hot and strong, so a dash must literally be just one or two drops. Marinated anchovy fillets are bought soaked in a vinegar liquor, making them packed with flavour and taste.

SERVES 4
FOR THE SALAD
6 little gem or 2 cos lettuces
12 marinated or 8 tinned anchovy fillets. drained

4 thick slices of wholemeal bread
Olive oil
25 g (1 oz) Parmesan, grated
50 g (2 oz) Parmesan flakes

FOR THE DRESSING
15 g ($^{1}/_{2}$ oz) anchovy fillets, drained and
   chopped
2 teaspoons capers
2 teaspoons Worcestershire sauce
$^{1}/_{2}$ teaspoon Dijon mustard
A dash of Tabasco sauce

Juice of $^{1}/_{2}$ lemon
$^{1}/_{2}$ garlic clove, crushed
2 tablespoons finely grated Parmesan
1 egg, boiled for 1$^{1}/_{2}$ minutes only
150–300 ml (5–10 fl oz) extra-virgin
   olive oil
Freshly ground black pepper

Break down the lettuces into separate leaves. Split the anchovy fillets into strips. Remove the crusts from the bread and cut into 1 cm ($^{1}/_{2}$ in) squares. These can be shallow-fried, toasted or (and this is what I do) sprinkled with olive oil and baked in a pre-heated oven at 200°C/400°F/gas 6. Keep turning them every minute or so until golden brown and crunchy. Cooking them this way prevents them from becoming soaked in oil. While still hot, toss in the grated Parmesan.

The quickest way to make the dressing is to place all the ingredients in a blender, using just 150 ml (5 fl oz) of oil to start with, and blitz until thick and creamy. Check for seasoning. Be careful of using any salt in this dressing because of the high salt content of the anchovies. The dressing can be pushed through a sieve or left rustic, which will give you more texture. If necessary, you can add more oil a little at a time. The consistency should be thick and emulsified, coating the back of a spoon.

To assemble the salad, toss the lettuce leaves in the dressing, making sure they are all coated. Add the anchovies, croûtons and half of the Parmesan flakes and divide between the salad bowls. Sprinkle with the remaining Parmesan and serve.

Niçoise Salad

This country-style salad starter has, over the years, almost become a chefs' 'designer salad'. The tomatoes are laid at 12 o'clock, 3 o'clock, 6 o'clock and 9 o'clock and all the other flavours follow suit at 10 minutes to and 10 minutes past. Chefs could argue all day over what should be included. Should there be tuna or anchovies or both?

Well, I'm going to give you my version, with the first five ingredients coming from the original recipe and the rest the optional extras. I include tuna fish, but it's going to be grilled fresh tuna fillet to sit on top of the finished salad. Of course this can be left out of the recipe or replaced with broken tuna fish tossed into the salad.

SERVES 4
12 very thin slices of French bread
4 tablespoons olive oil or garlic butter
1 head of soft lettuce or mixed salad
   leaves
8 black olives, stoned and quartered
2 plum tomatoes, seeded and cut into
   6–8 wedges

1 teaspoon small capers
100 g (4 oz) fine beans, crisply cooked
4–8 tinned or marinated anchovy
   fillets, drained
8 new potatoes, cooked and sliced
Salt and freshly ground black
   pepper
4 × 100 g (4 oz) tuna fillet steaks

FOR THE DRESSING
6–8 tablespoons olive oil
2 tablespoons tarragon vinegar
1/2 teaspoon Dijon mustard
Freshly ground black pepper
A pinch of salt
1/2 small garlic clove, finely
crushed

1/2 teaspoon snipped fresh chives
1/2 teaspoon chopped fresh
tarragon
2 hard-boiled eggs, roughly
chopped

To make the dressing, simply mix all the ingredients except the herbs and egg in a jar or bottle, only adding the fresh herbs just before finishing the salad. If the herbs are added too early the tarragon vinegar will discolour them.

Brush the bread with olive oil or garlic butter. Toast until golden and crisp on both sides. Separate the salad leaves and add the olives, tomatoes, capers, fine beans and anchovy fillets. Add the potato slices and season with salt and pepper.

Season the tuna with salt and pepper and start to grill or shallow-fry for about 1–1 1/2 minutes on each side, keeping the tuna medium rare to medium.

While the tuna fish is cooking, mix the salad dressing with the chopped herbs and chopped hard-boiled egg. Pour some over the salad and toss together with the toasts. Divide between plates and sit the tuna on top.

Poached Egg Salad with Sauté Potatoes, Black Pudding and Bacon

I have always wanted to do something with the Great British Breakfast, it has so many potential combinations. Here is an idea that acts as a starter for lunch, dinner or a complete meal on its own. The leaves listed below are good for this salad as they have different tastes and colours, but you can use any lettuces available to you. The most exciting part of eating this dish is breaking into the egg yolk and mixing it with the salad and sauce. It's tasty, rich and a delight to eat.

SERVES 4
1 tablespoon white wine or malt
vinegar (using white wine vinegar
prevents any discoloration)
4 eggs
225 g (8 oz) new potatoes, boiled and
sliced
50 g (2 oz) unsalted butter
175 g (6 oz) smoked bacon, rinded and
into strips

1/2 black pudding, cut into 1 cm
(1/2 in) pieces
A few lettuce leaves per person
(lollo rosso, oak leaf, curly endive,
rocket)
150 ml (5 fl oz) Basic Vinaigrette
(see p. 379)
150 ml (5 fl oz) Red Wine Sauce
(see p. 368) (optional)
Salt and freshly ground white pepper

Bring a large, deep pan of water to a rolling boil, add the wine vinegar, then crack the eggs into the water. Poach for about 4 minutes until the white has set. Remove from the pan with a slotted spoon and place in a bowl of cold water.

Fry the potato slices in the butter until golden and crisp on both sides. Remove from the pan and keep warm. Fry the bacon until crisp and nicely browned. Add to the potatoes. Fry the black pudding for a few minutes on both sides and keep warm with the bacon and potatoes.

Separate the lettuce leaves carefully and wash in a little salted water. Drain and shake off any excess water. Place in a bowl and dress with most of the vinaigrette.

The finishing of the salad is up to you. I like to almost 'build' my salad by firstly placing some potatoes, black pudding and bacon on to the plates or bowls and then the lettuce leaves followed by more potatoes etc., until I have what you might call a designer salad, but still looking quite natural. The simplest way is just to mix your garnishes with the salad leaves and separate on to plates.

While assembling the salad, warm the red wine sauce, if using, and re-heat the poached eggs for 1–2 minutes in a bowl of hot water. Drain the eggs well, place on top of the salad and sprinkle with a little of the remaining vinaigrette and a twist of pepper. Pour the red wine sauce around and serve.

Watercress, Spinach and Parmesan Salad with Cider Vinegar and Mustard Dressing

This is a great vegetarian starter, main course or side salad recipe; it really can be any of these. Its simple ingredients are complemented by a good sweet dressing that has a bite. The recipe makes about 350 ml (12 fl oz) of dressing; any left over will keep well, chilled, for a few days.

This is a very basic recipe that can have so many combinations: spring onions, garlic croûtons, French beans and lots more tastes can be added. The cider dressing can also be used in salads of your choice. I sometimes use it to season and flavour spinach to go with pork dishes.

SERVES 6–8 as a starter
2–3 bunches of watercress, about
    100 g (4 oz)
100 g (4 oz) baby spinach leaves
100 g (4 oz) Parmesan, flaked, or 50 g
    (2 oz) Parmesan, freshly grated

FOR THE CIDER DRESSING
1 1/2 tablespoons cider vinegar
1 heaped teaspoon caster sugar
1 egg
1 egg yolk
2 teaspoons Dijon mustard
300 ml (10 fl oz) groundnut oil
Salt and freshly ground black
    pepper

To make the dressing, warm the cider vinegar with the sugar, then allow to cool. Mix the egg and egg yolk with the mustard and add the sugared vinegar. Whisk the ingredients together, then gradually add the groundnut oil a drop at a time, whisking continuously, as you would when making mayonnaise. Season with salt and pepper.

Sprinkle the dressing over the mixed salad leaves and Parmesan, then divide between individual plates or serve in a large bowl for everybody to help themselves.

Pistou Salad

'Pistou' is really a Provençal soup made in a similar way to minestrone, but much simpler and without the dried haricots or butter beans. It's usually made with potatoes, French beans, onions and tomatoes, then finished with garlic, basil and Gruyère.

Well, I decided to take some of those flavours and treat this dish almost like a pistou/minestrone – no strict rules but containing the bare essentials. All these flavours except the salad leaves can be made into a soup with the addition of some vegetable stock.

SERVES 6–8

3–4 Pickled Red Onions (see p. 156)
8–12 small new potatoes, cooked and
   kept warm
Salt and freshly ground black pepper
Juice of 1/2 lemon
225 g (8 oz) fine French beans
4 tablespoons Pesto sauce
   (see p. 374)

4–6 small globe artichokes preserved
   in olive oil, quartered
1/2 bunch of spring onions, shredded
2–3 plum or salad tomatoes, cut into 8
   wedges
A few black olives, stoned and halved
50 g (2 oz) salad leaves, such as baby
   spinach and rocket
Parmesan flakes

Prepare the red onions, reserving the marinating liquor for the dressing. The new potatoes, should be halved, then seasoned before you squeeze the lemon over them. Blanch the French beans in boiling salted water for 1 minute, then drain well and refresh in iced water.

To make the dressing, mix the pesto sauce with 3–4 tablespoons of the red onion liquor to give you a richer and looser pesto dressing.

I prefer to keep just the potatoes and onions warm and mix and season with the other ingredients, adding the salad leaves at the last minute, then dressing carefully on plates. Finish with some Parmesan flakes and good crusty bread.

VARIATION

To make the recipe into a soup, just cook the onions in a little olive oil, add some cooked new potatoes, tomatoes, black olives and artichokes and cook for a few minutes. Top with some Vegetable Stock (see p. 400) and cook for 8–10 minutes. To finish, add the spring onions, French beans and pesto sauce. Serve the soup with Parmesan flakes and good crusty bread.

Simple Salad

This salad is as simple as its title. It eats very well as a vegetarian main course, starter, or goes with so many other dishes, such as Blackened Chicken (see p. 121). The chicken can be cooked on an open barbecue, then served sitting on this salad. A great dish all year round but especially good in the summer.

These are not strict measures for the ingredients, but give you an idea how to balance the flavours. It's really a handful of each mixed with salad leaves – Little Gems, rocket and baby spinach work very well. The artichoke hearts are to be found in delicatessens or large supermarkets. These are sold loose and are usually marinated in olive oil and herb dressing. If the salad is going to be a starter, then work on approximately half a choke per portion; for a main course, use one choke per portion. Adjust the quantity of leaves according to how you are serving the salad.

SERVES 4

175–225 g (6–8 oz) fine French beans

4 artichoke hearts preserved in oil

Mixed salad leaves, such as little gem, rocket and baby spinach

25 g (1 oz) black olives, stoned and halved

2 spring onions, shredded

2 plum or salad tomatoes, cut into 8 wedges

$^1/_2$ small red pepper, seeded and cut into wafer-thin strips

6 tablespoons Spicy Tomato Dressing (see p. 381)

The French beans must be topped and tailed, blanched for 1 minute in boiling salted water, then refreshed in cold running water to retain their rich colour and bite. All you need to do with the artichoke hearts is quarter them lengthways, including the stalk. Mix all the ingredients together in a bowl, spoon in the dressing and toss together gently so that it coats all the ingredients. The salad is ready to eat.

VARIATIONS

Other flavours that can be added to the salad or sprinkled on top are: chopped fresh herbs such as basil, tarragon or parsley; fried bread croûtons or toasts; freshly grated Parmesan.

Cooking the 'Perfect' Omelette

I'm sure we could all argue over this subject. What is the perfect omelette? Is it the one that's beautifully golden brown? Is it flat or round? Is it totally colourless? Is it firm? Is it slightly runny?

Well, I suppose the easiest answer is the most perfect is the way you like to eat it. Well why not? However, for me, the perfect omelette hasn't been eaten by many people. Making an omelette is really just a dish that involves the setting of eggs with the added flavour of your choice: crispy bacon; black pudding; cheese and onion; tomato and chive; smoked salmon, spring onion and chilli; button or wild mushrooms; mixed herbs; sweet peppers; spinach; potato; garlic, it's up to you. It's not really a cooking process, more of a 'warming' to thicken the egg, giving you a set scrambled effect with a complete soft and light finish with no colour.

Here's the recipe for a plain omelette as a main course.

SERVES 1–2
4 fresh eggs
Salt and freshly ground black pepper
A small knob of unsalted butter

It is very important to have a good non-stick, 15–20 cm (6–8 in) omelette pan.

Warm the pan on the stove. While the pan is warming, crack the eggs into a bowl and whisk with a fork. It's very important not to season the eggs until the omelette is about to be made. If eggs are salted too early they break down and become thin, runny and slightly discoloured, giving a dull look.

The omelette pan should now be hot enough to add the knob of butter. As the butter melts and becomes bubbly; season the eggs and pour them into the pan. This will now only take between 3–4 minutes to cook. To keep them light, keep the eggs moving by shaking the pan and stirring the eggs with a fork. This prevents them from sticking and colouring. You will soon have a scrambled look to the eggs. Now cheese can be added or any other flavour. Allow the eggs to set on the base for 5–10 seconds. The eggs will still be moist and not completely set in the centre. Holding the pan at an angle (down), slide and tap the omelette towards the edge, folding it over as you do so.

This can now be turned out on to a plate and shaped under a cloth to give a cigar shape. The omelette is now ready. It will have no colour but be filled with an almost soufflé texture. This makes it a dream to eat, with every mouthful melting.

Spicy Scrambled Eggs

This is a great quick snack dish that also holds well as a starter or canapé. The quantities of garlic and ginger may seem a lot for just a 3-egg omelette but, mixed together and cooked, they do balance the strength of both flavours.

SERVES 1–2
3 eggs, beaten
A knob of unsalted butter
$1/2$ heaped teaspoon crushed garlic
$1/2$ heaped teaspoon crushed fresh ginger root
1 tablespoon finely chopped onion

$1/2$ teaspoon seeded, chopped red chilli
$1/2$ teaspoon ground turmeric
1 tomato, seeded and diced
Salt and freshly ground black pepper
$1/2$ teaspoon chopped fresh coriander leaves (optional)

Heat a frying-pan and add the butter. Work the crushed garlic and ginger together to a paste.

Once the butter is bubbling, add the garlic and ginger paste, the chopped onion, chilli, turmeric and tomato. Cook for a few minutes until lightly softened. Add the beaten eggs and stir over the heat until the eggs have softly scrambled. Taste and season with salt and pepper, if necessary. Stir in the chopped coriander, if using, and serve.

Spanish Omelette

This must be one of the cheapest dishes to produce, and also one of the simplest to make. A Spanish friend of mine gave me this recipe and it works every time. Most tapas bars serve Spanish omelettes, but I've yet to have one as good as this. It can be served as a starter, snack or main course, and I like to serve it with Red Pepper and Anchovy Salad (see p. 29).

SERVES 4
2 large potatoes, thinly sliced
1 onion, sliced
Salt and freshly ground white pepper
Groundnut or vegetable oil for deep-frying

4 eggs, beaten
1 teaspoon olive oil
1 quantity Red Pepper and Anchovy Salad (see p. 29)
A handful of salad leaves

Mix the potatoes with the sliced onions and sprinkle them lightly with salt. Heat the groundnut oil to about 140–150°C (285–300°F) and blanch the potatoes and onions in batches in a deep-fat fryer for about 4–5 minutes, making sure you cook them without colouring. Make sure the oil is not too hot, and while the potatoes are blanching, turn with a fork to ensure even cooking. When cooked, drain off all excess oil. Mix the potatoes, onions and eggs and season with salt and pepper.

Heat a 15 cm (6 in) frying-pan with sloping sides and trickle in the olive oil. Pour in the potato and egg mixture and move with the fork as the first side is cooking. It should take a few minutes until it is golden brown. Turn the omelette on to a plate then slide it back into the pan to cook the other side. Leave to rest for a minute or two, as it is best eaten just warm.

Serve in wedges with a little of the red pepper and anchovy salad, on plates garnished with salad leaves.

Smoked Salmon and Asparagus with Poached Egg Hollandaise

Cold smoked salmon on warm toast with warm asparagus and a gently poached egg just breaking on top sounds – delicious – and it is. Lots of traditional flavours working together. This dish can be even better. I like to top the poached egg with a spoonful of Hollandaise Sauce (see p. 373). It eats beautifully and gives a good finish to the appearance of the dish.

SERVES 4

12–16 medium asparagus spears
Salt
25 g (1 oz) unsalted butter
4 thick slices of wholemeal bread

Horseradish sauce or cream
225 g (8 oz) sliced smoked salmon
4 poached eggs (see p. 38)
1 quantity Hollandaise Sauce
  (see p. 373)

The first job is to prepare and cook the asparagus. To be certain of them being tender, lightly peel them from half way down to the base of the spears and cut about 2.5 cm (1 in) off the root. The asparagus will now be deep green from the top, changing tones down to white.

Drop the asparagus into boiling, salted water and keep on full heat for 2–3 minutes, then drain. The spears will still have a nice bite in them. If you are cooking the asparagus in advance, simply drop them into ice-cold water to refresh them. To re-heat, just drop them back into hot water for 30–40 seconds, lift out, season with salt and pepper and brush with butter.

Toast the bread and spread with a thin layer of horseradish sauce or cream; the flavour works really well with smoked salmon. Cover the toast with the salmon and lay the asparagus tips on top. Sit the warm poached eggs on the asparagus and finish with hollandaise sauce.

VARIATIONS
Instead of the hollandaise, you can use some Basic Vinaigrette (see p. 379) with snipped fresh chives and just spoon it over the egg.

Open Leek Tart with Warm Poached Egg

This is a dish that has few ingredients but many flavours. Leeks themselves hold many tastes giving different strengths from the white to the green. If thin pencil leeks cannot be found, then simply buy standard leeks and split them lengthways. The crispy pastry base has a good texture, and sitting the warm poached egg on top and tasting the yolk mix with all the other flavours is sensational. On top of all that, it's also a wonderful vegetarian starter or main course dish.

SERVES 4
1/4 quantity Shortcrust Pastry
   (see p. 394)
8 pencil leeks, about 1 cm (1/2 in) thick
4 eggs
A knob of unsalted butter

Salt and freshly ground black pepper
About 4 tablespoons Red Wine
   Dressing (see p. 383)
4 teaspoons walnut oil
2 teaspoons roughly chopped fresh
   flatleaf parsley

Pre-heat the oven to 200°C/400°F/gas 6. Line a baking tray with greaseproof paper. Roll out the pastry 1–2 mm thick and cut into 4 × 10 cm (4 in) discs. Rest the pastry discs on the lined baking tray, then cook in the pre-heated oven for 8–10 minutes until golden and crispy. To keep them flat, cover with another sheet of greaseproof paper and a light ovenproof baking tray

The leeks should be trimmed and washed, leaving them whole. Bring a large pan of salted water to the boil and add the leeks. Cook for 1–3 minutes, depending on the size of the leeks. Drain, then refresh in iced water. Lightly squeeze the leeks to remove excess water, then cut into 6 cm (2½ in) sticks.

To poach the eggs, fill a small pan with a mixture of two-thirds water and one-third malt vinegar; the high quantity of vinegar will immediately hold the egg white around the yolk. Bring to the boil, then break in the eggs and poach for 3–3½ minutes. If you wish to cook these early, then simply refresh in iced water, then re-heat later in boiling water for about 1 minute

To finish the dish, melt a knob of butter in a pan, add the leeks, season with salt and pepper and heat through for 2–3 minutes. Sit the pastry discs in shallow soup bowls or on plates and spoon some of the red wine dressing around. Add the remaining dressing to the leeks, then divide them between the discs and sit the warm poached eggs on top. To finish, mix the walnut oil with the chopped parsley and trickle over the top.

Gruyère Cheese Flan

This is my basic flan recipe, but of course you can add any other ingredients you like. One of my favourites is to make this into a leek, mushroom and Gruyère flan by simply omitting one of the onions and replacing it with a shredded leek and 50 g (2 oz) of sliced mushrooms, both lightly cooked in butter. It then eats very well with a Spicy Tomato Sauce (see p. 374).

If you don't have the time to make your own pastry, both shortcrust and puff are easily found in most food stores, although they're not quite as good as home-made. I prefer to use puff pastry for this recipe as it cooks much more lightly and suits the flan. It eats very well as a starter or main course with salad.

SERVES 8
2 large onions, sliced
40 g (1 1/2 oz) unsalted butter
1 1/2 tablespoons groundnut or
   vegetable oil
2 eggs
1 egg yolk

150 ml (5 fl oz) double cream or milk
100 g (4 oz) Gruyère or Cheddar,
   grated
Cayenne pepper (optional)
175 g (6 oz) Puff or Shortcrust Pastry
   (see pp. 393 or 394)
Salt and freshly ground white
   pepper

To start the filling, cook the sliced onions in 1 tablespoon of the butter and 1/2 tablespoon of the oil until soft and transparent. Leave to cool. In a basin, beat the eggs and egg yolk together, then add the cream or milk and leave to one side. Melt the remaining butter and oil together until blended, then leave to cool. Mix the grated cheese with the eggs and cream and fold in the onions and the cool butter and oil mixture. Season with salt and pepper and a little cayenne, if you like. The mixture can be made the day before as it refrigerates very well.

Pre-heat the oven to 180°C/350°F/gas 4 and prepare a 24 cm (9 1/2 in) flan tin or a flan ring and a baking sheet.

Roll out the pastry and use to line the flan tin or ring. Line the pastry with greaseproof paper and fill with baking beans or dried rice. Bake blind in the pre-heated oven for 15–20 minutes, then allow to cool. Remove the beans and paper.

Reduce the oven temperature to 150°C/300–325°F/gas 2–3. Pour the filling mixture into the pastry base and cook in the oven for about 45 minutes until the flan is just set. The tart should colour during cooking. If it starts to over-colour, lightly cover with foil or greaseproof paper. The flan is best left to rest for 20–30 minutes before serving as this will help set the texture of the filling.

Welsh Rarebit

This recipe makes a large quantity but it is just as easy as making less, and can be more successful. It will keep in the fridge for up to ten days, so can be used in plenty of other dishes and it freezes really well. My favourite use is with the Smoked Haddock with a tomato salad (see p. 72). It's also delicious as a simple cheese on toast. The mix also freezes very well. When I make it at home, I divide it into four and freeze three batches for use later.

SERVES 16

700 g (1½ lb) mature Cheddar, grated
150 ml (5 fl oz) milk
25 g (1 oz) plain flour
50 g (2 oz) fresh white breadcrumbs
1 tablespoon English mustard powder

2 shakes of Worcestershire sauce
Salt and freshly ground white
   pepper
2 eggs
2 egg yolks

Put the Cheddar into a pan and add the milk. Slowly melt them together over a low heat, but do not allow the mix to boil as this will separate the cheese. When the mixture is smooth and just begins to bubble, add the flour, breadcrumbs and mustard and cook for a few minutes, stirring, over a low heat, until the mixture comes away from the sides of the pan and begins to form a ball shape. Add the Worcestershire sauce, salt and pepper and leave to cool.

When cold, place the mixture in a food processor, turn on the motor and slowly add the eggs and egg yolks. (If you don't have a processor or mixer, just beat vigorously with a wooden spoon.) When the eggs are mixed in, chill for a few hours before using. After it has rested in the fridge, you will find the rarebit is very easy to handle. You will find it has so many uses.

Mozzarella and Tomato Fried Sandwiches with Garlic Mushrooms

Egg-fried sandwiches work so well as starters or snacks. Basically they are sandwiches dipped in beaten egg, then fried in oil and butter until golden brown. The sandwich takes on a whole new texture and taste. These will give you a completely new croque monsieur, simply dip it into the egg and fry.

Of course, there are many combinations of savoury fillings, whether meat, fish or vegetarian. This recipe I'm going to give you is vegetarian, with an Italian feel.

Mozzarella is an Italian cheese that was made from water buffaloes' milk. A lot now is made from cows' milk. It is stored in its own milk and has a slightly rubbery texture. It is also used on pizzas and in Italian salads.

SERVES 2

4 × 25 g (1 oz) Mozzarella slices

4 thick slices of white or brown bread, buttered

1 tomato, sliced

Salt and freshly ground black pepper

2 tablespoons olive oil

A small knob of unsalted butter

2 eggs, beaten

25g (1 oz) Garlic Butter (see p. 18)

100 g (4 oz) button mushrooms, sliced

Lay the Mozzarella on 2 slices of bread, leaving a 5 mm (¼ in) border clear. Sit some slices of tomato on top of the cheese and season with salt and pepper. Cover with the remaining slices of bread, pushing all around the outside to seal in the cheese and tomato. Heat a frying-pan with the olive oil and butter. Dip the sandwiches in the beaten eggs, making sure the egg has soaked in. Fry over a medium heat for a few minutes on each side to a golden brown.

While the sandwiches are cooking, heat another frying-pan and add the garlic butter. Once it is bubbling, add the sliced mushrooms. Season with salt and pepper and cook on a fast heat to prevent them from becoming too soft and wet. Instead these should take on a good colour and be ready within minutes.

To serve the dish, place the sandwiches on plates and spoon some garlic mushrooms on top, pouring over any excess juices.

Ricotta and Spinach Gnocchi

Gnocchi is an Italian dish of little dumplings which can be made in three ways: with semolina, potato or flour and eggs. I'm using the latter with ricotta cheese, which is readily available and is probably the cheese most used in cooking in Italy.

SERVES 4

350 g (12 oz) fresh spinach, stalks removed

175 g (6 oz) ricotta, drained and diced

1 egg

50 g (2 oz) plain flour

25 g (1 oz) Parmesan, grated

A pinch of freshly grated nutmeg

Salt and freshly ground white pepper

Parmesan flakes, to serve

FOR THE DRESSING

150 ml (5 fl oz) olive oil

4 shallots or 1 large onion, finely chopped

1 large garlic clove, crushed

6 tomatoes, skinned, seeded and chopped

Juice of ½ lemon

1 bunch of fresh basil, chopped

Wash the spinach well to remove any grit then shake off any excess water. Place the spinach in a hot pan and cook in its own water for a few minutes until the leaves begin to wilt. Remove them from the pan and squeeze out any excess liquid. Blitz the spinach in a food processor or chop it very finely. Mix the spinach with the ricotta, egg, flour and Parmesan and season with nutmeg, salt and pepper. Leave the mixture to rest in the fridge for 20 minutes.

To make the dressing, warm the olive oil with the chopped shallots or onion and garlic and cook over a gentle heat for about 15 minutes. Add the chopped tomatoes and cook for a further 5 minutes. Season with salt and pepper and add the lemon juice. Keep the dressing warm while you cook the gnocchi.

Using floured hands, shape the gnocchi into small 2.5 cm (1 in) balls. Bring a large pan of salted water to the boil (or you could use vegetable stock, see p. 400) and drop the gnocchi into the boiling water. When the balls rise to the surface after just a few minutes they are cooked. Remove them from the pan using a slotted spoon and allow to drain well. Add the chopped basil to the dressing at the last minute, just before serving, then roll the gnocchi in the dressing and divide between four bowls. Sprinkle with some Parmesan flakes and serve.

Leek and Parmesan Risotto with a Warm Poached Egg

I like to serve risottos, and I write more about them in the chapter on Vegetarian Main Courses (see pp. 202–207). This one makes a very special starter which I like to serve in shallow bowls topped with the poached egg.

SERVES 4

1.2 litres (2 pints) Vegetable Stock (see p. 400) or Chicken Stock (see p. 399)
450 g (1 lb) leeks, trimmed and sliced
175 g (6 oz) unsalted butter
2 onions, finely chopped
1 small garlic clove, crushed

225 g (3 oz) Arborio rice
3–4 tablespoons grated Parmesan
Salt and freshly ground white pepper
4 poached eggs, (see p. 38)
2–3 tablespoons Basic Vinaigrette (see p. 379) or seasoned olive oil
1 tablespoon snipped fresh chives
Fresh Parmesan flakes (optional)

Bring the stock to the boil and add the sliced leeks. Bring back to the boil and drain the leeks off, reserving the leeks and stock separately. Melt the butter in a large pan, add the onions and garlic and cook for a few minutes without colouring until softened. Add the rice and cook for a further minute. Start to add the hot stock a ladle at a time and cook over a medium heat, allowing the rice to absorb almost all the stock before adding more stock. Continue to add, cook and stir until the rice is softening but not getting to a purée creamed stage; this will take about 20 minutes.

Stir in the Parmesan. The more you add, the richer the taste will become. The Parmesan will also thicken the risotto, so add more stock to give a loose consistency if necessary. Add the leeks, season with salt and pepper and warm through. Spoon into the bowls and sit a warm poached egg on top. Mix the dressing or olive oil with the chives and spoon a little over the eggs. Sprinkle with some Parmesan flakes to finish the dish.

Anchovy and Onion Pastry Pieces

These are lovely little appetizers: the strength of the anchovy contrasting with the rich sweetness of the onion on crisp puff pastry. To achieve the correct rich sweetness in the onions they must first be caramelized, a slow process, but worth it. I would suggest you prepare these the day before you need them.

SERVES 4

4–8 large onions, sliced
1 tablespoon water
Salt and freshly ground white
   pepper

175 g (6 oz) Puff Pastry (see p. 393)
1 egg, beaten
100 g (4 oz) tinned anchovy fillets,
   drained
Olive oil

Place the onions and water in a large pan over a very low heat and keep on a low heat for anything between 2 and 4 hours. This process allows all the natural juices and sugars from the onions to be released. Once the onions have really softened and broken down, the sugar content will slowly start to caramelize. The onions will start to change colour but they are only ready when at a deep golden stage. Season with salt and pepper.

Meanwhile, roll out the puff pastry very thinly and cut into 2.5 cm (1 in) wide strips. Rest the pastry in the fridge for 30 minutes to prevent it from shrinking while it is being cooled.

Pre-heat the oven to 220°C/425°F/gas 7 and grease a baking sheet.

Place the strips on the baking sheet and brush with beaten egg. Spoon some onions down the centre of the strips, leaving 3 mm (1/8 in) down each side. Lay the anchovy fillets head to tail down the centre of the onions. Bake in the pre-heated oven for 8–10 minutes, until the pastry is golden and crispy. Sprinkle with olive oil and cut into 2.5 cm (1 in) squares. Serve at once.

Tapenade

Tapenade comes from the word tapeno *which means 'caper' in Provençal. The paste is absolutely delicious and can be used for so many things. I like to spread it on toast to serve with Fillet of Red Mullet (see p. 107) but it is also great just to have on toast as a snack with drinks.*

MAKES about 350 g (12 oz)

225 g (8 oz) black olives, stoned

1 small garlic clove, crushed

50 g (2 oz) tinned anchovy fillets,
    drained

25 g (1 oz) capers, drained

2 tablespoons olive oil

1 teaspoon lemon juice

Freshly ground black
    pepper

Place the olives, garlic, anchovies and capers into a food processor and blend to a purée. While the motor is still running, slowly add the olive oil until the mix is pliable. You may need a little more olive oil. Add the lemon juice and season to taste with pepper. The tapenade is now ready to use or will keep for about a week in the fridge.

Mussels with Garlic, Almonds and Parsley

This is usually served as a starter, but it also makes a great main course.

SERVES 4

FOR THE BUTTER

6 shallots, finely chopped

1 large garlic clove, crushed

250 g (9 oz) unsalted butter, softened

FOR THE MUSSEL COOKING LIQUOR

1/2 onion, chopped

1 carrot, chopped

2 celery sticks, chopped

1 small leek, chopped

15 g (1/2 oz) unsalted butter

1 garlic clove, crushed

1 bay leaf

1 sprig of fresh thyme

1/2 bottle of dry white wine

600 ml (1 pint) Fish Stock (see p. 399)

1 kg (2 1/4 lb) mussels, scrubbed and
    bearded (see p. 17)

FOR THE GARNISH

50 g (2 oz) nibbed almonds, lightly
    toasted

2 tablespoons chopped fresh parsley

4 slices of white bread, crusts
    removed, crumbed and toasted until
    golden

Sweat the chopped shallots and garlic in 1 tablespoon of the butter until translucent, then leave to cool. Mix them with most of the remaining butter and keep aside for later.

To start the mussel liquor, sweat the chopped onion, carrot, celery and leek in the butter with the garlic, bay leaf and thyme for a few minutes. Add the white wine and boil to reduce until almost dry. Add the fish stock and bring to the boil, then add the mussels. Stir until the shells begin to open, then remove from the heat.

Strain the cooking liquor through a fine sieve and discard the vegetables. Remove the mussels from their shells, discarding any that have not opened, and remove any sinews from the mussels. Keep them moist in a little of the stock. Rinse the shells.

Boil the liquor to reduce it until a good mussel flavour is achieved, then gradually add the shallot and garlic butter in knobs. Add the mussels, toasted almonds and parsley. Place some of the shells in a circle on large individual bowls or plates. Spoon the mussels into the shells and pour over some of the cooking liquor. To finish the dish, sprinkle with the warm, golden toasted breadcrumbs.

Fried Cockle Salad

Eating deep-fried cockles is delicious. They get really crispy and tasty. Just be careful not to fry too many at once otherwise you'll almost have a popcorn situation. So it's best to use a deep-fat fryer, or certainly a large pan with a lid.

The crispy cockles eat very well with Salsa Dressing (see p. 385), although it is best to make the relish looser with more olive oil and lime juice, making it into more of a dressing.

You can buy cooked cockles in most fishmongers and supermarkets. If you buy live cockles, wash them well, removing any grit, then drop them into a pan of boiling water. The cockles will start to open after 30 seconds. Once they are open, drain off the water and leave the cockles to cool. Pick the cockles from their shells and leave to drain on a cloth.

Use whichever salad leaves you prefer. There's plenty of choice from lollo rosso and oakleaf to curly endive, rocket or lambs' lettuce.

SERVES 4
1 quantity Salsa Dressing (see p. 385)
2–3 tablespoons olive oil
Juice of 1/2 lime
Salt and freshly ground white pepper
Oil, for deep-frying

175–225 g (6–8 oz) fresh cooked cockles
2–3 tablespoons milk
2–3 tablespoons self-raising flour
Mixed salad leaves
A few drops of olive oil

Loosen the salsa relish recipe with some more olive oil and a few drops of extra lime juice. Check the dressing for seasoning with salt and pepper.

To cook the cockles, pre-heat the fat fryer to 180°C/350°F. Coat the cockles in milk, then roll lightly through the flour, shaking off any excess. Fry the cockles in the pre-heated oil for 1–2 minutes, until golden and crispy. Lift them from the fryer and sprinkle with salt.

Spoon the relish on to the plates and scatter over the crispy cockles. Mix the salad leaves with a few drops of olive oil and season with salt and pepper. Sit the leaves in a small pile in the centre of the plate. The leaves should be standing high with the dressing and cockles being visible all around the plate.

Griddled Scallops with Cabbage and Smoked Salmon

Scallops must be one of almost every chef's favourite ingredients. Fresh from the shell and cooked a minute later, you can't get much fresher.

One of the most important things to remember with scallops, as with most fish, is not to mask their delicate sweet flavour, only enhance it. With this dish I feel we're doing just that. It works and eats so well – all the tastes helping each other.

SERVES 4

12 large scallops, cleaned and
   trimmed
1/2 small Savoy cabbage, about 175 g
   (6 oz)
100 g (4 oz) smoked salmon

Oil, for frying
2–3 tablespoons water
A knob of unsalted butter
Salt and freshly ground black pepper
3–4 tablespoons Mustard Dressing
   (see p. 382)

Remove the dark outside leaves from the cabbage and cut the rest into quarters. The cabbage can now be sliced into 1 cm (1/2 in) strips. The slices of smoked salmon can now also be cut into similar-sized pieces or thinner julienne strips. The dish is now ready to finish.

Heat a frying-pan or griddle plate and trickle with a little oil. Place the scallops in the hot frying-pan or on the griddle. It is very important to cook scallops in a hot pan to seal in all the juices and not create a stewing effect. The scallops should be turned when half-cooked and seasoned with salt and pepper. Cook for no more than 1–2 minutes in total.

At the same time, heat a pan and add the water and butter. Once the water and butter are boiling, add the cabbage. Season with salt and pepper and keep turning in the pan. The cabbage will only take 1–2 minutes and it's best eaten when just becoming tender but still has some texture. Add the smoked salmon to the cabbage, check for seasoning and add the mustard dressing. This will mix with the cooking liquor which balances the mustard taste.

To serve, simply spoon the cabbage and smoked salmon at the top of the plates and finish with some of the mustard dressing liquor and griddled scallops sitting in front.

VARIATIONS

A drop of fresh lemon juice will fire up the liquor even more.

If you don't like mustard, then either leave it out altogether – the dish still eats well – or add a little grated fresh horseradish and snipped fresh chives. Both flavours work well with the cabbage and scallops.

If you can't find good fresh scallops, then simply use another fresh fish, such as monkfish, to go with the cabbage and smoked salmon.

Seared Scallops and Watercress Salad with Smoked Bacon and Parsley

This recipe uses two dressings that are featured in other dishes in the book but, when all is put together, you have a completely different finished result in texture and taste. This is one of the beauties of cooking, being able to turn flavours to each other and get different results with maximum flavour. The smokiness of the bacon working with the sweet-bitter flavour of seared scallops is sensational.

I have listed 1–2 bunches of watercress because bunches come in various sizes. A handful of sprigs will be enough per portion.

SERVES 4

12 large scallops, cleaned and trimmed

I–2 bunches of watercress

2 tomatoes, blanched and skinned

4 smoked streaky bacon rashers

Oil, for frying

A knob of unsalted butter

8 tablespoons Mustard Dressing (see p. 382)

1 tablespoon chopped fresh flatleaf parsley

Salt and freshly ground black pepper

3–4 tablespoons Cider Dressing (see p. 32)

The watercress should be picked into sprigs, removing only the coarse base of the stalks. Cut the skinned tomatoes into quarters, then into 5 mm (1/4 in) dice. Cut the rashers of bacon into thin strips. These can now be fried in a hot pan, literally just brushed with oil, as the fat content in the bacon strips will melt in the pan. The bacon will take 5–6 minutes to fry and become very crispy, almost a crackling texture.

The scallops can now be cooked in a very hot pan or griddle, also just brushed with oil and with a knob of butter added. The scallops will only take a few minutes to cook, giving an almost crisp edge and a very succulent centre.

To serve, warm the mustard dressing, adding the bacon, tomato and chopped parsley and seasoning with salt and pepper. Dress the watercress sprigs with the cider dressing. Spoon some of the finished mustard dressing on to the plates and sit three scallops per portion on top. Finish the dish with a handful of the watercress sprigs in the centre. It is now ready to eat and enjoy.

Sautéd Scallop and Fennel Salad

Scallops are available fresh from many fishmongers and supermarkets, or you might find some good-quality scallops frozen.

SERVES 4
4 fennel bulbs
Juice of 1 lemon
1 star anise (optional)
900 ml (1¹/₂ pints) water
Salt and freshly ground white pepper

50–75 g (2–3 oz) unsalted butter
1 tablespoon olive oil
12 scallops, trimmed and roes removed
Green salad leaves
Basic Vinaigrette (see p. 379)
1 tablespoon snipped fresh chives

Top and tail the fennel. Using a small knife, remove the core from the base of each fennel. Add the lemon juice and star anise to the water with a pinch of salt and bring to the boil. Add the fennel, cover and simmer over a medium heat for 15–20 minutes until just tender.

Pour off half of the cooking liquor and boil it to reduce to about 150 ml (5 fl oz). This will increase the flavour of the fennel. Add the butter to the liquor and whisk vigorously to make a butter sauce. For an even lighter and smoother sauce, use an electric hand blender to finish. This sauce can be kept warm and re-heated and blitzed before serving.

Slice the fennel 5 mm (¹/₄ in) thick lengthways. Heat a frying-pan and add a teaspoon of olive oil to the pan. Fry the fennel slices on both sides until golden brown. Season with salt and pepper.

To cook the scallops, heat a frying-pan with a few drops of olive oil and a knob of butter. It is very important to cook scallops in a hot pan. This will colour and seal them quickly. If the pan is only warm, the scallops will begin to poach in their own juices, creating a different texture and taste. Once coloured and seasoned on both sides, the scallops are ready; this should only take 2–3 minutes, depending on size.

To serve the dish, lay the fennel slices on the centre of a warmed serving plate and sit the scallops on top. Mix the salad leaves with a little vinaigrette and sit them in the centre of the scallops. Add the chives to the sauce and spoon around the plate.

Griddled Scallops with Crispy Aubergines

This dish shows another taste alternative with basic ingredients. The sweetness of the scallops mixed with an almost bitter/burnt flavour of the frying works really well with the tomato and olive taste. For a quick salad dressing, just mix a few drops of balsamic vinegar with some olive oil and season with salt and pepper. Alternatively, a good extra-virgin olive oil would be enough on its own.

SERVES 4
1 large aubergine
2–3 tablespoons plain flour
1 teaspoon cayenne pepper

Salt and freshly ground white pepper
Oil, for deep-frying
1 quantity Tomato Relish
(see p. 50)

6–8 black olives, stoned and finely
  diced
Basic Vinaigrette (see p. 379) or olive
  oil
25 g (1 oz) unsalted butter

12 large scallops, cleaned and
  trimmed
Mixed green salad leaves such
  as rocket, curly endive, baby
  spinach

Split the aubergine lengthways and slice across thinly. Mix the plain flour with the cayenne pepper and a pinch of salt. Sprinkle the flour over the aubergines and lightly dust off any excess. These can now be fried in hot fat until golden and crispy. Drain off any excess fat and sprinkle with salt. The aubergines can be cooked before you cook the scallops and will stay crispy and warm.

Warm the tomato relish, then mix the chopped black olives with a little vinaigrette or olive oil.

Heat a frying-pan until very hot but not burning, add a few drops of olive oil and a little butter. Sit the scallops in the pan, in batches if necessary, keeping the pan hot. If the pan is not hot enough, the scallops will simply begin to stew in their own juices, which will spoil their taste and texture. Once they have coloured golden brown on both sides, turn them out, season with salt and pepper and repeat the same process if you are cooking in batches. This will only take 2–3 minutes.

Season the salad leaves and toss with a little balsamic vinegar and olive oil, or just olive oil. Spoon the warm tomato relish into the centre of the plate, making a circular platform for the scallops. Spoon the black olive dressing around. Sit the scallops on to the relish and place the salad leaves in the centre. To finish the dish, simply arrange the fried aubergines on top.

Grilled King Prawns with Warm Spicy Relish

This dish is great as a starter or main course. King prawns can be cooked loose or made into kebabs (about five prawns per portion as a main course, or three or four as a starter) and cook really well on the open grill or barbecue. That's the beauty of a dish like this: it has so many combinations and options. The prawns taste delicious with the spicy relish, or you can just serve them on their own, with a squeeze of lemon or with mayonnaise. Also, you don't have to use king prawns. Just ordinary fresh prawns (or even frozen) will also eat really well with the warm relish. You can eat the whole lot cold, warm under the grill or toss in butter in a frying-pan. That's how simple and easy this dish can be.

This relish can be made several days in advance and kept chilled, then either served cold or simply re-heated. Oh, and by the way, the relish also eats well with other fish and also chicken, so have a go.

To save time, you can use a tin of chopped tomatoes for this recipe; it's never quite the same but it does work. You can simply drain off all liquid from the can and add the tomatoes to the mix, or you can boil the tomatoes to reduce all the excess liquid until thick and strong in flavour before adding this to the mixture.

SERVES 4–6

20 raw king prawns
Olive oil
Salt and freshly ground black pepper

FOR THE RELISH

8 plum or salad tomatoes
1 tablespoon olive oil
2 large red onions, finely chopped

1 garlic clove, crushed
2 green peppers, seeded and finely diced
2 fresh green chillies, seeded and very finely diced
1 teaspoon tomato purée
2 teaspoons demerara sugar
1 1/2 tablespoons malt vinegar
Salt

Pre-heat a grill or barbecue.

If the prawns are whole including heads, then firstly remove the heads, then pick the shells from the tails, leaving the base of tail intact. The prawns can be placed on wooden skewers or left loose. Brush the prawns with olive oil and season with salt and pepper. The prawns will take about 1 1/2–2 minutes per side on a hot open grill or barbecue, under a domestic oven grill or in a frying-pan.

To make the relish, remove the eyes from the tomatoes, then blanch them in boiling water for 8–10 seconds, then refresh in cold water and remove the skins. Quarter the tomatoes and remove all the seeds and water. Dice the flesh into 5 mm (1/4 in) dice.

Warm the olive oil in a pan and cook the chopped red onions over a low heat for a few minutes until they begin to soften. Add the garlic, peppers and chillies, increasing the heat to medium. Continue to cook for a few minutes. Add the tomatoes and tomato purée and cook for about 6–8 minutes. As the tomatoes cook, all excess water will be released, creating a tomato-sauce effect. However, this may seem a little too thin, so either continue to cook until a thicker tomato base is achieved or, and I think this is better, simply drain off all juices through a sieve and simmer the liquor on the stove until it begins to thicken, then remix with the other ingredients. You will now have a tasty warm chilli relish.

To finish it off and give a spicy effect, mix together the demerara sugar and malt vinegar and bring to the boil. This mix will only take a couple of minutes to boil and reduce in volume. The consistency should be like a thick syrup. Add this to the relish a little at a time, tasting until a sweet and sour flavour is achieved. Season with salt and pepper.

VARIATIONS

If you are using straightforward, small, frozen peeled prawns, then why not mix some cold spicy relish with mayonnaise and turn the whole dish into a spicy prawn cocktail. That's a starter to take to the table in no time at all.

Prawns and Sesame on Toast

Whenever I eat at a Chinese/Szechuan restaurant Ha To Sie are always my first choice. They have become regular favourites. I've always wanted to know exactly how the dish is made, so you can imagine how happy I was to get hold of this recipe. I'm sure there are endless different recipes for this dish but, as I have always said, that's one of the beauties of cooking.

This recipe is also easy to make. It's more or less just blitzed in a food processor, spread on toast and sprinkled with sesame seeds. Then just fry the toast. The bread is best when 1–2 days old. This allows it to dry slightly and move on from the doughy texture.

You can eat the toasts as starters, snacks or canapés. I like to eat them with just a squeeze of lemon but they also eat very well with Peanut Sauce (see p. 78).

SERVES 4–6
275 g (10 oz) raw prawns
2 tablespoons chopped spring onions
2 tablespoons chopped water chest-
   nuts
2 teaspoons grated fresh root ginger
1 teaspoon cornflour
1 egg white

2 tablespoons chopped fresh coriander
1/2 green chilli, seeded and finely
   chopped
A pinch of salt
6 slices of bread
2 tablespoons sesame seeds
Oil, for deep- or shallow-frying

Place all the ingredients except the bread and sesame seeds in a food processor or liquidizer and blitz till all are combined. The mix is now ready to spread on to the bread. Once the mix is on the bread, sprinkle a teaspoon or two of sesame seeds over each slice and cut off the crusts. The prawns on toast are now ready to cook. Another plus with this dish is how well it keeps, and it can be prepared several hours in advance then just chilled until needed.

Pre-heat the oil to 180°C/350°F. Fry the toasts for about 1–1 1/2 minutes on each side or until golden, then cut each slice into 8 triangles or fingers before serving.

NOTE

The raw prawns listed in the ingredients does mean raw and not the normal pink cooked prawns. This gives you a better paste texture to spread on the toasts. A good prawn to use is a raw frozen white king prawn. These come from Thailand and have a very thin, soft shell. They also come with the heads already removed. With the soft shell there is no need to peel them first. Simply blitz and the shell breaks down.

Basic pink peeled prawns can be used and will work, but you may find you will need egg white to help hold the mix together.

Smoked Eel Pâté

As you know by now, I love having as many variations as possible with all my recipes. Well, this recipe is no exception: its variations are plenty. I made this recipe in a limousine driving along Fifth Avenue in New York for my Christmas Special television show in 1995. I think that tells you just how easy this recipe must be.

Smoked eel is a fish we don't see and taste enough of. It has a very meaty texture and is succulent to eat. Although, of course, if don't have smoked eel, you can use any smoked fish for this pâté and it will taste equally delicious: smoked salmon, mackerel or trout will work just as well.

You can serve the pâté in many different ways. It can simply be set in a bowl and eaten immediately, or firmed in the fridge (if you're making it well in advance, then top it with the thinnest layer of melted butter). It can be rolled in cling film and chilled, then sliced into rounds, or set in a small or individual terrine moulds. It's a great dish to have as a starter, snack, canapé, or perhaps as a salad or part of your buffet. I also use it as part of a main course dish. Just some good fillet of fresh fish grilled, then topped with a slice of the pâté melting over. It looks really good and tastes even better.

SERVES 4
100 g (4 oz) smoked eel or other smoked fish fillet, chopped

50 g (2 oz) unsalted butter
3 tablespoons crème fraîche
Salt and freshly ground black pepper

The quickest way to make this is to blitz the smoked eel or fish in a food processor or liquidizer until puréed. Add the butter and blitz again. All you have to do now is add the crème fraîche and season with salt and pepper. If you are adding extra flavours (see Variations), work them in at the same time. Your pâté is now ready – it takes just minutes to make.

If you have used a food processor, the pâté will be of a smooth consistency. If you'd prefer a coarser texture, then simply dice the fish quite small and just work in the butter and crème fraîche with a spoon.

VARIATIONS

Any or all these flavours can be mixed in to sharpen and fire the taste of your pâté: a squeeze of fresh lemon juice; a pinch of cayenne pepper; 1 teaspoon English or Dijon mustard; 1 teaspoon snipped fresh chives; 1 teaspoon chopped spring onions.

Smoked Eel, Trout or Salmon with Potato Salad and Mustard Oil

This recipe has very different tastes from a basic potato salad. With this one I'm using horseradish (fresh or creamed) and red onions as flavours. It also doesn't have a mayonnaise base but instead the Mustard Dressing is being used. However, this can be made an awful lot quicker and still be very tasty by using a good-quality jar of mayonnaise mixed with creamed horseradish and a dot of mustard. So you can see cooking doesn't have to be too much of a chore. There are always alternatives.

SERVES 4

225–350 g (8–12 oz) smoked eel, smoked salmon or smoked trout fillets

FOR THE MUSTARD OIL

50 g (2 oz) dried mustard seeds

1 tablespoon water

1 teaspoon English mustard powder

5 tablespoons grapeseed oil

1 teaspoon ground turmeric

A pinch of salt

FOR THE POTATO SALAD

450 g (1 lb) cooked warm, small new potatoes

1 teaspoon finely grated horseradish or horseradish sauce

I red onion, finely chopped

1 tablespoon olive oil

A squeeze of fresh lemon juice

Salt and freshly ground black pepper

4–6 tablespoons Mustard Dressing (see p. 382) or mayonnaise

1 teaspoon chopped fresh parsley

Salad leaves, to serve (optional)

To make the mustard oil, roast the mustard seeds in a dry frying-pan over a moderate heat for a few minutes until golden. Allow to cool. Mix the water with the mustard powder, then blend all the ingredients together. Leave the mix for 24 hours to infuse the flavours. Then pass through a muslin cloth or very fine sieve to achieve a clear mustard oil.

Now make the potato salad. As soon as the potatoes are cooked, cut them in half and add the horseradish, red onion, olive oil, lemon juice and season with salt and pepper. To finish, simply add the mustard dressing, or mayonnaise and chopped parsley. To serve the dish, sit the potato salad on plates and top with the smoked fish, or serve at the side. Finish the dish with a trickle of the mustard oil. Salad leaves can also be used, if liked, dressed with a little mustard oil.

Smoked Eel Kedgeree

This dish could also be called a smoked eel risotto because it's made by the risotto method, but it holds all the flavours of a good old-fashioned kedgeree. I serve it as a starter, but it can be a total meal in itself. Hard-boiled eggs are traditionally used, but having a warm poached egg sitting on top of the rice and just breaking the yolk over it is a dream. The recipe for the Curry Cream Sauce is on page 369, but you can buy a ready-made one just to make the dish a little easier. If you really cannot find smoked eel, you can make the dish with smoked haddock.

SERVES 4
900 g (2 lb) smoked eel

FOR THE EEL STOCK
1 onion, chopped
1 leek, chopped
2 celery sticks, chopped
6 mushrooms or 50 g (2 oz) mushroom
    trimmings
1 bay leaf
1 sprig of fresh thyme
2 sprigs of fresh tarragon
A few black peppercorns
50 g (2 oz) unsalted butter
300 ml (10 fl oz) dry white wine
1.2 litres (2 pints) Fish Stock
    (see p. 399) or water

FOR THE KEDGEREE
2 onions, finely chopped
100 g (4 oz) unsalted butter
50 g (2 oz) bone marrow, chopped
    (optional)
1 garlic clove, crushed
225 g (8 oz) Arborio or long-grain rice
1/2 quantity Curry Cream Sauce
    (see p. 369)

TO SERVE
4 eggs, poached (see p. 38)
3 tablespoons olive oil
2 teaspoons snipped fresh chives

Smoked eel is one of my favourite smoked fish. Firstly it has to be filleted and skinned. Hopefully your fishmonger will do this for you, but if not, simply cut off the head and position the knife against the top half of the central bone. Carefully cut along the bone removing the fillet of fish. Turn the fish over and repeat the same process.

Now the skin can be removed: slide your finger or thumb under the skin at the head end and it should tear off all the way along. The fillets may need a little trimming down the sides to remove any excess skin. Turn the fillets on their back to show the centre. From the head end to half-way down there will be some bones. Simply position the knife under these bones, and cut away from the flesh. You now have two long, clean fillets of eel. Cut these into 2.5 cm (1 in) pieces and put in the fridge.

To make the eel stock, chop all the bones, skin and trimmings. Place the chopped vegetables, herbs and peppercorns in a large, warmed pan with the butter and cook them gently for 10 minutes without letting them colour. Add the bones and trimmings and continue to cook for a further 5 minutes. Add the white wine and boil to reduce until almost dry. Add the fish stock or water. (Fish stock will give you a stronger and better taste. If you are using water, ask the fishmonger to give you some fish bones as well to cook with the eel.) Bring the stock to the simmer and cook for 20 minutes. Strain through a sieve and stock is ready.

For the kedgeree, cook the chopped onions in the butter with the bone marrow, if using, and the garlic for 5–6 minutes until softened. Stir in the rice and cook for 2 minutes, then start to add the hot eel stock a few tablespoons at a time, stirring continuously. This will create a steam and help the cooking process. Wait for the stock to be absorbed before adding more, and keep adding the stock and stirring until the rice is just softening – this will take about 15–20 minutes. The rice should be tender and the mixture still moist.

When the rice is cooked, stir in half the curry sauce and taste. At this stage it becomes a matter of personal choice; some more or all of the curry sauce can be added if you want a stronger taste.

Add the pieces of chopped eel to the kedgeree and stir in to warm through. Warm the poached eggs for a few minutes in a bowl of boiling water, then drain well. Spoon the kedgeree into four bowls and sit a poached egg on top of each one. Spoon a little olive oil over the eggs and sprinkle with the snipped chives. The dish is now ready to serve.

Crumbled Baked Sardine Fillets

This dish can only really be made with fresh sardines. Sardines are great for grilling whole on a barbecue or under the grill, but the small bones can often be too much hard work. So for this dish, ask your fishmonger to scale and fillet them for you. If they are from large sardines you will only need three or four fillets a portion as a starter. Some of the small bones within the fillets can be removed with a small knife or tweezers. Any remaining ones are quite edible as for tinned sardines. The 'crumble' is a breadcrumb and fresh herb mix sprinkled on top and grilled. Once crumbled, the sardines can be served on a simple salad or just with a squeeze of lemon.

SERVES 4
6–8 sardines, filleted
Mixed green salad leaves
Olive oil
A few drops of lemon juice

FOR THE CRUMBLE TOPPING
25 g (1 oz) unsalted butter
1 large shallot or 1/2 onion, finely chopped
4 slices of white bread, crusts removed, crumbed
1 teaspoon chopped fresh parsley
1/2 teaspoon chopped fresh tarragon
1/2 teaspoon chopped fresh basil
Salt and freshly ground white pepper
Juice of 1/2 lemon

FOR THE ANCHOVY DIP
6 tinned anchovy fillets, drained
1 egg
25 g (1 oz) capers
1 garlic clove, crushed
2.5 cm (1 in) root ginger, peeled and chopped
1 bunch of fresh basil leaves
Juice of 1 lemon
1/2 teaspoon chopped fresh thyme
A pinch of sugar
50 ml (2 fl oz) warm water
225 ml (7 1/2 fl oz) olive oil
225 ml (7 1/2 fl oz) groundnut oil

Pre-heat the grill and butter and season a baking tray

To make the crumble topping, melt the butter with the chopped shallot or onion and cook without colour for 1–2 minutes. Mix the breadcrumbs and chopped herbs and season with salt and pepper. Mix some of the shallot butter into the crumbs until a crumbly texture is formed; you may not need all the shallot mixture. Add a few drops of lemon juice to the mix.

Sit the sardine fillets skin-side up on the tray. Sprinkle the crumble crumbs on top of each fillet. Place the sardines under a hot grill. Once the crumbs have become golden brown and crispy the fillets will be cooked; it will take just a few minutes.

Meanwhile, to make the anchovy dip, place all the ingredients, except the oils, in food processor and blitz to a paste. With the processor still running, slowly add the oil as you would for mayonnaise. Season the dressing with salt and pepper and push through a fine sieve. The dressing will have a mayonnaise sauce consistency, with a hint of green from the basil and capers.

Toss the salad leaves in some olive oil with salt and pepper and a few drops of lemon juice.

Spoon the anchovy dip on to the plates, forming a circular pattern. Sit the salad leaves on the centre of the sauce and place the crumbled fillets on top of the lettuce. The dish is ready.

Grilled Sardine Fillets on Tomato Toasts

This is a similar dish to Grilled Mackerel with Stewed Tomatoes, Pesto and Onions (see p. 69) but with this we've created different tastes and textures. It's not just an alternative, therefore, but a dish quite rightly out on its own. It may sound a little complicated but believe me, it's simple and tasty, so try it.

SERVES 4
8 fresh sardines, scaled and filleted
4 tablespoons olive oil
Juice of 1/2 lemon
Salt and freshly ground white pepper
4 × 1 cm (1/2 in) slices of crusty or
   onion bread

1 quantity Stewed Tomatoes, Pesto
   and Onions (see p. 69)
300 ml (10 fl oz) Hollandaise Sauce
   (see p. 373, optional)

In a dish large enough to hold the sardines in one layer, mix the olive oil with the lemon juice and season with salt and pepper. Lay the sardine fillets into the oil and leave for 1–2 hours to take on the taste.

Brush the bread slices with a little of the marinade oil. These slices can now be toasted on both sides until golden. Warm the stewed tomatoes with pesto.

Pre-heat the grill to hot. Season the sardine fillets with salt and pepper and lay them on a tray or grill rack and place under the hot grill. Just cook until slightly coloured. Providing the grill is hot this will only take 2–3 minutes.

To serve, spoon some hollandaise sauce, if using, on to four plates or into bowls, spreading it a little into a circle. Sit the toasts on top, and spoon the tomatoes with pesto on to them. Sit the sardines overlapping on top and just pour a little of the excess oil from the tray over the fish.

Crab and Salmon Fritters

These are a wonderful savoury starter than can also be cooked for hot canapés. The crab and salmon go together very well but chopped prawns and cod or lots of other combinations could be substituted for either. Once cooked until golden and crispy, I like to serve with a soured cream lemon or lime dip, made by flavouring some soured cream with lemon or lime juice, salt and pepper. This recipe comes in two parts: the crab and salmon filling and the choux pastry to bind it.

SERVES 6–8

FOR THE PASTRY
150 (fl oz) water
50 g (2 oz) butter
100 g (4 oz) plain flour
2 eggs, beaten
A pinch of salt

FOR THE FILLING
225 g (8 oz) salmon fillet
Salt and freshly ground white pepper

1 glass of white wine
15 g (^{1}/2 oz) unsalted butter
2 teaspoons olive oil
1 green pepper, seeded and finely diced
1 red pepper, seeded and finely diced
^{1}/2 bunch of spring onions, finely diced
15 g (^{1}/2 oz) root ginger, finely grated
225 g (8 oz) cooked white crab meat
1 teaspoon chopped fresh dill
Tabasco sauce

Pre-heat the oven to 200°C/400°F/gas 6 and grease and season a baking tray.

To make the pastry, bring the water and butter to the boil. Remove from the heat and add the flour. Return to the pan to a moderate heat and cook, stirring vigorously, until the paste comes away from the sides of the pan. Leave to cool. Gradually beat the eggs into the dough with the salt, leaving you with a smooth choux pastry mix with a dropping consistency.

To cook the salmon, sit it in the baking tray and add the glass of white wine. Cover with foil and bake in the pre-heated oven for 10–15 minutes, depending on the thickness of the fish. To check the salmon, it should be just firming to the touch, cooked like a medium steak, still pink in the middle. Once cooked, allow to cool. Reserve any cooking liquor.

Melt the butter with the olive oil. When it begins to bubble, add the peppers, spring onions and ginger and cook for 1–2 minutes. Remove from the pan and allow to cool.

The crab meat can be bought cooked and prepared (it's also possible to buy it frozen). Break it down and checked through for any broken shell. Add the salmon, peppers and dill and season with salt, pepper and a few drops of Tabasco sauce. Bind together with the choux pastry

Heat the deep-frying oil to 180°C/350°F. Spoon the fritter mix straight from the bowl into the fryer or on to a floured tray before cooking. This gives a rustic natural shape. Fry the fritters until golden brown and crispy. If they seem to be cooking too quickly, then turn the fryer down to 150°C/300°F.

NOTE

The fritters should be no bigger than a soup spoon size. This will ensure they cook evenly. For little tasters, the size of a teaspoon should be just right.

Crab Dumplings

Here's another dish that has come from one recipe, had a small change and become something completely different. This was originally a Bone Marrow Dumplings (see p. 403). It can also be made with horseradish to go with tuna (see p. 105 Grilled Tuna on Greens with Horseradish Dumplings and Red Wine Dressing). These dumplings will go so well with the Red Mullet Broth (see p. 19), Mulligatawny Soup (see p. 15), home-made Crab Bisque (see p. 22) or even just tinned bisque. Or perhaps you could feature these as a fish starter, using a tin of bisque finished with a squeeze of fresh lemon juice and dot of cream or crème fraîche as your sauce. They also eat very well with the Spinach with Soured Lime Cream and Spicy Curry Dressing from the halibut recipe on p. 99.

MAKES 4 large or 8 small dumplings
100 g (4 oz) white crab meat
100 g (4 oz) fresh white breadcrumbs
2 tablespoons double cream
3 egg yolks

Salt and freshly ground black pepper
Freshly grated nutmeg
600 ml (1 pint) Fish Stock (see p. 399)
or water for poaching

Place the breadcrumbs, double cream and egg yolks in a food processor or liquidizer and season with salt, pepper and nutmeg. Blitz until thoroughly mixed. Before adding the crab meat, make sure it has been checked for any shell. Fold the crab into the mix, then chill for 1 hour before cooking.

Once set, heat the fish stock or water to simmering point. The dumplings can now be shaped between two serving spoons or rolled into balls by hand and dropped into the liquor. Bring back to the simmer and cook large dumplings for 8–10 minutes and small for 5–6 minutes. Remove from the stock with a slotted spoon and serve immediately.

VARIATION

The dumplings also work very well shallow-fried for about 5 minutes.

Crab Risotto

Seafood risottos are really delightful to eat. In Italy, meat or fish are almost always included in the dish rather than served with it, making the risotto a complete meal in itself.

For the maximum crab flavour; it's best to use fresh crab cooked in fish stock. This will leave you with a good crab stock to lift the flavour. If you are using fresh crab, follow the cooking method from Crab Bisque (see p. 22). Otherwise, cooked white crab meat can be obtained from most fishmongers or supermarkets, either fresh or frozen.

I also like to serve the risotto finished with a border of Crab Bisque. This is well worth the effort; it totally lifts the whole dish. But remember that tinned crab bisque is available – one or two tablespoons will be enough.

SERVES 4–6

1.2 litres (2 pints) Fish Stock
  (see p. 399)
100–175 g (4–6 oz) unsalted butter
1 tablespoon olive oil
2 onions, finely chopped
25–50 g (1–2 oz) bone marrow, chopped
  (optional)
225 g (8 oz) Arborio rice

225 g (8 oz) white crab meat, shredded
Salt and freshly ground white pepper
1–2 tablespoons finely grated
  Parmesan (optional)
Crab Bisque (see p. 22) or tinned
  (optional)
Parmesan flakes (optional)
Olive oil

Bring the fish or crab stock to the simmer. Melt 100 g (4 oz) of the butter with the olive oil, add the onions and cook for 3–4 minutes, without colouring. As the onions begin to soften, add the bone marrow, if using. Add the rice and cook for 2–3 minutes. Now add two ladles of hot stock, keeping the rice over a medium heat. The hot stock will create a steam and immediately begin to evaporate. Because you only add a ladle at a time, the rice will absorb the stock without becoming totally encased. This is the process that helps cream the risotto.

Continue to add the stock a little at a time until the rice is tender; this will take about 20 minutes. The finished texture of the rice should have the slightest bite to it.

Add the crab meat and the remaining butter and season with salt and pepper. I also like to add a little Parmesan to lift the taste. The consistency should not be at all stodgy but rich and creamy. Some crab bisque can be added to the finished risotto to improve the flavour and consistency even more; you will need to use only a few spoonfuls.

The risotto is now ready to serve. If you are using crab bisque, spoon the risotto into bowls and pour some more bisque around. The risotto can also be garnished with Parmesan flakes and a trickle of olive oil.

VARIATIONS

This recipe can be used for lobster, prawn or shrimp risotto. Mussels also make a good risotto. Clean them (see p. 17) and then cook them first in fish stock, using the resulting mussel stock for the risotto which will make it really full of flavour. Don't add the cooked mussels to the rice until the end of the cooking time otherwise they will be overcooked and tough.

Tuna Carpaccio

Fresh tuna fish must be one of the most versatile fish to cook with. I has a fillet steak texture and eats so well when cooked medium rare to medium.

Carpaccio is most commonly known using beef, as in the recipe on p. 80. It's simply raw beef sliced very thinly and then served with a tasty dressing. Well, this dish is going to be very similar, but instead of serving the tuna completely 'raw' I almost cure it, as you would when making gravadlax. This really helps the flavour of the tuna, giving you the strong flavours of salt, sugar and fresh dill.

As a garnish for this dish, giving you more texture, a green salad will work; or how about trying Crispy Spinach (see p. 225)? I prefer to serve the spinach. This does give you two totally different textures, with the 'raw' tuna and crispy spinach. I normally serve just a small pile of the spinach at the top of the plate.

This dish can also become a sort of canapé by rolling some of the spinach in the tuna. Biting through the very tender succulent fish into the crispy spinach is wonderful.

SERVES 6–8
450 g (1 lb) tuna fillet
25 g (1 oz) coarse sea salt
50 g (2 oz) demerara sugar
1 heaped teaspoon pink peppercorns,
    chopped or crushed

2 teaspoons chopped fresh dill, plus
    more for dressing (optional)
Finely grated zest of $1/2$ lemon
A pinch of freshly ground black pepper
150 ml (5 fl oz) olive oil

Trim the tuna of all skin, leaving just pure tuna meat. Mix together the sea salt, demerara sugar, pink peppercorns, chopped dill, grated lemon zest and black pepper and spread over the fish, then pour over the olive oil. Cover and chill, turning occasionally, for 48 hours.

During this time the salt and sugar will dissolve and cure the fish. Lift the fish from the oil which will not be used for the dressing. It is now ready to serve or can be wrapped in cling film and frozen until needed.

Pour the oil into a pan and bring to the boil. Pour it through a sieve and leave to cool. This will leave you with a strongly flavoured dressing. When using the dressing, some more chopped dill can be added to lift the flavour.

To serve, slice the tuna *very* thinly, allowing 3–4 slices per portion. If you have frozen the fillet, it's best to slice on a machine and then arrange and allow to thaw on the serving plates. To finish, spoon the marinade dressing over and serve with a spoonful of crispy spinach.

Seared Tuna with Garlic and Almond Cream

I like to eat tuna just like a steak, medium rare, keeping the meat moist and succulent with a good texture and taste. Searing the fillet in a good, hot pan will give me just that – it's virtually in and out. If you prefer the tuna well done, then just pan-fry the fish for a little longer on both sides. The garlic and almond cream spread on top and glazed gives an even better taste.

If you can't get tuna, this recipe will work with most other fish. They will, however, need to be properly pan-fried and not just seared.

For a good finish to this dish, I sit the hot, grilled tuna on top of a French Bean and Sesame Salad (see p. 214).

SERVES 4
4 × 175 g (6 oz) tuna fillet steaks

FOR THE GARLIC AND ALMOND CREAM
3 garlic cloves, crushed
A pinch of salt
2 medium slices of white bread, soaked in water
2 teaspoons white wine vinegar
2 egg yolks
150 ml (5 fl oz) olive oil
65 g (2¹/₂ oz) ground almonds
1–2 drops of soy sauce (optional)

To make the garlic and almond cream, crush the garlic with the salt. Squeeze the excess water from the bread, then blitz it in a food processor or liquidizer with the garlic. Whisk the white wine vinegar with the egg yolks, then gradually whisk in the oil a drop at a time as you would when making mayonnaise. Mix the garlic and bread mixture with the mayonnaise and blitz in the ground almonds. Enhance the flavour with the soy sauce, if liked.

Pre-heat the grill.

The tuna should now be seared on both sides in a hot pan. Spread the cream on top, being fairly generous. All you need to do now is glaze the cream under the hot grill and the fish is ready to sit on top of the prepared French bean and sesame salad.

Grilled Tuna with Salsa Dressing or Sauerkraut

As you can see in the title, there's already two options for the tuna in this recipe, both of which are excellent. This dish also eats well as a main course. The tuna is best cooked and served as medium rare steak, still nice and pink in the centre, to help the taste and texture. The tuna can be grilled or pan-fried, and should be served warm with the cold salsa dressing or with the warm sauerkraut (p. 171 – half the recipe will be enough for 4–6 starter portions).

If fresh tuna is unavailable or hard to get hold of, then other fish can be used – salmon, red mullet, trout or more. Tinned tuna can also be used and broken down with a fork and then mixed with the salsa dressing, this eats very well with a salad or even just a sandwich filling. The sauerkraut will only really work with fresh tuna steaks. The sauerkraut version is best served warm on the plate, topped with some salad leaves and then the tuna steak sat on top. A good basic dressing with chopped chives goes very well with this dish.

The salsa is best served just sat next to the tuna with some green leaves (see p. 385).

SERVES 4–6

4 × 100–175 g (4–6 oz) tuna fillet steaks
Olive oil
Salt and freshly ground black pepper

Green or mixed salad leaves
Basic Vinaigrette (see p. 379)
Salsa Dressing (see p. 385) or
 1/2 quantity Sauerkraut (see p. 171)

To cook the tuna, lightly brush the fish with olive oil and season with salt and pepper. The fish can now either be grilled on a hot grill or barbecue or pan-fried in a hot frying-pan. If the thickness of the steaks is 1 cm (1/2 in), the fish will only take 1–2 minutes on each side before it is ready to serve.

Toss the salad leaves in a little vinaigrette and arrange on plates with the steak.

Now all you have to do is decide – salsa or sauerkraut?

Seared Peppered Salmon

This dish has very few ingredients but the method and preparation give lots of texture and taste. It's like eating warm salmon gravad lax with a fiery bite from the finely ground pepper.

The salmon can just be sliced and eaten, but the raw black pepper is very strong. The purpose of the searing is to take away that rawness, create texture and give aroma and bite. I like to eat it with Cucumber Pickle (see p. 390) – the classic salmon and cucumber combination with a difference.

SERVES 4–6
450 g (1 lb) salmon fillet, with skin
1 tablespoon finely ground black
   pepper

1 tablespoon salt
1 tablespoon caster sugar
Olive oil
Lemon or lime juice

Trim the salmon fillet and remove any bones. Along the fillet run several 'pin' bones; these can easily be removed with tweezers or small pliers. The black pepper must be finely ground. You can do this in a food processor or in a pepper mill. Shake the pepper through a sieve to leave you with a fine grind. Mix with the salt and sugar and sprinkle over the salmon so that it is covered in one layer of ground black pepper. Wrap the salmon in cling film and chill. The salmon will be 'cooked' by the salt and sugar mix. This curing process can take as little as 1–2 hours, but I like to make this in the morning for eating in the evening.

   Remove the cling film and cut the salmon into 2–3 cm (3/4–1 1/4 in) thick slices. Pre-heat a frying-pan and brush with olive oil. Make sure the pan is hot. Sit the salmon in the pan and sear for about 15–20 seconds on one side. Providing that the pan is hot, the salmon will be almost raw but just coloured, with very slightly burnt tinges burnt on the pepper. Serve the salmon as a starter with a squeeze of lemon or lime juice or try it sitting on the cucumber pickle.

Potted Salmon

This a good summer dish which can be made and set in a serving dish and used as a starter or main course. Always be careful when cooking salmon, as the fish is delicate. It needs very little cooking and should always be pink in the centre to keep it moist and succulent.

To make the clarified butter, simply melt 350 g (12 oz) of unsalted butter until it foams, then let the foam die. Don't allow it to brown. Remove from the heat and leave to stand until the milky residue sinks to the bottom. Strain off through muslin.

You can make the salmon pots a few days in advance, but always serve them at room temperature. This will allow the butter to become softer and a lot tastier.

SERVES 4
450 g (1 lb) salmon fillet
300 ml (10 fl oz) clarified butter
2 shallots, finely chopped
1 small garlic clove, crushed
1/2 teaspoon ground mace
1/2 teaspoon salt

Freshly ground white pepper
1 tablespoon chopped fresh parsley
1 tablespoon chopped fresh tarragon
A few salad leaves
1 lemon, cut into wedges
Warm toast, to serve

Trim the salmon fillet and cut into 1 cm (1/2 in) cubes. Warm the clarified butter to simmering point and add the chopped shallots. Cook for a few minutes until the shallots have softened. Add the garlic, mace, salt and pepper. Carefully spoon the salmon into the butter and return to a *low* heat. The salmon can now only be stirred very carefully to avoid breaking. As soon as the salmon has a light opaque colour, after about 5–6 minutes, remove it from the heat and allow to cool. Add the chopped parsley and tarragon.

Spoon the salmon into individual 7.5 cm (3 in) serving moulds, making sure that the shallots and herbs are evenly distributed between the moulds. Top up with the remaining butter. You may find that you have some butter left. This can be used for cooking fish, or frozen until the next time. Cool and chill the moulds until set.

Remove from the fridge and allow to return to room temperature. Turn out the moulds on to plates and garnish with salad leaves and lemon. This dish also eats well with warm thick toast.

Seared Salmon on Soured Baked Potato

Fresh or smoked salmon, or even both, can be used with this dish. I like to use smoked salmon as its smoky flavour, half cooked, works so well with the sharp, tangy, sour taste.

SERVES 4

4 × 5 mm (^{1}/$_2$ in) slices of smoked salmon, each about 75–100 g (3–4 oz)
^{1}/$_2$ quantity Soured Baked Potatoes (see p. 234)

1 tablespoon olive oil
A squeeze of fresh lemon juice
1 tablespoon chopped fresh parsley or snipped fresh chives

Make the soured baked potatoes, filling all four of the half-skins so you have a smaller quantity than you would for a main course. All you then have to do is sear the salmon in a hot pan on one side only to cook just half-way through and give a golden edge to the fish. Sit a soured baked potato on a plate and arrange the salmon on top. Trickle with some olive oil, lemon juice, parsley or chives and you have a finished dish.

Mackerel Croquettes

These croquettes can be made with other fish: salmon, cod, prawns or shrimps. To the mackerel fillets in this recipe, I've also added some smoked mackerel. This is not essential, but it does enhance the whole flavour of the fish without being overpowering.

SERVES 4–6

4 mackerel fillets, skinned

2 shallots or 1 small onion, finely
   chopped

Salt and freshly ground white pepper

1 glass of white wine

1 bunch of spring onions, chopped

1 smoked mackerel fillet

225–350 g (8–12 oz) Mashed Potatoes
   (see p. 230), without milk, butter or
   cream

Cayenne pepper

2 tablespoons plain flour

1 egg, beaten

100 g (4 oz) breadcrumbs

25 g (1 oz) unsalted butter and cooking
   oil, or oil for deep-frying

1 lemon or lime, cut into wedges

1 quantity Lemon Butter Sauce
   (see p. 371)

Pre-heat the oven to 200°C/400°F/gas 6 and butter a roasting tray.

To remove the central bones from the mackerel fillets, cut either side of the bones straight through the fish. This will leave eight strips of mackerel. Sit the fish on the tray with the chopped shallots, and season with salt and pepper. Add the white wine and cook in the pre-heated oven for about 6–8 minutes; the mackerel should only be just cooked. Drain off any excess liquor into a small pan, bring to the boil and boil to reduce by at least half. When the liquor has reduced, add the chopped spring onions and cook for 30–60 seconds until only just beginning to soften.

Flake the smoked and cooked mackerel fillets and add the spring onion reduction. Fold in 225 g (8 oz) of the mashed potatoes, which will be enough to bind. The texture can be loosened by adding more potato. Season with salt and cayenne pepper. Shape into balls or croquettes about 6 × 2 cm (2$^{1}/_{2}$ × $^{3}/_{4}$ in). Leave to chill in the fridge.

Dust the croquettes lightly in flour, then pass through beaten egg. Roll in bread-crumbs and re-shape gently, if necessary, with a palette knife. To shallow-fry, heat the butter and oil over a medium heat and fry for 2–3 minutes until golden on all sides. To deep-fry, heat the fat to 150°C/300°F and fry until golden. Serve with lemon or lime wedges and lemon butter sauce.

VARIATIONS

Soured cream, flavoured with fresh lime juice, salt and pepper, makes a tasty dip to serve with the croquettes.

Grilled Mackerel with Mussel Stew

You can leave out the first stage in cooking the mussel stew, if you wish, and simply cook the mussels in fish stock, but the pre-cooking does give a lot more flavour to the cooking liquor.

SERVES 4
4 mackerel fillets
25 g (1 oz) unsalted butter
Salt and freshly ground black
   pepper

**FOR THE MUSSEL COOKING
LIQUOR**
1 tablespoon unsalted butter
1 carrot, diced
1 onion, diced
1 celery stick, diced
1 bay leaf
1 sprig of fresh tarragon
300 ml (10 fl oz) dry white wine
600 ml (1 pint) Fish Stock (see
   p. 399)
900 g (2 lb) fresh mussels, washed and
   bearded (see p. 17)

FOR THE STEW
2 tablespoons olive oil
100 g (4 oz) unsalted butter
2 large carrots, cut into 5 mm (1/4 in)
   dice
2 onions, cut into 5 mm (1/4 in) dice
3 celery sticks, cut into 5 mm (1/4 in)
   dice
1 bouquet garni (a few fresh basil and
   tarragon leaves and 1 star anise
   tied in a muslin bag) or bouquet
   garni sachet
300 ml (10 fl oz) dry white wine
2 teaspoons Pesto Sauce
   (see p. 374)
2 large tomatoes, skinned, seeded and
   diced
1 teaspoon chopped fresh parsley

Butter and season a baking tray.

Trim the mackerel fillets and remove all central bones. This can be done easily by cutting either side of the bones down to the skin but not cutting through. Pick from the head and pull out the central bones; they will come away from the skin in one piece. Place the fillets on the prepared tray, skin-side up. Brush the skin with butter and season with salt and pepper, then place in the fridge.

To cook the mussel liquor, melt the butter in a pan and add the carrot, onion, celery, bay leaf and tarragon and cook gently, without colour, until softened. Add the white wine and boil until the liquid has almost evaporated. Add the stock and bring to a rapid simmer.

Drop the cleaned and bearded mussels into the cooking liquor. Bring the liquid back to the boil, stirring frequently. As soon as the mussels begin to open, drain in a colander, reserving the stock. This should now be drained through a fine sieve. Pick the mussels from their shells and check that they are clean from all impurities. Discard any that have not opened.

Warm a pan and add the olive oil and 25 g (1 oz) of the butter. Add the diced vegetables with the bouquet garni. Cook without colouring until they begin to soften. Add the white wine and reduce until almost dry. Add enough of the mussel stock to cover the vegetables; you may not need all of the stock so just add a little at a time. Bring to a simmer and cook until the vegetables are tender. This will take about 8–10 minutes.

Pre-heat the grill.

Cook the mackerel fillets under the pre-heated grill until the skin is crisp. The fish will only take 4–6 minutes.

While the mackerel is cooking, whisk the remaining butter into the liquor and add some pesto sauce to taste, the diced tomatoes, chopped fresh parsley and, of course, the mussels. Warm through and spoon into large bowls, distributing the garnish equally. Sit the mackerel on top and serve.

Fillet of Mackerel with Caramelized Onions and Sweet Peppers

In this recipe, the mackerel is 'cooked' in a sousing liquor made with white wine, white wine vinegar and water and flavoured with pickling spices, star anise and herbs. The combination of the sharp, soused taste and the sweetness of the onions and peppers works really well. I like to present this dish on very thin short pastry discs. This gives the dish another texture, almost like eating on open flan.

SERVES 4

1 quantity Shortcrust Pastry
(see p. 394)

4 mackerel fillets, skinned and
trimmed

2 tablespoons Basic Vinaigrette
(see p. 379)

A few drops of balsamic vinegar

2 teaspoons fresh chives, snipped 1 cm
(1/2 in) long

FOR THE PEPPERS AND ONIONS

4 large onions, sliced

1 tablespoon water

1 large red pepper, seeded and cut into
strips

1 tablespoon olive oil

Salt and freshly ground black pepper

FOR THE SOUSING LIQUOR

2 teaspoons olive oil

1/2 onion, roughly chopped

1 small carrot, roughly chopped

1 celery stick, roughly chopped

1 sprig of fresh thyme

1 sprig of fresh tarragon

1 bay leaf

1 star anise (optional)

2 teaspoons pickling spice

85 ml (3 fl oz) white wine

85 ml (3 fl oz) white wine vinegar

450 ml (15 fl oz) water

A pinch of salt

Juice of 1/2 lemon

Pre-heat the oven to 190°C/375°F/gas 5.

Roll out the pastry very thinly, cut into 7.5–10 cm (3–4 in) discs and leave to rest in the fridge for 20 minutes. Bake in the pre-heated oven for about 10 minutes until cooked through and crisp.

To caramelize the onions, simply place them in a pan with a tablespoon of water and cook, uncovered, over a low heat for about 2 hours until all the natural juices and sugars from the onions begin to colour to a rich, golden brown. This can be done in advance.

Cook the red peppers in the olive oil for 2–3 minutes, until softened. Add to the caramelized onions and season with salt and pepper.

Meanwhile, make the sousing liquor. Warm the olive oil and add the onion, carrot, celery, thyme, tarragon, bay leaf, star anise and pickling spice. Cook for a few minutes, until the vegetables begin to soften. Add the white wine, wine vinegar and water with a pinch of salt and the lemon juice. Bring to the simmer and cook for 15–20 minutes. Strain.

Place the mackerel fillets in the warm sousing liquor and bring almost to the simmer. This will just warm them through, keeping the fish succulent and juicy.

Sweeten the dressing with a little balsamic vinegar and add the chives.

Spoon the warm onion and pepper mix on to the pastry discs and lay the mackerel fillets on top. Spoon the dressing over and around the mackerel.

VARIATIONS

If you haven't got enough time to make the caramelized onions, simply fry 2 or 3 sliced onions in butter until golden brown and almost burnt. This will give a more bittersweet taste that will become a lot sweeter when added to the red pepper.

Soused Mackerel with Warm Potatoes

Sousing or pickling is usually associated with raw fish. This recipe is slightly different. the mackerel is heated briefly in its spicy liquor, then served warm with the potatoes. This makes the liquor a sauce, and the addition of potato makes the mackerel a complete dish.

SERVES 4
1 small fennel bulb, very thinly sliced
2 carrots, thinly sliced
2 celery sticks, thinly sliced
1 leek, thinly sliced
2 shallots or onion, thinly sliced
1 bouquet garni (1 bay leaf, 1 star
    anise, a few fresh basil leaves, 2
    sprigs each of fresh thyme and
    tarragon tied in a square of muslin
    or a strip of leek leaves) or bouquet
    garni sachet
6 black peppercorns

50 ml (2 fl oz) olive oil
100 g (4 oz) unsalted butter
150 ml (5 fl oz) dry white wine
150 ml (5 fl oz) white wine vinegar
600 ml (1 pint) water
4 mackerel fillets, all bones removed
Salt and freshly ground white pepper
1 quantity Mashed Potatoes (see
    p. 230)
1 shallot, finely diced
Juice of 1 lemon
1 tablespoon chopped fresh
    parsley

Cook all the sliced vegetables in a pan with the bouquet garni, peppercorns, olive oil and half the butter for a few minutes. Add the white wine, wine vinegar and water and simmer for about 10–12 minutes until the vegetables are cooked. This is your sousing liquor. Allow to cool and remove garni.

Place the fillets in a lightly buttered flameproof dish and cover with the liquor and vegetables. Season with salt and pepper. Bring slowly to the simmer then remove from the heat. The fish is now ready.

Fry the shallot in a knob of butter, without colouring and add to the hot mashed potatoes, with the lemon juice. Mix and spoon some into serving bowls. Sit the mackerel on top. Stir the remaining butter and the parsley into the cooking liquor. Spoon the vegetables and sauce round the fish and serve.

Grilled Mackerel with Stewed Tomatoes, Pesto and Onions

Here we are looking at simple ingredients, and we all know that tomatoes, onions, garlic and basil work well together. I have added the slight Italian influence, using pesto sauce. This has so many uses: as a seasoning, a sauce on its own, or to flavour cream sauces or tomatoes. It can be made at home, but good pesto can be found in almost any supermarket or delicatessen.

I use the mackerel as a starter and so only serve one fillet a portion, but like most dishes this would also make a good main course for two.

SERVES 4

FOR THE TOMATOES, PESTO AND ONIONS
2–3 tablespoons olive oil
3 onions, thinly sliced
12 tomatoes, preferably plum, skinned
    and quartered
1 tablespoon Pesto Sauce (see p. 374)

FOR THE MACKEREL
Salt and freshly ground white pepper
Oil, for deep-frying (preferably
    groundnut)
25 g (1 oz) unsalted butter
4 mackerel fillets, all bones removed
1 tablespoon plain flour
Curly endive leaves
1–2 tablespoons Basic Vinaigrette
    (see p. 379)

Pour the olive oil into a pan and add one-third of the sliced onions. Allow to cook gently for about 10 minutes until the onions are soft but not coloured. Add the quartered tomatoes and continue to cook for 15–20 minutes until the tomatoes have stewed with the onions, creating their own sauce. Add the pesto sauce to taste (approximately a tablespoon will be enough) and season with salt and pepper.

Pre-heat the grill to moderate and heat the oil for deep-frying. Brush a tray with a little of the butter and season it with salt and pepper. Lay the mackerel fillets on top and brush with butter. Cook the fillets under the grill for about 5–6 minutes until the skin is crisp. Meanwhile, lightly dust the remaining onions with flour. Fry in the deep hot oil until golden and crisp. Drain well and season with a little salt.

Spoon some of the warm tomato mixture on to individual plates. Dress the curly endive with a little vinaigrette and place a few leaves on to each tomato mound. Lay the mackerel fillets on top and finish the dish with the crispy onions.

Grilled Mackerel with Pickled Red Cabbage and Creamy Anchovy Sauce

There are so many ways of pickling foods. In this recipe, the ingredients are prepared in the morning and will be ready to eat in the evening. Many other recipes have to be planned well in advance: ingredients steeped in cold vinegar with spices can take up to six weeks to mature. The vinegar used can be natural or sweetened. Also the strength of the pickle can be determined by the spices and quantity of dried chillies used.

There's also hot and cold pickling. Cold pickling is probably best if you're using onions or cabbage to be eaten at a later date, as this will keep them crisper. A hot method is better for pickling fruits.

In this recipe, I'm using the hot technique so the cabbage will be ready within hours. You can leave out the muslin bag of pickling spices if you prefer. Also, I prefer to leave this recipe unsweetened but, if you like sweeter pickles, then simply add 15–25 g (½–1 oz) of white sugar to the vinegar before boiling.

The cabbage and dressing work very well together, but so do just the mackerel and the cabbage on their own. Or you could try Mustard Dressing (see p. 382) or Cider Dressing (see p. 32).

SERVES 4
4 mackerel fillets
A knob of unsalted butter
Salt and freshly ground black pepper

FOR THE PICKLED RED CABBAGE
½ red cabbage, approximately
   225–350 g (8–12 oz)
A pinch of salt
50 ml (5 fl oz) red wine vinegar
1 teaspoon dried pickling spices, tied
   in muslin

FOR THE DRESSING
2 egg yolks or I hard-boiled egg
25 g (1 oz) anchovy fillets, drained and
   chopped
2 teaspoons capers
2 teaspoons Worcestershire sauce
1 teaspoon Dijon mustard
A dash of Tabasco sauce
Juice of ½ lemon
1 small garlic clove, crushed
2 tablespoons finely grated Parmesan
   (optional)
Freshly ground black pepper
150 ml (5 fl oz) olive oil

The cabbage must be made several hours in advance. Cut the cabbage into three and remove the core and stalk. Shred the cabbage very finely and add a pinch of salt. Bring the red wine vinegar to the boil with the pickling spices. Once boiling, pour on top of the cabbage, stirring to make sure the cabbage is covered. Place a lid on top, remove from the heat and leave to steep for several hours. When the cabbage is ready to use, remove and squeeze the muslin bag to release all the flavours. Warm just to room temperature.

Pre-heat the grill.

The dressing can be made very quickly in a food processor or liquidizer. Blitz the egg yolks or hard-boiled eggs with all other ingredients except the olive oil. The oil can then be added slowly as the mix is blending. Once all oil has been added, just push the dressing through a sieve to give a creamy consistency. You should have about 300 ml (10 fl oz) of dressing.

To cook the mackerel, lightly butter and season the fillets before sitting under the pre-heated grill. The fillets will take between 4–6 minutes, leaving the skin crispy.

To serve, spoon some pickled red cabbage on to the centre of the plates and pour the creamy dressing around before sitting the crispy hot grilled mackerel on top.

RED WINE VINEGAR

A lot of the basic red wine vinegars available in most supermarkets and food stores are thin and not very red-wine-flavoured. They will work but will not give you the fullest of flavours. Good red wine vinegar is now available at most large superstores and delicatessens. The way to check is to look for the hallmarks of a good wine. For instance, a red Bordeaux vinegar is made from Appellation Contrôlée Bordeaux wines. Of course, these are more expensive and could also become too strong and powerful. I always find it best to use two-thirds basic red wine vinegar and one-third strong red wine vinegar. So if you see some, do try it – you will not be disappointed with the results.

Kipper Rarebit on Toast

Kippers simply cooked in milk with butter or just grilled eat really well. The wonderful, silky soft texture of the flakes work in salads, risottos and now with my cheese on toast.

Of course, this dish doesn't have to be just a snack, it eats well as a starter or main course. I sometimes like to serve the poached flakes of kipper on spinach topped with some rarebit and glazed until golden, then finished with a warm poached egg. When you break the egg and eat it with the rarebit, kipper and spinach – well, it's a dream.

Here's the recipe for 'kipper cheese on toast'. It also eats well if tomatoes have been sliced and laid on the toast first.

MAKES 6 slices
2 kippers
150–300 ml (5–10 fl oz) milk
A knob of unsalted butter
6 thick slices of bread

FOR THE RAREBIT
225 g (8 oz) Cheddar
2 tablespoons milk

1 small garlic clove, crushed
Fine pinch of paprika
1 tablespoon plain flour
1 tablespoon fresh white
  breadcrumbs
1 teaspoon English mustard powder
A few shakes of Worcestershire sauce
Freshly ground black pepper
1 egg, beaten

Place the kippers in a pan and cover with milk and butter. Bring to the boil, remove from the heat and leave to stand for 5–6 minutes. Lift the kippers from the pan and trim off all skin and bones. You should have 225 g (8 oz) of flesh.

To make the rarebit, melt together the Cheddar and milk with the garlic and paprika. When the mixture becomes smooth, add the flour, breadcrumbs and mustard powder and cook for a few minutes until the mixture comes away from the sides of the pan. Add the Worcestershire sauce and season with pepper. Leave to cool slightly. While just warm, beat in the egg. The mix is now ready.

Pre-heat the grill. At this stage, the kipper should be broken into flakes. Now add enough of the rarebit to the kipper to bind together. Toast the bread. Spoon and spread the kipper rarebit on the toast and place under the grill until golden. The dish is ready to eat.

NOTE

The remaining rarebit mix will keep for up to a week refrigerated, or it can be frozen.

Smoked Haddock with Welsh Rarebit

This has to be one of my favourites – possibly a signature dish and, hopefully, a classic. It's lovely as a starter or main course. Cheese and tomato are a great combination, so placing the haddock on to a tomato salad works really well and, of course, gives us those hot and cold tastes. Choose really good tomatoes – plum are much the best.

I have chosen natural smoked haddock which is quite white in colour. The yellow-dyed haddock is not really needed as the cheese is, of course, already that colour – and you know that I like natural tastes, textures and colours.

SERVES 4
6 ripe plum or salad tomatoes
Salt and freshly ground white pepper
**4 × 100 g (4 oz) slices of natural
  smoked haddock**
175 g (6 oz) Welsh Rarebit mix (see p. 40)

**1 tablespoon finely snipped fresh
  chives**
**150 ml (5 fl oz) Basic Vinaigrette
  (see p. 379)**

Pre-heat the oven to 180°C/350°F/gas 4 and pre-heat the grill to medium.

Firstly, remove and discard the eyes from the tomatoes. Blanch the tomatoes in boiling water for 5–6 seconds, Cool them quickly in iced water and the skins should peel off easily. Slice the tomatoes and arrange, overlapping in the centre of individual plates. You'll need about 1½ tomatoes per portion, and this should make a nice circle. Sprinkle with a little salt and a twist of pepper.

Arrange the haddock portions in a buttered flameproof dish. Split the rarebit into four pieces, pat out on your hands to about 2–3 mm (1/8 in) thick and lay on top of the haddock (the mix should be quite pliable and easy to use). Colour under the grill until golden then finish the haddock in the pre-heated oven for 3–4 minutes.

Add the chives to the vinaigrette and spoon over the tomatoes. When the haddock is cooked, just sit it on top of the tomatoes and serve.

Cod Brandade with Warm Poached Egg

This dish needs a lot of planning and thinking time, but really is worth every effort. The basic mixture makes more than you need for four, because 75 g (3 oz) will be enough per starter portion. The rest of the mixture can be stored in the fridge for a day or so and can be rolled into balls and coated with breadcrumbs then deep-fried as for the Salmon Fish Cakes (see p. 109).

SERVES 4
900 g (2 lb) cod fillet, with skin
Rock salt
8 black peppercorns
1 sprig of fresh thyme
1 bay leaf
200 ml (7 fl oz) olive oil
1 large garlic clove, finely chopped
1–1.5 kg (2–3 lb) Mashed Potatoes
    without cream or butter (see p. 230)

2 tablespoons chopped fresh parsley
Freshly ground white pepper

TO SERVE
Milk
4 eggs, poached (see p. 38)
300 ml (10 fl oz) Brandade Dressing
    (see p. 384)
Olive oil

Sprinkle the cod liberally with rock salt, cover and place in the fridge for 48 hours, turning it at least once. After the fish has been salted, it needs to be washed to remove the salt, then soaked for 12 hours in cold water.

Drain the fish well and cut it into eight pieces. Place in a pan with the peppercorns, thyme and bay leaf and just cover with cold water. Bring to the boil then remove from the heat and allow to cool. Remove the cod from the liquid, take off the skin and pick out any bones. Flake the flesh.

Warm the olive oil in a large pan then add the cod. While it is cooking for a few minutes, add the garlic and break up the fish with a wooden spoon. Add some mashed potatoes, working on a ratio of two parts potato to one part cod. Add the parsley and season with white pepper. This mixture can now be left to cool, then chilled.

To serve the brandade, place it in a pan with a little milk over a gentle heat until warmed through. While the cod is warming, poach the eggs. Then spoon the cod on to the centre of the plates and sit the warm poached eggs on top. Spoon the dressing generously all around and trickle a little extra olive oil over the eggs.

Grilled Trout Fillets on Almond Toasts or Trout and Almond Toasts

This recipe is taking a classic combination of flavours – trout and almonds – and giving you two different ways of eating them.

The first alternative is to toast the almond cream on toast, and then sit the grilled fillet on top. The other alternative is to steam the trout lightly and then, once cold, break it down and add it to the cream. Both work very well. The fillet of fish gives you a coarser texture and the steamed version gives you many options for eating it as a starter, snack or on small toast canapés.

SERVES 4

4 × 100 g (4oz) trout fillets, with skin

$1/2$ quantity Garlic and Almond Cream (see p. 61), made without garlic or with just $1/2$ clove

8 × 1 cm ($1/2$ in) slices of good-quality bread

A knob of unsalted butter

Salt and freshly ground black pepper

4 tablespoons olive oil

Juice of $1/2$ lemon

$1/2$ teaspoon chopped fresh parsley (optional)

2 teaspoons broken flaked almonds, toasted (optional)

Salad leaves, to garnish (optional)

Pre-heat the grill.

First prepare the almond cream. Once ready to eat and serve, toast the bread. Butter the trout fillets and season with salt and pepper. These can now be placed under the grill and cooked for 4–6 minutes until cooked and crispy. While the fish is cooking, generously spread some almond cream on to the toasts and glaze under the grill.

Whisk together the olive oil and lemon juice and season with salt and pepper. The chopped parsley and toasted almond flakes can also be added to create an interesting texture.

Sit the golden toasts on plates and top each with a fillet of trout. Garnish the plate with a few salad leaves, if liked, and then spoon some of the dressing over the salad and fish.

VARIATION

For the steamed version, simply steam the seasoned fillets on butter paper over boiling water for 3–4 minutes. Once cooked, allow the fillets to cool before removing the skin. Then simply break them down into flakes and mix with the almond cream. Spoon and spread on the toasts and finish under the grill. The same garnishes can be used on this method.

Devilled Herring Fingers

Devilled whitebait must be one of the first dishes you're taught at catering college. It's a real classic and a dish that I still enjoy. However, eating fish heads, tails and so on is not to everyone's taste. So something that I do from time to time is replace the whitebait with herring fillets. These just need to be cut into fingers, dipped in milk and flour and fried.

Whitebait is often served as a starter with just a squeeze of lemon, but the herring fingers can be the dish of your choice: perhaps a crispy fried herring salad or with a barbecue dip. The herrings also work well as a garnish for another fish dish, such as roasted salmon with spicy crisp herrings.

I like to eat the fingers as appetizers. They really get the taste buds going when served in a bowl with a good lemon mayonnaise or soured cream dip.

SERVES 4

4–6 large herring fillets, trimmed and
   cleaned
4 heaped tablespoons plain flour

2 teaspoons cayenne pepper
4 tablespoons milk
Oil, for deep-frying
Salt

Cut the herring fillets diagonally across into 5 mm (1/4 in) strips.

Mix the flour with the cayenne pepper. Dip the 'fingers' through the milk, then into the flour, shaking off any excess. The herring is now ready to be dropped into hot oil and deep-fried for about 1 minute until golden and crispy. Remove from the oil, drain on kitchen paper and sprinkle with salt. It really is as easy as that. Now you all you have to do is eat them.

The Rhodes 'Open' Club Sandwich

A club sandwich was one of the first dishes that I ever had to make – this was at the Amsterdam Hilton. The coffee shop was always packed, and the club sandwich was one of the most popular choices. This is my version and I hope you enjoy it. It's having just one slice of toast that makes this 'Open'. Make it as a starter for dinner parties – nobody will expect to be served a sandwich.

MAKES 2 sandwiches
2 slices of bread of your choice
Soft butter
1 chicken breast, skinned
Salt and freshly ground white pepper
1 tablespoon olive oil (if necessary)
2 smoked or green back bacon
   rashers, rinded

$^1/_2$ iceberg lettuce, shredded
1 tablespoon finely chopped onion
2 tablespoons Mayonnaise (see p. 380)
2–3 tomatoes, thinly sliced
2 tablespoon Basic Vinaigrette
   (see p. 379)
1 teaspoon chopped fresh parsley
2 poached eggs, warmed (see p. 38)

Pre-heat the grill to hot. Butter the bread on both sides and then toast it under the grill until golden brown.

Split the chicken breast lengthways through the middle and season with salt and pepper. Grill, or pan-fry in the olive oil, for a few minutes on each side until cooked. Grill the bacon until crisp. Mix the shredded lettuce and onion with the mayonnaise and season with salt and pepper.

Lay the tomato slices on top of the two pieces of toast and sprinkle with some of the vinaigrette. Divide the lettuce mixture between the two and top with the bacon and chicken breast halves. Sit the warmed poached eggs on the chicken breasts and mix the chopped parsley with the remaining vinaigrette and sprinkle over them.

Grilled Ham, Cheese and Tomato Toasts

This recipe is a designer sandwich which I often make from leftovers or as a complete supper meal. The cooked ham I'm using here is from Boiled Bacon with Pearl Barley and Lentils (see p. 174) – there always seems to be some left over. Of course, you don't have to cook bacon or ham just for this recipe; I'm sure you can buy some good cooked ham at the shops. Welsh rarebit, however, is a must for this dish. Plain melted cheese just isn't the same.

SERVES 4

4 slices of crusty bread
50 g (2 oz) unsalted butter
4 slices of cooked bacon or ham
  (see p. 174)
4 plum or salad tomatoes, sliced
Freshly ground black pepper

175 g (6 oz) Welsh Rarebit mix
  (see p. 40)
4 eggs, poached (see p. 38)
1 teaspoon chopped fresh parsley
50 ml (2 fl oz) Basic Vinaigrette
  (see p. 379)

Pre-heat the grill to hot. Butter the slices of bread and toast them on both sides. Lay the ham on to the buttered side. Cover with the sliced tomatoes and season with pepper. Split the rarebit into four pieces, pat out on your hands to the size and shape of the toast and lay on top of the tomatoes. Sit the toasts under the hot grill and colour the rarebit mix golden brown. Warm the poached eggs for a few minutes in a bowl of boiling water. Put the toasts on individual plates and top each one with a poached egg. Mix the chopped parsley with the vinaigrette and spoon over the top.

Chicken Wing Salad

If you have chicken wings left after preparing chicken breasts, this is a great way to use them. Barbecued chicken wings make a quick and easy snack, salad or lunch dish and are very moreish. The wings also eat well with soured cream, as a dip.

SERVES 4
900 g (2 lb) chicken wings
1 tablespoon paprika
Juice of 1–2 lemons

2 tablespoons soy sauce
Olive or cooking oil
Mixed salad leaves

Dust the chicken wings lightly with paprika. Add the lemon juice and soy sauce and toss together well. You can cook the wings now, but I prefer to leave them to take on the taste for anything from a few hours to a few days.

Lift the wings from the marinade. The best way to cook the wings is on an open barbecue. If you cannot do this, pre-heat the oven to 220°C/425°F/gas 7. Pre-heat a roasting tin on top of the stove with a little olive or cooking oil. Fry the wings until well coloured (even with a few burnt tinges), then transfer to the oven for 10–15 minutes.

Once the wings are cooked, pour over the marinade and bring to the boil. Remove from the heat and stir well. This will give the wings a paprika, lemon and soy glaze. Serve the wings on top of a mixed salad as a starter or in a big bowl for everyone to help themselves. They are also very good served with Peanut Sauce (see p. 78).

Chicken or Pork Satay Sticks

Here's a quick and easy marinade for chicken or pork (fish can also be used) that lifts the whole flavour of the complete dish, rather than the sauce trying to do that simply on its own.

For the meat to really take on the taste it's best to make at least 8 hours in advance and for a really strong flavour, 24 hours.

This recipe will give you approximately 16 half-filled 15 cm (6 in) bamboo skewers (a starter portion will need 3–4 sticks). If you prefer pork, I always use loin or pork fillet; both are very tender when cooked.

SERVES 2–4
4 chicken breasts or 450–675 g
 (1–1 1/2 lb)
pork loin or fillet

FOR THE MARINADE
6 tablespoons soy sauce
6 tablespoons teriyaki sauce/marinade
1 large garlic clove, crushed
1 teaspoon finely chopped fresh root
 ginger
1 teaspoon chopped fresh coriander

FOR THE PEANUT SAUCE
225 g (8 oz) crunchy peanut butter
3 garlic cloves, crushed
15 fresh coriander leaves
50 ml (2 fl oz) soy sauce
2 tablespoons Japanese sake
1/4–1/2 teaspoon chilli oil
120 ml (4 fl oz) coconut milk

Cut the chicken or pork into a small dice no bigger than 1 cm (1/2 in). These cubes can now be pushed on to soaked 15 cm (6 in) bamboo skewers, only covering half of each skewer with the meat.

Mix together all the marinade ingredients. The kebabs can now be placed in the marinade, covered with cling film and chilled for a minimum of 8 hours to achieve a good taste. If you can leave them for 24 hours you really will have the maximum taste. The quantity of marinade should be enough to cover all the meat. If all is not covered, then simply turn every 2 hours.

To make the sauce, blend the peanut butter with the garlic and coriander in a food processor or liquidizer. In a separate jug, mix the soy sauce, sake, chilli oil and coconut milk. With the motor running, pour the mixture slowly into the processor until all the liquid has blended in. The sauce should be thick but not set like peanut butter. If the sauce is too thick, just loosen it by adding a tablespoon of water at a time.

The kebabs are now ready to cook. The cooking process is really now up to you. These can be brushed in oil or butter and then fried, grilled or barbecued, taking 6–8 minutes. Meanwhile, warm the sauce in a pan, or serve it cold if you prefer (either eats very well).

Chicken Liver Parfait

This is a great dish for a starter or a main item on a cold buffet. I like to serve a slice on a plate with some good, thick toast, a few lettuce leaves and home-made Grape Chutney (see p. 386) or Green Tomato Chutney (see p. 386). I always cook this parfait in a loaf tin or porcelain terrine mould but, of course, individual 7.5 cm (3 in) moulds can be used.

SERVES 8–10

750 g (1¹/₂ lb) chicken livers, soaked for at least 24 hours in cold milk

1 garlic clove, crushed

Pinch of freshly grated nutmeg

Salt and freshly ground white pepper

3 eggs

900 ml (1¹/₂ pints) double cream

3 tablespoons brandy

About 3 tablespoons Veal *Jus* (see p. 387) or bought alternative (see p. 401) (optional)

Pre-heat the oven to 160°C/325°F/gas 3. Butter a 30 × 8 × 8 cm (12 × 3 × 3 in) terrine dish with a lid, a 900 g (2 lb) loaf tin, or eight to ten 7.5 cm (3 in) ramekin dishes and line them all with greaseproof paper.

Soaking the livers in milk removes any bitter taste. Drain the milk from the livers and discard the milk. For the best results with this recipe you will need a food processor or liquidizer. Blitz the livers in the processor with the garlic, nutmeg, salt and pepper until smooth. Add the eggs and blitz for a further 1 minute. Add the cream, brandy and *jus*. if using. (The *jus* is optional for this recipe, but I find it gives a little depth and flavour to the parfait.) Continue to blitz for a few seconds and then check for seasoning. The parfait should now be pushed through a fine sieve to give a smoother consistency. You will find the mix to be quite liquid.

Pour the mix into the prepared terrine or moulds and cover with a lid. Stand in a tray filled with warm water to come half-way up the sides of the terrine to ensure a slow, steady cooking, and cook in the pre-heated oven for about 1¹/₂ hours. Make sure the parfait is checked after 30 minutes and 1 hour. After 1 hour, check every 10 minutes until the parfait is just firming to the touch. It will, of course, continue to cook once removed from the oven until it has completely cooled. Remove from the water bath and leave to cool then chill for 2–3 hours.

To serve the parfait, dip the mould into hot water and turn it over on to a chopping board. Remove the greaseproof paper and slice as needed. The parfait can be wrapped in cling film and kept in the fridge for 2–3 days.

Duck Rillettes

Duck rillette is almost like a home-made coarse pâté. You can make it with pork or goose, as well.

Other flavours can be added to the duck before cooking to help flavour the cooking fat which will be used to hold the duck together. Orange peel can be left in (as for canard à l'orange), or a clove of garlic, a bay leaf and a sprig of fresh thyme. It's also possible to add some chicken or duck stock to this recipe for a moister flavour.

Duck rillettes are best served with slices of thick, hot toast.

SERVES 4   **2 teaspoons rock sea salt**
4 duck legs   **900 g (2 lb) duck fat**

To make the rillette, simply follow the recipe for Confit of Duck (see p. 127 or 128), cooking for a minimum of 2 hours. The duck meat has to be very tender and on the point of being overcooked.

Once cooked but still warm, take the duck legs from the cooking fat and remove the skin. Take all the meat from the bone, then break down the duck flesh, pulling it apart with two forks so that the meat is shredded rather than making a purée. Once the duck is reasonably finely shredded, start to add some of the strained cooking fat. This will give the meat a coarse pâté texture. After 150 ml (5 fl oz]) has been added, check the seasoning with salt and pepper: season generously as the mix will be served cold. The duck rillettes should be moist and rich to eat. More fat can be added to make the pâté even richer (300 ml/10 fl oz would be the maximum for this quantity). Spoon the rillettes into individual ramekins or one larger bowl and set in the fridge.

Once set, spoon a little of the liquid fat on top of the moulds and allow to set. This will keep the rillettes fresh as long as they are chilled. I suggest, however, that you keep them no longer than a week. Because of the high fat content, the pâté will set quite firmly in the fridge so take out about an hour before eating to appreciate the full flavour.

Beef Carpaccio

This dish originated in the 1950s and was named after the Italian painter, Vittore Carpaccio, known for the reds and whites in his work. It has now become a favourite starter across the world. Here is my version.

SERVES at least 8   **5 tablespoons Worcestershire sauce**
900 g (2 lb) topside of beef   **4 garlic cloves, chopped**
50 g (2 oz) Parmesan   **1 bunch of fresh basil**
Freshly ground black pepper   **1/2 bunch of fresh thyme**
                                                15 black peppercorns, crushed
FOR THE MARINADE   **300 ml (10 fl oz) dry white wine**
150 ml (5 fl oz) balsamic vinegar   **600 ml (1 pint) olive oil**
5 tablespoons soy sauce   **15 g (1/2 oz) coarse sea salt**

Trim the beef of any fat and sinew, which will leave you with 750–800 g (1^1/$_2$–1^3/$_4$ lb) of meat.

Mix together all the marinade ingredients, reserving a few basil leaves to finish the dish. Roll the beef in the marinade, cover and leave to steep in the fridge for 4–5 days to achieve the maximum taste. The beef should be turned in the marinade every day. If the beef is kept in the oil in the fridge, you could leave it for up to 10–12 days.

After the marinating process, remove the meat from the marinade and wrap in cling film. Freeze it, if you like, to use later, or it can even be sliced from frozen on a slicing machine. It can also be kept in the fridge and sliced very thinly with a sharp knife as you want it. Push the marinade through a sieve to use as the dressing.

To serve the carpaccio, slice it very thinly and place the slices on to the serving plate, covering the whole surface (about three to four slices if cut by hand, four to five if cut on a machine). Chop the remaining basil leaves and add to the dressing. Brush this over the meat and twist on some freshly ground black pepper. The Parmesan can be shaved and laid on top, or it can be grated and served separately.

Black Pudding Fritters

This isn't really a new recipe. I'm sure in many parts of the country you will find this dish in fish and chip shops. However, I thought I would include it because it's such a fun dish (and, of course, very tasty) and works so well as a snack, canapé, in finger buffets, as a starter or even as a main course with mashed potatoes and peas.

Well, these fritters do go very well with Home-made Tomato Ketchup (see p. 377) or a mayonnaise-based sauce. A good tartare sauce works very well: that's basically mayonnaise with chopped capers, gherkins, parsley and onions or shallots. The acidic flavour from the capers and gherkins almost electrify the black pudding. Other good mayonnaise flavourings are horseradish cream or purée, Dijon or grain mustard or a beetroot purée. In fact, the beetroot purée mixed with mayonnaise and then spiced with fresh or tinned horseradish is a real winner to go with this dish.

SERVES 2–4

1 × 225 g (8 oz) black pudding, peeled

FOR THE BATTER
225 g (8 oz) self-raising flour

300 ml (10 fl oz) lager
Plain flour, for dusting
Oil, for deep-frying
Salt

Pre-heat the oil to 180°C/350°F.

The first thing you have to do is prepare the black pudding. This can be cut into 12 × 2.5 cm (1 in) pieces – these are really the perfect size for snacks – or split the pudding through the middle, then cut in half to give you quarters. These are a good size for a starter or part of a main course.

The next stage is to make the batter. Sift the self-raising flour into a bowl and whisk in the lager, making sure you are left with a good thick consistency. This will increase the lightness of the finished dish, creating an almost soufflé effect. Lightly dust the black pudding with the flour and then dip in the batter. This is best done with a cocktail stick, completely covering the pudding itself while preventing your hands from becoming covered.

Providing that the oil has been heated to 180°C/350°F, the cooking time will be 3–5 minutes, until crispy and golden brown. Remove from the fryer, shaking off any excess fat. Lightly sprinkle with salt and serve with the sauce of your choice.

Mushroom Risotto with Crispy Black Pudding

Mushrooms and black puddings are a traditional British combination, usually served at breakfast. They work together very well in this recipe, contrasting the creaminess of the risotto with the crispy, rich black pudding. The best mushrooms to use are the open cup or flat which have an almost meaty texture and a much better flavour.

SERVES 4–8
100–175 g (4–6 oz) unsalted butter
1 tablespoon olive oil
2 onions, finely chopped
25–50 g (1–2 oz) bone marrow, chopped
(optional)
1.2 litres (2 pints) Vegetable Stock
(see p. 400) or Chicken Stock
(see p. 399)

225–350 g (8–12 oz) open-cup or flat
mushrooms, sliced
225 g (8 oz) Arborio rice
1 black pudding, cut into
1 cm (1/2 in) die
1–2 tablespoons freshly grated
Parmesan
Salt and freshly ground black pepper
Parmesan flakes

Melt the butter with the olive oil in a large pan. Add the chopped onions and chopped bone marrow, if using, and cook without colouring for 2–3 minutes. Meanwhile, bring the stock to the boil. Add the sliced mushrooms to the onions, increasing the heat of the pan. Allow the mushrooms to cook for 2–3 minutes. Add the rice and continue to cook over a medium heat for a further minute. Add the hot stock a ladle at a time, allowing it to become absorbed in the rice and evaporate before adding another ladle. Continue this process, stirring almost continuously to keep an even cooking. This will take 20–30 minutes. When the risotto is almost cooked, the black pudding can be either pan-fried until crispy or cooked under the grill.

Once the risotto is cooked, add some grated Parmesan and check the consistency is of a rich creamy texture. Season with salt and pepper and spoon on to a plate. Sprinkle with Parmesan flakes, crispy black pudding and a few drops of olive oil.

Breast of Pigeon Wrapped in Cabbage on a Warm Potato Salad

Try to find squab pigeons to make this dish. These are specially reared young pigeons, and are very tender and plump. By doubling the quantities this could also be served as a main course. As a variation, a pigeon red wine sauce can be made by adding the pigeon carcasses to the reduction of the Red Wine Sauce (see p. 369) and then continuing with the recipe. The legs and carcass will infuse the sauce, giving it a rich, gamey flavour.

SERVES 4

2 squab pigeons
225 g (8 oz) mushrooms, minced or finely chopped
2 chicken livers, chopped
4 chicken hearts (optional), chopped
50 g (2 oz) wild mushrooms (optional), chopped
Salt and freshly ground black pepper
1 egg yolk
4 large green cabbage leaves
100 g (4 oz) pig's caul, soaked in cold water for 24 hours (optional)
50 g (2 oz) unsalted butter

FOR THE WARM POTATO SALAD
450 g (1 lb) new potatoes, cooked
2 tablespoons olive oil
300 ml (10 fl oz) Red Wine Vinaigrette (see p. 379)
1/2 teaspoon chopped fresh parsley
1/2 teaspoon chopped fresh tarragon
1/2 teaspoon snipped fresh chives

Remove the legs and breasts from the pigeon carcasses. Skin the breasts but keep them whole. Cut up all the meat on the legs.

Place the minced or chopped mushrooms in a pan and cook over a low heat until almost dry. Allow to cool. Mix in the chopped leg meat, and the chopped chicken livers, and wild mushrooms, if using. Season with salt and pepper and bind with the egg yolk.

Blanch the cabbage quickly in boiling, salted water and then refresh in cold water and dry on a cloth. Lay them flat and sit the pigeon breasts on top of each one. Spread about 5 mm (1/4 in) of the minced filling on top of each breast and fold over the cabbage until you have a small cabbage parcel. Cut the pig's caul, if using, into four and wrap a piece around each cabbage parcel. The parcels are now ready to cook.

Heat the butter in a frying-pan and cook the pigeon parcels for about 5–6 minutes on each side until golden brown.

While the cooked potatoes for the salad are still warm, peel and slice them and mix with the olive oil, then season with salt and pepper. Keep them warm. Mix the red wine vinaigrette with the chopped herbs. Divide the potatoes between the four plates and spoon the dressing over each portion. Make two or three cuts through the parcels, arrange them on top of the potatoes and serve.

Sautéd *Foie Gras* on Sweet Mashed Potatoes with Crispy Cabbage

Foie gras *isn't everyone's cup of tea or, for that matter, very easy to get hold of. But don't be put off by that because this recipe works very well as a starter or main course with many other flavours. Chicken livers can be used as a replacement, or even lambs' or calves' liver if the dish is served as a main course. On top of that, many fish will work very well.*

Sauternes is a classic sweet white wine to accompany foie gras, *so reducing shallots with that wine to flavour the mashed potato is very exciting. If you can't get Sauternes, then buy another sweet white wine and increase the quantity by half again.*

SERVES 4

4 × 75–100 g (3–4 oz) slices of *foie gras*

4 tablespoons chopped shallots

300 ml (10 fl oz) Sauternes

225 g (8 oz) Mashed Potatoes (see p. 230), made with butter but without cream

Salt and freshly ground black pepper

Oil, for deep-frying

6–8 large Savoy cabbage leaves, cut into 1 cm (1/2 in) strips

2 tablespoons Veal or Beef *Jus* (see p. 398) or bought alternative (see p. 401, optional)

Mix the chopped shallots with the Sauternes and bring to a simmer. Reduce until all the wine has been absorbed by the shallots. Mix with the mashed potatoes and season.

Heat the oil to 180°C/350°F and deep-fry the Savoy cabbage for 30 seconds–1 minute until golden-edged and crispy. As soon as the cabbage has been dropped in the oil, cover with a lid to prevent any spitting created from the cabbage water content. After the first 15–20 seconds, the lid can be lifted. Once cooked, drain and lightly salt.

All we have to do now is cook the *foie gras*. Heat a frying-pan and season the *foie gras* with salt and pepper. Place the *foie gras* in the pan. It's important to cook in a hot pan, as this will seal the *foie gras* and give a good golden colour. The *foie gras* will need just 1 1/2–2 minutes on each side. Quite a lot of excess fat will be left in the pan. Pour off and reserve half of this fat, leaving the rest in the pan.

To present the dish, spoon some Sauternes shallot potatoes on to plates and sit the *foie gras* on top. You can now add the *jus* or gravy, if using, to the remaining fat in the pan. This creates a sauce for the dish. It will come to the boil very quickly. Season with salt and pepper and pour a tablespoon over each portion. Now just top the dish with the crispy cabbage to finish.

The remaining *foie gras* fat can be kept chilled or frozen and used as a cooking fat for many dishes. It's very good just melted and mixed with mashed potatoes instead of butter.

Fish
Main
Courses

Pan-fried Fish with Anchovy Cream Noodles, Crispy Bayonne Ham and Parsley

The reason this is just titled pan-fried 'fish' is because there are so many you can use: sea bass, tuna, salmon, John Dory and monkfish to name but a few.

SERVES 4

4 × 175–225 g (6–8 oz) fish fillets

225–350 g (8–12 oz) fresh or dried
    noodles, cooked

A good handful of fresh parsley

Oil, for deep-frying

4 slices of Bayonne or Parma ham,
    or streaky bacon if either is
    unavailable

Plain flour, for dusting

A knob of unsalted butter

Salt and freshly ground black
    pepper

FOR THE ANCHOVY CREAM SAUCE

A knob of unsalted butter

1 onion, finely chopped

1/2 leek, shredded

1 bay leaf

1/2 garlic clove

1 glass of dry white wine, about
    150 ml (5 fl oz)

300 ml (10 fl oz) Fish Stock (see p. 399)

150 ml (5 fl oz) double cream

50 g (2 oz) tinned anchovies, well
    drained and chopped

A squeeze of fresh lemon juice

Pre-heat the grill.

To make the sauce, melt the butter in a pan and add the onion, leek, bay leaf and garlic. Cook over a moderate heat for a few minutes, until softened. Add the white wine and boil to reduce by two-thirds. Add the fish stock and boil to reduce by half. Add the double cream and the anchovy fillets and cook for a few minutes. The sauce can now be blitzed in a food processor or liquidizer or with a hand blender, then pushed through a sieve. Check for seasoning and add just a few drops of lemon juice to lift the finished flavour.

The parsley can be cooked in a deep-fat fryer or in 1 cm (1/2 in) of hot fat in a frying-pan. It's important to use a lid and check all excess water is shaken off before cooking.

Cut the ham into 1 cm (1/2 in) strips and pan-fry them for I–2 minutes, then finish crisping the strips under the grill. The noodles can now be re-heated in the anchovy cream sauce.

Whichever fish is being cooked can be lightly floured on the presentation side, brushed with butter and seasoned with salt and pepper. Now all you have to do is cook the fish until tender in a hot pan; the timing will, of course, depend on the type of fish you choose.

To present the dish, divide the noodles and sauce between bowls or plates. Sit the fish on top, then sprinkle with the crispy Bayonne or Parma ham and parsley.

Fish on Spinach with a Cider and Mussel Sauce

I've just called this 'fish' because so many fish work well with this recipe: cod, halibut, sea bass, red mullet, turbot, brill – the list could go on. However, make sure which-ever fish you choose, it is well filleted with all the bones removed. White fish should be skinned as well.

SERVES 4

4 × 175–225 g (6–8 oz) fish fillets
2 tablespoons plain flour
75 g (3 oz) unsalted butter
900 g (2 lb) fresh spinach, picked and
   washed

FOR THE MUSSEL COOKING LIQUOR

15 g (1/2 oz) unsalted butter
1 onion, roughly chopped
1 carrot, roughly chopped
2 celery sticks, roughly chopped
1/2 leek, roughly chopped
1 bay leaf (optional)
1 sprig of fresh thyme

1 star anise (optional)
2 glasses of dry white wine
600 ml (1 pint) Fish Stock (see p. 399)
   or water
900 g (2 lb) fresh mussels, scrubbed
   and bearded (see p. 17)

FOR THE CIDER SAUCE

350 g (12 oz) shallots or onions, sliced
   into rings
25 g (1 oz) unsalted butter
A pinch of saffron (optional)
1–2 bottles of dry cider
85–120 ml (3–4 fl oz) double cream
Salt and freshly ground white
   pepper

To cook the mussels, melt the butter and fry the vegetables, bay leaf, thyme and star anise, if using for 8–10 minutes without colouring. Add the wine and boil to reduce until almost dry. Add the stock or water, bring to the boil and cook for a few minutes. Add the mussels and bring to the boil, stirring. Once the stock is boiling, the mussels will be opening and cooking. Drain and reserve the cooking liquor. Discard any mussels that have not opened and pick the rest from their shells. Keep them in a few spoonfuls of cooking liquor to keep them moist.

To make the cider sauce, soften the shallots in a knob of butter with the saffron, if using. Add the cider and boil to reduce by three-quarters. Add the mussel stock and continue to reduce by half. Add half the cream, bring to a simmer and simmer for a few minutes. Check for taste and consistency and season with salt and pepper. If the sauce is too thin, reduce a little more. Add a knob or two of butter to enrich the flavour.

The fish should be seasoned and lightly dusted in flour before being pan-fried, or just seasoned if being grilled. Cod will take 3–4 minutes on each side.

While the fish is cooking, melt the butter in a large pan and add the spinach. Cook and stir for 2–3 minutes until tender. Add the mussels to the fish sauce and warm through. Spoon the spinach on to plates and sit the fish on top. Spoon the sauce over the fish, forming a small pile of shallots on top of each fillet.

Pan-fried Sea Bass with Spring Onions and Creamy Potatoes

There's more to the spring onions than the title of this recipe is telling you. They have been mixed with soy sauce, five-spice powder, red chillies and mirin. Mirin is a Japanese sweet rice wine which is available in major supermarkets, oriental food stores and some delicatessens. If you can't find it listed as mirin, then buy a basic rice wine or rice vinegar – the recipe will work with either.

Should sea bass be difficult to find, this dish works just as well with any other fish. For this dish I prefer to have the sea bass skinned, but I don't waste the skin – I deep-fry it to serve with the fish and call it Sea Bass Crackling. The creamy mashed potatoes should be very creamy, only just holding their shape. When you eat them with the fish they are like a thick cream sauce. You will notice that I am using whipping or single cream; basically this is because double cream would thicken the potatoes rather than loosen them to the creamy consistency I am after.

SERVES 4

4 × 175–225 g (6–8 oz) sea bass fillets, skinned and skins reserved
3 tablespoons soy sauce
3 tablespoons mirin (sweet rice wine)
A small pinch of five-spice powder
3 tablespoons olive or sesame oil
Salt and freshly ground black pepper
1 bunch of spring onions, finely shredded
1 red chilli, seeded and very finely chopped
Plain flour, for dusting

A knob of unsalted butter
1–2 tablespoons oil
Oil, for deep-frying

FOR THE CREAMY MASHED POTATOES

675 g (1½ lb) Mashed Potatoes (see p. 230), made without butter or cream
75 g (3 oz) unsalted butter
150–300 ml (5–10 fl oz) whipping or single cream
Salt and freshly ground black pepper
Freshly grated nutmeg

To make the dressing, boil the soy sauce, mirin and five-spice powder together, then remove from the heat. Mix with the olive or sesame oil and season with salt and pepper, if necessary. Mix the spring onions with the chopped chilli.

To fry the sea bass, lightly flour on the skin side and season with salt and pepper. Heat a frying-pan and add the butter. Once the butter is bubbling, cook the bass on the floured side for 2–3 minutes, then turn it over and continue to cook for a further 3 minutes. The fish could take a little longer to cook – this really depends on the thickness of the fillets. Once the fish has been turned over, heat 2–3 tablespoons of the dressing and add the spring onions and chilli. This must be cooked on a high heat and stirred to ensure even cooking. The spring onions will take 1–2 minutes to cook.

To finish the mashed potatoes, add the butter, then 150 ml (5 fl oz) of the cream. Season with the salt, pepper and grated nutmeg. The remaining cream can now be added a little at a time until a loose consistency is achieved.

Dry the reserved fish skin on a cloth and cut into 2.5–5 cm (1–2 in) pieces, then lightly flour and deep-fry until golden and crisp. Drain on kitchen paper and season with salt. For safety, always use a lid when deep-frying to prevent any spitting of hot fat.

To present the dish, spoon or pipe some creamy potatoes at the top of the plate and top with a crispy skin. Sit the sea bass at the front of the plate and spoon the spring onion and chilli mix on top. The dish can now be finished with a trickle of the remaining dressing around the fish.

Grilled Sea Bass with Fettucine and Ratatouille Sauce

This is a very colourful dish which features many styles – English, Italian and French – many textures and, of course, many flavours. If you do not have the time to make your own pasta, there are many good-quality fresh and dried pastas available in the shops.

SERVES 4
450 g (1 lb) Pasta Dough (see p. 395)
50 g (2 oz) unsalted butter
Salt and freshly ground black pepper
4 × 175–225 g (6–8 oz) sea bass fillets
25 ml (1 fl oz) olive oil

FOR THE RATATOUILLE SAUCE
1 red pepper, seeded
1 green pepper, seeded
2 shallots
1/2 aubergine
1 courgette
25 g (1 oz) unsalted butter
25 ml (1 fl oz) olive oil
300 ml (10 fl oz) Red Pepper Coulis
** (see p. 376)**

To make the fettucine, roll the dough through a pasta machine several times until it becomes about 1 mm (1/16 in) thick, then pass through the noodle cutter and leave to rest. If you do not have a pasta machine, it can be divided, rolled several times until very thin then cut by hand into ribbons; a pizza wheel is the easiest way to cut the pasta.

Pre-heat the grill to medium and butter and season a flameproof baking tray.

To make the ratatouille, cut the vegetables into 5 mm (1/4 in) dice. Melt the butter with the olive oil in a large pan. Add the diced vegetables and cook for about 3–4 minutes, until just softened. In another pan, warm the red pepper coulis then add the vegetables. Season with salt and pepper.

Lay the sea bass fillets on the prepared tray, skin side up, and cook under the medium grill for about 8 minutes.

While the fish is cooking, boil a large pan of water with the olive oil and a pinch of salt. When boiling, drop in the pasta and move it around with a fork. If it is fresh, it will only take a few minutes to cook. For dried pasta, just follow the instructions on the packet. Drain through a colander, season with salt and pepper and toss with the remaining butter to loosen.

Warm the ratatouille sauce and spoon it on to hot plates. Sit the fettucine in the middle and lay the grilled sea bass on the top.

Sea Bass on Minestrone

This sauce is almost like a minestrone soup, with flavour of all vegetables cooked in a tomato liquor. The dish eats well with noodles or with the fish on mashed potatoes. Sea bass is not the only fish that can be used. Red mullet or most white fish will also eat well. A seafood minestrone of scallops, prawns, mussels and cockles is a real winner.

SERVES 4

50 g (2 oz) unsalted butter

I tablespoon olive oil

2 carrots, diced

I large onion, diced

2 celery sticks, diced

1 garlic clove, crushed

1 medium courgette, diced

1/2 leek, diced

2 glasses of white wine

150 ml (5 fl oz) Fish Stock (see p. 399)

150 ml (5 fl oz) Tomato Coulis (see
    p. 375)

4 × 175 g–225 g (6–8 oz) sea bass fillets

2 tomatoes, skinned and diced

8–10 fresh basil leaves, cut into
    squares

12–15 fresh tarragon leaves, cut into
    squares

1–2 teaspoons Pesto Sauce
    (see p. 374) (optional)

Melt half the butter with the olive oil, then add the carrots, onion, celery and garlic. Cook without colouring for a few minutes. Cook the courgette and leek separately In a knob of butter so that they retain their green colour. Once cooked, allow them to cool, then add them towards the end of cooking. Once the vegetables have softened, add the white wine and boil to reduce until almost dry. Add the stock and boil to reduce by half. Add the tomato coulis and simmer for 10–12 minutes, until the sauce has a broth consistency.

Arrange the fish on a buttered and seasoned tray and cook under a hot grill for 5–10 minutes, leaving the skin golden and crispy.

While the fish is cooking, add the tomatoes, herbs, courgettes and leeks to the minestrone, bring to the simmer and add the remaining butter. Finish with the pesto sauce, if liked. Spoon the minestrone sauce into some bowls and sit the fish on top.

VARIATIONS

To make this into a more complete meal, cook some noodles and toss in butter. Sit them in the centre of bowls and spoon the sauce around. Arrange the fish on top.

Try serving the dish with mashed potatoes, leaving out the pesto sauce, and spooning some of the sauce on to the mash before sitting the fish on top and spooning the remaining sauce around.

Grilled Sea Trout with Soured New Potatoes and Watercress Dressing

Sea Trout is not the easiest of fish to get hold of, but do try it if you can; the flavour and texture is so good. If you don't get hold of it, then just replace it with salmon, red mullet, halibut, bass or cod – just about any fish will work. If you're choosing cod, leave the skin on and crisp it under the grill – it's delicious. I love the combination of the trout with the soured new potatoes – this recipe has so many possible variations leading to other dishes. When you take a look you'll see why.

SERVES 4

4 × 175–225 g (6–8 oz) sea trout fillet portions (from a 1.75–2.75 g/4–6 lb) fish), trimmed of all bones, with skin
Salt and freshly ground black pepper

A knob of unsalted butter
1/4 quantity Watercress and Herb Dressing (see p. 381)
1 quantity Soured New Potatoes (see p. 234)

Pre-heat the grill.

Lightly butter a baking sheet and arrange the fillets on it, skin-side up. Season the skin with salt and pepper and dot with a little butter. Sit under a hot grill and cook until the skin becomes crispy. It will only take 5–6 minutes until the fish are cooked. Spoon some watercress dressing on to the centre of a plate and top with the soured new potatoes and crispy sea trout.

Roast Cod on Potatoes with Fried Anchovies

This has to be my favourite fish dish in the book. As with most of the recipes, another fish can be used or you can leave the fish out and serve the dish as a warm potato salad with crispy anchovies. Marinated anchovies are sold loosely, not in tins.

Because I'm roasting this cod, I want to keep the skin on. When shallow-fried then roasted, cod skin comes up very crisp and tasty; it's good enough to eat on its own.

SERVES 4

450 g (1 lb) new potatoes

Salt and freshly ground white pepper

150 ml (5 fl oz) Vierge Dressing
   (see p. 380) or olive oil

Juice of 1 lemon

25 g (1 oz) unsalted butter

2 teaspoons cooking oil

4 × 175–225 g (6–8 oz) cod fillets

12 marinated anchovies

1 teaspoon self-raising flour

1/4 teaspoon cayenne pepper

2–3 tablespoons milk

Oil, for deep-frying

1 tablespoon fine or chopped
   capers

2 shallots or 1/2 onion, very finely
   chopped

1/2 teaspoon chopped fresh parsley

1 teaspoon chopped fresh
   coriander

1 teaspoon chopped fresh tarragon

1 teaspoon chopped fresh basil

A few green salad leaves (optional)

Pre-heat the oven 200°C/400°F/gas 6.

Cook the new potatoes, then peel off the skin. Cut into 5 mm (1/4 in) slices while still warm, then season with salt and pepper. Add 1–2 tablespoons of dressing or olive oil and the juice of 1/2 lemon. Season again with salt and pepper and keep warm.

Melt the butter and oil in a hot pan. Season the cod with salt and pepper and place in the pan skin-side down. Cook until deep in colour, then turn over and finish cooking in the oven for 5–8 minutes, depending on the thickness of the cod.

Split the anchovies through the centre. Mix the flour with the cayenne and a pinch of salt. Dip the anchovies in the milk, then roll in the cayenne flour. Deep-fry in hot oil until very crispy. If you don't have a deep-fat fryer, cook them in about 5 mm (1/4 in) of hot oil in a frying-pan, but don't let it get so hot so that it smokes, and keep turning the fish in the pan until they are crispy.

To finish the dish, warm the remaining dressing or oil and add the capers and shallots or onion with a squeeze of lemon juice and the herbs. Season with salt and pepper. The dressing should be served warm.

Spoon some potatoes on to plates and top with a few green salad leaves. Spoon the dressing all around and sit a few fried anchovy fillets on top of the dressing. Finish the dish with the roasted cod fillet on top with the crispy-skin side showing. Brush with a little butter to finish.

Pan-fried Cod on Fennel and Potato Salad with Tartare Dressing

Cod, chips and tartare sauce is probably Britain's most famous and classic fish dish, and cooked well with a good, crispy batter and a tartare made with fresh mayonnaise, you can't beat it. I decided to use nearly all of those tastes in this dish: the fresh cod, potatoes and tartare sauce flavour without the mayonnaise. To this I've added some fresh fennel which, with its slight aniseed flavour, really helps the potatoes and fish. You can, of course, leave out the fennel and I promise you'll still enjoy this lighter version of our old favourite.

SERVES 4
4 × 175–225 g (6–8 oz) cod fillets
2 tablespoons plain flour
50 g (2 oz) unsalted butter
1 tablespoon olive oil

FOR THE DRESSING
2 teaspoons capers
2 teaspoons chopped cocktail gherkins
2 teaspoons chopped shallot or onion

1/2 bunch of fresh parsley
1–2 tablespoons olive oil
Salt and freshly ground black pepper

FOR THE FENNEL AND POTATOES
2 large fennel bulbs
2 lemons
275 g (10 oz) new potatoes
50 ml (2 fl oz) Basic Vinaigrette
** (see p. 379)**

To make the dressing, place the capers, gherkins and shallot or onion in a food processor and blitz until almost puréed. Add the parsley and 1 tablespoon of olive oil. Continue to blitz until the parsley is finely chopped. Season with salt and pepper. If the dressing is very thick, simply add more olive oil. This dressing keeps well for 24 hours in the fridge.

To cook the fennel, top and tail the bulbs and remove some of the core at the base. Bring about 1.2 litres (2 pints) of water to the boil (enough to cover the fennel) with the juice of 1 lemon and a pinch of salt. Place the fennel into the water and cover with a lid, bring back to the boil, then simmer until just tender; this will take 15–20 minutes. Leave to cool. Cut the fennel in half lengthways, then each half into 5–6 slices lengthways.

Meanwhile, boil the potatoes until tender, then drain, peel off the skins and cut the potatoes in half. Mix the basic dressing with the juice of the remaining lemon and add to the new potatoes and fennel slices. Season with salt and pepper and bring up to the simmer.

To cook the cod, lightly flour and season each fillet and brush with butter on the skin side. Heat a frying-pan with a little olive oil. Lay the cod butter-side down into the pan and cook until golden brown. Turn the fish in the pan and continue to cook. The cod will take about 6–8 minutes to cook.

To serve, spoon the tartare dressing into bowls or plates and sit the fennel and potatoes on top. Finish by sitting the cod on to the garnish.

Deep-fried Cod in Batter

This must be the quickest batter to make. It's just lager and some salt and self-raising flour. The only secret is to make sure the batter is very thick, almost too thick. As the cod is cooking, the batter will soufflé, keeping it light and crisp. If the batter is too thin, it tends to stick to the fish and become heavy. You can use the same recipe for any deep-fried fish, sausages or whatever. It also eats well with Tomato Sauce (see p. 380).

SERVES 4
450 g (1 lb) self-raising flour
Salt and freshly ground black pepper
4 × 175–225 g (6–8 oz) cod fillets,
    skinned and boned
600 ml (1 pint) lager
A pinch of salt
Oil, for deep-frying

FOR THE TARTARE SAUCE
300 ml (10 fl oz) Mayonnaise
    (see p. 380)
25 g (1 oz) gherkins, chopped
25 g (1 oz) capers, chopped
25 g (1 oz) onion, finely chopped
2 teaspoons chopped fresh parsley
A squeeze of lemon juice

Season a spoonful of flour with salt and pepper. Lightly dust each fillet in the flour

Whisk half the remaining flour into the lager with a pinch of salt, then gradually add the flour a spoonful at a time to make a thick batter. Dip the cod into the batter. Heat the oil to 180°C/350°F, then fry the cod until golden.

To make the sauce, mix all the ingredients together and season with lemon juice, salt and pepper. Serve with the crispy fried cod.

Pan-fried Cod on Pecorino Mashed Potatoes and Spinach

You don't have to stick to cod with this recipe: halibut, haddock, turbot or brill can all be used and taste just as good.

Pecorino is an Italian ewes' milk cheese with a similar texture to Parmesan. I like to use smoked Pecorino for extra taste. Pecorino cheeses were introduced to me by Giovanni, an Italian friend who lives in South Wales. Giovanni makes his own 'Pecorinos' with Welsh ewes' milk – and it works. If you can't find Pecorino, just use a Parmesan.

All I do with this recipe is add grated smoked Pecorino to hot mashed potatoes to give you a delicious cheesey mash. Of course, you can use the cheesey mash with so many other things: top your shepherds' pie with it, make a cheesey champ (see p. 232), or serve it with sausage and beans.

SERVES 4
1 tablespoon plain flour
Salt and freshly ground white pepper
4 × 175–225 g (6–8 oz) cod fillets,
    skinned
1 tablespoon cooking oil
100 g (4 oz) unsalted butter

3–4 tablespoons Fish Stock
    (see p. 399) or water
900 g (2 lb) spinach, picked and
    washed
Juice of 1/2 lemon
450 g (1 lb) Mashed Potatoes
    (see p. 230)
100–175 g (4–6 oz) Pecorino, grated

Lightly flour and season the cod with salt and pepper. Heat a frying-pan with the oil and 25 g (1 oz) of the butter. When the pan is hot and the butter bubbling, add the cod and cook for about 3–4 minutes on each side, keeping the pan hot, until the fish is golden brown. Always cook the presentation skin-side down first. When the fish colours, it will show every line of the fillet and also hold the fish together a lot better.

While the fish is cooking, bring the stock or water to the boil with 25 g (1 oz) of butter. Add the spinach leaves and stir for 2–3 minutes. The spinach will cook quickly and create a spinach liquor in the pan. Season with salt and pepper, drain off the spinach and re-boil the liquor. Whisk in the remaining butter to make a spinach butter sauce. Taste and adjust the seasoning if necessary and add the lemon juice to lift the flavour.

Warm the mashed potatoes with 100 g (4 oz) of cheese. Taste and add the remaining cheese, or more if you wish.

Spoon the potatoes on to plates and sit some spinach on top. Arrange the fish on top. Pour the spinach butter sauce around and serve.

Cod with a Parsley Crust

The cod for this recipe is best cut from the middle of large fillets, giving good, rectangular pieces of fish. The best way to serve the fish is sitting on a bed of mashed potatoes with a lemon butter sauce drizzled around. Finishing the dish this way creates three complementary textures with the crust, the fish and the potatoes.

SERVES 4
75g (3 oz) unsalted butter
2 shallots, finely chopped
4 tablespoons chopped fresh parsley
**1/2 large white sliced loaf, crusts
    removed, crumbed**
**Salt and freshly ground white
    pepper**

4 × 175–225 g (6–8 oz) cod fillets

TO SERVE
**1 quantity Mashed Potatoes
    (see p. 230)**
**1 quantity Lemon Butter Sauce
    (see p. 371)**

Pre-heat the grill to medium, pre-heat the oven to 180–200°C/350°–400°F/gas 4–6, butter and season a flameproof dish.

Melt the butter with the chopped shallots, which should just soften, then remove from the heat. Add the chopped parsley to the breadcrumbs and season with salt and pepper. Gradually mix this with the shallot butter to form a light paste. Lay the fish on the prepared dish and cover each cod fillet with the parsley crust. Cook the cod under the grill, not too near the heat. It will take about 8–10 minutes. As the crust slowly colours, the fish will be cooking. When the fish under the crust turns opaque and milky and the crust is golden brown, it is ready. Finish in the pre-heated oven for a few minutes to make sure the fish is completely cooked.

Divide the mashed potatoes between four hot plates, sit the fish on top and pour the warm sauce around.

Cod with Cabbage, Bacon and Peas

This dish holds all the simplest ingredients, yet is packed with textures and tastes. We all keep cabbage, bacon and peas, so all you have to do now is buy the cod.

SERVES 4
4 smoked back bacon rashers, rinded and cut into strips
2 onions, finely shredded
100 g (4 oz) unsalted butter
1 tablespoon olive oil
600 ml (1 pint) Chicken Stock (see p. 399)
1/2 green cabbage, finely shredded
100 g (4 oz) cooked fresh or frozen peas

Salt and freshly ground white pepper
1 tablespoon plain flour
4 × 175–225 g (6–8 oz) cod fillets, skinned
A little vegetable oil

TO SERVE
1 quantity Mashed Potatoes (see p. 230)

Cook the bacon and onions in 25 g (1 oz) of the butter and the olive oil, until soft. Add the chicken stock and bring to the boil. Allow to simmer for a few minutes then re-boil and add the cabbage. This will only need to cook for a few minutes until it is tender but with a little bite to it; it must be kept boiling to prevent the cabbage from stewing. Now add the peas and 50 g (2 oz) of the remaining butter, cut in pieces. Check for seasoning.

Lightly flour the skinned side of the cod and brush with the remaining soft butter. Brush a frying-pan with a little oil. Pan-fry the cod, skinned side down, for about 5–6 minutes. The underside, or skinned side, is the presentation side.

Divide the hot mashed potato between four hot plates. Sit the fish on top of the potato and spoon the broth and vegetables around.

Roast Cod with Crispy Shrimps and Gremolata Mashed Potatoes

Starting to pan-fry cod, and then finishing by roasting in the oven, works so well, especially if you leave the skin on the fillet to give you a crispy topping to very succulent fish underneath. Leaving the skin on also protects the flesh and holds the fillet together. Small brown shrimps are the best for the crispy shrimps. They have to be picked and trimmed, just leaving the tails encased in shell. Frying them in nut-brown butter makes them even crisper and very tasty to eat with a squeeze of fresh lemon juice. If the small brown shrimps are unavailable, you can use shelled shrimps or just peeled prawns – all will work.

SERVES 4

4 × 175–225 g (6–8 oz) cod fillets, with
   skin
2 tablespoons plain flour
50 g (2 oz) unsalted butter
50–100 g (2–4 oz) Gremolata
   (see p. 402)
450 g (1 lb) Mashed Potatoes
   (see p. 230), made without butter

100–175 g (4–6 oz) brown shrimps,
   preferably tails, with shell left on
A squeeze of fresh lemon juice
Salt and freshly ground black
   pepper
1/2 quantity Lemon Butter Sauce
   (see p. 371), warm (optional)

Pre-heat the oven to 200°C/400°F/gas 6.

Lightly dust the skin side of the cod fillets with flour and brush each with a little butter. Heat an ovenproof frying-pan and add half the remaining butter. Once bubbling, sit the cod fillets in, skin-side down. Allow to fry for 2–3 minutes until the skin becomes golden and is starting to crisp. Turn the fish fillets over in the pan, leaving skin-side up, then finish in the pre-heated oven for 4–6 minutes, depending on the thickness of the fillet.

While the fish is cooking, the gremolata can be worked into the hot mashed potatoes. The quantity depends on the richness of lemon, garlic and parsley you would prefer in the potato. I like to make sure that all these flavours are quite powerful in the finished dish

To cook the shrimps, heat a small frying-pan and add the remaining butter. Once it starts to bubble, add the brown shrimps. Allow the shrimps to fry and crisp for approximately 1 minute. Add a squeeze of fresh lemon juice and season with salt and pepper.

To finish and serve the dish, shape the potatoes between two large serving spoons and place at the top of the plate. Sit the roasted cod at the front of the plate and spoon over the crispy shrimps. Lemon butter sauce can also be used to give a creamy finish to the dish by spooning some of the warm sauce around the fish and shrimps. The warm gremolata potatoes can also be served separately.

Roast Cod with Horseradish Yorkshire Pudding and Shrimp Gravy

Does this dish sound familiar? Well, you may have heard the idea before but the result is completely different.

Roast beef with Yorkshire pudding must be the most classic British dish. All over Europe and probably the world, whenever British cooking is mentioned, guess what? Yes, the next line always includes roast beef.

It was really Yorkshire pudding that was the starting point for this dish. Yorkshire pudding is not just for beef. In this recipe, I've fired it up with horseradish cream to give an extra bite. The gravy is made with fish bones to give a completely different taste while retaining the body and strength of that classic sauce. Fish or chicken stock can be used: both will work, but obviously the fish stock will give you a stronger fish flavour. And, of course, there's the wonderful flavours to come through of the cod itself with crispy skin and succulent flakes.

SERVES 4

4 × 175–225 g (6–8 oz) cod fillets, with
   skin
Salt and freshly ground black pepper
1 tablespoon plain flour
A knob of unsalted butter
Sprigs of watercress

FOR THE YORKSHIRE PUDDINGS

1/2 quantity Yorkshire Pudding batter
   (see p. 247)
Finely grated zest of 1 lemon
2 tablespoons horseradish cream, or
   more
A drop of oil

FOR THE FISH GRAVY

450 g (1 lb) fish bones or shrimp shells,
   chopped
A few parsley stalks
A drop of oil
1 glass of white wine, about 150 ml
   (5 fl oz)
300 ml (10 fl oz) Fish Stock or Chicken
   Stock (see p. 399)
150 ml (5 fl oz) Veal or Beef *Jus*
   (see p. 398) or bought alternative
   (see p. 401)
100 g (4 oz) peeled shrimps
1 tablespoon roughly chopped fresh
   flatleaf parsley

Pre-heat the oven to 200°C/400°F/gas 6. Heat 4 × 10 cm (4 in) moulds, 2.5 cm (1 in) deep with a teaspoon of oil in each.

To make the gravy, fry the chopped fish bones with the parsley stalks in the oil until golden. Or the bones can also be coloured in a hot oven. Add the white wine and boil to reduce until almost dry. Add the stock, bring to the boil and reduce by half. Add the *jus* or gravy and bring to a simmer. This can now be gently simmered for 20 minutes before being strained through a fine sieve. Check the consistency and seasoning of the gravy; you should have about 300 ml (10 fl oz). The sauce should not be too thick and heavy as this will overpower the cod. A looser consistency is best.

To make the puddings, add the lemon zest to the batter, with horseradish cream to taste. Two tablespoons gives it a fiery taste. At raw stage, the mix will taste stronger than at finished cooked stage. Pour the finished batter into the hot moulds and cook in the pre-heated oven for 20–25 minutes.

To cook the fish, first season with salt and pepper and lightly dust the skin side with plain flour. Brush the floured side with butter. Heat an ovenproof frying-pan or roasting tin. Trickle some cooking oil into the pan and sit the fish in on top of the stove skin-side down. The butter will melt, crisping the skin as it does. Once golden brown (this will take 2–3 minutes), turn the fish in the pan and finish by roasting in the pre-heated oven for 6–8 minutes. Don't put the fish in the oven until the Yorkshire puddings are about 8 minutes from ready.

Add the shrimps to the warm gravy. Once they are added, the gravy should not be heated past a mild simmer or this will toughen the shrimps. A squeeze of juice from the zested lemon will lift all the flavours from the gravy. Once the Yorkshire puddings and cod are cooked, sit the pudding at the top of the plate and the cod in front. Add the chopped parsley to the gravy and spoon the sauce over or around. The dish can be finished with a sprig of watercress to complete a classic garnish. The whole thing work so well, the horseradish and lemon Yorkshires helping to mop up the shrimp gravy and contrasting with crispy roast cod – sounds good to me.

NOTE

It is important to add the horseradish and lemon at the last minute as this will prevent the acidity from both flavours breaking down the batter consistency.

Steamed Halibut on Spinach with Soured Lime Cream and Spicy Curry Dressing

This recipe has three definite flavours that all work together very well. The fish itself is delicious to eat simply pan-fried or steamed on its own but also works well with other tastes. The spinach and soured cream could well stand up as a vegetarian dish on their own. As for the spicy dressing, this is powerful. It's really the flavours associated to a curry paste that have been loosened by the oils. The sharp/hot taste is quietened down by the spinach with the soured cream. Consequently, both are helping lift the halibut taste without spoiling it.

Please promise me you won't use this dressing just for this dish because it will work with so many dishes. A good rich, spicy salad or barbecued lamb, pork or chicken are just a few to think about.

Although this recipe may appear long-winded, it is, in fact, really very simple.

Once the dressing is made – before you add the tomato and coriander – it will keep up to 2 weeks in the fridge. The soured cream mix also keeps well for a few days.

SERVES 4

4 × 175–225 g (6–8 oz) halibut fillets, skinned

675 g (1 1/2 lb) spinach, picked and washed

A knob of unsalted butter

Salt and freshly ground black pepper

3–4 tablespoons Soured Cream, Lime and Mint Yoghurt (see p. 385)

FOR THE SPICY CURRY DRESSING

1/2 teaspoon chopped fresh thyme

1/2 teaspoon crushed dried chillies

1/2 teaspoon cumin seed or ground cumin

1 star anise

6–8 shallots or 1 small onion, finely chopped

150 ml (5 fl oz) sesame oil

5 tablespoons olive oil

4 teaspoons soy sauce

4 teaspoons teriyaki sauce

2 teaspoons Worcestershire sauce

1–2 drops of Tabasco sauce

1/4 teaspoon finely chopped fresh root ginger

1/2 garlic clove, crushed

1/2 teaspoon ground turmeric

1/2 teaspoon cayenne pepper

1/4 teaspoon paprika

1/4 teaspoon ground mixed spice

1 teaspoon clear honey

2 tomatoes, blanched and skinned

1 heaped teaspoon chopped fresh coriander

To make the dressing, tie the thyme, chillies, cumin and star anise in a piece of muslin. Then all that has to be done is mix together all the ingredients except the tomatoes and coriander and place over a low heat, bringing the dressing to a gentle simmer. This can now be left to cook for 8–10 minutes. The dressing should then be left to cool slightly and should only ever be served warm to appreciate all the flavours. Once cooled, the muslin bag can be squeezed and removed. This dressing will keep very well in the fridge for 2 weeks.

The blanched and skinned tomatoes will also be mixed with the dressing when the dish is being finished. Halve the tomatoes, removing all the seeds and water. The tomato flesh can now be cut into 5 mm (1/4 in) dice.

The spinach can be prepared in advance if you wish. To cook the spinach, simply plunge into boiling, salted water for about 1 minute, and then drain and refresh under cold water. Once it is cold, lightly squeezed out any excess water.

Arrange a piece of butter paper in a steamer and season with salt and pepper. Place the halibut on top and steam over the boiling water. The cooking time will vary depending on the thickness of the fillets: an average time will be approximately 5–6 minutes. While the fish is steaming, warm the spinach in a little butter and season with salt and pepper. Once hot, add the soured cream, lime and mint yoghurt. Once this has been added, just warm, do not re-boil or the yoghurt cream will thicken and become almost dry.

Add the diced tomatoes and chopped coriander to the dressing. Sit the soured lime cream spinach on to the plate with the steamed halibut on top and finish with 1–2 tablespoons of spicy dressing per portion.

Fingers of Skate with Potatoes, Fennel and Braised Artichokes

This dish really doesn't have to be difficult. The potatoes and fennel are quick and easy to prepare and, if the artichokes sound like too much hard work (but it's worth a try), there are good-quality tinned artichoke bottoms available. Mixed bags of salad leaves are also available in supermarkets.

SERVES 4

225 g (8 oz) new potatoes, boiled
1 onion, finely chopped
100 ml (3¹/2 fl oz) Basic Vinaigrette (see p. 379)
2 fennel bulbs, trimmed
Salt and freshly ground white pepper
Juice of ¹/2 lemon
1 quantity Braised Artichoke Bottoms (see p. 224)
50 g (2 oz) unsalted butter
700 g (1¹/2 lb) skate wing fillets
Plain flour, for coating
1 tablespoon olive oil
A handful of green salad leaves (rocket, curly endive, lamb's lettuce etc.)

FOR THE DRESSING

1 egg
25 g (1 oz) capers, drained
6 tinned anchovy fillets, drained
1 garlic clove
1 × 2.5 cm (1 in) piece of fresh ginger root, peeled
1 bunch of fresh basil leaves
Juice of 1 lemon
¹/2 teaspoon chopped fresh thyme
A pinch of sugar
50 ml (2 fl oz) warm water
225 ml (7¹/2 fl oz) olive oil
225 ml (7¹/2 fl oz) groundnut oil
Salt and freshly ground black pepper

To make the dressing, place all the ingredients except the oils in a food processor and blitz to a paste. With the motor running, slowly add the oils, as you would for mayonnaise. Push the dressing through a fine sieve then season to taste with salt and pepper.

Slice the new potatoes while still warm and mix with the chopped onion. Add about 2 tablespoons of the vinaigrette to moisten.

To cook the fennel, plunge it into boiling, salted water with the lemon juice and simmer for about 20 minutes until tender. Allow to cool in the liquor. When cool, halve the fennel and slice into long strips.

Warm the potatoes, fennel and artichokes together in half the butter.

Cut the skate into fingers, allowing five pieces per portion. Lightly flour the skate and fry in the remaining butter and the olive oil for a few minutes on each side.

Mix the dressing with the potatoes, fennel and artichokes and spoon on to the centre of the plates. Sit the skate fingers on top and finish with some salad leaves tossed in the remaining vinaigrette. Any leftover dressing can be kept in the fridge and used for simple mixed salads.

Fillet of Skate with Red Peppers, Potatoes, Capers and Bayonne Ham

Filleting skate is quite unusual – skate wings are normally cooked on the bone – but it really suits this dish. It's a simple recipe with not too many flavours, just enough to help each other. Bayonne is a cured ham usually made in Orthez near Béarn in south-west France. It has a similar texture to Parma ham but the flavours are different. Bayonne is usually lightly smoked to lift the taste. If you can't find any, substitute Parma ham. Cut the thin slices into 1 cm (1/2 in) strips ready to fry until crisp.

SERVES 4

2 red peppers
Juice of 1 lemon
6 tablespoons olive oil
Salt and freshly ground white pepper
225–350 g (8–12 oz) new potatoes,
   peeled, cooked and sliced
2 teaspoons fine capers

4 × 175 g (6 oz) skate fillets
1 tablespoon plain flour
25 g (1 oz) unsalted butter
4–6 slices Bayonne ham, cut into
   pieces
Mixed salad leaves
2 tablespoons Basic Vinaigrette
   (see p. 379)

Core and halve the peppers lengthways, remove the seeds and cut into 1 cm (1/2 in) slices lengthways. Mix the lemon juice with 4 tablespoons of olive oil, season with salt and pepper, and pour over the potatoes. Fry the peppers in a little olive oil, colouring and softening slightly, then mix with the potatoes and capers.

Dust the skate with flour, brush with butter and season with salt and pepper. Pre-heat a frying-pan and brush with olive oil. Sit the fillets in the pan, presentation side down, and fry quickly for 2 minutes, then turn and cook for a further minute.

Meanwhile, heat another pan and fry the ham in virtually no fat, cooking and tossing until crisp.

Divide the potatoes and peppers between the plates. Toss the salad leaves in a little dressing and arrange on top. Sit the skate on the leaves and spoon the crisp ham over the top

NOTE

Salad leaves are not essential for any of the fish dishes, but they do always help to give the dish texture.

Pan-fried Skate with Ratatouille Salad

This is another recipe in which skate is filleted, but below I give a variation for it cooked on the bone.

SERVES 4

2 red peppers
1 green pepper
2 small courgettes
1 large onion, thickly sliced
2 tablespoons olive oil
50 g (2 oz) unsalted butter
2 large, flat mushrooms, sliced
Salt and freshly ground white
   pepper

1 tablespoon plain flour
4 × 175 g (6 oz) skate fillets
250 ml (8 fl oz) Basic Vinaigrette
   (see p. 379)
6 fresh basil leaves (optional)
1–2 teaspoons Pesto Sauce
   (see p. 374) (optional)
Green salad leaves
1 aubergine, sliced and fried
   (see p. 48)

Core and halve the peppers lengthways, remove the seeds and cut into 1 cm (½ in) slices lengthways. Slice the courgettes at an angle to give oval slices. Fry the onion and peppers in a heavy-based pan in a little olive oil and butter until softened. Add the courgettes and cook for 1 minute then remove from the heat. Cook the mushrooms separately in a very hot pan in a little olive oil, then add to the other vegetables. Season with salt and pepper.

Lightly flour the skate fillets and brush with butter. Heat a frying-pan and brush with oil. Sit the fillets buttered-side down into the pan and fry quickly for 2 minutes on one side, then 1 minute on the other until golden brown.

Mix the vinaigrette with the basil leaves or pesto, if using, and use a little to dress the salad leaves. Add the ratatouille to the dressing and spoon on to plates. Sit the leaves on top and finish with the fish and aubergines.

VARIATIONS

Another skate dish that I enjoy is one that is cooked on the bone. The skate is shallow-fried in olive oil and butter for 3–4 minutes on each side until the flesh is crisp and golden brown. Arrange the skate on a plate and surround with some Lemon Butter Sauce (see p. 371), finishing with some crunchy brown shrimps and parsley in nut brown butter.

The best shrimps to use are the small, brown variety. To pick them, simply pull off the heads and small tails and leave the rest of the shell on the tail itself. The shell is crispy without being too hard. To make the butter nut brown, heat a frying-pan and add some butter. It should be bubbling and beginning to colour almost immediately. When it's just turning brown but not burnt, add the shrimp tails, a squeeze of lemon juice and season with salt and pepper. Finish with chopped fresh parsley and spoon over the skate.

Roast Skate with Mustard Seed Butter and Toasted Crumbs

Skate with black butter is the most classic of all skate dishes, and you can't get much simpler than that.

Skate can lend itself to so many different fish dishes whether they are starters or main courses, on or off the bone. Filleting skate seems to be fairly modern idea but for this dish it's going to be on the bone. In many respects, with almost all fish you will get better results if they are cooked on the bone, keeping all the flavour and juices in the flesh. However, eating fish on the bone can become a chore and fiddly. Well, with skate you won't really have that problem; the fillets more or less just slide off.

SERVES 4
4 × 350 g (12 oz) skate wings on the bone
Salt and freshly ground black pepper
2 tablespoons plain flour
25 g (1 oz) unsalted butter
50 g (2 oz) fresh white breadcrumbs

1 glass of red wine, about 150 ml (5 fl oz)
1 teaspoon chopped fresh parsley

FOR THE MUSTARD SEED BUTTER
50 g (2 oz) unsalted butter, softened
50 g (2 oz) grain mustard

Pre-heat the oven to 200°C/400°F/gas 6. Pre-heat the grill. Grease a baking tray.

Season the skate wings with salt and pepper and lightly dust with flour on the top (presentation) side. Heat a large frying-pan and add a knob of butter. Colour the presentation side first, and then turn in the pan before transferring the fish on to the baking tray. The fish can now be finished in the pre-heated oven for about 10–l2 minutes.

To make the mustard seed butter, simply mix the two ingredients together. This can now be kept chilled or used immediately.

Toast the breadcrumbs under the grill to give a golden and slightly crunchy texture, turning occasionally until evenly golden.

A minute or so before the fish has finished cooking, remove it from the oven, place a tablespoon of the mustard butter on each skate wing and spread evenly, then return to the oven. Once cooked, remove from the oven and sprinkle the toasted crumbs on top.

Sit the fish on plates, ready to serve. Heat all the butter and juices left on the tray and add the red wine. Bring to the boil and check for seasoning. The consistency may be a little thin. If so, just add some more mustard seed butter for a smoother finish. Add the chopped parsley and spoon around the fish. The flavour of the red wine adds body and strength to the juices and butter.

Grilled Tuna on Greens with Horseradish Dumplings and Red Wine Dressing

Tuna is looked on as the 'meat' of fish, cooked medium-rare to medium as for a fillet steak. With this in mind, I wanted to give it the garnish of a steak and serve it almost like roast beef – the greens and dumplings obviously being the garnishes for the beef and red wine the dressing for the steak. The dumpling recipe is really the same as Bone Marrow Dumplings (see p. 403), with the addition of freshly grated horseradish. You will need this quantity of horseradish to give the real strength of the radish although, of course, you can make it even more fiery by simply adding more. If fresh horseradish is unavailable then add bottled grated horseradish, mixing and stirring until you have the right strength. This dish can also work with other fish and meats: beef steaks, chicken breasts or turbot would go well.

The dumpling recipe should always be made 1–2 hours in advance to allow the mix to set. The mix will, in fact, keep chilled for 3–4 days, so if you have some left over, simply roll into dumplings and cook them either separately or in your stew.

SERVES 4

4 × 175–225 g (6–8 oz) tuna steaks
675 g (1 1/2 lb) spring greens
Salt and freshly ground black
    pepper
25 g (1 oz) unsalted butter
8 tablespoons Red Wine Dressing
    (p. 383)

FOR THE DUMPLINGS

100 g (4 oz) fresh bone marrow
100 g (4 oz) fresh white breadcrumbs
2 tablespoons double cream
3 egg yolks
3–4 tablespoons grated fresh
    horseradish
A pinch of freshly grated nutmeg
About 600 ml (1 pint) Fish Stock
    or Chicken Stock (see p. 399) or
    water

To make the dumplings, break down the bone marrow in a food processor or liquidizer, then add the breadcrumbs. Add the cream and egg yolks with the grated horseradish. Season with nutmeg, salt and pepper and chill for minimum 1 hour before shaping into 8 large or 4 small dumplings. I like to shape the mix into ovals between 2 tablespoons. Drop the dumplings into simmering stock or water and poach for 10–15 minutes. Remove with a slotted spoon and drain on kitchen paper.

The greens should have any thick stalks removed and be cut down into 1 cm (1/2 in) thick strips. Blanch in boiling salted water for 1–2 minutes until the greens feel tender. Now you can either simply drain off the water, season with salt and pepper and lightly butter, providing they are to be eaten immediately, or refresh under cold water, and then toss in butter in a hot pan or microwave later.

As for the tuna, this can be cooked on a grill plate or pan-fried in a knob of butter, seasoned with salt and pepper. The tuna will only need 2–3 minutes on each side.

To serve the dish, sit the greens in the centre of the plate and top with the tuna and a dumpling. Spoon the red wine dressing around to finish.

VARIATION

The dressing can be made stronger by boiling it and adding 1 glass of red wine (about 150 ml/5 fl oz) and then reducing it by half.

Steamed Fillet of Turbot on Green Vegetables with Ginger and Lime

Once you have all the ingredients together for this, it's so quick and easy to cook.

SERVES 4

4 × 175 g (6 oz) turbot or cod fillets
Salt and freshly ground white pepper
150 ml (5 fl oz) dry white wine
50 g (2 oz) unsalted butter or goose fat
450 g (1 lb) oyster or button mushrooms, sliced
450 g (1 lb) leeks, sliced
450 g (1 lb) fresh spinach, stalks removed
1/2 teaspoon grated fresh ginger root
1/2 bunch of fresh flatleaf parsley, picked
8 asparagus spears, blanched and cut into 5 cm (2 in) lengths
Juice of 1 lime

Pre-heat the oven to 220°C/425°F/gas 7 and grease and season a shallow baking tray. Place the fillets in the tray, add the white wine and cover with buttered grease-proof paper. Place the tray in the pre-heated oven and the fish will begin to steam. They will take only 5–6 minutes to cook and will be just firm to the touch.

Meanwhile, heat a wok or frying-pan and add the butter or goose fat. Add the sliced mushrooms, leeks, spinach and ginger and stir-fry for about 2–3 minutes until almost cooked. Add the parsley and asparagus, season and add the lime juice.

To serve, divide the vegetables between four hot plates. Sit the turbot on top of the vegetables and spoon a little of the fish cooking liquor over the top.

Grilled Tuna on Potato and Onion Salad

Fresh tuna is a beautiful, meaty fish, but if you would prefer not to use it or just can't find anywhere to buy it, this dish can work very well with turbot, brill, bass and many other fish. The tuna medallions have a very similar texture to fillet of beef. Tuna fillet eats best when cooked medium rare to medium.

SERVES 4

8 large onions, sliced

2 tablespoons water

350 g (12 oz) new potatoes, boiled

175–200 ml (6–7 fl oz) Basic Vinaigrette
   (see p. 379)

A few fresh basil and tarragon leaves,
   chopped

4 × 175 g (6 oz) medallions of tuna
   fillet

1 curly endive, separated, or a handful
   of lettuce leaves per person

Place the onions and water in a pan and allow to cook very slowly until the natural sugar from the onions starts to caramelize and then brown, stirring occasionally. This will take at least 1 hour of slow cooking.

Pre-heat the barbecue or grill to hot. Slice the warm new potatoes and sprinkle liberally with some of the vinaigrette. Mix with the onions and chopped herbs. This mixture should be kept just slightly warm.

The tuna would now best be cooked on an open barbecue to give a good grilled taste, but it can also be cooked under a pre-heated grill (or pan-fried in some butter and olive oil). It will take about 3–4 minutes per side, depending on the thickness of the fillet.

Spoon the potato and onion salad on to the centre of the plates. Dress the salad leaves with some of the vinaigrette. Sit some leaves on top of the potatoes and finish with the tuna. Spoon some of the dressing over and serve.

Fillet of Red Mullet on Tapenade Toasts

Red mullet is perfect for this dish, which looks and certainly tastes very good and very Mediterranean. I particularly like to use an onion bread for the toasts.

SERVES 4

4 × 175 g (6 oz) red mullet fillets,
   scaled and all bones removed

25 g (1 oz) unsalted butter, melted

Salt and freshly ground black pepper

4 slices of onion or crusty bread

4 tablespoons Tapenade (see p. 43)

1/2 curly endive, separated into leaves

150 ml (5 fl oz) Vierge Dressing
   (see p. 380)

2 tomatoes, skinned, seeded and diced

6 fresh basil leaves, chopped

Pre-heat the grill to hot and butter a flameproof tray. Lay the mullet fillets on the buttered tray, skin side up, brush with the butter and season with salt and pepper. Place the fish under the hot grill and allow the red skin to crisp. This will only take 3–4 minutes.

Toast the slices of bread and spread the tapenade on each slice. Place the toasts on hot plates. Toss the curly endive in a little of the vierge dressing and sit it on top of the toasts. Place the fillets on top of the lettuce. Mix the diced tomatoes and basil with the remaining vierge dressing and spoon over and around the fish.

Seared Salmons on Tartare Potato Cake with Warm Poached Egg

The plural 'salmons' is used for this dish because I'm using fresh and smoked salmon, both cooked. This gives a great combination of flavours that go so well with the tartare potato cake. I've named the potato cake 'Tartare' because basically I'm using some of the ingredients associated with tartare sauce: shallots or onions, capers and, with this recipe, marinated anchovy fillets. You can buy marinated anchovy fillets at delicatessens, and they are the best variety to use in this dish. Tinned anchovies can also be used but the full flavour won't quite be achieved. Of course the anchovies, capers and shallots are all optional extras, but the sharp flavour of these ingredients works so well with the salmon.

To sum the whole dish up, I can promise you that when you break the poached egg on to the salmon the richness of the yolk and smoky taste working with the fresh salmon and potatoes is very exciting and certainly not to be missed.

SERVES 4

4 × 75–100 g (3–4 oz) slices of fresh salmon, about 5 mm (^{1}/4 in) thick
4 × 75–100 g (3–4 oz) slices of smoked salmon, about 5 mm (^{1}/4 in) thick
3 large jacket potatoes, boiled in their skins until completely cooked
Salt and freshly ground black pepper
2 shallots or 1 small onion, finely chopped
1 tablespoon fine or chopped capers
12 marinated anchovy fillets, chopped
25 g (1 oz) unsalted butter
4 eggs
1 teaspoon chopped fresh flatleaf parsley
^{1}/2 quantity Lemon Butter Sauce (see p. 371)

Pre-heat the oven to 200°C/400°F/gas 6. Butter 4 × 10 cm (4 in) rings for the potatoes. Peel the potatoes and slice into rounds. Sit the first layer of potatoes in the base of the rings, season with salt and pepper and sprinkle on the chopped shallots or onion, capers and anchovies. To finish simply top with another layer of potato. These potato cakes can be make up in advance and chilled.

To cook the potato cakes, melt half the butter in a frying-pan and with a spatula or fish slice lift the cakes from the rings into the pan. These can now be pan-fried for 4–5 minutes until golden on one side. Turn over the cakes and finish cooking in the pre-heated oven for approximately 15–20 minutes.

To poach the eggs, fill a small pan with a mixture of two-thirds water and one-third malt vinegar; the high quantity of vinegar will immediately hold the egg white around the yolk. Bring to the boil, then break in the eggs and poach for 3–3^1/2 minutes. If you wish to cook these early, then simply refresh in iced water, then re-heat later in boiling water for about 1 minute.

To cook the salmons, heat a frying-pan and add the remaining butter. The fresh salmon must be the first as this will take slightly longer than the smoked. Season the fresh salmon with salt and pepper and the smoked with just pepper. Lay the fresh salmon in the pan and cook for I–2 minutes before turning and adding the smoked salmon. The smoked salmon should be cooked on one side only for 1–2 minutes. This will also finish the cooking time for the fresh salmon.

To present the dish, add the chopped parsley to the warm lemon butter sauce and re-heat the poached eggs in boiling water. Sit the potato cakes on plates and top with a slice of each salmon and a warm poached egg. To finish, just spoon some lemon butter sauce over and serve.

Salmon Fish Cakes

These are fish cakes with a difference. They are simple to make but good to look at and great to eat. They go very well with a green salad.

SERVES 4–6
Salt and freshly ground white pepper
2 shallots, finely chopped
450 g (1 lb) salmon, filleted and skinned
1 tablespoon unsalted butter
150 ml (5 fl oz) dry white wine
1 tablespoon chopped fresh parsley
350 g (12 oz) Mashed Potatoes without cream or butter (see p. 230)

2 tablespoons plain flour
2 eggs, beaten
100 g (4 oz) fresh breadcrumbs, for coating
Vegetable oil, for deep-frying
1 quantity Lemon Butter Sauce (see p. 371)

Pre-heat the oven to 200°C/400°F/gas 6 and butter and season a baking tray.

Sprinkle the finely chopped shallots on to the prepared baking tray, sit the salmon on top and season again with salt and pepper. Add the white wine, cover with foil and cook in the pre-heated oven for about 8–10 minutes until the fish is just cooked. The salmon should be just firm on the outside and still pink in the middle.

Sit the salmon in a colander over a pan to collect all the cooking juices. When all the juices have been collected, boil to reduce them to a syrupy consistency.

Break up the salmon with a wooden spoon, then add the syrupy reduction and the chopped parsley. Fold in 225 g (8 oz) of the potato, and then add it a spoonful at a time until you have a binding texture. Check for seasoning then roll into 12 to 18 balls about 4 cm (1$^{1}/_{2}$ in) in diameter. Three cakes per portion will be enough. Lightly pass through the flour, beaten eggs and then the breadcrumbs; repeat the process of egg and breadcrumbs once more.

The fish cakes are now ready for deep-frying which cooks them well and gives a good all-rounder colour. Heat the vegetable oil to 180°C/350°F then fry the fish cakes for about 4–5 minutes. Drain well on kitchen paper.

To serve, just pour the warm lemon butter sauce into individual serving dishes or bowls and sit three fish cakes in the middle of each one.

Smoked Haddock Tart with Grilled Halibut

This is a delicious combination – the grilled halibut with its own sauce flavoured with tomato and tarragon eats so well with the tart, I just had to include it in this recipe – but the tart can stand quite happily as a complete dish on its own. The basic tart recipe itself is an old favourite of mine because, with the taste of smoked haddock travelling through the whole tart, well, it's sensational. If you are not serving the tart with the halibut and sauce, simply cook the smoked haddock in the cream rather than the stock.

The dish can also take on so many combinations. Add mushrooms, leeks, spring onions or fresh herbs. It can also be finished by topping with Welsh or Stilton Rarebit (see p. 40 and p. 197), both going very well with smoked haddock and giving you a golden, almost crispy, cheesy topping. If the tart is to be served on its own, then I feel it eats well with the Spicy Tomato Dressing (see p. 381).

For a change, I sometimes mix half quantities of the cream sauce with Lemon Butter Sauce (see p. 371). This gives a rich creamy, buttery sauce, almost velvety in consistency.

The most important thing is that you have a go at this dish – it's a must.

MAKES 4–6 × 10 cm (4 in) tarts or 1 × 25–30 cm (10–12 in) flan

FOR THE TART
1 quantity Shortcrust Pastry (see p. 394) or Puff Pastry (see p. 393)
275–350 g (10–12 oz) smoked haddock fillet
300 ml (10 fl oz) water or Fish Stock (see p. 399)
A knob of butter
2 onions, sliced
2 eggs, beaten
300 ml (10 fl oz) double cream
2 tablespoons freshly grated Parmesan

FOR THE GRILLED HALIBUT
4 × 225 g (8 oz) halibut fillets
Plain flour
Salt and freshly ground black pepper
A knob of butter

FOR THE GRILLED HALIBUT SAUCE
150–300 m (5–10 fl oz) smoked haddock stock liquor (from above)
150 ml (5 fl oz) double cream
A knob of butter
A squeeze of fresh lemon juice
1–2 tomatoes, blanched, skinned, seeded and diced
1 teaspoon chopped fresh tarragon

Pre-heat the oven to 200°C/400°F/gas 6. Grease and line 4–6 × 10 cm (4 in) tart tins or 1 × 25–30 cm (10–12 in) flan tin.

Roll out the pastry and use to line the tins. Fill with greaseproof paper and baking beans or rice and bake for about 15–20 minutes. Remove the paper and beans.

Lightly poach the smoked haddock before making the tart mix. To do this, sit the haddock fillet in the water or stock and bring to a soft simmer, then cook for 2 minutes. Leave to cool, then remove the haddock. Reserve the stock for the sauce.

Melt the butter in a pan and add the sliced onion. Cook for a few minutes until softened. Beat the eggs into the cream, then add the Parmesan. The cream mix can now be added to the sliced onions. Cook this on a moderate heat for a few minutes, just to thicken. Remove from the heat.

Break the haddock into flakes and divide between the pastry cases. Top each tart with the cream and egg mix and finish in the pre-heated oven for 10–15 minutes for individual tarts or 25–30 minutes for a large tart.

The tart mix can be made in advance, mixing the fish flakes with the tart mix and then leaving to cool and chilling. If this is done, the tarts will take an extra 5–10 minutes to cook from cold in the oven.

The halibut eats very well 'grill-marked' and then cooked under the grill for a few minutes. Of course it can be just pan-fried or grilled without the markings. To 'grill-mark', lightly dust the presentation side of the fish with plain flour and season with salt and pepper. Now a thin metal skewer/kebab stick can be heated on an open gas. Once *red* hot, simply lift (using an oven cloth) and mark the fillet, re-heating the skewer or stick between each marking. The fillets can now be placed on a buttered tray, brushed with butter and cooked under a hot grill for 3–5 minutes, depending on the thickness of the fish.

To make the sauce, boil the haddock stock and add the double cream. Bring to the simmer and cook for a few minutes, stirring. Whisk in the knob of butter and check for seasoning with salt and pepper. Add a squeeze of lemon juice with the diced tomato flesh and chopped tarragon.

To serve, spoon the sauce over and around the tart before sitting the halibut on top.

Grilled Herrings with Braised Lentils and Mustard Seed Sauce

Grilled herrings whole on the bone with a separate hot English mustard sauce was one of the very first dishes I was taught as a young chef. They were very nice to eat, but hard work. So, to simplify everything for the diner, I decided to take them off the bone and try them just with the sauce. I then needed something to eat with them, and mashed potatoes worked very well, but I find lentils even tastier.

SERVES 4
8 large herring fillets
Melted butter

FOR THE BRAISED LENTILS
50 g (2 oz) unsalted butter
25 g (1 oz) carrot, finely diced
25 g (1 oz) celery, finely diced
25 g (1 oz) onion, finely diced
25 g (1 oz) leek, finely diced
1 small garlic clove, crushed
100 g (4 oz) green lentils (lentilles de Puy)
450 ml (15 fl oz) Chicken Stock (see p. 399) or Vegetable Stock (see p. 400)
Salt and freshly ground black pepper

FOR THE MUSTARD SEED SAUCE
2 shallots, finely chopped
1 celery stick, chopped
1/2 leek, chopped
1 bay leaf
50 g (2 oz) unsalted butter
300 ml (10 fl oz) dry white wine
600 ml (1 pint) Fish Stock (see p. 399)
300 ml (10 fl oz) double cream
About 2 teaspoons Meaux grain mustard

Pre-heat the oven to 200°C/ 400°F/gas 6 and butter and season a small flameproof baking tray.

To cook the lentils, melt the butter in a small ovenproof braising pan. Add the diced vegetables and garlic and cook for a few minutes. Add the lentils, stirring well. Cover with the stock and bring to the simmer. Cover with a lid and braise in the pre-heated oven for about 30–35 minutes, until the lentils are tender and all the stock has been absorbed. Make sure they are tender before taking them from the oven. Season with salt and pepper.

To make the sauce, sweat the vegetables and bay leaf in the butter for a few minutes. Add the white wine and boil to reduce until almost dry. Add the fish stock and continue to boil until reduced by three-quarters. Pour on the cream and cook slowly until the sauce is thick enough to coat the back of a spoon. Strain through a fine sieve. Stir in the mustard, a teaspoon at a time, until the right taste is achieved – mustardy but not overpowering.

To cook the herring fillets, place them on a greased baking tray and brush with butter. Cook under the hot grill for about 5–6 minutes. As soon as the fillets have coloured they will be ready to serve.

To serve, spoon the green lentils on to the centre of four hot plates, pour the mustard sauce around and sit the herring fillets on top of the braised lentils. The dish is now complete.

Stuffed Herrings

This dish eats well on its own simply with a squeeze of lemon or served with a mustard cream sauce (see Herrings with Spring Onion and Bacon Potato Cakes, page 113).

SERVES 4
4 herrings, filleted
Pig's caul (optional)

FOR THE STUFFING
4 medium slices of white bread
1 tablespoon melted butter
1 large onion, finely chopped
2 smoked streaky bacon rashers,
  finely diced

1/2 teaspoon chopped fresh sage
1/4 teaspoon chopped fresh thyme
1/2 teaspoon chopped fresh parsley
25 g (1 oz) bone marrow, finely diced
  (optional)
2 tablespoons dried shredded suet
Salt and freshly ground black
  pepper

Pre-heat the oven to 200–220°C/400–425°F/gas 6–7.

To make the stuffing, remove the crusts from the sliced bread and crumb the slices. Melt the butter, add the chopped onion and cook without colouring for 2–3 minutes. Add the bacon and herbs and continue to cook for 2 minutes. Allow to cool. Mix with the breadcrumbs, diced bone marrow, if using, and suet. Season with salt and pepper. The texture of this stuffing should just hold and bind together if squeezed in your hand.

The herrings should be filleted and as many fine bones removed as possible. Lay out four fillets and divide and spread the stuffing over them. Cover with the other fillets. Before cooking, the fish can be wrapped in pig's caul (or in a layer of buttered foil), then pan-fried in a little olive oil and butter until golden brown on both sides. Finish them in the pre-heated oven for a few minutes. (However, if you have used foil, simply bake them in the oven for 12–15 minutes.) Once cooked, the caul will be almost invisible. It is used only to hold the fillets together.

Herrings with Spring Onion and Bacon Potato Cakes

These herring fillets are grilled and arranged on top of potato cakes. They can then be served with a wedge of lemon or with a mustard cream sauce.

SERVES 4
8 herring fillets
Olive oil or unsalted butter
4 Spring Onion Potato Cakes with
  bacon (see p. 230)

FOR THE MUSTARD CREAM SAUCE
50 g (2 oz) unsalted butter
1 shallot, chopped

1 carrot, chopped
1 celery stick, chopped
1 bacon rasher, chopped
A few tarragon leaves
2 glasses white wine
300 m (10 fl oz) Fish Stock
  (see p. 399)
50–85 ml (2–3 fl oz) double cream
1–3 teaspoons grain mustard

Melt 15 g (1/2 oz) of butter and cook the vegetables, bacon and tarragon without colouring until they soften. Add the white wine and boil to reduce until almost dry. Add the stock and boil to reduce by half. Add the cream and cook for 8–10 minutes. Strain the sauce and whisk in the remaining butter. Add the mustard a little at a time until you have the right strength.

Meanwhile, brush the herrings with a little oil or butter and cook under a hot grill for 5–6 minutes.

Sit the potato cakes in the centre of the plates, spoon the sauce around and lay the herring fillets on top.

VARIATIONS

The potato cake works well using spinach instead of bacon and spring onions (see p. 230). Cook 450 g (1 lb) of picked and washed spinach in 25 g (1 oz) of butter for a few minutes until tender, then drain, cool and chop. Add the spinach to the potato mix and proceed as for that recipe. They eat particularly well with fish dishes.

Cooked mushrooms, bacon, onion and many other ingredients can also be added to the potato cakes.

Poultry and Game Main Courses

Chicken Balti

The spices used for this recipe can be made in quantity and then kept in an airtight jar until needed.

You'll also notice this recipe is for four people but in the ingredients the chicken breasts are listed as 4–6. This is basically because you need a little extra whenever chicken breasts are diced and used in a stew or curry. As you can see, this dish is simple and easy to make, and all you need now is a good rice dish to go with it, such as Braised Rice (see p. 240).

SERVES 4

4–6 chicken breasts, cut into 2 cm (3/4 in) dice

4 tablespoons cooking oil

1 large onion, finely chopped

1 garlic clove, crushed

2 teaspoons cardamom pods or crushed cardamom seeds

2 teaspoons cumin seeds

2 tablespoons ground coriander

1/2 teaspoon ground cloves

1/2 teaspoon turmeric

1/2 teaspoon paprika

1 teaspoon salt

2 green chillies, seeded and chopped

1 × 400 g tin of evaporated milk

1 heaped teaspoon chopped fresh coriander

Salt and freshly ground black pepper

Heat a non-stick pan and add the cooking oil. Add the chopped onion and garlic and cook for a few minutes, allowing them to colour. Add all the spices, salt and green chillies and continue to cook for a few minutes.

Add the diced chicken and turn in the pan until completely sealed on all sides. Now it's time to add the evaporated milk. Bring to the simmer, stirring to prevent the milk from sticking. Once simmering, reduce the heat, allowing the chicken to cook gently for 15–20 minutes, until the chicken is tender and the sauce has thickened. It is important to stir this dish regularly. This will prevent the evaporated milk from catching and burning in the pan. As the curry is cooking, the sauce will take on all the flavours and also thicken. The total cooking time will be 35–40 minutes.

To finish the dish, simply add the freshly chopped coriander and check for seasoning with salt and pepper.

Chicken with Wild Mushrooms, Grapes and Tarragon

This dish can be a fricassee, as here, or the chicken can simply be roasted and the sauce served separately. Oyster or pleurote mushrooms have become fairly common, but if you have any problem finding them, just substitute button mushrooms.

SERVES 4

1 chicken, about 1.5–1.75 kg (3–4 lb)

350 g (12 oz) oyster or button
    mushrooms

1 bunch of fresh tarragon

25 g (1 oz) unsalted butter

1 tablespoon olive oil

175 g (6 oz) seedless grapes, peeled

Salt and freshly ground white
    pepper

FOR THE SAUCE

4 shallots, chopped

1 carrot, chopped

2 celery sticks, chopped

1 bay leaf

1 sprig of fresh thyme

50 g (2 oz) unsalted butter

300 ml (10 fl oz) dry white wine

1.2 litres (2 pints) Chicken Stock
    (see p. 399)

450 ml (15 fl oz) double cream

For a fricassee, the chicken must be cut into four portions, removing the breasts and legs from the carcass. Split the drumsticks from the thighs, but leave the breasts whole. The carcass should be chopped and used in making the sauce.

Pre-heat the oven to 200°C/400°F/gas 6.

Pick over the oyster mushrooms, removing and reserving the stalks, and slice the mushroom caps. Remove the stalks from the tarragon and reserve them for the sauce.

To make the sauce, sweat the tarragon stalks, chopped shallots, carrot, celery, bay leaf and thyme in half the butter. Add the chopped chicken carcass and the mushroom trimmings and cook for a few minutes. Pour on the white wine and boil to reduce until almost dry. Add the chicken stock and boil to reduce by three-quarters. Add the cream and simmer for 20 minutes. Strain the sauce through a sieve.

Fry the chicken pieces in the butter and olive oil until coloured then transfer to the pre-heated oven and cook for 20 minutes, checking the breasts after 10 minutes; they may be ready and can be removed. When the chicken is cooked, leave it to rest for 15 minutes. Add the sliced mushroom caps, tarragon leaves and grapes to the sauce and warm them through until the mushrooms are tender. Season with salt and pepper.

Cut the chicken breasts in half and divide the chicken, giving a piece of breast and leg for each portion. Spoon over the sauce and serve.

Chicken with Paprika, Lemon and Soy Sauce

This dish eats very well with my Mashed Potatoes (see p. 230), which can be spiced up with a little olive oil, chopped onion, garlic, even chopped parsley for that extra taste and colour.

SERVES 4

1 chicken, about 1.5–1.75 kg (3¹/2–4 lb)

1 garlic clove, halved

150 ml (5 fl oz) olive oil

Salt and freshly ground white pepper

1 sprig of fresh thyme, chopped

2 heaped tablespoons paprika
2 tablespoons plain flour
Juice of 3 lemons

50 ml (2 fl oz) soy sauce
50 g (2 oz) unsalted butter

Pre-heat the oven to 220°C/425°F/gas 7.

Cut the chicken into eight pieces: split the legs in half; remove the breasts from the carcass and cut each into two pieces. Rub the chicken pieces with the garlic and some of the olive oil. Season with salt and pepper and sprinkle with chopped thyme. Mix the paprika and flour together and cover the chicken pieces liberally with the mixture. Mix together the lemon juice and soy sauce and cover the chicken with half of this mixture.

Pre-heat a large flameproof baking pan and add some of the olive oil and half the butter. Add the chicken and fry over a high heat to crisp the skin until it is almost burnt black. Turn the chicken pieces in the pan and add the remaining lemon juice and soy sauce and a little more of the paprika mix. Place in the pre-heated oven for about 20 minutes, by which time the chicken will have a very crispy skin.

Remove the chicken from the oven and the pan and drain the liquor through a sieve into another pan. Warm this liquor and add the remaining butter. The sauce will now almost have a sweet and sour taste from the lemon, soy sauce and paprika. Pour it over the chicken and serve. Or, if you are serving it with mashed potatoes, divide them between individual plates, sit the chicken on top and pour the juices over.

Grilled Chicken Breast with Noodles in Creamy Mushroom Sauce

This is a variation on a great old Italian classic: noodles, mushrooms and a cream sauce. It's a great way of turning a simple chicken breast into a wonderful dish, and is best served with a mixed or green salad. The marinated chicken breasts can be cooked on an open barbecue and served with a salad, and the cream sauce can be used with other dishes, even just with noodles on their own. If you don't have time to make your own fettucine, you can use shop-bought fresh or dried.

SERVES 4
4 chicken breasts
Salt and freshly ground white pepper
450 g (1 lb) Fettucine (see p. 89)
A little olive oil
1 teaspoon chopped fresh parsley

FOR THE MARINADE
300 ml (10 fl oz) olive oil
Juice of 2 lemons
1 garlic clove, crushed
1/2 teaspoon chopped fresh thyme
1/2 teaspoon chopped fresh basil
1/2 teaspoon chopped fresh tarragon

FOR THE CREAM SAUCE
4 chicken wings (optional)
1 carrot, coarsely chopped
1 onion, coarsely chopped
2 celery sticks, coarsely chopped
1 small leek, coarsely chopped
50 g (2 oz) unsalted butter
1 small garlic clove
1 sprig of fresh thyme
1 bay leaf
A few fresh basil leaves
300 ml (10 fl oz) dry white wine

900 ml (1½ pints) Chicken Stock
   (see p. 399)
600 ml (1 pint) double cream

FOR THE GARNISH
2 large onions, sliced
6 smoked back bacon rashers, rinded
   and chopped
225 g (8 oz) button mushrooms, sliced
50 g (2 oz) unsalted butter

Mix together all the marinade ingredients, season with salt and pepper and pour over the chicken breasts. The breasts are best left in the marinade for 48 hours to allow them to take on the tastes.

Pre-heat the grill to medium.

To make the cream sauce, cook the chicken wings and chopped vegetables in the butter with the garlic and herbs, until softened. Add the white wine and boil to reduce until almost dry. Add the chicken stock and boil to reduce by two-thirds. Add the cream, slowly bring to the simmer and then simmer the sauce gently for about 30 minutes. Push the sauce through a sieve, check for seasoning and keep to one side in a large pan.

Remove the chicken breasts from the marinade and grill them until cooked through and tender, or pan-fry them in a little butter and olive oil.

The pasta can be made as for the sea bass recipe (see p. 89), or finer spaghetti noodles can be made or bought for this. It just needs to be boiled in salted water with a little oil until tender.

For the garnish, cook the sliced onions, bacon and mushrooms in the butter until they are soft.

To serve, place the pasta and garnish in the sauce, bring to the simmer and allow it to warm through for 2 minutes. Divide the pasta and garnish between four large bowls and spoon some of the sauce over each one. The grilled or pan-fried chicken breasts can now be carved into two pieces, cutting at an angle through the middle. Sit the chicken on top of the noodles. Pour 8–10 tablespoons of the marinade through a sieve into a bowl and add the chopped parsley. Spoon a little over each chicken breast just before serving.

Jambonette de Volaille

This is a classic French dish and really is just a stuffed chicken leg. When totally finished, the shape resembles a small ham, which is where the name jambonette comes from. This recipe may look time-consuming, but it is very straightforward and

worth every effort. The jambonette eats well with Braised Butter Beans (see p. 245)
Ratatouille (see p. 192), or Tomato and Onion Flavoured Gravy (see p. 367).

SERVES 4

4 chicken legs

225 g 8 oz pig's caul, soaked in cold
  water for 24 hours (optional)

2 tablespoons olive oil

FOR THE STUFFING

225 g (8 oz) button mushrooms, minced
  or finely chopped

2 small chicken breasts, skinned

50 g (2 oz) fresh spinach, stalks
  removed, leaves blanched and
  drained

1 large onion, finely chopped

2 smoked bacon rashers, rinded and
  finely diced

1 garlic clove, crushed

A few fresh basil leaves, chopped

100 g (4 oz) oyster mushrooms
  (optional), sliced

25 g (1 oz) unsalted butter

Salt and freshly ground white pepper

1 egg

TO SERVE

Braised Butter Beans (see p. 245) or
  Ratatouille (see p. 192)

Tomato and Onion Flavoured Gravy
  (see p. 367)

Firstly, the chicken legs must be boned. Lay the leg skin-side down, and cut along the thigh bone only. Scrape down the bone towards the joint and the thigh meat will start to fall from the bone. Continue to scrape until the bone is free of any meat. Keep the point of the knife close to the knuckle joint and cut round carefully. The joint will now be clean. Continue the same process and scrape down to the next joint. At this point, the bone can be broken or cut and the leg will be boned. Repeat the same process for all the legs, just leaving the knuckle on the end of each one.

To make the stuffing, heat the minced mushrooms on their own in a pan until they become totally dry. Allow to cool. Mince or finely chop the chicken breasts with the blanched spinach then mix into the mushrooms and chill in the fridge. Heat the onion, bacon, garlic, basil and oyster mushrooms, if using, in the butter for a few minutes until softened, then allow to cool. Add to the chicken and mushroom mixture, season with salt and pepper and mix in the egg.

Fill the boned legs with the stuffing, filling them enough to re-shape into a chicken leg, and folding the skin and meat under to seal the leg. They can now be wrapped in pig's caul, if using, or simply use wooden cocktail sticks to hold the legs together. Leave the legs to rest for at least 1 hour in the fridge to set, then they will be ready to roast.

Pre-heat the oven to 200°C/400°F/gas 6.

Fry the chicken legs on the curved side in the olive oil in a flameproof baking pan until golden brown, then turn in the pan and cook in the pre-heated oven for 20–25 minutes.

Put the hot butter beans or ratatouille on hot plates. Cut the *jambonette* into 4–5 slices and arrange on the beans or vegetables and serve with the tomato and onion sauce poured around.

Spicy Fried Chicken

This chicken dish is simple to make and so easy to cook. The chicken is dry-fried. This basically means it doesn't have any sauce but the instant marinade keeps it moist to eat with lots of flavours happening. Looking at the seasoning ingredients you'd think it was going to need marinating for several hours before cooking. Well it doesn't. You literally just mix the chicken in the 'marinade' and fry. The dish will eat very well with a straightforward salad or boiled or fried basmati rice.

SERVES 4

4–6 chicken breasts

Groundnut or sesame oil for frying

A squeeze of fresh lemon juice
(optional)

1 tablespoon chopped fresh coriander
(optional)

A sprinkling of Garam Masala
(see p. 402) (optional)

FOR THE MARINADE

4 tablespoons natural yoghurt

3 tablespoons lime juice

$3/4$ teaspoon ground turmeric

$3/4$ teaspoon paprika

2 garlic cloves, crushed

3 cardamom pods, crushed

$1/2$ teaspoon salt

Mix all the marinade ingredients together. Cut the chicken into thin strips and spoon and mix the marinade on to the chicken. Heat a large frying-pan with just a drop of the cooking oil. The pan must be hot before frying the chicken. Fry, tossing the chicken to give an all-over golden brown finish. Providing that the chicken has been cut into thin strips, it will only take 4–5 minutes to cook.

To finish the taste, squeeze a trickle of lemon juice on to the chicken and add the chopped coriander. To finish the dish totally, just sprinkle with garam masala and serve. This is not essential but will give an even fuller taste.

NOTE

It is best to fry a handful of chicken at a time as this prevents the heat being lost from the pan and the meat stewing.

Blackened Chicken

This recipe is so called because the spice mixture used to season the meat leaves it with a black finish with plenty of spice flavours. The same spice recipe can be used on fish. Once made, the spices can be kept in an airtight jar for use another day.

Try the chicken dish with different combinations of flavours. It goes very well with Simple Salad (see p. 34), especially during the summer when the chicken has been cooked on an open barbecue. It also eats well with stir-fried rice or pasta dishes. I particularly like to eat it as a topping and extra to an open BLT (bacon, lettuce, tomato) sandwich: a really good lunchtime dish.

SERVES 4

4 chicken breasts

1 tablespoon oil

A knob of unsalted butter

FOR THE BLACKENED SPICE MIX

1 tablespoon salt

1^1/$_2$ teaspoons garlic powder

1^1/$_2$ teaspoons freshly ground black pepper

1 teaspoon ground white pepper

1 teaspoon onion powder or granules

1 teaspoon ground cumin

1/$_2$ teaspoon cayenne pepper

1/$_2$ teaspoon paprika

Pre-heat the oven to 200°C/400°F/gas 6.

Mix all the spices together. The chicken breasts can now be either completely rolled in the spices or just coated on the skin side.

To cook the chicken, either pan-fry or grill. If you are pan-frying, then simply heat a pan and add the oil and butter. Once the butter is bubbling, add the chicken breast skin-side down and cook for a few minutes until blackened, then turn the chicken and continue to cook until blackened, if liked, on the other side. The chicken will take 10–12 minutes to cook completely. If you are grilling, brush with oil and butter and grill until blackened on all sides and then season. Finish in the pre-heated oven for about 10 minutes until cooked through. It's now up to you how you want to serve it.

NOTE

I prefer just to 'blacken' and season the skin side.

Roast Chicken on Cabbage with Crispy Pancetta and Lemon and Thyme Dumplings

Roast chicken and bacon are common company, usually helped along with sausages and bread sauce, a favourite for the Great British Sunday Lunch. I wanted to take a classic like this and turn it into something more than just a Sunday Lunch.

Pancetta is an Italian cured bacon that can be found in most delicatessens. The fat that almost dissolves in the cooking gives a wonderful full flavour to the bacon. A good smoked or unsmoked streaky bacon can be used instead. You'll notice I have mentioned corn-fed chicken. Basically this has a fuller flavour than the basic battery-fed chickens that are mostly available to us.

SERVES 4

1 corn-fed or oven-ready chicken, about 1.75 kg (4 lb)

12 rashers pancetta or 8 rashers streaky bacon

75 g (3 oz) carrots, diced

75 g (3 oz) onions, diced

75 g (3 oz) celery, diced

75 g (3 oz) leek, diced

1 sprig of fresh thyme or a pinch of
    dried thyme (optional)
150 ml (5 fl oz) dry white wine
300 ml (10 fl oz) Chicken Stock
    (see p. 399)
300 ml (10 fl oz) Veal or Beef *Jus*
    (see p. 398) or bought alternative
    (see p. 401)
1 medium Savoy cabbage
Cooking oil
A knob of unsalted butter
Salt and freshly ground black pepper

FOR THE DUMPLINGS
100 g (4 oz) fresh bone marrow
100 g (4 oz) white breadcrumbs
2 tablespoons double cream
3 egg yolks
A pinch of grated nutmeg
1 heaped teaspoon chopped fresh
    thyme
Finely grated zest and juice of
    1 lemon
Chicken Stock (see p. 399) or water

When you cut up the chicken, make sure you keep all the bones for stock. Remove the legs at the joint and split the drumstick from the thigh. Trim off the knuckle ends of the drumsticks and remove the bones from the thighs on the meat side, leaving the skin attached. The thighs can now be rolled or folded and held together with a cocktail stick. The breasts can now be left on the bone, removing the back bone carcass; the wings can be trimmed back to a single bone attached to the breast. This can be cleaned and trimmed, exposing the bone itself.

The carcass bones can now all be roughly chopped and either roasted or coloured in a pan with the diced carrot, onion, celery and leek – specific quantities are not too important. Also a sprig or pinch of thyme can be added. Once the chicken and vegetables are coloured, add the wine and bring to the boil, then boil to reduce until almost dry. Add the chicken stock and also boil to reduce by two-thirds. Now the *jus* or gravy can be added and brought to a simmer. Once simmering, cook for 20–30 minutes without reducing as this would make the sauce too strong. The sauce can now be strained through a sieve. You now have about 300 ml (10 fl oz) of a well flavoured chicken sauce to go with the roast.

While the sauce is cooking, make the dumpling mix. Break down the bone marrow in a food processor or mixer. Add the breadcrumbs, cream, egg yolks, nutmeg and thyme. Add the lemon zest and juice and season with salt and pepper. Once the lemon has been added, a curdled texture may appear. This should just be ignored; once cooked the dumpling will gel together and not separate. You will have about 350 g (12 oz) of mix. The mix is best left chilled for at least 2 hours before cooking. It keeps very well for 3–4 days; the lemon juice will change the colour of the mix, making it almost salmon pink, but this will disappear once cooked.

Pre-heat the oven to 200°C/400°F/gas 6.

Cut the cabbage into 2 cm (3/4 in) thick strips. Rinse carefully and drain in a colander.

To roast the chicken, heat a roasting pan with a trickle of cooking oil and a small knob of butter. Season the bird with salt and pepper. Colour all the pieces golden in the pan. Remove the drumsticks and thighs, then sit the breasts on the bone in the pan and cook in the pre-heated oven for 10 minutes before adding the drumsticks and thighs and cooking for a further 10–15 minutes or until completely golden and crispy. During the cooking time, baste the chicken with its own cooking fat to keep it moist and help the colouring. Once cooked, remove from the oven and leave to rest for a few minutes.

While the chicken is cooking, cook the dumplings and cabbage. Shape the dumpling mix into 4 ovals between 2 tablespoons or roll into balls before dropping into simmering chicken stock or water and cooking for 10–15 minutes, depending on the size. Any excess dumpling mix can be left refrigerated and used for another dish.

Melt a knob of butter in a pan with 2 teaspoons of water. Once bubbling, add the cabbage and turn up the heat, stirring all the time. Once beginning to soften, season with salt and pepper. The cabbage will only take 2–3 minutes to become tender without becoming overcooked and floppy.

While the chicken is resting, grill the rashers of pancetta or bacon until crisp.

Now the breasts can be taken off the bone. Divide the cabbage between plates or bowls. Sit the rashers of pancetta or bacon on top, then the portions of chicken. Spoon the hot gravy over the chicken pieces, and then finish with a lemon and thyme dumpling.

Grilled Chicken Breast with Braised Pearl Barley, Lemon and Thyme

This really is a simple dish, not too many ingredients but packed with textures and tastes. Instead of simmering the barley on the stove, it cooks evenly if you put in a pre-heated oven at 180°C/350°F/gas 4.

SERVES 4

1 large onion, finely chopped
175–225 g (6–8 oz) unsalted butter, softened but not melted
900 ml (1¹/₂ pints) Chicken Stock (see p. 399)
1 leek, sliced or diced

100 g (4 oz) pearl barley
1 teaspoon chopped fresh thyme
Juice of 1–2 lemons
4 chicken breasts
Salt and freshly ground black pepper

To braise the barley, cook the chopped onion in 50 g (2 oz) of the butter, without colouring, until softened. Bring 600 ml (1 pint) of the chicken stock to the boil, add the leeks and cook for 30 seconds. Strain, reserving both stock and leeks. Add the pearl barley to the onions and cook for another 1–2 minutes. Add the stock and bring to the simmer. Cover with a lid and cook over a low heat, stirring continuously, until the barley becomes tender; this will take 30–40 minutes. Add more stock if the barley becomes dry. The remaining 300 ml (10 fl oz) of chicken stock can be boiled until reduced by half to leave you with a good, strong stock.

Mix 100–150 g (4–5 oz) of the butter with the thyme and lemon juice. (This can be made at any time and will keep in the fridge for as long as the butter will last.)

The chicken breasts eat very well if cooked on a grill pan or open barbecue. They can also be pan-fried or cooked under the grill. They will take about 15 minutes.

To finish the barley, add a knob of butter and the leeks and warm through. If there is still a lot of excess chicken stock, simply pour it off. Re-boil the reduced chicken stock, then gradually add and whisk in enough of the lemon and thyme butter until you have a smooth sauce consistency. Season with salt and pepper. Spoon the barley on to the centre of a warmed serving plate and pour the sauce around. Slice the chicken breast through the middle and place on top of the barley.

Grilled Chicken on Red Wine, Onions and Mushrooms

This dish is very rich; the flavour of the red onions cooked in red wine eats beautifully. Use flat or open-cup mushrooms; both have a good flavour and texture. This mushroom and red wine garnish also works well with lamb and beef.

SERVES 4

50 g (2 oz) unsalted butter

8–10 large red onions, sliced

50 g (2 oz) demerara sugar

300 ml (10 fl oz) red wine vinegar

Salt and freshly ground black pepper

1 bottle of red wine

2 tablespoons *crème de cassis* (optional)

8–12 flat or open-cup mushrooms

4 chicken breasts

300 ml (¹/₂ pint) Red Wine Sauce (see p. 368)

Pre-heat the oven to 200°C/400°F/gas 6.

Melt half the butter in a large pan, add the onions and cook for a few minutes without colouring until they begin to soften. Add the sugar and red wine vinegar and boil to reduce until almost dry. Season with salt and pepper. Add the wine and also reduce until almost dry. Season again with salt and pepper and stir in the *crème de cassis*, if using.

Remove the stalks from the mushrooms and tear off the outer skin from the mushrooms. This is not essential but makes them even more tender. Lay them upside-down on a buttered and seasoned tray, brush with butter and season again. Cook under the grill for 4–6 minutes.

Meanwhile, cook the chicken on an open grill or on a grill plate, or just fry in a little butter until golden, then finish in the pre-heated oven for 8–10 minutes. Warm the red wine sauce.

To serve the dish, divide the onions between four bowls (there might well be enough for more), then sit the mushrooms on top. Carve the chicken through the centre and arrange on top of the mushrooms. Pour the warm sauce around.

VARIATIONS

For a lighter sauce, take any of the red onion trimmings from slicing them and cook in a knob of butter for a few minutes until softened. Add 600 ml (1 pint) of red wine and reduce until almost dry. Add 450 ml (15 fl oz) of chicken stock and reduce by half. Strain through a sieve and whisk in 50–75 g (2–3 oz) of unsalted butter. This will give you a lighter red wine sauce that can be blitzed with a hand blender to make it even lighter.

Crispy Roast Duck Breasts with Parsnip Purée

The duck breasts I use for this recipe are called magrets. This is a duck breast that has been completely removed from the bone and has no wing attached. This breast can then have the skin removed or left on. I prefer to leave the skin on, as this gives a crispy finish. Magret duck breasts usually come vacuum-packed from France and are ready to cook. If you can't get magrets, simply roast duck breasts still on the carcass, then remove them from the bone once cooked and rested.

SERVES 4

4 *magret* duck breasts
1 tablespoon vegetable or olive oil
Salt and freshly ground black pepper

4 teaspoons clear honey
450 g (1 lb) parsnips
50 g (2 oz) unsalted butter
1 quantity Cranberry Gravy (see p. 368)

Pre-heat the oven to 200°C/400°F/gas 6.

First score the fat on the duck breasts with a sharp knife all the way across (right to left) about 1–2 mm (1/8 in) apart. The fat only needs to be scored and not cut through into the flesh. Pre-heat a roasting pan on top of the stove with the oil. Season the scored duck breasts with salt and pepper. Sit the breasts skin-side down in the pan. This will create some spitting from the pan as all the water from the fat will cook out. Once the breasts are cooking fast, turn the heat down to medium and continue to cook the breasts fat-side down until dark and almost burnt. The layer of skin will have cooked right down almost like a confit. Turn the breasts over and finish in the pre-heated oven for 6–10 minutes, until the flesh is cooked to medium, depending on the thickness of the breast; a large, thick breast will take 8–10 minutes. Once cooked, the skin will be dark, rich and crispy, almost like duck crackling.

This can now be made even tastier if honey is spooned on top and glazed under the grill. Before serving the breasts, it's best to leave them to rest for 5–10 minutes as this will allow the meat to become more tender.

To make the parsnip purée, peel and split the parsnips lengthways into quarters, and cut out the woody centres. Boil in salted water for about 15 minutes until tender, drain and shake dry. Add the salt and pepper and butter and mash the parsnips. Push through a sieve to get a smooth-textured purée. The *magrets* can be left whole or sliced diagonally and arranged on a plate. Serve the parsnip purée separately or shape it between two large spoons to give an oval shape and sit on the plate with the duck. Pour some of the cranberry gravy on to the dish and serve.

Confit of Duck (Marinated Version)

Confit comes from the French word meaning 'to preserve'. It is a classic regional dish from Gascony in south-west France. The technique can be applied to various different meats, but duck, goose and pork are the most common. So many tastes and textures can be achieved in the dish, but it will, of course, depend on how long you marinate the meat, how slowly you cook it, how you store it and what actually goes into the marinade. I'm going to give you my version, with various ways of serving it. I cook it in goose fat, which is quite expensive to buy, but the dish will work very well with rendered pork fat or lard. It really is worth making the effort for a good confit. The recipes that follow are just a few ideas of what to eat with confit. If you don't fancy any of these, confit is wonderful with a good salad.

SERVES 4
4 duck legs
2 teaspoons rock salt
1–1.5 kg (2–3 lb) goose or pork fat, to cover
4 tablespoons clear honey

FOR THE MARINADE
A few sprigs of fresh thyme
1 bay leaf
6 fresh basil leaves

12 black peppercorns
1 garlic clove, sliced
2 shallots or 1 onion, chopped
2.5 cm (1 in) fresh ginger root, peeled and grated
2 teaspoons Worcestershire sauce
2 teaspoons soy sauce
2 teaspoons balsamic vinegar
1 tablespoon white wine vinegar
1 tablespoon extra virgin olive oil

Mix together all the ingredients for the marinade. Rub each duck leg with the rock salt. Place the legs in the marinade, cover and leave for at least 3–4 days in the fridge. The longer the legs marinate, the stronger the flavour will become.

Pre-heat the oven to 160–180°C/325–350°F/gas 3–4.

To cook the duck legs, melt the fat in a deep flameproof baking dish or tray. Add the duck legs to the fat and cook in the pre-heated oven for about 2 hours. When cooked slowly the legs take on more flavour. Check them during cooking: if you try to separate the leg from the thigh and it starts to give easily, then they are ready. Leave to cool in the fat.

The legs can be eaten immediately after cooking. Or at this stage, they can be transferred to a suitable container, covered with the cooking fat and chilled. They will keep for weeks, even months, and the flavour will be developing all the time. When you are ready to serve them, simply remove them from the fat and cook in the low oven for about 20 minutes. I always like to finish my *confit* with a tablespoon of honey on each leg and then crisp it under the grill.

Confit of Duck (Salted Version)

This is a classic French dish that can also work with goose or pork. In Confit of Duck (Marinated Version) (see p. 127) the duck legs are steeped in a marinade for a few days. Well, this recipe is even simpler; you do without the marinade and these duck legs will just be salted for 24 hours before cooking.

SERVES 4
4 duck legs
2 teaspoons rock sea salt
900 g (2 lb) lard or goose fat, melted

Trim the legs of any remaining feather stalks and remove the knuckle on the under-side of the thigh. The skin can also be scored around the top of the drumstick knuckle so this will shrink while cooking and reveal the bone. Salt the legs on the skin side and chill for 24 hours. This will draw any water from the fat and ensure that the skin is crisp when the legs are cooked.

Pre-heat the oven to 160°C/325°F/gas 3.

Sit the legs in a braising dish and cover with melted lard. Bring just to a light simmer, cover with a lid and cook in the oven for 1½–2 hours. To check the legs, remove one from the fat and push the skin side. When you feel the meat is starting to become tender and give, remove from the heat and leave to cool in the fat.

Transfer the legs to a clean dish and cover completely in fat. They will keep chilled almost indefinitely.

To roast the legs, pre-heat the oven to 200°C/400°F/gas 6. Remove the legs from the fat and cut off the end knuckle. Cook in the pre-heated oven for 15–20 minutes until crispy.

Confit of Duck with Red Cabbage and Apples

SERVES 4

4 apples, peeled and cored

1/2 red cabbage, shredded

2 onions, sliced

65 g (2 1/2 oz) unsalted butter

150 ml (5 fl oz) red wine vinegar

25 g (1 oz) demerara sugar

150 ml (5 fl oz) red wine

Salt and freshly ground black pepper

TO SERVE

1 quantity Confit of Duck (Marinated
   Version) (see p. 127)

1 quantity Red Wine Sauce (see p. 368)

Chop two of the apples. Sweat the red cabbage and onions in 50 g (2 oz) of the butter for a few minutes until softened. Add the chopped apples and cook for a further few minutes. Add the wine vinegar and cook until it evaporates. Add the sugar and red wine and season with salt and pepper. Cover with a lid and continue to cook for about 30 minutes, until the cabbage is tender.

Slice the remaining apples in to 12 rings. Melt the remaining butter and fry the apple rings in a hot pan, browning on both sides.

Spoon the cabbage on to hot plates and sit three apple rings on top. Arrange the hot, glazed duck *confit* on the apples and pour the red wine sauce around.

Confit of Duck with Cabbage, Onions and Beansprouts

The flavours in the dish give an oriental taste similar to the classic Peking duck.

SERVES 4

1/2 green cabbage, shredded

225 g (8 oz) beansprouts

2 onions, sliced

25 g (1 oz) butter

1 tablespoon olive oil

Salt and freshly ground black pepper

A pinch of five-spice powder

300 ml (10 fl oz) Veal *Jus* (see p. 398) or
   bought alternative (see p. 401)

1 quantity Confit of Duck (Marinated
   Version) (see p. 127)

1–3 tablespoons Plum Purée Sauce
   (see p. 370)

Blanch the cabbage and beansprouts separately in boiling salted water then refresh under cold water and drain well. Melt the butter with the olive oil in a wok or frying pan. Fry the onions in the butter and olive oil until softened and golden brown. Add the cabbage and beansprouts and season with salt, pepper and five-spice powder. Stir-fry for 2–3 minutes.

Bring the veal *jus* to the simmer and gradually add the plum purée sauce until a rich, spicy plum flavour is achieved. One tablespoon may well be enough, the quantity all depends on your taste buds.

Spoon the cabbage mixture on to the hot plates, sit the hot, glazed *confit* on top and pour the sauce around.

Confit of Duck with Orange Sauce and Buttered Spinach

This is a variation on the original Confit of Duck (see p. 128). When salting the duck legs, add the pared rind of one orange and leave it with the legs during the cooking stage. This will help infuse the orange taste. To add even more orange taste to the duck, finely grate the zest of an orange, add it to some clear honey and use to glaze the roasted duck confit and give a sharp orange flavour.

SERVES 4
4 Confit of Duck legs (Salted Version)
    (see p. 128)

FOR THE ORANGE SAUCE
300 ml (¹/2 pint) Red Wine Sauce (see
    p. 368)
Pared rind of 1 orange
Juice of 1 orange

FOR THE BUTTERED SPINACH
900 g (2 lb) spinach, picked and
    washed
50 g (2 oz) unsalted butter
Salt and freshly ground black
    pepper

To make an orange sauce, start with a red wine sauce. During the cooking of the vegetables, add the orange rind and follow the recipe until the red wine has reduced in volume. Add the orange juice and boil until reduced by three-quarters. Continue with the recipe, adding the veal *jus* or alternative, and cook for 20–30 minutes, pushing the finished sauce through a sieve. The orange sauce is now ready and has a richness helped by the red wine.

To cook the spinach, make sure all excess water has been shaken off the leaves. Melt the butter in a hot pan. Once the butter begins to bubble, add the spinach and stir with a wooden spoon, keeping the pan at a high temperature. The spinach will cook very quickly. After 2–3 minutes, season the spinach with salt and pepper. Drain off any excess liquor and the spinach is ready.

To serve spinach with the duck, it's nice to divide the spinach between individual plates or bowls and sit each glazed duck leg *confit* on top. Just finish by pouring the orange sauce around.

Peppered Confit of Duck with Peppercorn Sauce

Cook the duck legs as for Confit of Duck (Salted Version) (see p. 128). Once they are cooked and removed from the fat, sprinkle finely crushed black peppercorns on top of each leg. The legs can now be roasted and glazed.

SERVES 4

4 Confit of Duck legs (Salted Version)
   (see p. 128)
Finely crushed black peppercorns

FOR THE PEPPERCORN SAUCE
2 teaspoons green peppercorns, lightly
   crushed

2 shallots, finely chopped
25 g (1 oz) unsalted butter
50 ml (2 fl oz) brandy
1 glass of dry white wine
300 ml (10 fl oz) Veal *Jus* (see p. 398) or
   alternative (see p. 401)
150 ml (5 fl oz) double cream

To make a peppercorn sauce, cook the peppercorns and shallots in the butter until just softened. Add the brandy and boil to reduce until almost dry. Add the white wine and boil to reduce until almost dry. Add the veal *jus* or alternative, bring the sauce to the simmer and cook gently for 20 minutes. Add the double cream (it will not curdle) and continue to cook and simmer for a few minutes. You should now have a good sauce consistency with a *café au lait* (milky coffee) colour.

Shredded Duck or Grilled Fish with Thai Noodles

This dish suits both meat and fish and, in particular, duck. I make a duck confit, and shred it, just before serving, over the spicy noodles. As an alternative to the duck, grilled sea bass, cod, turbot, halibut or perhaps a king prawn kebab will all work well with this dish. The noodles I normally use are fettucine. These can either be home-made, bought fresh or dried. Thai fish sauce, or nam pla, is a fish sauce used throughout south-east Asia as a seasoning, similar to soy sauce, for many savoury foods. It is made from salted fish and so consequently has a salty, anchovy taste.

SERVES 4

4 × 100–225 g (4–8 oz) portions of
   Confit of Duck (see p. 127) or
   4 × 100–250 g (4–8 oz) fish fillets
350–450 g (12–16 oz) noodles, cooked
   and tossed in a little dressing
A knob of unsalted butter
Salt and freshly ground black pepper

FOR THE THAI SAUCE
5 tablespoons Champagne or white
   wine vinegar
3 tablespoons Thai fish sauce
   (*nam pla*)
120 ml (4 fl oz) olive oil
1 large garlic clove, crushed
1 teaspoon very finely chopped fresh
   ginger root

Juice and grated zest of ¹/₂ small lemon

Juice and grated zest of ¹/₂ small orange

1 small red chilli, seeded and finely chopped

1 teaspoon crushed black peppercorns

1 lemon grass stick, finely chopped

TO FINISH THE DISH

1 large red onion, chopped

8–10 fresh basil leaves

8–10 fresh mint leaves

8–10 sprigs of fresh coriander

Make the duck *confit* as described on p. 127. It needs to be marinated a few days in advance, if possible.

To make the Thai sauce, mix together the Champagne or wine vinegar with the fish sauce. Whisk the olive oil into this mix a drop at a time, as for a mayonnaise. Add all other ingredients, making sure anything cut is very finely chopped. This can now be kept bottled until needed. You will have about 300 ml (10 fl oz).

Pre-heat the oven to 200°C/400°F/gas 6.

To roast the duck confit, remove the duck legs from the fat. In a hot pan, colour the duck on the fat side until golden, then finish in the pre-heated oven for 15–20 minutes, until crispy.

To cook the fish, you can pan-fry or grill. Most 100–225 g (4–8 oz) portions of fish fillet will only take approximately 6–8 minutes once coloured.

To finish either dish, warm the noodles in a knob of butter and season with salt and pepper. Add the red onions, herbs and Thai sauce to moisten all the pasta. This can now be spooned into bowls. If you are serving grilled fish, then simply sit the portions on top of the pasta. The duck can now be either left whole and placed on top, or shredded down with a spoon and fork (as is done in Chinese restaurants to go in pancakes) and sprinkled over the top.

NOTE

To guarantee a really crispy duck skin, cook the *confit* legs, skin-side down, in 1 cm (¹/₂ in) oil (almost deep-frying) until golden and crispy. The legs can then be finished by cooking in the oven for 10–15 minutes.

VARIATIONS

Roast duck breasts can also be served with this dish, or chicken, pork, lamb, beef, shrimps, prawns, lobster, crab, mussels …

Turkey Saltimbocca

Saltimbocca is an Italian dish using a veal escalope that has been wrapped in Parma ham with sage leaves. Well, this is exactly what I'm doing using an escalope of turkey breast instead. An escalope is actually just a slice of meat or fish. When using meat, depending on which cut and variety, you may find that it will need to be slightly batted out between pieces of cling film. This will give you a thin slice that will cook quite quickly when pan-fried.

This dish came to me when I was looking for Christmas lunch alternatives. I wanted to stick with turkey – capturing all the traditional Christmas tastes – but at the same time make a complete dish that doesn't need the endless garnishes that we all have. I wanted to keep things lighter and easier, instead of roast turkey and pork with bacon, sausages, stuffing, bread sauce, cranberry sauce, roast potatoes, sprouts, parsnips, carrots, gravy. I'm worn out writing it, let alone eating it. And remember that's just the main course.

But you certainly don't have to think about just keeping this recipe to serve at Christmas; the turkey can be eaten at any time of the year. Or you could perhaps replace the turkey with chicken breast batted out into an escalope and prepared with the Parma ham and sage, then served with some cheesy noodles and olive oil. If you find it difficult to get Parma or Bayonne ham, then just use some smoked or unsmoked rashers of back or streaky bacon – it still eats well.

To make sure the dish really is complete, I'm serving it with Braised Pearl Barley, Cranberry Sauce with Orange and Crispy Cabbage. Mustard Dressing is used to bind with the barley to give it a risotto-style consistency. If you really don't like mustard, then just use a splash of cream and a squeeze of lemon juice to help the taste and consistency.

I feel I've just written a book about this recipe. So, here it is: it's worth every word and minute.

SERVES 4

4 × 100–175 g (4–6 oz) turkey breast
   escalopes, about 5 mm (1/4 in) thick
4–8 slices of Parma ham or bacon
1/2 bunch of fresh sage
A knob of unsalted butter
Salt and freshly ground black pepper

1 quantity Braised Pearl Barley
   (see p. 245)
2–3 tablespoons Mustard Dressing
   (see p. 382)
1 quantity Cranberry Sauce with
   Orange (see p. 371)
1 quantity Crispy Cabbage (see p. 220)

The turkey can be prepared well in advance and kept chilled. Wrap the turkey escalopes in 1 or 2 rashers of Parma ham or bacon with a large sage leaf on the outside, reserving the rest of the sage for later. This can be held on with a cocktail stick. Set aside until needed. Season and pan-fry the escalopes in a knob of butter in a hot pan for a few minutes on each side, giving a golden brown colour on each side and crisping the Parma ham. Remove the cocktail sticks.

Chop the remaining sage while the turkey is cooking. Warm the pearl barley and add the sage. Moisten to taste with the mustard dressing.

You can serve the dishes separately if you like, but the way I like to serve this dish is to spoon some cranberry sauce around the outside of the plate. In the centre of the plate, spoon some pearl barley, sit the turkey on top and finish with the crispy cabbage sitting on top of the turkey. For a little extra taste, I like to trickle some extra mustard dressing over the cranberry sauce. The dish is now finished – it really is easy to make and, as you can see, it looks exciting and, of course, tastes delicious.

Roast Turkey Breast with Lemon and Herb Stuffing

Christmas Day cooking can be quite a nightmare, especially if you only finished wrapping the presents at midnight on Christmas Eve, went to bed at 1 a.m., then the children (if you have them) woke you at 6.30 a.m. Christmas morning wanting to unwrap their presents. The next thing you know, it's 9 a.m., your guests are arriving in three hours and you haven't even started cooking.

You've eventually served lunch at 2.30 p.m., first a starter, then the main course – roast turkey, stuffing, bread sauce, cranberry sauce, gravy, bacon, chipolatas, sprouts, carrots, parsnips, roast potatoes and probably even more. Of course, pudding hardly gets a look in because we're already too full.

Well, this recipe keeps things a bit simpler; it won't give so many headaches but certainly will give you the traditional flavours. You'll have the lovely lemon-flavoured turkey with carrots all from the same pan. I would be tempted just to serve one other vegetable, perhaps French beans or Brussels sprouts with chestnuts, along with good roast potatoes. If you want to serve the other basic garnishes, such as chipolatas, bacon and cranberry sauce, you can include them as well. Cooking and carving this dish is like having another Christmas present. When you make the first cut the lemon and herb flavours just hit you. A great surprise – Happy Christmas.

SERVES 6–8

1 × 1.75 kg (4 lb) turkey breast
6–8 large carrots, halved lengthways
300 ml (10 fl oz) Chicken Stock (see p. 399)
2–3 tablespoons Veal or Beef *Jus* (see p. 398) or bought alternative (see p. 401)

FOR THE LEMON, ONION AND HERB STUFFING
1¹/₂ tablespoons cooking oil
4 large onions, finely chopped
1 garlic clove, crushed (optional)
Grated zest of 3 lemons
1 heaped teaspoon chopped fresh sage
¹/₂ teaspoon chopped fresh thyme
¹/₂ teaspoon chopped fresh tarragon
450 g (1 lb) fresh white breadcrumbs
Salt and freshly ground black pepper
Freshly grated nutmeg
Juice of 1–1¹/₂ lemons
1–2 eggs, beaten
A knob of unsalted butter

To make the stuffing, warm half the cooking oil in a pan and add the finely chopped onions with the crushed garlic, if using. Soften the onions over a medium heat. Add the lemon zest and chopped fresh herbs and continue to cook for 6–8 minutes until the onions are tender. Leave to cool. Once cooled, add the breadcrumbs and season with salt, pepper and nutmeg. Then mix in the juice of 1 lemon. Taste the stuffing, it should be rich in flavour with a bite from the lemon. If you feel it needs a little more bite, then add the juice of the remaining 1/2 lemon. Now add enough egg to ensure that the stuffing holds together once cooked.

It's best to stuff the turkey a few hours before cooking, even the night before. Place the turkey breast on the work surface and make an incision with a long, sharp knife to make room for the stuffing at the thick end of the breast, not cutting quite through to the sides or other end. The turkey can now be filled with the stuffing. This will almost double the size of the breast. To hold the stuffing in the cut end during cooking, several methods can be used.

1. Simply hold together with 3 or 4 cocktail sticks.
2. Brush egg white on the turkey and press together. This will seal and set once hot. (It's a good idea to do this, then also use some cocktail sticks to be sure.)
3. The turkey can be sealed by sewing with cooks' string.
4. The turkey can also be wrapped in buttered foil. This will hold in the stuffing and also prevent the meat from becoming dry.

Any leftover stuffing can be placed in an ovenproof dish and cooked separately.

Pre-heat the oven to 200°C/400°F/gas 6.

To cook the turkey, first colour the turkey in a roasting pan with the remaining oil and knob of butter until golden. This will work even if the meat is wrapped in foil. If you want to be completely sure of good colouring, then colour the turkey before wrapping. Once coloured, I like to place the carrots in the pan and sit the turkey on top. This will prevent the meat from colouring too much on its base and becoming dry and leathery. Cover the turkey with some butter papers and place in the pre-heated oven. The turkey will take approximately 1 1/4–1 1/2 hours. This will roast the bird and also cook and set the stuffing. During the cooking process, baste the breast every 10 minutes, not wasting any flavour.

Once cooked, remove the turkey from the oven and allow to relax for a further 15–20 minutes before carving. The carrots will also be roasted and full of turkey taste. These, of course, can be served as a vegetable. The juices left in the pan can be used as a gravy. Warm the pan on top of the stove and add the chicken stock. Bring to boiling point, releasing all the flavours in the pan. This can now simply be poured through a sieve and used as a cooking liquor or boiled to reduce by half and some *jus* or alternative added to give a sauce consistency. Then just slice the turkey and serve.

Roast Pigeon and Pea Tarts

The wood pigeon is the most common and easily available type of pigeon and can certainly be used in this recipe. However, I prefer to use squab pigeons. Squab pigeon is a specially reared young pigeon that, when cooked, is beautiful and tender without being over-strong in taste. The breasts are very meaty and squabs are now a lot easier to get hold of. Of course, there's always one drawback and in this case it's price. A wood pigeon will be less than half the price of a squab. Whichever you choose, the recipe still works. The pea tarts are made using cooked 7.5 cm (3 in) diameter shortcrust flan moulds and the peas are braised split peas cooked to a purée. As for the pigeon sauce, we'll be making that from the carcasses of the pigeons.

The pea purée and sauce can both be prepared and cooked a day before, if you wish, and will warm with no loss of taste.

SERVES 4
4 pigeons, wood or squab
225 g (8 oz) Shortcrust Pastry
   (see p. 394)

FOR THE PEAS
50 g (2 oz) green split peas
75 g (3 oz) mixed carrot, onion, celery,
   chopped into 5 mm (¹/₄ in) dice
A knob of unsalted butter
150–300 ml (5–10 fl oz) Vegetable Stock
   (see p. 400) or Chicken Stock
   (see p. 399)
Salt and freshly ground black pepper

FOR THE SAUCE
The central carcasses of the pigeons
A little oil
2 glasses of red wine, about 300 ml
   (10 fl oz)
1 sprig of fresh thyme
1 bay leaf
300 ml (10 fl oz) Veal or Beef *Jus*
   (see p. 398) or bought alternative
   (see p. 401)

Pre-heat the oven to 200°C/400°F/gas 6.

To prepare the pigeons, remove the legs and then remove the central carcass, leaving the breasts still attached to the breast bone. Roasting the breasts on their part of the carcass will prevent them from shrinking and will also keep them moist. The legs can be roasted separately and served (only if using squab pigeon – wood pigeon legs are even smaller) with the rest of the pigeon. I personally just chop them up and use when making the sauce. Another alternative is to cook (*confit*) them in oil in a pan in the oven for 15–20 minutes. This will make them very tender, but still with little meat.

To cook the peas, cook the vegetables in a small flameproof casserole with a small knob of butter for 1–2 minutes before adding the peas. Cover with the stock and bring to a simmer. Cover with paper and a lid and cook in the pre-heated oven for 30–40 minutes. During the cooking time, check and stir to ensure even cooking. If at any time the mix appears to be a little too dry, then add more stock. At the same time be careful not to allow the mixture to be too thin, this will result in a soup consistency when puréed. When completely cooked and breaking when stirred, season with salt and pepper and blitz to a purée with an electric hand blender or push through a sieve. The peas are now ready.

To make the sauce, chop the carcasses (and legs) and fry in a little oil in a pan until brown and sealed. Add the red wine, thyme and bay leaf. Boil to reduce the wine by three-quarters, then add the *jus* or gravy. Bring to a simmer and cook on a low heat for 15–20 minutes. If the sauce is becoming too thick, then loosen with water. Check the sauce for seasoning with salt and pepper and then strain through a sieve. The sauce will now have a good pigeon/game flavour.

While the sauce is simmering, pre-heat the oven to 200°C/400°F/gas 6. Butter and lightly flour 4 × 7.5 cm (3 in) tartlet moulds.

Roll out the shortcrust pastry and use to line the moulds. Line the pastry with greaseproof paper, fill with baking beans or rice and bake in the pre-heated oven for 15–20 minutes, until golden and crispy. Remove the paper and beans.

To roast the pigeons, season with salt and pepper. Colour in a frying or roasting pan and then roast in the pre-heated oven with the breasts sitting up for 12–15 minutes. Once cooked, remove from the oven and leave to rest and relax.

To serve the dish, fill the tartlets with pea purée. Remove the breasts from the bone and slice each into three and arrange on top of the peas, allowing two breasts (one pigeon) per portion. Sit the tarts on plates and simply finish by pouring the rich sauce around.

NOTE

The breasts can be left whole and just set on top of the tarts. If you are using pigeon legs, then simply serve them on top of the tart with the breasts. The pigeon can also be roasted for 8–10 minutes (particularly if you are using wood pigeons) for a more pink finish.

Stewed Venison with Vegetables in Red Wine

Venison for stewing should come from the haunch, or you can use neck. I like to cut the meat into larger pieces rather than dice. It takes a little longer to cook but the texture and taste are better.

SERVES 4

900 g (2 lb) haunch of venison
1 tablespoon cooking fat or oil
450 g (1 lb) onions, sliced
1 sprig of fresh thyme

1 bay leaf
A few juniper berries, lightly crushed
A few black peppercorns, lightly crushed
1 bottle of red wine

900 ml–1.2 litres (1¹/₂–2 pints) Veal
Jus (p. 398) or alternative
(see p. 401)
Salt and freshly ground black
pepper

FOR THE GARNISH
225–275 g (8–10 oz) button onions
1 tablespoon cooking fat
3 carrots
4 celery sticks
6 flat or open-cup mushrooms

Cut the venison into chunks and colour in the fat in a hot frying-pan until completely sealed; remove from the pan. Cook the onions with the thyme, bay leaf, juniper berries and peppercorns for a few minutes. Add half the red wine and boil to reduce until almost dry. Add the *jus* and venison, bring to the simmer, then cook gently for 1¹/₂–2 hours, skimming occasionally. Add a tablespoon or two of water if the sauce becomes too thick.

When the stew is almost ready, fry the onions until well coloured. While they are colouring, quarter the carrots lengthways, then cut at an angle into 2 cm (³/₄ in) pieces. Slice the celery and quarter the mushrooms. Remove the onions from the pan. Add the carrots and celery and colour lightly. Add them to the onions. Add the mushrooms to the pan and fry for a few minutes, then return all the vegetables to the pan and cover with the remaining wine. Boil to reduce until almost dry. The vegetables should now be cooked.

Remove the meat from the sauce and strain the sauce through a sieve. Return the meat to the sauce and check for seasoning with salt and pepper. Add the vegetables to the meat and serve the dish as a stew, or sit the meat in bowls and top with the braised vegetables with the sauce spooned over.

VARIATIONS

To enrich the stew, redcurrant jelly can be added to sweeten the sauce; or a spoonful of Dijon or English mustard or a dash of Worcestershire sauce or mushroom ketchup.

The dish can also be turned into a pie by spooning the stew into a pie dish and topping with Shortcrust Pastry (see p. 394) or Puff Pastry (see p. 393).

You can adapt the recipe to use pheasant, grouse or other game birds.

Another venison dish I enjoy is roasted loin cooked pink, then carved and set on top of a basic Bubble and Squeak (see p. 237) or Beetroot Bubble and Squeak (see p. 229). Pour some Red Wine Sauce (see p. 368) around and the dish is ready.

Venison also eats well with Celeriac and Potato Dauphinoise (see p. 232).

Fillet of Venison Wellington

This dish is usually associated with fillet of beef, but I've tried it with venison, adding some chestnuts to the stuffing and serving it with a slightly sweetened sauce, and found it really delicious. You can, of course, follow this recipe for fillet of beef but omit the chestnuts and cook for an extra 20 minutes. Two dishes from one recipe. Ask your butcher to bone the venison for you and trim the fillet of all sinew. Take the bones home to add flavour to the sauce.

Another way to serve this is to make the Bubble and Squeak on p. 237, either cooked as per the recipe or in individual cakes. The venison slices can then be placed on top of the cakes and the sauce poured around.

SERVES 4

1 × 450–750 g (1–1½ lb) boned loin of
   venison from a saddle of fallow deer
275 g (10 oz) Puff Pastry (see p. 393)
50 g (2 oz) unsalted butter
Salt and freshly ground white pepper
4–6 thin Savoury Pancakes (see
   p. 395)
1 egg, beaten

FOR THE STUFFING
225 g (8 oz) mushrooms, minced or
   finely chopped
1 onion, finely chopped
2 smoked back bacon rashers, rinded
   and finely diced
1 garlic clove, crushed

A pinch of chopped fresh sage
A pinch of chopped fresh thyme
25 g (1 oz) unsalted butter
50 g (2 oz) shelled chestnuts,
   chopped
25 g (1 oz) fresh white breadcrumbs
1 teaspoon chopped fresh parsley
1 large chicken breast, skinned and
   minced or very finely chopped
Salt and freshly ground white pepper
1 egg, beaten

FOR THE SAUCE
Venison bones (optional)
600 ml (1 pint) Red Wine Sauce
   (see p. 368)
1–2 teaspoons cranberry jelly

To make the stuffing, cook the mushrooms on their own in a pan until almost dry. Cook the chopped onion, bacon, garlic, sage and thyme in the butter for a few minutes without colouring. Leave to cool. Add the chestnuts, breadcrumbs and parsley. Season the chicken with salt and pepper, gradually mix in the egg and mix until firm to the touch. Stir in the mushrooms and the onion mixture and check for seasoning.

The sauce can be made in advance. If you have the venison bones, pre-heat the oven to 220°C/425°F/gas 7. Chop the bones and roast in the pre-heated oven for about 30 minutes until browned. Add them to the reduction for the red wine sauce (see p. 368) before adding the veal *jus*, then cook in the normal way. Once the sauce has been pushed through a sieve a good venison flavour will have developed. Stir in the cranberry jelly to give a slightly sweeter taste.

Roll out the puff pastry until large enough to wrap the venison; the thinnest should be 3 mm (⅛ in) and the absolute thickest is 5 mm (¼ in). Leave to rest in the fridge.

Season the venison and fry in the butter in a hot pan until coloured on all sides but not cooked. Leave to cool.

To make the Wellington, lay two of the pancakes on the centre of the pastry and spread some of the stuffing over to cover them. Lay the meat on top and spread some more of the stuffing on top. Fold the pancakes around the meat and lay the other two on top. Brush the edges of the pastry with beaten egg and fold over to enclose the meat and stuffing. Trim off any excess pastry and turn the parcel over on to a dampened roasting tray. Leave to rest in the fridge for 30 minutes.

Pre-heat the oven to 220°C/425°F/gas 7.

Brush the pastry with a little more beaten egg. The pastry can be decorated with pastry trimmings or left plain. Roast in the pre-heated oven for 20–25 minutes. This will leave the meat still pink inside. Leave to rest for 10–15 minutes.

Slice the Venison Wellington, allowing three slices per portion, and serve with the hot, rich sauce.

Meat Main Courses

Peppered Roast Beef with Beetroot Crisps

At first impression, you might think the pepper flavour would mask the flavour of the beef, which can happen with a peppered steak because the whole of the outside of the cut is covered. When you pepper a joint of beef, however, it is going to be served sliced. This means that the beef itself has the predominant taste, with a fire of pepper just round the edges to lift it. So for your next beef roast, have a go at this recipe. The best cuts of beef to use are sirloin, topside or rib. If using a rib of beef, ask just for the eye of the joint, which will give you a better cut with few trimmings.

Peppered roast beef is also very good served cold or just warm with a raw Pickled Red Cabbage (see p. 70) or a good beetroot salad with horseradish dressing. The beetroot crisps provide a tasty garnish. The quantities are not really important for this recipe; make as much as you like.

SERVES 8
675–900 g (1¹/₂–2 lb) topside, sirloin or
   rib of beef
2–3 tablespoons black peppercorns,
   finely crushed
Salt
Cooking fat or oil

FOR THE BEETROOT CRISPS
2 raw beetroots
Plain flour, for dusting
Oil, for deep-frying
Salt

Pre-heat the oven to 220°C/425°F/gas 7.

Roll the beef in the crushed peppercorns until completely covered. Season with salt. Seal the meat in a hot roasting pan, then place in the pre-heated oven. A joint of this size will take 20–40 minutes to cook, but this very much depends on how you would like to eat it. Cooking for 20 minutes will keep it rare, 30 minutes medium and 40 minutes medium to well done. Once cooked, leave the meat to rest for 15–20 minutes before carving. This will relax the meat and it will become even more tender.

To make the beetroot crisps, first peel the raw beetroot and slice absolutely paper thin, using a mandoline, the slicer on a food processor or a very sharp knife. Dry on a cloth. Heat the oil in a deep-fat fryer or heavy-based pan to 180°C/350°F. Lightly dust the beetroot slices in flour and deep-fry in batches for 15–20 seconds. Drain and lightly salt before serving.

Steak with Spinach and Café de Paris Butter

A good grilled or fried steak – whether it is a sirloin, rump or rib-steak – still seems to be one of the most popular main courses in the UK. Well, there's nothing wrong with that; a good tasty tender steak will suit me any day of the week. This recipe just takes a basic dish a bit further and certainly makes the steak worthy of any special occasion or dinner party.

I'm not really quite sure where the Café de Paris butter originated from but it's one that has been around for some time. This recipe makes about 350 g (12 oz).

SERVES 4

4 × 225–350 g (8–12 oz) steaks (your choice!)

A knob of unsalted butter

2 tablespoons water

A pinch of salt

900 g (2 lb) spinach, pickled and washed

Salt and freshly ground black pepper

FOR THE CAFÉ DE PARIS BUTTER

225 g (8 oz) unsalted butter

1 bay leaf, finely crushed

A pinch of chopped fresh thyme

1/2 teaspoon snipped fresh chives

1/2 teaspoon chopped fresh tarragon

1/2 teaspoon chopped fresh chervil

A pinch of cayenne pepper

3/4 teaspoon Madras curry powder

1 large gherkin, finely chopped

1 heaped teaspoon chopped capers

1 garlic clove, crushed

1 teaspoon chopped fresh parsley

2 egg yolks

2 shallots or 1 small onion, finely chopped

Put all the Café de Paris butter ingredients, except the egg yolks and shallots or onion, into a food processor or liquidizer and blend together. The shallots and egg yolks can now be added. Shape the butter into a 15 × 5 cm (6 × 2 in) cylinder, wrap in cling film and chill.

To cook the steaks, just heat a grill plate or frying-pan and cook them to your liking. For rib and rump steaks I find it best to eat them between medium rare and medium. This helps break down the coarser texture. Cooking them rare can result in chewy steaks. It's always best to allow some resting time for the steaks after they have been cooked; a few minutes will be sufficient. This relaxes the meat, making it more tender.

While the steaks are cooking, melt a knob of butter in a pan and add the water. Bring to the boil and add the spinach. This will now take just a few minutes to cook, stirring from time to time. Do not cook with a lid on as this will result in the loss of colour from the spinach. Season the spinach with salt and pepper.

Pre-heat the grill. Finish the dish by putting 1 cm (1/2 in) slices of the Café de Paris butter on top of the steaks. Pop these under the grill for 1–2 minutes so the butter begins to melt. Divide the spinach between plates and sit the steaks on top. Pour any excess butter on top.

Beef Stew and Dumplings

This is a classic British dish which is a total meal in itself. You've got the meat, the vegetables and the dumplings all in one dish. The chestnuts are optional but I really enjoy the nutty taste they give the dish.

SERVES 4–6
900 g (2 lb) braising steak, trimmed and
  cut into 2.5 cm (1 in) dice
Salt and freshly ground black pepper
100 g (4 oz) beef dripping
4 large onions, diced
1 garlic clove, crushed
1 sprig of fresh thyme
25 g (1 oz) unsalted butter
1/2 bottle of red wine
1.75 litres (3 pints) Veal *Jus*
  (see p. 398) or bought alternative
  (see p. 401)
6 carrots
6 celery sticks
4 large potatoes, peeled
350 g (12 oz) button mushrooms
1 tablespoon tomato purée (optional)

FOR THE DUMPLINGS
1 onion, finely chopped
4 smoked back bacon rashers, rinded
  and diced
1 teaspoon chopped fresh thyme
25 g (1 oz) unsalted butter
100 g (4 oz) chestnuts, cooked, shelled
  and chopped (optional)
225 g (8 oz) plain flour
2 teaspoons baking powder
100 g (4 oz) fresh or dried beef suet,
  shredded
150 ml (5 fl oz) water
Chicken Stock (see p. 399) or water

Season the meat with salt and pepper and fry in the beef dripping until brown. Leave to drain in a colander. Meanwhile, in a large flameproof casserole, sweat the diced onions, garlic and thyme in the butter for a few minutes until soft. Add the red wine and boil until reduced by two-thirds. Add the *jus*, bring to the boil, and add the steak. Cover and leave to simmer gently for 1 1/2 hours.

Cut the carrots, celery and potatoes into large dice and add them to the stew with the whole button mushrooms and tomato purée. Continue to cook for another 15–20 minutes until the vegetables are soft. Check for seasoning.

Meanwhile, make the dumplings. Sweat the chopped onion, bacon and thyme in the butter until soft. Add the chopped chestnuts, if using, then allow the mixture to cool.

Mix together the flour, baking powder and suet. Add a pinch of salt and the onion mixture and mix to a dough with the water. The dumplings can now be rolled into balls 2.5–4 cm (1–1 1/2 in) in diameter. Bring the chicken stock or water to the boil, add the dumplings and simmer for 20 minutes. Serve the stew in hot bowls, and to finish top with the dumplings.

Steak and Kidney Pudding

There are many recipes for steak and kidney puddings. This one is a little more involved, but I think gets the best results. It's best to have some fresh and some dried suet but, if not, you can use just the dried.

SERVES 6–8

900 g (2 lb) braising steak, trimmed and cut into 2.5 cm (1 in) dice

450 g (1 lb) ox or lambs' kidneys, trimmed and cut into 2.5 cm (1 in) dice

50–75 g (2–3 oz) beef dripping

6 celery sticks, diced

6 carrots, diced

8 onions, diced

225 g (8 oz) mushrooms, quartered (optional)

1 garlic clove, crushed

1/2 teaspoon chopped fresh thyme

50 g (2 oz) unsalted butter

300 ml (10 fl oz) Guinness

1.75 litres (3 pints) Veal *Jus* (see p. 398) or bought alternative (see p. 401)

Salt and freshly ground white pepper

FOR THE SUET PASTRY

450 g (1 lb) plain flour

25 g (1 oz) baking powder

100 g (4 oz) fresh suet, chopped

100 g (4 oz) shredded dried suet

300 ml (10 fl oz) water

Grease two 1.2-litre (2-pint) pudding basins or six 400 ml (14 fl oz) moulds.

For the steak and kidney filling, fry the beef and kidney in the dripping, allowing it to colour well on all sides.

In a separate large pan, sweat the diced vegetables and mushrooms, if using, garlic and herbs in the butter for a few minutes until soft. Add the Guinness and boil to reduce until almost dry. Add the meat and cover with the *jus*. Bring to the simmer, cover, and simmer for 1–1½ hours, until the meat is tender. Check the seasoning and allow to cool.

While the meat is cooking, make the suet pastry. Sieve the flour, baking powder and a pinch of salt into a bowl. Mix in the suets then fold in the water to form a fairly firm dough. Allow the dough to rest for about 20 minutes. Roll out the dough and use the majority to line the pudding moulds; you will need some left for the lids. Keep in the fridge until needed. When the filling is cold, fill the moulds with the meat mixture, using a slotted spoon. You need only a little liquid in the filling. Roll out the remaining pastry and cover the moulds, trim and press together. Top with pieces of buttered foil.

Stand the puddings in a steamer or a pan half-filled with hot water, cover and steam for about 1 hour for the smaller puddings and 1½–2 hours for the larger ones, topping up with boiling water as necessary.

The liquid left from the stew can be re-boiled, pushed through a sieve and used as the gravy.

To serve, trim round the tops. Turn the individual puddings out on to hot plates and cover with the gravy. From the larger basins, cut and spoon on to hot plates and cover with gravy.

Home-made Corned Beef

You may be surprised to find that this really is a simple recipe. It just needs a little advanced planning as the beef must be soaked for three days before cooking. Corned beef is readily available for everyone, but it's so good to eat it home-made. The texture is similar to a standard corned beef, but this recipe isn't quite as pink in colour. The pig's trotters are optional but will help to create a jelly in the cooking liquor.

Corned beef is lovely to eat with chutney for tea or supper, or to break into pieces to make American Corned Beef Hash, fried with onions and potatoes (see p. 147). Hash is good for a cooked breakfast or lunch/supper dish.

The recipe I'm giving is using 2.25 kg (5 lb) of beef. You can reduce the size by up to half but any smaller quantities than that won't really give you the right balance of beef meat and fat.

SERVES 8
2.25 kg (5 lb) beef flank
1.75 litres (3 pints) cold water
75–100 g (3–4 oz) salt

2 pig's trotters (optional)
25 g (1 oz) gelatine leaves or powder
   (optional)

Trim the beef flank of all visible sinews but leave it as a whole piece. Mix the water and 75 g (3 oz) of salt to create a brine. To test the strength of the brine, sit a raw new potato in the water; the potato should float. If it won't float, simply add the remaining salt, or more if needed. Sit the beef in the brine and chill for 3 days.

Remove the meat from the brine and wash it, discarding the salt water. Place the meat in a clean pan with the pig's trotters, if using. Top up with fresh cold water. Bring to the boil, then simmer for 2$\frac{1}{2}$–3 hours, skimming any impurities from the liquor.

Once cooked, remove the meat from the liquor. Strain the cooking liquor through a fine sieve and taste; it should have a good beef flavour. Discard the trotters. Bring the stock to the boil and boil to reduce in volume, and increase its flavour and jelly content. Test the stock/jelly by spooning on to a small plate and placing in the fridge. The jelly must set very firmly to enable it to hold the beef together. If it doesn't set firmly enough, then add some or all of the gelatine to the mix. Only about 600–900 ml (1–1$\frac{1}{2}$ pints) of finished jelly stock will be needed. Make sure you do test the stock/jelly first as the dish is better if only set using natural jellies.

While the beef is still warm, break it down into pieces. The meat will almost separate itself between sinew strips. Any excess sinew can be removed, but make sure that all fat content is kept. The meat can now be pushed through a large mincer plate (5–10 mm/$\frac{1}{4}$–$\frac{1}{2}$ in) or chopped by hand with the fat. Mix the meat with 600 ml (1 pint) of reduced liquor and check the consistency. The meat should absorb the liquor and be left reasonably loose. If the mix is too firm, add another 300 ml (10 fl oz) of stock. Taste the corned beef before setting in a mould and correct the seasoning with salt and pepper. The mix can now be pressed firmly into a terrine mould or bowl and set in the fridge overnight.

Once set, turn out the corned beef and serve with a salad and pickle, fried for breakfast or turn it into a corned beef hash.

American Corned Beef Hash

The classic method for making corned beef is on p. 146. I used to believe that was really the only way to make it and there could be no other corned beef dish without using that. Well, how wrong I was. It's absolutely true you can never stop learning in this job; there's always another method to learn.

While I was in New York I just had to try a good corned beef hash and guess what? I found it. The beef itself is still salted for 3 days but after that it's simply boiled and left to cool. All you do then is simply shred it finely and then fry it. Could it be easier and tastier? I don't think so.

For me this is the best way to eat a good corned beef hash and the dish certainly has many options when to serve it. It eats very well as breakfast, lunch or dinner especially with fried eggs 'sunny-side up' or 'over easy'.

SERVES 6–8
900 g (2 lb) beef skirt
2 large jacket potatoes, about 900 g (2 lb)

Salt and freshly ground black pepper
3 onions, sliced
A knob of unsalted butter

You can buy the meat already salted, but if you want to do it yourself, it is quite simple. It's very important to order well in advance as the meat must be soaked for 3 days before cooking. Simply add enough salt to some water (enough to cover the beef) to keep a new potato afloat, cover and soak in the fridge for 3 days.

Once soaked, remove the beef and discard the water. Rinse the meat to release any excess salt. Cover the beef skirt with cold water in a pan and bring to a simmer. Cook for about 2$\frac{1}{2}$ hours until completely tender. Once cooked, leave to cool in the cooking liquor.

Now it's time to take the beef from the stock. The beef can now be chilled and kept for several days or used immediately.

Peel the potatoes and cut into 5–10 mm ($\frac{1}{4}$–$\frac{1}{2}$ in) dice. These should now be cooked in boiling salted water for 3–4 minutes, until tender. Pour off the water and leave the potatoes to one side. Shallow-fry the onions in the butter until golden brown.

Using a sharp knife, shred the beef, including all fat content, as thinly as possible. This will keep it very tender and moist. The beef can now be seasoned with salt and pepper and then fried with the onion and the pre-cooked potatoes. Once all has warmed, increase the heat and continue to fry until a crispy golden base has formed. The hash can now be turned over and fried till you have an equally crispy base on the otherside. It's not essential to form an omelette-style cake, but the change in textures from crispy to succulent is certainly very important.

You now have American Corned Beef Hash. And to keep with American traditions, why not serve it with the Home-made Ketchup on p. 377?

Beef Olives with Black Pudding

The stuffing for the beef olives is made from the same base as for the Jambonette de Volaille (see p. 119), using onions, mushrooms, garlic and herbs. The black pudding works very well in the recipe, and can be broken down with a wooden spoon if mincing is impossible. The beef olives can be served plain or some garnish can be added. I've chosen the button onions, mushrooms and bacon to give extra flavours and texture to the dish.

SERVES 4
700 g (1 1/2 lb lean beef topside or rump
Salt and freshly ground white pepper
225 g (8 oz) pig's caul, soaked in cold
    water for 24 hours (optional)
1.2 litres (2 pints) Red Wine Sauce (see
    p. 368) or Veal *Jus* (see p. 398) or
    bought alternative (see p. 401)
50 g (2 oz) beef dripping

FOR THE STUFFING
225 g (8 oz) black pudding, skinned and
    minced
1 chicken breast, minced or finely
    chopped

1 egg
3 onions, finely chopped
2 garlic cloves, crushed
A few fresh sage leaves, chopped
1/2 teaspoon chopped fresh thyme
50 g (2 oz) unsalted butter
175 g (6 oz) button mushrooms, minced
    and cooked until dry

FOR THE GARNISH
100 g (4 oz) button onions
100 g (4 oz) unsalted butter
100 g (4 oz) bacon, rinded and diced
100 g (4 oz) button mushrooms
2 teaspoons chopped fresh parsley

To make the stuffing, mix together the black pudding and chicken breast, season with salt and pepper and add the egg. Fry the chopped onions, garlic and herbs in the butter until softened, then allow to cool. Cook the mushrooms in a separate pan until dry then leave to cool. When cold, mix all the ingredients and beat together well. Check for seasoning and adjust to taste with salt and pepper.

Cut the meat into eight thin slices and sit each slice between two sheets of cling film. These can now be batted with a rolling pin to stretch the meat. Divide the filling between the slices then roll them up, folding in the sides to form a cylindrical beef olive shape. Wrap them individually in the pig's caul, if using, to keep the shape of the meat, or pierce and hold them in shape with cocktail sticks.

Start to warm the red wine sauce or *jus* in a large, lidded braising pan, making sure the sauce is not too thick; when the olives are slowly cooking in the sauce, it will thicken.

Fry the beef olives in the dripping for a few minutes until well coloured on all sides. Drain off any excess fat and sit the beef olives in the red wine sauce or gravy. Bring to the simmer and cook gently for about 1^1/$_2$ hours. Check the meat: it should start to feel soft and give when pinched. Simmer for a further 30 minutes, then the olives will be tender and ready.

Drain the sauce into a pan and re-boil, skimming off any excess fat or impurities if necessary. Return the beef olives to the sauce to warm through.

To make the garnish, fry the onions in butter until soft and golden brown. Remove from the pan and add the bacon and mushrooms. These can be fried together on top of the stove until the bacon is brown and crispy. Add the garnishes to the sauce.

To serve, remove the cocktail sticks, if using, from the beef olives, and serve the olive into hot bowls, allowing two per portion. Spoon the garnish and sauce over and sprinkle with the chopped parsley.

Irish Stew

This dish can be prepared and cooked in many different ways. You can look in a dozen cookery books and you'll find an equal number of varying recipes. Well, this is my version.

SERVES 4

750 g (1¹/₂ lb) middle neck of lamb, cut into cutlets

100 g (4 oz) unsalted butter

4 onions, sliced

450 g (1 lb) potatoes, peeled and cut into 2.5 cm (1 in) dice

1 garlic clove

1 bouquet garni (1 bay leaf, 1 sprig each of fresh rosemary and thyme tied in a square of muslin or strip of leek) or bouquet garni sachet

1.5 litres (2¹/₂ pints) Chicken Stock (see p. 399) or water

175 g (6 oz) carrots, diced

6 celery sticks, cut into 2.5 cm (1 in) dice

225 g (8 oz) Savoy cabbage, shredded

Salt and freshly ground white pepper

2 teaspoons chopped fresh parsley

Cover the meat with cold water in a large pan and bring to the boil. Drain off the water and refresh the meat in cold water. Drain well.

Melt the butter in a large braising pan and add the sliced onions, half the diced potatoes and the garlic. Add the bouquet garni to the pan and sweat for 2 minutes. Add the lamb cutlets and cover with the chicken stock. Bring the stock to the simmer, cover and cook for 30 minutes. The meat will be half-cooked and the potatoes will have started to purée and thicken the stock. Add the diced carrots and continue to cook for a further 10 minutes. Add the remaining potatoes and the diced celery and cook for 15–20 minutes. At this stage we do not want to purée the potatoes but just cook them until soft. Add the cabbage and cook for another 2–3 minutes until the meat and vegetables are tender. Season with salt and pepper, remove the bouquet garni and serve in individual bowls or one large bowl. Finish with the chopped parsley. You now have a complete meal.

Lancashire Hot-pot

This is a Great British Classic. It's usually just neck of lamb, kidneys, onions, potatoes and gravy, but I've tried to refine it, by adding more textures and tastes. It also looks a lot nicer when presented, and just shows how good ordinary lamb chump chops

can be. The chops should be lean with the little bone and fat left on. The vegetables have to be chopped into very small dice, which may sound tiresome but it's worth doing. You will need a shallow flameproof braising dish to hold the chops in one layer.

SERVES 4

2 carrots, finely diced

2 celery sticks, finely diced

2 onions, finely diced

1 leek, finely diced

50–75 g (2–3 oz) unsalted butter

1/2 garlic clove, crushed

2 large sprigs of fresh rosemary

4 thick, lean lamb chump chops

150 ml (5 fl oz) dry white wine

900 ml (1 1/2 pints) Veal *Jus* (see p. 398) or bought alternative (see p. 401)

4 large potatoes, peeled

1 tablespoon lamb fat or beef dripping

Salt and freshly ground white pepper

A sprinkling of chopped fresh parsley

Pre-heat the oven to 200°C/400°F/gas 6.

Lightly cook the diced vegetables in the butter with the garlic and rosemary for a few minutes until softened. Drain and keep to one side. Fry the chops in the butter remaining in the pan for about 3–4 minutes on each side until golden. Remove and drain. Add the white wine to the pan and boil to reduce until almost dry. This will help release all the flavours into the sauce. Add the *jus*, bring just to the boil, then strain through a sieve.

Shape the potatoes into cylinders and slice them 3 mm (1/8 in) thick. You will need about ten slices per chop. Fry the potatoes in the fat or dripping until golden, then drain well.

Place the chops in the braising dish and spoon the vegetables on top, covering all the lamb. Season with salt and pepper. Layer the potatoes on top of the vegetables, overlapping them almost to resemble fish scales. Pour the gravy around and bring to the simmer. Place in the pre-heated oven and allow to braise for about 40–45 minutes. The potatoes should be crisp and golden.

Remove the chops with the vegetables and potatoes still on top. Bring the sauce to the boil, skimming off any impurities. It should be rich and dark, just thick enough to coat the back of a spoon. Place the chops in hot bowls, pour the sauce around and sprinkle with chopped parsley.

Chump of Lamb Marinated with Red Wine and Orange

There are many ways of cooking and serving this dish. The lamb cooks beautifully on a barbecue grill, leaving it nicely burnt outside and still pink in the centre. This gives a lovely bitter-sweet taste that will eat well with a mixed or green salad. But for this recipe, I'm going to roast the lamb and make a sauce with the marinade.

Lamb chumps are taken from the saddle of lamb towards the tail end. They can be cut into chump chops or left as one piece, rolled and tied. For this recipe they are going to be just that, like individual roasts. One of my favourite dishes to go with this is Buttered Spetzli with Leeks (see p. 249).

SERVES 4
4 chumps of lamb, each about 225–275
    g (8–10 oz), rolled and tied
25 g (1 oz) lard
600 ml (1 pint) Veal *Jus* (see p. 398) or
    bought alternative (see p. 401)
    (optional)

FOR THE MARINADE
1/2 bottle of red wine
2 shallots or 1 onion, chopped
2 garlic cloves, sliced
Grated zest of 1 orange
1 sprig of fresh thyme
1 sprig of fresh rosemary
1 sprig of fresh tarragon
A few black peppercorns, crushed

Mix all the marinade ingredients together in a dish large enough to hold the chumps in one layer. Add the chump roasts, cover and leave to marinate. The flavour gets better if left longer. I prefer to marinate in the fridge for up to 5 days for the best results. You will find that the lamb is now deep red in colour.

Pre-heat the oven to 220°C/425°F/gas 7. Pre-heat a roasting tray and fry the chumps in the lard on top of the stove until almost burnt and crisp. Then place the tray in the pre-heated oven and roast for 15–20 minutes. Remove from the oven and leave to rest for 6–8 minutes.

While the lamb is roasting, boil the marinade until reduced by three-quarters. Add the *jus*, if using, then simmer for 15 minutes. Pass the sauce through a sieve.

The lamb chumps can now be sliced and served with the sauce.

Home-made Lamb Pasties

This is not a Cornish pasty recipe – or at least so I've been told – so I've changed its name to 'home-made'. It's my version of a pasty – light, crisp and very tasty. If you do not have time to make your own pastry, you can use a shop-bought puff or flaky pastry. Should you have any filling left over, this will keep in the fridge and can be eaten just as mince or made into a shepherd's pie.

MAKES 8 PASTIES
750 g (1 1/2 lb) Puff Pastry (see p. 393)
1 egg, beaten

FOR THE FILLING
450 g (1 lb) lean lamb, coarsely minced
    or chopped
25 g (1 oz) beef dripping or lamb fat
1 garlic clove, crushed

1/2 teaspoon chopped fresh thyme
1/2 teaspoon chopped fresh sage
100 g (4 oz) onions, cut into 1 cm
    (1/2 in) dice
100 g (4 oz) carrots, cut into 1 cm
    (1/2 in) dice
100 g (4 oz) celery, cut into 1 cm
    (1/2 in) dice

Salt and freshly ground white pepper

25 g (1 oz) plain flour

900 ml (1½ pints) Chicken Stock (see p. 399) reduced to 300 ml (10 fl oz)

100 g (4 oz) swede, cut into 1 cm (½ in) dice

100 g (4 oz) parsnip, cut into 1 cm (½ in) dice

600 ml (1 pint) Veal *Jus* (see p. 398) or bought alternative (see p. 401) (150 ml/5 fl oz for mixture and optional 450 ml/15 fl oz for gravy)

2 potatoes, cooked in their skins

Worcestershire sauce

Fry the minced lamb in the dripping, colouring on all sides and separating the grains. Add the garlic, herbs, diced onions, carrots and celery, cover and cook for about 10 minutes. Season with salt and generously with pepper. Add the flour and continue to cook for a few minutes. Add one-third of the reduced chicken stock and cook for 10–15 minutes. Add the parsnips and swedes and another one-third of the stock and cook for 10 minutes. Check for seasoning and add the remaining stock and 150 ml (5 fl oz) of veal *jus*.

Peel the boiled potatoes and cut into 1 cm (½ in) dice. Add them to the meat and cook for 5–6 minutes. Check for seasoning with salt and pepper once again, and add 2–3 drops of Worcestershire sauce for an extra spicy flavour. Allow the mix to cool.

Roll out the puff pastry and cut into six to eight 15 cm (6 in) squares. When the filling mix is cold, spoon some on to each square of pastry slightly off-centre. Brush around the edges with the beaten egg and fold over diagonally to make a triangle. Trim to a semi-circle, shape and then pinch with thumb and forefinger all the way round the edges to seal. Brush over each of the pasties with beaten egg and leave in the fridge for about 20 minutes before baking.

Pre-heat the oven to 200°C/400°F/gas 6 and dampen a baking sheet.

To cook the pasties, just sit them on the prepared baking sheet and bake in the pre-heated oven for about 30 minutes. They should be crisp and golden brown. These can now be eaten as they are or served with the remaining hot *jus*.

Roast Fillets of Lamb on Aubergine with Provençale Onions

The best end of lamb is positioned between the saddle of lamb and the middle neck. It is one of the most popular cuts of lamb. At most butchers they are sold 'French trimmed', which means they are cut and cleaned to show the individual bones – the best way to buy them. You can cook them as racks of lamb or cut them into individual lamb cutlets. Another alternative is to remove the meat from the bones so that you are left with two fillets, which is what you want here. These can now be halved to give you four portions. The fat will just tear off leaving the meat clean.

SERVES 4
2 small aubergines
Salt and freshly ground black pepper
25 g (1 oz) beef dripping or lamb fat
2 best ends of lamb, boned
2 tablespoons olive oil
450 ml (15 fl oz) Tomato and Onion
   Flavoured Gravy (see p. 367)

FOR THE PROVENÇALE ONIONS
2 tablespoons olive oil
2 large onions, finely chopped
2 garlic cloves, crushed
1/2 bunch of fresh basil, chopped
1/2 bunch of fresh tarragon, chopped
450 g (1 lb) button mushrooms, sliced
300 ml (10 fl oz) dry white wine
150 ml (5 fl oz) Tomato Coulis
   (see p. 375) or 2 teaspoons
   tomato purée

Pre-heat the oven to 220°C/425°F/gas 7.

Slice the aubergines into six pieces each, sprinkle with some salt and leave them to drain in a colander for about 30 minutes.

To make the Provençale onions, heat the olive oil in a pan and add the chopped onions and garlic. Cover with a lid and cook over a low heat for 5 minutes. Remove the lid and add the chopped herbs and sliced mushrooms. Continue to cook for 5–6 minutes. Add the white wine, increase the heat and boil to reduce until almost dry. Add the tomato coulis or purée and bring to the simmer. Season with salt and pepper. The sauce should be fairly thick. Keep the sauce warm.

Pre-heat a small roasting tray and add the dripping or fat. Season the lamb with salt and pepper and fry in the fat until coloured on all sides, then put the lamb in the preheated oven and roast for about 10–12 minutes. After this cooking time, the meat will just give when pressed between thumb and forefinger; at this stage it will be medium rare to medium. Remove the lamb from the oven and leave to rest in a warm place for 10 minutes before slicing.

While the lamb is resting, lightly rinse the salt from the aubergines and dry on a cloth. Heat the olive oil in a frying-pan and cook the aubergines until golden on both sides. Drain well on kitchen paper. Heat the tomato and onion gravy through gently.

Lay the aubergine slices on to hot plates, three slices per portion, and spoon the Provençale onions on top. Carve the lamb lengthways, allowing five to six slices per fillet. Overlap the slices on the onions and pour the tomato and onion gravy around.

Roast Loin of Lamb with Lemon, Garlic and Mint

The three flavours of lemon, garlic and mint all work so well with lamb. However, it's not often you find three that work well on their own that can also be mixed and work even better. You'll find that all three flavours can be recognized without overpowering the sweetness of the lamb.

For this recipe you'll notice that I am using loins of lamb. This is the cut of meat taken from the best end (lamb cutlets). This gives you individual portions. These flavours also work very well on a roast leg of lamb, making a gravy from the residue left in the pan. I'm sure you can imagine the flavours you'll achieve.

I like to serve the loins on spinach warmed through with the cream sauce. The spinach and cream certainly prevent the predominant flavours taking over the lamb. The gravy is really an optional extra. I like just to serve a tablespoon over the top of each portion of spinach. It does eat very well, making the dish even richer.

SERVES 4

2 boned loins of lamb, cut in half to make 4 portions

Finely grated zest of 2 lemons

1 large garlic clove, crushed

1 tablespoon chopped fresh mint

Pig's caul to wrap loins (optional), soaked overnight in cold water

A knob of unsalted butter

Salt and freshly ground black pepper

900 g (2 lb) spinach, picked and washed

FOR THE CREAM SAUCE

1 shallot or 1/2 onion, chopped

2 garlic cloves, roughly chopped

1 glass of white wine, about 150 ml (5 fl oz)

Juice of 1–2 lemons

300 ml (10 fl oz) Chicken Stock (see p. 399)

150 ml (5 fl oz) double cream

Salt and freshly ground black pepper

FOR THE GRAVY

150 ml (5 fl oz) Veal or Beef *Jus* (see p. 398) or bought alternative (see p. 401)

5 tablespoons Home-made Mint Sauce/Reduction (see p. 378) or mint sauce

Pre-heat the oven to 220°C/425°F/gas 7. To make the sauce, place the chopped shallot or onion in a pan with the garlic. Add the white wine and bring to the boil, then boil to reduce by two-thirds. Add the juice of 1 lemon and the chicken stock. Bring to the boil, then boil again to reduce by half. It's now time to add the double cream. The sauce can now be brought to the simmer and cooked for a few minutes. Taste the sauce for consistency and seasoning. It's not a thick cream sauce that we are after, just one that barely coats the back of a spoon. The overall taste should give you the flavour of garlic and natural acidity of lemon. Once you feel the flavour is right, simply strain through a sieve to leave you with a smooth cream sauce. You should have about 300 ml (10 fl oz).

To make the gravy, all you have to do is bring the *jus* or gravy to the boil and add the mint sauce reduction or mint sauce from a jar. If you do this, strain the sauce through a sieve. You should have about 150 ml (5 fl oz). Any not used will set when cold and can be refrigerated or frozen.

To cook the spinach, plunge it into boiling, salted water and cook only for 1–2 minutes before straining off and refreshing in ice-cold water. This will keep the deep green and freshness of the spinach. It also means it can be cooked well in advance and re-heated when needed. Spinach microwaves very well once cooked. Another option for cooking it is to melt a knob of butter in a pan. Once bubbling, add the spinach and cook quickly on a fast heat. The spinach, after being washed, will have some water content. This will help create a steam and cook the spinach a lot quicker. With this method, the spinach should be served immediately.

To prepare the lamb, mix the lemon zest with the garlic and chopped mint. Roll the lamb in the lemon mix to give a thin coating of all the flavours. This can be done several hours in advance or just before cooking.

I then like to cover the lamb in pig's caul. This is quite difficult to get hold of but holds all the mix on to the lamb. Pig's caul must be soaked in cold water, this makes it easier to use, then drained. It's almost like using cling film, just roll it around the meat and it will cling. If caul is unavailable, cook without a covering or wrap foil around the lamb before cooking.

To cook the lamb, heat a roasting pan and add a knob of butter or cooking oil. Season the lamb with salt and pepper, then colour and seal in the pan. The meat must now be finished in the pre-heated oven. Loins of lamb will only take 8–12 minutes to cook to a medium rare to medium stage. For completely well done, cook for 15–20 minutes. Whenever roasting meats, whether they be individual portions or complete joints, it's important to allow resting time. This relaxes the meat after cooking in a hot oven. These portions will need 5–10 minutes, legs of lamb or beef joints should always have 20–30 minutes.

Warm the spinach and add the cream sauce. The creamed spinach eats so well, every bite of spinach gives you the creamy garlic lemon flavour.

Spoon the spinach on to plates or bowls. Pour a tablespoon of the gravy, if using, on top of each spinach portion. The portions of lamb can now be cut into three, giving you three medallions of pink lamb per portion. Sit them on top of the spinach and serve. It looks a very simple dish that releases so many textures and tastes.

Roast Chumps of Lamb with Spring Greens and Pickled Red Onions

Chumps of lamb are normally sold as chump chops. These aren't; they are the chump joint taken off the bone, the same place the chops come from (rear end of the saddle), but to be served as individual portion roasts. They need trimming of some fat and tidying, then you have lamb with just 1–2 mm of fat covering and ready for roasting.

The pickled red onions are really good. I promise you, when you've made these once you'll be designing dishes to go with them – I have. They will keep very well chilled and can be used for many other dishes and salads. You will notice that we don't have a sauce or gravy here. The marinade from the onions works well enough. Also any excess oil, vinegar can be used again.

SERVES 4
4 lamb chumps, trimmed
Salt and freshly ground black pepper
675 g (1¹/₂ lb) spring greens, stalks
  removed and cut in 1 cm (¹/₂ in)
  strips
A knob of unsalted butter

FOR THE PICKLED RED ONIONS
450 g (1 lb) red onions
95–120 ml (3–4 fl oz) olive oil
95–120 ml (3–4 fl oz) groundnut oil
90–120 ml (3–4 fl oz) balsamic vinegar
A squeeze of fresh lemon juice

The red onions can be made well in advance. Cut the onions into 6 or 8, making sure the core is kept intact as this holds the onions together. Bring a pan of water to the boil, add the onions and cook for 1–2 minutes. Meanwhile, warm together the oils, balsamic vinegar and lemon juice. When the onions are ready, drain off the liquid and add the onions to the vinegar mix, keeping them off the heat. Season with salt and pepper. The onions are now marinating and should be turned over every now and again to ensure even flavouring. It's best to make these at least 1–2 hours before eating. They should then only be served warm; if they become too hot the real flavour is lost.

Pre-heat the oven to 200°C/400°F/gas 6.

The lamb should now be seasoned and started in a roasting pan on top of the stove over a medium heat. Add the lamb, fat-side down, and start to colour and cook for a few minutes, before turning in the pan until each side is sealed and browned; then cook in the pre-heated oven for 12–15 minutes for a pink finish, depending on the size of the cut. It's very important to give chumps of lamb a good 8–10 minutes resting time once cooked, to relax the meat.

While the lamb is resting, the spring greens can be blanched in boiling, salted water for 30 seconds to 1 minute, before draining off the water and adding a knob of butter and seasoning with salt and pepper.

To serve, spoon the greens at 6 o'clock on the plate with the red onions and some of the dressing at 12 o'clock. Now all we need to do is carve the chumps of lamb and sit them on top of the greens.

NOTE
The pickled red onions and spring greens will also complement roast lamb for a really satisfying Sunday lunch.

Another great idea is to add the pickled red onions to the roasting pan for the last 10 minutes so that they absorb the wonderful flavours of the roast itself.

Pot-roast Shoulder of Lamb

This is a variation of a Great British dish, using a classic cooking method of pot-roasting, slowly braising to allow the meat to take on all the flavours of the ingredients and become more and more tender at the same time. This recipe takes on one or two spices to give it a whole new taste. Shoulder of lamb is one of the tastiest cuts of lamb. For this recipe, it has been boned, rolled and tied, removing any excess fat from the centre. Marinating the lamb for two or three days with all the ingredients helps to increase the flavour.

SERVES 4–6

1 shoulder of lamb, boned and rolled, about 675 g (1¹/₂ lb)

1 orange, cut into 6–8

1 lemon, cut into 6–8

1 cinnamon stick

6 cloves

10 black peppercorns

2 star anise

2 tablespoons demerara sugar

2 glasses of dry sherry, about 150 ml (5 fl oz)

100 ml (3¹/₂ fl oz) soy sauce

450 ml (15 fl oz) water

Pre-heat the oven to 160°C/325°F/gas 3.

Mix together all the ingredients except the lamb and the water. The lamb can be marinated in this mix and kept chilled for 2–3 days. It is now ready to pot roast.

Sit the lamb in a deep ovenproof dish with the marinade and add the water. This will cover the lamb half-way. Bring the pan to a simmer, then cover with a lid. Place the dish in the pre-heated oven and cook for 2¹/₂–3 hours, basting every 20 minutes, until the lamb is totally moist and tender through the whole joint. For the last hour of cooking, remove the lid. This will allow the liquor to reduce, and the continual basting will help the lamb become golden brown and glazed.

Once cooked, drain off any excess liquor. This will have some fat content from the lamb. Strain the liquor through a sieve into a pan and bring to a simmer, skimming off any excess fat that rises to the top. This cooking liquor can be used as a natural *jus* for the 450 ml (15 fl oz) in all. If the sauce is too strong, simply add water.

A boned and rolled shoulder is ideal for carving. I like to carve straight through, giving good rounds of succulent, rich lamb. It also eats well just sitting on top of mashed potatoes with the rich savoury liquor poured on top.

Breast of Lamb with a Mustard and Herb Crust

Breast of lamb is a cut of meat taken from the belly. It's quite cheap and is packed with flavour. When buying lamb breasts, make sure the lamb has been skinned, boned and any excess fat has been removed. One breast will give you enough for two portions. Once cut in two, roll the lamb lengthways and tie tightly. Lamb breasts are usually roasted or cut into chunks and braised. This dish holds several cooking methods: frying, braising and grilling. It's braised in a stock and can be cooked a few days in advance and kept in its jellied stock. You can add any lamb bones to the stock during cooking to increase the lamb flavour.

SERVES 4

4 portions of lamb breast, rolled and
    tied
2 tablespoons lamb fat or cooking oil
50 g (2 oz) unsalted butter
1 garlic clove, crushed
1 sprig of fresh thyme
1 sprig of fresh rosemary
A few fresh sage leaves
1 onion, diced
2 carrots, diced

2 celery sticks, diced
1/2 leek, diced
1.2–1.75 litres (2–3 pints) Chicken
    Stock (see p. 399)
A few lamb bones (optional)
1 teaspoon chopped mixed thyme,
    sage and rosemary
1 quantity Basic Crumble Mix
    (see p. 193)
2–4 teaspoons Dijon or grain mustard
150 ml (5 fl oz) double cream

Heat a frying pan and colour the lamb breasts in the fat or oil. Melt half the butter in a braising pan and fry the garlic, herbs and vegetables slowly for a few minutes. Add the stock and lamb bones, if using. Bring to the simmer. Add the lamb breasts and simmer until tender; this will take about 2 hours.

Once cooked, the lamb can be left in the stock and jellied (to use later) or taken out of the stock and finished with the crust.

Add the chopped mixed herbs to the crumble mix and flavour with 1–2 teaspoons of mustard.

Cut the meat into 1 cm (1/2 in) slices and separate into portions. Push the slices together, just slightly parted at an angle. Top with the herb crust and crisp under a hot grill until golden brown.

To make the sauce, reduce some of the cooking liquor to about 300 ml (10 fl oz). Thicken with the remaining butter and add the double cream, cooking for 5–10 minutes, then add 1–2 teaspoons of mustard and serve.

Roast Best End of Lamb with a Parsnip Crumble

The best end of lamb can be ordered from your butcher. If you ask for a pair of best ends and want them chined (split), this will leave you with two best ends, which are like two fillets of lamb with bones attached. If you cut between the bones, this gives you lamb cutlets and, although you can use cutlets for this recipe, I prefer to leave the meat on the bone or as whole fillets before roasting; this will give a totally different taste and texture to the meat. Ask for the lamb to be French-trimmed to the eye of the meat and all fat removed; this means that the bones are clean. You now have the two meat fillets with individual bones attached. Split both through the middle leaving four roasting joints with about three bones attached on each (any excess bones can be cut off).

SERVES 4
2 best ends of lamb, split, French-
    trimmed and fat removed
Salt and freshly ground black pepper
1 tablespoon cooking fat

1 quantity Parsnip Crumble
    (see p. 195)
300 ml (10 fl oz) Red Wine Sauce
    (see p. 368)

Pre-heat the oven to 200°C/400°F/gas 6.

Season the meat with salt and pepper, then colour it in the cooking fat in a hot pan on top of the stove. Once the meat has coloured, transfer to a roasting tin in the pre-heated oven and roast until medium rare. This will take 8–10 minutes, longer if you prefer the lamb a little more cooked. To test the meat, simply press between thumb and forefinger; the meat should feel tender and just give when pressure is applied. The lamb should now be left to rest for another 10 minutes before carving and serving, as this will give the meat a softer texture and make it more tender.

Meanwhile, shape the crumbles in individual rings. Finish in the hot oven or under the grill until golden and crunchy.

Carve between the bones, giving three roasted cutlets per portion. Place the lamb on top of the individual parsnip crumbles and then pour the red wine sauce around.

Roast Best End of Lamb with a Leek and Mustard Crumble

Here is a good way of serving the best end of lamb. It's simple to cook. Just follow the lamb preparation and cooking instructions in Roast Best End of Lamb with a Parsnip Crumble (see p. 159).

Best ends of lamb also eat well and cook a little quicker if the meat is off the bone. Providing that the lamb is French-trimmed, you can simply cut the meat away from the bone, leaving lamb fillets. Once cooked, these can be sliced either across or lengthways.

The Leek and Mustard Crumble works very well as part of the main dish or as a separate vegetable accompaniment.

SERVES 4
2 best ends of lamb, split, French-
    trimmed and fat removed
1 quantity Leek and Mustard Crumble
    (see p. 194)

300 ml (10 fl oz) Red Wine Sauce
    (see p. 368)

Roast the lamb (see previous recipe) and prepare and cook the crumbles in individual rings, as explained in Roast Parsnip and Chestnut Crumble on Bubble and Squeak (see p. 196). Arrange the crumbles on a serving plate and sit the roast lamb on top. Pour the red wine sauce around.

Peppered Lamb Fillet with Mint and Caper Sauce

The pepper flavour works really well with the sweetness of lamb, without being over-powering. This dish is packed with lots of different flavours, all of which you can still identify and taste. I use a standard pepper mill to grind the peppercorns, then shake them through a sieve to keep out any large pieces. The lamb fillet I use is from the best end of lamb, which is the joint lamb cutlets come from. All I've done is take the meat completely off the bone.

You don't have to follow this recipe to the letter. The same idea can be used for roasting a leg of lamb. Roll the leg in the pepper and roast it as normal. When you come to carve the joint, every slice will have a wonderful peppery taste. You can make the same sauce to accompany it, or just flavour your lamb gravy with mint and capers.

Spinach eats very well with this dish, as do Fondant Potatoes (see p. 231), which help to mop up the sauce.

SERVES 4
2 fillets from best end of lamb
Black or white peppercorns, crushed and sieved
Salt and freshly ground black pepper
1 tablespoon cooking oil or fat

FOR THE SAUCE (SERVES 8–10)
1 large shallot or 1/2 onion, roughly chopped
1 carrot, roughly chopped
1 celery stick, roughly chopped
1 tablespoon unsalted butter
12 fresh mint leaves
2–3 glasses of red wine
600 ml (1 pint) Veal *Jus* (see p. 398) or bought alternative (see p. 401)
1 bay leaf
2 teaspoons fine capers

Pre-heat the oven to 220°C/425°F/gas 7.

To make the sauce, cook the vegetables and bay leaf in the butter until softened and lightly coloured. Add the mint and wine and boil to reduce by three-quarters. Add the *jus* or gravy, bring to the boil and simmer gently for 20 minutes. Season with salt and pepper and strain. The sauce should have a slight mint flavour. Add the capers just before serving.

Meanwhile, cut the fillets in half, giving you four individual portions. Roll them in the crushed peppercorns, shaking off any excess. Season with salt. Heat a roasting pan with the oil or fat and fry the lamb for 1–2 minutes, sealing and colouring all over. Finish the lamb in the pre-heated oven for about 6–8 minutes, to cook the lamb to medium. If you want the meat rarer than that, cook for 5 minutes, or allow 10–12 minutes if you like it well done.

Always allow meat to rest for 5–10 minutes once it is cooked; this will make it more tender to eat. Carve the meat into slices and serve with the caper *jus*.

VARIATIONS

You can make the sauce without adding any of the vegetables. Simply reduce the red wine with the mint, and then add the *jus*.

Roast Leg of Pork

Roasting must be one of Britain's most popular cooking methods, especially on Sundays, and pork is a particular favourite. In fact it was one of the meats served at Christmas before turkeys were introduced from America. Roast pork and apple sauce is delicious if the pork has been cooked so that it stays succulent and the skin turns to crackling. You can also mix apple sauce with cranberry sauce to eat with pork (or as a dip for the crackling). When I'm cooking pork, I like to sit the leg on pork bones (see if you can get them) to protect the meat, or you can use halved onions. The quantity of pork here serves at least ten people but you can, of course, use a smaller cut to suit your own needs.

SERVES 10 OR MORE
3.5–4.5 kg (8–10 lb) leg of pork
Lard or cooking oil
Salt
Pork bones (optional)

4 onions, halved
600 ml (1 pint) Veal *Jus* (see p. 398) or
bought alternative (see p. 401)
Salt and freshly ground black pepper

Pre-heat the oven to 200°C/400°F/gas 6.

To achieve a good, crisp crackling, the skin on the leg must be scored just deep enough to break through. Brush with lard or cooking oil and sprinkle fairly liberally with salt.

Sit the leg on a few pork bones in a roasting pan. Alternatively, sit the pork on halved onions with the skin left on, placing them face down. The onions not only protect the meat but also slowly cook, absorbing some of the pork juices. Leaving on the skins holds them together. Roast the pork for about 20–30 minutes, by which time the pork will have started colouring and crisping. Once it has reached the golden stage, loosely sit a piece of foil on top to prevent it from becoming too dark; don't overtighten it or the leg will create steam underneath and you won't get a crispy crackling. Roast for a further 3 hours, then remove the foil and finish cooking for about 30 minutes until the meat is tender and the crackling has crisped even more. Allow the meat to rest for 20–30 minutes before removing the crackling and carving the meat. A leg of pork this size will always take at least 4 hours to cook.

Once the pork has cooked, pour off any excess fat and add some gravy to collect all the taste from the cooking juices. The onion flavour comes through to lift the gravy.

Spoon the onions out of their skins, season with salt and pepper and serve as a vegetable to go with the pork; they are packed with flavour.

Pork Crackling and Scratchings

Roast pork is so good to eat, but I think the best bit is the crackling – good, crunchy, salted pork flavour.

To get good, crispy crackling, the skin has to be scored with a sharp knife just deep enough to break through. Brush the skin lightly with cooking oil or lard, then sprinkle liberally with salt before roasting. The salt will draw any water from the skin and leave a very crisp finish.

I also like to make crackling or scratchings without any meat attached. Ask the butcher for some pork rind, preferably from the loin, and cut off any excess fat underneath. Score and salt the skin and roast in a pre-heated oven at 200°C/400°F/gas 6. The rind will take 30–40 minutes to become crunchy.

To make scratchings, instead of scoring the rind, remove the fat and cut it into 5 mm (1/4 in) strips, then sprinkle with salt. Bake in the pre-heated oven for about 30 minutes. It's nice to offer your own scratchings with pre-dinner drinks or use them in a starter for a meal. I like to make a pork scratching and apple salad. Simply quarter some apples and cut again into eight. Fry and toss them in butter, giving a little colour, for 2–3 minutes. Sit them around the plate with warm pork scratchings and mix some snipped fresh chives with Basic Vinaigrette (see p. 379) to spoon over. Dress the centre of the plate with mixed salad leaves tossed in dressing.

At Christmas, if you've got some roast pork and crackling left over, use up the crackling in this salad. You can also spoon some Cranberry Sauce (see p. 371) into the centre of the plate, dressing the salad leaves on top.

Seared Spicy Pork Belly

Pork belly is quite a cheap cut of meat and, I think, highly under-rated. Belly slices are wonderful roasted or barbecued, they have a great balance of meat and pork fat content which helps them 'crisp up' during cooking. Well, for this recipe I'm not using the strips but instead squares of belly that have all bone and skin removed. It should be no problem to ask the butcher to cut some for you, but make sure they do remove all skin and bone. The squares should be about 7.5 cm (3 in). Teriyaki marinade is available in most large supermarkets; you'll find it near the soy sauce. The pork almost tastes Chinese; it has a good spicy flavour and eats very well with just buttered noodles or with Fried Spinach, Mushrooms and Beansprouts (see p. 226).

SERVES 4

4 pork belly squares, prepared as
  above
1 tablespoon olive oil

4 teaspoons clear honey
4–5 tablespoons Basic Vinaigrette
  (see p. 379)
4–6 spring onions

FOR THE SPICY MARINADE
150 ml (5 fl oz) teriyaki marinade
85 ml (3 fl oz) soy sauce
1 teaspoon Tabasco sauce

3 tablespoons Worcestershire sauce
2 garlic cloves, sliced
50 g (2 oz) ginger root, finely diced or
grated

Score the pork belly squares diagonally on the fat side about 3 mm (^{1}/8 in) deep. They should also be scored very lightly underneath. The pork is now ready for marinating.

To make the marinade, simply mix all the ingredients together. Reserve 3 table-spoons to use in the finished dressing, then pour the rest over the pork, turning from time to time. The pork only needs to marinate for 24 hours before cooking. It can, of course, be left longer but this will increase the taste of the spices, which could become too strong.

Pre-heat the oven to 200°C/400°F/gas 6.

To cook the pork, heat the olive oil in a roasting pan and add the pork, fat-side down, over a medium heat. The fat will start to colour almost immediately, giving a rich roasted/seared colour. Continue to colour until quite dark. Turn the pork and cook in the pre-heated oven for about 15–20 minutes. The cooking time will really depend on the thickness of the belly.

Once cooked, spoon the honey on top and glaze under a hot grill. Remove the pork and leave to rest for a few minutes. Mix any excess honey in the pan with the reserved marinade and the vinaigrette dressing and strain through a sieve. Cut the spring onions into small, thin oval pieces. Slice the pork into thin slices and sit in the bowl. Spoon the marinade dressing over and sprinkle with the spring onions.

Knuckles and Hocks, Hands and Scrag Ends

Knuckle, hocks and hands of pork or lamb scrag ends are all 'rough' cuts of meat. Although cheap, they are are packed with flavour, especially when slowly roasted and served with gravy.

Any of these cuts can be roasted in a medium oven at about 180°C/350°F/gas 4 for 2–2^1/2 hours.

Hand of pork (from the shoulder, with the trotter removed) can be bought on or off the bone. Once scored and tied, it is ready to cook. If it's salted and slowly roasted, you will have some very crispy crackling and moist pork underneath. Sliced and served with mustard or apple sauce, it eats really well. It's a brilliant cut to roast and just sit and pick at, or break off crackling, tear the meat and eat it in a French stick sandwich with the bread soaking up all the juices. The same can be done with the other joints.

Scrag ends of lamb are normally casseroled, but a knuckle is for roasting and eats well if glazed with honey and mint.

These are cuts of meat we should use more often. If you have four knuckles of lamb roasted for a Sunday lunch and you sit them in a bowl and plonk them on the table, I promise you everyone will be excited and delighted by the messy eating.

Home-made Pork Pie

The meats I use for this recipe are pork shoulder and back fat. Pork belly can also be used, maintaining the same total weight. The filling must be made before the pastry, as hot water crust has to be moulded while still warm. To finish the pie, a home-made pork jelly can be made using pigs' trotters. Alternatively, home-made chicken stock can be used and set with leaf or powdered gelatine; 25 g (1 oz) per 600 ml (1 pint) stock will guarantee a good setting consistency. For a richer, golden jelly, the pig's trotters can first be coloured in a hot pan along with the vegetables before simmering.

It's best to make the pork pie at least 48 hours before serving. This will give the filling time to mature, with all the spices impregnating the pork stuffing.

The home-made Piccalilli on p. 386 eats very well with this dish.

SERVES 8–12

25 g (1 oz) butter
2 large onions, finely chopped
1 teaspoon chopped fresh sage
1 teaspoon chopped fresh thyme
1 level teaspoon ground mace
1 teaspoon dried English mustard
1 teaspoon mixed spice
1 kg (2 lb 2 oz) trimmed shoulder pork
    (or pork belly)
175 g (6 oz) pork back (or pork belly)
Salt and pepper

FOR THE JELLIED STOCK
3 pig's trotters or 2 ham hocks
1 onion
1 carrot
2 celery sticks
Few black peppercorns
Sprig of fresh thyme
I bay leaf
1.8 litres (3 pints) water
25 g (1 oz) gelatine (or 2 leaves), if
    needed for 1.2 litres (2 pints) stock

FOR THE PASTRY
150 ml (¼ pint) milk
150 ml (¼ pint) water
175 g (6 oz) lard
675 g (1½ lb) plain flour
1 teaspoon salt
1 egg, beaten, to glaze

The mould used for this recipe is a loose-bottomed or spring-clip tin 20 cm (8 in) in diameter and 6.75–7.5 cm (2½–3 in) deep.

First, make the jellied stock. Place all the ingredients except for the gelatine, in a saucepan and bring to the simmer. Cook for 3 hours, before passing the stock through a sieve. Boil the stock and reduce to 600–900 ml (1–1½ pints). Test a spoonful or two by refrigerating until cold and well set. If the jelly is still a little loose, add 1 or 2 leaves of gelatine to the stock.

Now make the filling. Melt the butter in a saucepan. Once bubbling, add the chopped onions and cook for a few minutes, without colouring, until they begin to soften.

Remove from the stove and add the sage, thyme, mace, mustard and mixed spice. Leave to cool. Meanwhile, chop the pork shoulder and back fat into 5 mm (¼ in) rough dice, or break the meat down in a food processor or mince coarsely. However, dicing maintains the maximum moisteness of the meat. Mix the cooked onions with the chopped pork, seasoning well with salt and pepper. Refrigerate until needed.

Now, make the pastry. Pre-heat the oven to 220°C/425°F/gas 7. Grease the pie mould and place it on a baking sheet. Bring the milk, water and lard to the boil. Sift the flour with the salt into the bowl, leaving a well in the centre. Pour in the boiling lard liquor and stir into the flour to form a dough, kneading lightly by hand. Keep a quarter of the pastry warm to one side, then work or roll the rest of the pastry on a lightly floured surface until just large enough to fill the mould and approximately 5 mm (¼ in) thick. Sit the pastry in the mould, gently pushing it out to make it fill to just above the top of the mould. Trim the edges.

Fill the lined mould with the pork filling, packing it just above the top. Fold the pastry around the top on to the mix and brush with the beaten egg. Roll out the remaining pastry to the same thickness and sit on top of the pie, pressing the edges together and cutting away any excess. Using a 1 cm (½ in) plain metal piping nozzle, cut a cross in the centre, pressing the nozzle in to create a hole and leaving it in place. Decorate the pie, if wished, with any pastry trimmings. The border can also be pinched with a fork to give a simple patterned edge. Brush the pie with the beaten egg.

Bake the pie immediately in the hot oven for 30 minutes. Reduce the oven temperature to 190°C/375°F/gas 5 and cook the pie for a further hour. Once the pie reaches a golden brown stage, gently cover with foil to prevent the pastry from burning. Check the pie at this stage by inserting a skewer through the nozzle, which should come out hot and clean. If not, continue to cook for a further 15–20 minutes. Once cooked, lift the pie from the oven and relax for 15 minutes before removing from the mould. Brush the pastry with the beaten egg. Return to the oven for a further 15 minutes until the pie has a golden glaze.

Remove from the oven and allow the pie to rest for 30 minutes. The pie filling will have shrunk slightly during the cooking process, leaving a space to be filled with the jelly. Using a jug and funnel, pour a little of the jelly stock into the pie. This will be absorbed slowly by the meat, giving it a moister finish. Repeat this process until the pie has cooled. Now refrigerate before adding more cold jelly, and the pie is full. Any remaining jelly can be frozen, ready for your next pork pie.

Pork and Black Pudding Patties

Every recipe has alternatives and this one certainly isn't going to miss out. It's a basic recipe for minced pork patties with the addition of black pudding. The black pudding gives a different texture to the dish and a lot more flavour.

As far as the alternatives are concerned, this recipe can be rolled into dumpling balls and braised with mushrooms, onions and red wine. Or go very British by braising them in beer and serving with spinach and mashed potatoes.

There's also a very quick and easy way of making this recipe. Simply buy a pound of good-quality pork sausages, squeeze them out of their skins and mix them with 100–175 g (4–6 oz) of chopped black pudding and the mix is made.

SERVES 4

175 g (6 oz) black pudding
450 g (1 lb) pork belly, including fat, coarsely minced
2 small or 1 large onion, finely chopped
1 garlic clove, crushed
^{1}/2 teaspoon chopped fresh sage
A knob of unsalted butter
1 egg, beaten
1 thick slice of white bread, crumbled
Salt and freshly ground black pepper

The black pudding should first be peeled, and then either crumbled by hand or chopped before adding to the minced pork. Cook the onion, garlic and sage in a knob of butter for 2–3 minutes, until softened. Leave to cool. Once cooled, mix with the pork and black pudding, add the egg and breadcrumbs and season with salt and pepper. The mix can now be shaped into 4 × 175–225 g (6–8 oz) patties approximately 2.5 cm (1 in) thick. The patties can now be cooked by either grilling (perhaps on a barbecue) or pan-frying for 6–7 minutes on each side until completely cooked through. Now to serve the patties there are endless alternatives.

I like to serve them topped with my Welsh Rarebit mix (see p. 40) and sitting on Irish Potato Cakes (see p. 237) with Apple and Mustard Seed Relish (see p. 388). A good mustard sauce also works very well with mashed potatoes, or why not just eat them in a good roll with salad and chips.

VARIATIONS

Here's a great alternative for this recipe – do you remember meat loaf, mashed potato and gravy from school dinner days? Well, that's exactly what this recipe can be turned into. Just follow the recipe and ingredients until the mix is made. Now instead of dividing it into patties, take a square of buttered foil and make the mix into a bloomer loaf. Wrap the foil around, then allow to set and firm in the fridge for 30 minutes. The next stage is to pan-fry in the foil for a few minutes. All you have to do now is remove the foil, slice into 4–6 portions and serve. The mix can also be spiced up with Worcestershire sauce or perhaps add some chopped chestnuts and thyme for a Christmas supper. Adding some Dijon mustard to the accompanying mashed potatoes works very well, as does Onion Gravy (see p. 367). Strain off the onions, once cooked, to give a smooth, onion-flavoured sauce. This will be the best school dinner you'll have ever had.

NOTE

It is best to leave some of the black pudding in 1 cm (^{1}/2 in) pieces mixed with the pork. This gives a better texture and an exciting bite to the patties.

Confit of Pork Belly with Rich Sherry Lentils

A confit of any meat really means a preserve. This is a process of cooking the meat in fat, then storing the meat encased and covered in the fat. Kept chilled, the meat will keep for at least a month. There is, of course, more to the technique than just preserving. The method of slow cooking in the fat keeps the meat very moist and tender. The pork belly should be bought already portioned. Simply ask your butcher to prepare it for you, boned and skinned.

I like to serve the dish with Rich Sherry Lentils or noodles. Or, for a starter, cook some smaller portions of pork and sit them on top of my Sweet Pepper and Chilli Relish (see p. 389).

SERVES 4

900 g (2 lb) lard

4 × 225 g (8 oz) pork belly portions,
   each a 10 cm (4 in) square
   (1 cm/^{1}/$_2$ in squares for starters)

A knob of unsalted butter

2 tablespoons clear honey (optional)

1 quantity Rich Sherry Lentils
   (see p. 243)

Pre-heat the oven to 190°C/375°F/gas 5.

Melt the lard in a flameproof, ovenproof dish and add the squares of pork. Bring to a simmer, then cover and place in the pre-heated oven to cook for 1–1^1/$_2$ hours. After the first hour, pierce the pork belly with a knife. If it feels tender right through, then just remove from the oven and allow to cool. If not, leave for a further 20 minutes, then test again.

If you want to keep them chilled, then leave until cold. Remove the pork from the fat and place in a bowl or tray, then strain the fat back on top to cover the meat completely. It will keep refrigerated for at least 1 month.

When you are ready to eat the pork, pre-heat the oven to 180°C/350°F/gas 4.

Remove the meat from the fat and score the fat side diagonally with a knife. Heat a little butter in an ovenproof frying-pan, sit the pork in, fat-side down, and fry for a few minutes until golden. Turn the pork over and cook in the pre-heated oven for about 15 minutes until golden and heated through. The *confit* of pork is now ready. To make it even richer, spoon a little honey on top and glaze under a hot grill.

To serve, spoon the hot lentils into a large soup plate and sit the golden pork belly on top.

Caramelized Pork Fillets

These pork fillets are quick and easy to prepare. The caramelizing is created by seasoning with granulated sugar as well as salt and pepper. On contact with the hot pan, the sugar begins to dissolve and caramelizes, giving you an almost burnt look to the pork but with a rich, bitter-sweet taste.

I prefer to eat pork fillets pink inside and, for best results, you should leave them to relax while you make a quick sweet and sour sauce from the residue in the pan.

SERVES 4–6
2 × 450 g (1 lb) pork fillets
Salt and freshly ground black pepper
1 tablespoon groundnut oil
50 g (2 oz) granulated sugar

FOR THE SAUCE
2 tablespoons white wine vinegar

1 teaspoon tomato purée or ketchup
150 m (5 fl oz) Chicken Stock
(see p. 399) or water
A knob of unsalted butter (optional)
A dash of Worcestershire sauce
(optional)
A dash of Tabasco sauce
(optional)

Pre-heat the oven to 200°C/400°F/gas 6.

Season the pork fillets with salt and pepper. Heat a frying-pan with the oil until hot. Coat the pork with the sugar, then add it to the pan. As the pork is caramelizing, turn in the pan to ensure equal colouring. Once a rich golden colour, which will only take a few minutes, finish in the pre-heated oven for 12–15 minutes (or 6–8 minutes longer if you like them well done) until cooked to your liking. Remove the pork from the oven and pan and leave to rest.

Now it's time to make a quick sweet and sour sauce. Add the white wine vinegar to the pan and boil to reduce. This will happen immediately due to the heat of the pan. Add the tomato purée or ketchup and the chicken stock or water. Bring to the boil and cook for a few minutes. The sauce can now be sieved and finished with a knob of butter and spiced with a little Worcestershire and Tabasco sauce, if liked. The pork fillets can now be sliced and served with the sauce.

Home-made Pork Sausages

There are so many varieties of sausage available in the shops, good ones, too, that you're probably wondering why I'm making my own. Well, they've become a Great British Classic, and I like making classic dishes. They give me a great sense of achievement and taste really good too.

If you do decide to make the sausages, speak to your butcher a day or two before and order the pigs' cheeks and sausage skins. The cheeks are totally fat free and have great flavour; you need just the centre, meaty part. Also make sure the shoulder is boned and rindless. You can make life even easier, however, by replacing the shoulder, cheeks and back fat with trimmed pork belly. I like to serve the sausages with Split Pea Fritters (see p. 244), arranging two sausages on top of each fritter. I also like to serve them with an Onion Gravy (see p. 367), which you may well want to pass through a sieve for a smoother sauce.

MAKES ABOUT 16 SAUSAGES

900 g (2 lb) boned and rinded shoulder
   of pork
4 pigs' cheeks, trimmed
225 g (8 oz) rinded pork back fat
2 onions, very finely chopped
25 g (1 oz) unsalted butter
1/4 teaspoon chopped fresh thyme
1/4 teaspoon chopped fresh sage
1 garlic clove, crushed

Salt and freshly ground black pepper
A pinch of ground mace
2 slices of white bread, crusts
   removed and crumbed
1 egg, beaten
Worcestershire sauce
About 4 metres (4 1/2 yards) sausage
   skins, soaked in cold water
50 g (2 oz) lard

Mince the shoulder, cheeks and back fat through a medium mincer. I like to keep the mix fairly coarse and only mince the meat once. For a smoother texture mince once more.

Sweat the chopped onions in the butter with the herbs and garlic for 2–3 minutes until soft. If there is any excess liquid once the onions are cooked, turn up the heat and boil to reduce until dry. Leave to cool. When the onions are cold, mix them with the pork meat and season with salt, pepper and ground mace. Add the breadcrumbs and egg. A few drops of Worcestershire sauce will now finish the taste.

The skins will have been preserved in salt and will need to be well soaked and rinsed in cold water. Cut the skin into sixteen 25 cm (10 in) lengths and tie a knot in one end. Fill a piping bag with the sausage meat and pipe into the skin. Fill to the size of a standard pork sausage, then tie a knot in the other end. This will leave 5–8 cm (2–3 in) of spare sausage skin which will shrink during cooking. Repeat the process with the remaining sausage mix. Rest the sausages in the fridge for 30 minutes.

The sausages are now ready to cook. They must be treated carefully during cooking and not fried on a high heat. Melt the lard and cook the sausages over a medium heat for about 10 minues until browned on all sides. The sausages are now ready to eat. They can be simply placed on top of the pea fritters and the onion sauce poured around, or even just eaten in a roll.

Boiled Collar of Bacon with Home-made Sauerkraut

Sauerkraut is a warm pickled cabbage. I used to eat sauerkraut a lot when I lived in Amsterdam in the late 1970s and also when visiting my brother who lived in Germany. We would always have grilled bratwurst sausage with sauerkraut in a roll. I think these were the German answer to hotdogs and ketchup.

Sauerkraut is often cooked with bacon to help the flavour. I decided to keep the sauerkraut 'vegetarian' and cook it with the marinade. Serve it with the boiled bacon and mustard seed sauce.

SERVES 4-6
900–1500 g (2–3 lb) bacon collar, boned, skinned, rolled and tied
1 onion, roughly chopped
2 carrots, roughly chopped
2 celery sticks, roughly chopped
1 bay leaf
Chicken Stock (see p. 399) or water to cover bacon
150 ml (5 fl oz) double cream
25 g (1 oz) unsalted butter
1–2 teaspoons mustard seed
Salt and freshly ground white pepper

FOR THE SAUERKRAUT
1 medium white cabbage, finely shredded
150 ml (5 fl oz) white wine
150 ml (5 fl oz) white wine vinegar
Bouquet garni (2 teaspoons pickling spice, 2 teaspoons lightly crushed juniper berries, a pinch of thyme)
25 g (1 oz) unsalted butter
3 onions, sliced

To start the sauerkraut, place the shredded cabbage in a bowl with the wine and vinegar. Tie the bouquet garni ingredients in a square of muslin and add to the bowl. Leave to marinate for 48 hours, turning occasionally to make sure all the cabbage is marinated. This will give it a good pickly texture and taste.

Soak the bacon in water for 24 hours before boiling. Soaking the bacon releases excess salt content, leaving a better and less salty taste.

Once soaked, remove and wash the collar, and place in a pan with the vegetables, bay leaf and stock or water. Bring to the simmer and continue to simmer for 1–1½ hours. Once cooked, the bacon should be left to rest in the liquor for 20 minutes to relax the meat and make it more tender.

To make the mustard seed sauce, take 600 ml (1 pint) of the cooking liquor and boil to reduce by half. Add the cream and cook for 10 minutes. Add the butter and mustard seed to taste. Check for seasoning with salt and pepper.

To finish the sauerkraut, drain off the liquor and keep to one side. Melt the butter in a pan and add the sliced onions. Allow to cook on a medium heat with no browning until slightly softened. Add the white cabbage, bouquet garni and 2–3 tablespoons of the liquor and cover with a lid. Cook on a medium heat, stirring from time to time. As the cabbage is cooking the pickling liquor will start to evaporate. Add some more liquor a little at a time until the cabbage becomes tender. This will take about 20 minutes. The cabbage should be tender but still have a slight bite. Season with salt and pepper.

To serve the dish, spoon some sauerkraut on to plates. Remove the bacon from the liquor and carve, allowing either one thick or two thinner slices per person. Sit the bacon on top of the cabbage and spoon some liquor over to add some extra moisture to the meat. The dish can now be finished with either extra liquor or the mustard seed cream sauce.

Boiled Collar of Bacon on Mustard Mashed Potatoes, with Chive Liquor

I enjoy boiled bacon dishes. The beauty of boiling meat is that it creates its own stock as it cooks, which then becomes the base for the sauce.

Mashed potatoes go well this dish. I normally don't tamper with mash, but mustard and bacon are good friends and using them to flavour the potatoes gives them a real bite. You can choose whatever mustard you prefer, but I recommend grain, Dijon or English. My favourite is Dijon mash; not too hot but packed with flavour.

The combination of mustard mashed potatoes and bacon works so well. The potatoes eat equally well with almost any form of pork – roast leg or loin, sausages, or braised belly are just a few.

SERVES 4–6

900 g–1.5 kg (2–3 lb) smoked bacon collar, rolled and rinded
1 onion, roughly chopped
2 carrots, roughly chopped
2 celery sticks, roughly chopped
1/2 leek, roughly chopped
1 bay leaf
1.2–1.75 litres (2–3 pints) Chicken Stock (see p. 399) or water
100 g (4 oz) unsalted butter
Salt and freshly ground white pepper
675–900 g (1 1/2–2 lb) Mashed Potatoes (see p. 230)
About 1 tablespoon Dijon mustard
1 tablespoon snipped fresh chives

Soak the bacon in water for 24 hours before cooking, to reduce the salt content.

Sit the bacon in a pan with the vegetables and bay leaf. Cover with the stock or water. Bring to the simmer and continue to simmer for 1–1 1/2 hours. Leave to rest in the liquor for 20–30 minutes.

Drain off 600 ml (1 pint) of the stock, bring to the boil and boil until reduced by half. Whisk in a spoonful of butter at a time to make a creamy sauce; you may find that 75 g (3 oz) is enough. You can use a hand blender to give a creamier consistency. Season with salt and pepper.

Add some mustard to the mashed potatoes a teaspoon at a time, tasting as you go until you have the mustard flavour you want. Spoon the potatoes on to plates. Add the chives to the liquor and spoon round the mash. Carve the bacon, two slices per portion, and arrange on top of the potatoes.

Boiled Bacon with Pearl Barley and Lentils

There are so many alternative ways of serving boiled bacon. It eats well with split peas, broad beans and even just parsley sauce, but this is one of my favourite ways of serving it. It could even be used as a winter soup. The bacon can also be served with Braised Split Peas (see p. 244), with just a little stock spooned over. Any leftover stock can be frozen for soup-making, some sauces, or even your next boiled bacon.

SERVES 4

1.8 kg (4 lb) unsmoked rolled bacon collar, rinded
5 carrots
4 onions
2 celery sticks
1 leek
1 sprig of fresh thyme
1 bay leaf
About 1.75–2.25 litres (3–4 pints) Chicken Stock (see p. 399)
50 g (2 oz) pearl barley
1 large swede
2 parsnips
100 g (4 oz) unsalted butter
1 garlic clove, crushed
50 g (2 oz) Braised Lentils (see p. 242)
1 tablespoon chopped fresh parsley
Salt and freshly ground black pepper
1 quantity Mashed Potatoes (see p. 230)

Soak the rolled bacon in water for 24 hours before cooking. This will reduce the salt content.

Put the bacon in a large pot. Coarsely chop two of the carrots, one of the onions, the celery and leek and add to the pot with the herbs. Cover with chicken stock, bring to the simmer, skim off any impurities, cover and cook gently for about 1 1/2 hours until cooked. Allow to rest for 30 minutes in the stock.

Cook the pearl barley in some of the cooking liquor for about 15–20 minutes until soft. Cut the remaining vegetables into 1 cm (1/2 in) dice and sweat in half the butter with the garlic. Add the pearl barley and a little more stock, if necess\ary, to give a soup consistency. Allow this to simmer for about 15 minutes until all the vegetables are tender. Add the cooked lentils, the remaining knobs of butter and the chopped parsley to create a barley, lentil and vegetable stew. Check for seasoning.

To serve, sit the warm mashed potatoes in the centre of the serving plates and spoon some of the stew around. Slice the bacon, allow two slices per portion, and place on the potatoes. Finish with a spoonful of stock on top of the meat and serve.

Jellied Bacon with Parsley

This is a very tasty, traditional English dish. It can simply be spooned on to a plate and served with lettuce leaves and a potato salad, the recipe for which is to be found on p. 216.

SERVES 4
1.8 kg (4 lb) unsmoked bacon collar
2 carrots
1 onion
2 celery sticks
1 leek
1 bay leaf
**1.2–1.75 litres (2–3 pints) Chicken
Stock (see p. 399)**
6 shallots or 3 onions, finely chopped
150 ml (5 fl oz) dry white wine
150 ml (5 fl oz) white wine vinegar
2 teaspoons chopped fresh parsley
Salt and freshly ground black pepper

Cooking the bacon is best done either in the morning or the day before. Put the bacon, carrots, onion, celery, leek, bay leaf and chicken stock in a pan, making sure the stock covers the meat. Bring to the simmer, cover and simmer gently for 1 hour until the bacon is cooked. Allow the bacon to cool in the stock then transfer it to a clean container. Pass the cooking liquor through a fine sieve; it will set to a jelly.

While the stock is setting, cover the chopped shallots with the white wine and wine vinegar in a small pan. Boil to reduce until dry then leave to cool.

Taste the jelly, and if it is a little bland, it may now need to be re-boiled and reduced for a stronger taste. When it is ready, sit it on a bowl of ice and allow it to cool almost to setting point. It will have almost jellied.

Trim the bacon of any excess fat; the meat will be nice and moist. Slice and shred the bacon into thin strips and mix with the parsley and shallots. Check for seasoning and add the stock. Pour the mix into a bowl or tray and chill in the fridge until set.

Venison Dumplings

You can make these dumplings to serve with the Stewed Venison (see p. 137). The offal will give a good, strong, gamey flavour, but if you're not too keen on offal, replace it with 175 g (6 oz) of finely chopped or minced black pudding. This will give a strong flavour and can be used in so many other stews or braised dishes, with pork, chicken, duck or lamb.

SERVES 4

50 g (2 oz) venison heart, coarsely
  minced
50 g (2 oz) venison liver, coarsely
  minced
50 g (2 oz) venison kidney, coarsely
  minced
2 tablespoons finely chopped onion,
  cooked in butter
1/2 teaspoon chopped fresh sage and
  thyme

100 g (4 oz) shredded dried suet
225 g (8 oz) self-raising flour
4–5 juniper berries, crushed
A pinch of salt
50–85 ml (2–3 fl oz) water
1 egg
300 ml (10 fl oz) Chicken Stock
  (see p. 399) or water

Mix the offal with the chopped onions, herbs, suet, flour, juniper berries and salt. Mix with the water and egg to a reasonably firm dough. Roll into balls and poach in stock or water for 20 minutes. The dumplings can then be added to a stew.

Grilled Calves' Liver Steak with Spiced Potatoes

If calves' liver is hard to find, then simply replace it with lambs' liver, which eats equally well in this dish. In fact, the spiced potatoes, or 'Aloo Bhaji', work with so many other meats, fish and vegetarian dishes.

SERVES 4

4 × 175 g (6 oz) calves' liver steaks or
  slices, 2.5 cm (1 in) thick
Oil, for frying
Salt and freshly ground black pepper
1/2 quantity Soured Cream, Lime and
  Mint Yoghurt (see p. 385)

FOR THE SPICED POTATOES

4 tablespoons oil
1 onion, sliced
2 garlic cloves, crushed
2 teaspoons black mustard seeds
1 1/2 teaspoons ground coriander
1/2 teaspoon ground turmeric

Pinch of chilli powder

$^1/_4$ teaspoon ground ginger

A pinch of salt

450 g (1 lb) potatoes, peeled and cut into 1 cm ($^1/_4$ in) dice

150–300 ml (5–10 fl oz) water

To make the spiced potatoes, warm the oil and add the sliced onion, garlic and all the spices and cook for 2–3 minutes. Add the potatoes and continue to cook for a few minutes before adding the water, just enough almost to cover the potatoes. Bring to a simmer and cook until the potatoes are tender. This will take 15–20 minutes. As the potatoes are simmering, stir gently for an even cooking. The water will reduce, being absorbed by the potato. Do not add any more during cooking or you will be left with a bland potato soup. However, if the liquor does seem to be too thin, then once cooked, drain off the excess stock and boil the stock to reduce before returning it to the potatoes. This will give you a better consistency and taste.

The calves' liver can now be brushed lightly with oil and seasoned with salt and pepper. These eat very well cooked on a grill or pan-fried. I like to eat liver at medium stage. This will take 2–3 minutes cooking on each side, or 4–5 minutes for well done.

To finish the dish, mix 1–2 tablespoons of the soured cream with the hot spiced potatoes and divide on to plates. The liver steaks can now be sliced into three and layered on top. Serve with the remaining soured cream.

NOTE

I also like to serve Red Wine Dressing (p. 383) over each portion of liver.

Calves' Liver with Onion Gravy and Mashed Potatoes

This has to be the most popular main course on my menu. It's simple, it's tasty, but of course calves' liver isn't the easiest offal to find. I also enjoy lambs' liver, so this recipe can be used with the liver of your choice. The liver also eats very well with the bacon just plain, without the sauce or potatoes. You can then serve your own choice of vegetables to go with it.

SERVES 4

700 g (1$^1/_2$ lb) calves' liver

700 g (1$^1/_2$ lb) Mashed Potatoes (see p. 230)

600 ml (1 pint) Onion Gravy (see p. 367)

4 smoked middle bacon rashers, rinded

50 g (2 oz) unsalted butter

The liver can be bought already sliced, but if you wish to cut your own, make sure the film of soft sinew covering the meat is removed first. Cut the liver into about eight thin slices.

Pre-heat the grill to hot.

Prepare the mashed potatoes and onion gravy and keep them hot on the stove. Grill the bacon until crispy.

The ideal way to cook the liver is on an open grill for the maximum taste. If you don't have a grill, pan-fried liver will be equally good. Pre-heat a frying-pan very hot. Add the butter and the liver. If the liver has been sliced 5 mm (1/4 in) thick, it will only take 1 1/2 minutes on both sides. It will now be a good colour and still slightly pink inside, making it moist to eat.

To serve the dish, spoon the potatoes towards the top of hot plates and cover the rest of the plate with onion gravy. Lay the liver on the potatoes and gravy, allowing two slices per portion. To finish, just sit the bacon rashers on top.

Faggots in Onion Gravy

I usually use the trimmings from cuts of beef for this when I make them. Pig's caul (the lining of a pig's stomach) is the classic wrapping for faggots, and your butcher should be able to get some for you. (It needs to be soaked in cold water for 24 hours before use.) Alternatively, you can fry the faggots without the caul, as for meatballs, but the finish and flavour won't be quite the same. The best dishes to serve with faggots are Colcannon (see p. 238) or Mashed Potatoes (see p. 230).

SERVES 4

2 onions, finely chopped
1 garlic clove, crushed
1/2 teaspoon fresh thyme leaves
1/2 teaspoon chopped fresh sage
1/2 teaspoon chopped fresh parsley
50 g (2 oz) unsalted butter
300 ml (10 fl oz) Veal *Jus* (see p. 398) or bought alternative (see p. 401)
175 g (6 oz) lean beef rump or topside, well trimmed
175 g (6 oz) ox heart, trimmed
175 g (6 oz) ox kidney, trimmed

175 g (6 oz) lambs' liver, trimmed
Salt and freshly ground black pepper
1 egg
450 g (1 lb) pig's caul, soaked in cold water for 24 hours

TO FINISH
1.2 litres (2 pints) thin Veal *Jus* or Stock (see p. 398) or bought alternative (see p. 401)
25 g (1 oz) beef dripping
1 quantity Onion Gravy (see p. 367)

Cook the chopped onions, garlic and herbs in the butter until soft. Add the veal *jus* and boil to reduce by two-thirds. Leave to cool, then allow to set in the fridge.

Mince the meats through a medium cutter. Place all the minced meat in a mixer and beat slowly, adding salt and pepper to taste. The salt will also thicken the meat, giving a gelatinous texture. Add the egg and the reduced, cool onion mix. The faggot mixture is now ready, and is best left chilled for 2–3 hours to set more firmly.

To form the faggots, squeeze any excess water from the caul and cut it into 8 × 20 cm (8 in) squares. Spoon about 75 g (3 oz) of the faggot mixture into the centre of each square and wrap and turn the caul around the meat to form firm ball shapes.

When you are ready to cook the faggots, warm the veal *jus* or stock. Fry the faggots in the dripping until brown on all sides, then place them in the *jus* or stock and simmer very gently for 12–15 minutes, until just starting to firm up. Remove the pan from the heat and leave to rest. The faggots can now be allowed to cool, left in the cooking liquor, and chilled. The liquor will set like a jelly and keep the faggots for up to a week in the fridge.

When you want to serve the faggots, remove them from the jelly and heat through for 15–20 minutes in the onion gravy on top of the stove. To serve, lift the faggots from the gravy and arrange on hot plates. Sit the onions on top and spoon over the gravy.

Pigs' Cheeks Stew

Pigs' cheeks are certainly an unusual cut of meat, not very often used. You'll have to know your butcher and ask him to save some for you. What you want is just the meaty part of the cheek. This is a classic recipe for stewing them but, if cheeks are unavailable, replace with large chunks of lean pork. The cheeks are best served with Mashed Potatoes (see p. 230) and Glazed Carrots (see p. 227) or Spinach with Cream and Garlic (see p. 224).

SERVES 4

1.5 kg (3 lb) pigs' cheeks, trimmed of all sinews
Salt and freshly ground black pepper
50 g (2 oz) plain flour
25 g (1 oz) beef dripping or lard
450 g (1 lb) shallots or onions, sliced
225 g (8 oz) bacon rind, cut into strips
6 garlic cloves, halved
A few black peppercorns
1 bottle of red wine
600 ml (1 pint) Veal *Jus* (see p. 398) or bought alternative (see p. 401)

1 bouquet garni (1 bay leaf, 1 sprig of fresh thyme, 2 sprigs of fresh sage wrapped and tied in a strip of leek) or bouquet garni sachet

FOR THE GARNISH

225 g (8 oz) button onions
100 g (4 oz) unsalted butter
225 g (8 oz) button mushrooms
175 g (6 oz) smoked bacon, rinded and cut into strips

Season the cheeks with salt and pepper and lightly dip in flour. Pre-heat the lard in a frying-pan and fry the cheeks until coloured on both sides. Remove from the pan and place in a large flameproof casserole. Add the sliced shallots or onions to the frying-pan and fry until tender. Transfer the shallots or onions to the casserole using a slotted spoon. Add the bacon rind to the frying-pan and fry for a few minutes then transfer to the casserole. Add the garlic and peppercorns to the frying-pan and pour on the red wine and *jus*. Bring to the simmer, then pour over the cheeks and add the bouquet garni. Cover and allow to cook gently for about 1 1/2–2 hours until tender.

Meanwhile, prepare the garnish. Fry the button onions in the butter until softened and golden brown. Add the mushrooms and bacon strips and continue to fry for a few more minutes. Leave to drain of any excess fat in a sieve or colander.

When the cheeks are tender, remove them from the sauce and strain the sauce through a sieve into a pan. Boil the sauce until reduced to a thicker consistency, skimming once or twice, if necessary, to remove any impurities. Once re-boiled, mix with the cheeks again, add the drained garnishes and re-heat gently before serving.

VARIATION

This recipe can also be used for duck legs. Allowing one leg per portion, simply remove the skin, separate the thigh from the drumstick and quickly fry in fat. Soak the legs in red wine and chill for a few days to enhance the taste, or cook straightaway as for the cheeks. The legs will take about 2 hours to cook in the liquor, and they eat particularly well with the Spinach with Cream and Garlic (see p. 224).

Braised Oxtail

This dish is more than just traditional British, in fact it has become my signature dish. I find it exciting to cook and even more exciting to eat. You can pick up the tails and eat them with your hands and just dip your bread in the sauce to collect all the tastes. The tails are also very good served with creamy Mashed Potatoes (see p. 230).

SERVES 4–6

4 oxtails, trimmed of fat
Salt and freshly ground black pepper
100 g (4 oz) beef dripping
225 g (8 oz) carrots, chopped
225 g (8 oz) onions, chopped
225 g (8 oz) celery sticks, chopped
225 g (8 oz) leeks, chopped
450 g (1 lb) tomatoes, chopped
1 sprig of fresh thyme
1 bay leaf
1 garlic clove, crushed

600 ml (1 pint) red wine
2.25 litres (4 pints) Veal Stock
  (see p. 398) or bought alternative
  (see p. 401)

FOR THE GARNISH

1 large carrot, finely diced
1 onion, finely diced
2 celery sticks, finely diced
1 leek, finely diced
6 tomatoes, skinned, seeded and diced
2 tablespoons chopped fresh parsley

For this recipe, the veal stock should not have been reduced to a sauce consistency, as this tends to become too strong when braising the tails. Oxtails can be used in place of veal bones when making the stock for extra beef flavour.

Pre-heat the oven to 200°C/400°F/gas 6.

Firstly, separate the trimmed tails between the joints and season with salt and pepper. In a large pan, fry the tails in the dripping until brown on all sides, then drain in a colander. Fry the chopped carrot, onion, celery and leek in the same pan, collecting all the residue from the tails. Add the chopped tomatoes, thyme, bay leaf and garlic and continue to cook for a few minutes. Place the tails in a large braising pan with the vegetables. Pour the red wine into the pan and boil to reduce until almost dry. Add some of the stock then pour on to the meat in the braising pan and cover with the remaining stock. Bring the tails to a simmer and braise in the pre-heated oven for 1½–2 hours until the meat is tender.

Lift the pieces of meat from the sauce and keep to one side. Push the sauce through a sieve into a pan, then boil to reduce it, skimming off all impurities, to a good sauce consistency.

While the sauce is reducing, quickly cook the diced garnish carrot, onion, celery and leek in a tablespoon of water until soft. When the sauce is ready, add the tails and vegetable garnish and simmer until the tails are warmed through. Add the diced tomato and spoon into hot bowls, allowing three or four oxtail pieces per portion. Sprinkle with chopped parsley and serve.

Braised Lambs' Tongues

Lambs' tongues are a cheap cut of meat which don't get used very often. They take a while to cook, but are simple and worth every minute. This recipe is similar to the Irish Stew (see p. 150) in its basic ingredients, but there are many additions that can change the whole dish: Meaux mustard can be added at the end; mushrooms and bacon can be cooked with the vegetables; celeriac, swede and parsnip can all be used to lift the dish. This eats very well with the Mashed Potatoes (see p. 230) or just some crusty bread.

SERVES 4–6
12 lambs' tongues
1.75 litres (3 pints) Chicken Stock (see p. 399)
3 large onions
450 g (1 lb) carrots
8 celery sticks
675 g (1½ lb) potatoes, peeled
50 g (2 oz) unsalted butter

2 tablespoons olive oil
2 garlic cloves, crushed
1 bouquet garni (1 bay leaf, 1 sprig each of fresh thyme, rosemary and sage, wrapped and tied in a strip of leek) or bouquet garni sachet
Salt and freshly ground black pepper
1 tablespoon chopped fresh parsley

Cover the tongues with cold water in a large pan and bring to the boil. Drain, then refresh under cold water. Return the tongues to the same pan and cover with chicken stock. Bring to the simmer, cover and cook slowly for 2–2½ hours in the stock. Make sure they are covered with liquid all the time, adding more stock or water if necessary. Check after 2 hours. Remove one tongue from the stock and pinch or pierce with a knife; it will either give slightly or the knife will pierce easily if it is cooked. If not, continue to cook for a further 30 minutes then re-check. When cooked and still warm, remove them from the stock and take off the skins. These will peel off very easily. Strain and reserve the cooking liquor.

Cut the vegetables into 2.5 cm (1 in) pieces. Melt the butter and olive oil in a separate pan and cook the vegetables, garlic and bouquet garni for 5–10 minutes. Add the reserved cooking liquor, season with salt and pepper, bring to the simmer and cook for 15 minutes.

Cut the tongues into two or three pieces and add to the vegetables. Bring back to the simmer and continue to cook for a further 5–10 minutes. Remove the bouquet garni and taste for seasoning. Sprinkle with parsley and the stew is ready. The tongues will be tender and the vegetables will have taken on the flavours of the cooking liquor.

Ox Cheek Stew with Neeps and Tatties

Ox cheeks are an unusual cut of beef with a good, open texture which is ideal for braising or stewing as it enables the beef to absorb all the sauce and liquor. If you can't find a butcher to offer you the cheeks, then just use large pieces of chuck steak.

SERVES 4–6
1.1–1.5 kg (2$^{1}/_{2}$–3 lb) ox cheeks, trimmed of all fat and sinew
Salt and freshly ground black pepper
2 tablespoons cooking fat
2 large onions, sliced
1 small garlic clove, crushed
1 sprig of fresh thyme
1 bay leaf
1 bottle of red wine

900 ml–1.2 litres (1$^{1}/_{2}$–2 pints) Veal *Jus* (see p. 398) or bought alternative (see p. 401)
450 g (1 lb) shallots
2 tablespoons unsalted butter

FOR THE NEEPS AND TATTIES
450 g (1 lb) swedes
450 g (1 lb) potatoes
100 g (4 oz) unsalted butter

Season the ox cheeks with salt and pepper. Pre-heat a frying-pan and add a little cooking fat. Fry the cheeks until well coloured on all sides. Remove from the pan and drain off excess fat or liquor. Colour the sliced onions in a braising pan until well coloured. Add the garlic, thyme, bay leaf and half the red wine. Bring to the boil and boil to reduce until almost dry. Add the veal *jus* and ox cheeks and bring to the simmer. Braise the cheeks slowly for 1$^{1}/_{2}$–2 hours until tender.

While the cheeks are cooking, split the peeled shallots in half lengthways and cook in a very little butter until well coloured (almost burnt). Add the remaining red wine and reduce until almost dry.

Meanwhile, cook the swedes and potatoes separately in boiling, salted water until tender. (I also like to add carrots to this recipe, which gives a slightly sweeter flavour.) Drain and leave to dry for a few minutes. Lightly mash the vegetables or stir with a wooden spoon to give a coarse purée. If you prefer a smoother finish push the vegetables through a sieve. Add the butter and season with salt and pepper.

Once the cheeks are cooked, remove them from the sauce and drain the sauce through a sieve. Re-heat the cheeks in the sauce and spoon into bowls. The shallots can be mixed with the stew or sat on top to finish. Serve with the neeps and tatties.

Home-made Haggis

This traditional Scottish dish goes back to the 1600s, although it didn't really become a common dish until the mid 1700s in Edinburgh. It's not one that's going to be made on a daily basis but, if you do feel like having a go and you've never eaten haggis before, you will be more than pleasantly surprised.

Haggis has a faggot-like consistency that isn't short of flavour. I personally love to eat a good haggis with mashed turnips, the real Scottish way. The mashed 'turnips' in Scotland are, in fact, mashed 'swedes' to us in England. Mixing the swedes with mashed potatoes eats very well with this dish.

This recipe was first cooked for me by Stuart Busby, a chef I've worked with for many years. It was Burns Night, 25 January – well what else can you eat?

I like to make this recipe into individual portions. It can also be made into a steamed haggis pudding by simply making the recipe and placing it in two 1.75-litre (3-pint) pudding basins. Cover it with buttered foil and then steam for 3^1/2 hours. This can then be served with gravy made from the cooking liquor.

SERVES 4–6

1 × sheep's pluck (lungs, heart and
   liver)
Chicken Stock (see p. 399) or water
Carrot, onion, celery and leek, chopped
   (optional)
6 large onions, finely chopped
25 g (1 oz) unsalted butter
A drop of oil
175 g (6 oz) pinhead oats
100 g (4 oz) shredded dried suet
1/2 teaspoon chopped fresh thyme
1/2 teaspoon chopped fresh sage

2 teaspoons salt
A pinch of cayenne
A pinch of black pepper
Finely grated zest and juice of 1 lemon
   (optional)
225–450 g (8–16 oz) pig's caul, to wrap
   the haggis (optional, needed if not
   using pudding basins), soaked
   overnight in cold water

TO SERVE
Mashed swede
Mashed potatoes (see p. 230)

If it is difficult to buy a complete sheep's pluck (containing the lungs, heart, liver and lights), then simply buy a sheep's heart, lung and liver separately. These can then be cooked in the same way. Wash the pluck, place in a pan and cover with chicken stock or water. Obviously chicken stock will give you a stronger flavour and more of a jellied finish. It's best to add some chopped carrot, onion, celery and leek to the stock or water to increase the flavour. The windpipe from the pluck should be left hanging out of the pan and left to drip into an empty pan. This can now be simmered for 1^1/2 hours. Once cooked, leave to cool in the pan, then set in stock overnight.

The windpipe can now be removed. The hearts, lung, lights and liver can now be minced through a medium mincer or chopped; you will need about 1.1 kg (2½lb) in total. The liver obviously has a very powerful taste; I prefer only to use half to balance the flavours.

The cooking liquor should be tasted for flavour and seasoning. Should it taste a little weak, then simply return to the boil and boil to reduce and increase the depth of flavour. Up to 600 ml (1 pint) of stock may be added to the haggis mix to give a good moist texture.

The onions can be lightly softened without colour in the butter or drop of oil, then allowed to cool. The pinhead oats can be toasted to a golden brown colour. All the ingredients can now be mixed together, including the herbs, salt, pepper and cayenne. The stock can now be added to finish the mix. The mix should be well seasoned, giving a full flavour with a bite from the cayenne pepper. Lemon zest and juice can also be added to this mix to lift the other flavours.

If you are using pig's caul, drain the soaked caul, squeeze out excess water and lay it on a chopping board. Divide the mix into 8–10 portions and wrap each portion in the caul to make oval shapes. To keep the shape and prevent the caul from splitting, also wrap each portion in buttered foil. If pig's caul is unavailable, then simply wrap each portion in cling film twice, then also in foil. Alternatively, you can use two 1.75-litre (3-pint) pudding basins or 300 ml (½ pint) ones for individual portions.

To cook, simply boil any remaining stock with the addition of water to give enough quantity to cover the haggis. The haggis portions can now be cooked in the simmering liquor for 45–60 minutes. Once cooked, they will keep hot in the stock. Some stock can be strained off and made into a gravy for the haggis. I always like to eat them straight from the stock, the mix being moist enough because of the added stock.

Of course, while it was cooking the mashed turnips/swedes will also be on the stove along with mashed potatoes to finish the dish.

VARIATION

While I was staying in Glasgow and feeling peckish – it was probably 9.30–10.00 p.m. – I decided to pop into a fish and chip shop for a bite to eat. To my surprise I ended up eating the speciality of the house. It was Battered Deep-fried Haggis with Curry Sauce. Certainly a dish I hadn't tried before and probably what worried me was that I really loved it.

So there's another option, if you have any haggis left over. Once it's cold just lightly flour, dip in batter (lager mixed with self-raising flour to a thick consistency makes a brilliant batter), and deep-fry until golden. Now just serve a good curry sauce to go with it.

Lambs' Kidneys 'Chasseur' and Others

Eating offal isn't everyone's favourite, but liver and kidneys seem to be on every household menu at some point. Kidneys can make a very quick and easy dish, just diced and sautéd in hot fat with mustard, or served with a paella-style rice dish with peas, peppers and mushrooms.

A classic chasseur is normally made with onions or shallots, mushrooms, tomatoes, tarragon and parsley in a white wine sauce. This one can be just that, but I thought about having the garnish 'dry': roasted button onions, sautéd button mushrooms and maybe garlic cloves roasted in their skins. Pea purée makes a good vegetable accompaniment.

As for the 'others', well, kidneys eat very well in a mushroom risotto; roasted and sliced on top of the Pea Tart (see p. 136); or served with Spring Greens and Pickled Red Onions (see p. 156). Kidneys can also be roasted encased in their own fat, which protects them and gives you nothing more than good, succulent meat inside, or sautéd in some of their own fat for a few minutes, keeping them rich and moist. Veal kidneys can be used and cooked in exactly the same way.

SERVES 4

10–12 lambs' kidneys

2 glasses of dry white wine, about
    300 ml (10 fl oz)

300 ml (10 fl oz) Veal or Beef *Jus*
    (see p. 398) or bought alternative
    (see p. 401)

2 tomatoes, blanched, skinned and
    diced

1 teaspoon chopped fresh tarragon

25 g (1 oz) unsalted butter

12–16 button onions

8 garlic cloves, with skin on
    (optional)

16–20 button mushrooms

Salt and freshly ground black
    pepper

To make the sauce, boil the white wine until reduced by three-quarters. Add the *jus* or alternative, bring to simmer, then add the tomatoes and tarragon.

Remove the fat from the kidneys if you have not bought them already trimmed. Halve them lengthways and remove any sinew from the centre. These can now be left at this size, this will give you between 5–6 halves per portion, or halved again. If you have some kidney fat, then save it for sautéing them in.

Heat a frying-pan and add one or two knobs of kidney fat or butter. Add the kidneys, making sure the pan stays very hot, otherwise the kidneys will begin to stew. Fry, turning them in the pan for 2–3 minutes, then remove and keep warm. This pan can now be used to cook the button onions. Add a little more fat and pan-fry until the onions are golden brown. Add the garlic and continue to cook until they are also golden. Now add the mushrooms, making sure the pan stays hot. Season with salt and pepper. The cooking time for the mushrooms will be 3–4 minutes, during which time the onions and garlic will finish cooking. Add the kidneys to re-warm. The sauce can now be served separately or all mixed together.

VARIATIONS

If you prefer to serve the kidneys in the sauce, just use 1/2 crushed garlic clove. Boil the white wine with the crushed garlic to reduce by three-quarters. Add the *jus* or alternative and bring to a simmer, then cook for 8–10 minutes before adding the cooked mushrooms, button onions, tarragon and diced tomato. The sauce is now ready just to have the kidneys added and served.

If you wish to try roasting kidneys, it's best to buy them totally encased in their own fat. This can be coloured on the outside in a roasting pan, then finished in a pre-heated oven at 200°C/400°F/gas 6. Lambs' kidneys will only take about 20 minutes, large veal kidneys will take between 50 minutes to 1 hour. Once cooked, simply remove the fat, carve and serve.

NOTE

If using whole garlic cloves, the raw flavour can be weakened by blanching them four or five times in boiling water and then sautéing them to give a milder finish.

Vegetarian Dishes

Savoury Tarts

I could make this almost a separate chapter; the combinations go on and on. These tarts make perfect vegetarian dishes as well as just good starters, main courses or snacks. They have a different texture to traditional quiche lorraine and are very easy to make. You can make this in one large flan ring or as individual tartlets.

The basic tart mix is made up of eggs, cream and cheese. I am using grated, fresh Parmesan to give a good, strong flavour and a smooth consistency. Other cheese can be used, from Cheddar and Gruyère to a smoked cheese – Italian Pecorino works well. When cooking the tart mix, it's important not to let it boil or this will scramble the eggs.

You can use puff or shortcrust pastry (see p. 394) for your tarts, both of which are available at most supermarkets. I prefer puff pastry as it gives a lighter, cleaner finish. Turn to p. 393 for details on how to make and blind bake puff pastry cases.

Basic Tart Mix

This recipe has almost unlimited combinations. It also has to be one of the quickest and easiest tart mixes to make. The quantity of this basic recipe can easily be adjusted, it really depends on what the filling is going to be. This amount will be enough for six 10 cm (4 in) individual or one 25 cm (10 in) case.

SERVES 6
300 ml (10 fl oz) double cream
2 heaped tablespoons freshly grated Parmesan

2 eggs, beaten
Salt and freshly ground black pepper

Beat the cream, Parmesan and eggs and season with salt and pepper. The mix is now ready to use.

Almost any filling can be bound and finished with this mix, but all the fillings must be previously cooked or blanched before adding to the Parmesan cream. The filling can then be warmed until it thickens, making sure it does not boil as this will scramble the eggs. The mixture can then be spooned into tart cases and cooked in the oven until set, or chilled to be used later.

Onion and Mushroom Tart with a Parsley Garlic Crust

This tart cooks almost like a crumble with the garlic and parsley crust. It eats very well with a tomato salad or Tomato and Mustard Seed Salad (see p. 191).

SERVES 6

25 g (1 oz) unsalted butter

1 tablespoon olive oil

4 onions, sliced

225 g (8 oz) button mushrooms, sliced

Salt and freshly ground black pepper

1 quantity Basic Tart Mix (see p. 188)

6 × 10 cm (4 in) or 1 × or 1 × 25 cm
(10 in) Puff Pastry cases, blind
baked (see p. 393)

1/2 quantity Basic Crumble Mix
(see p. 193)

2 tablespoons chopped fresh parsley

1 large garlic clove

Pre-heat the oven to 200°C/ 400°F/gas 6.

Melt the butter with the olive oil, add the sliced onions and cook over a moderate heat for 2–3 minutes. Add the button mushrooms, increasing the heat, and cook for a further 2–3 minutes. Season with salt and pepper. Add the basic tart mix and cook without boiling for 15–20 minutes. The filling is now ready to use, or it can also be cooled and kept chilled for a few days.

Spoon the mix into the cooked pastry cases and finish in the pre-heated oven for 15–20 minutes. One large flan will need 30–35 minutes.

While the tart is cooking, start to make the crumble topping. Add the crushed garlic to the shallots in the original recipe and cook in the butter. Add the chopped parsley to the breadcrumbs and finish as per recipe.

Once the flans are cooked, sprinkle the parsley and garlic crust on top, covering the flan completely. Finish slowly under a grill, until golden and crispy.

Provençale Tart

This is similar to the Ratatouille Tart (see p. 192), using onions, courgettes red and green peppers, but they both eat very differently with different textures, tastes and sauces. You can make the filling in advance and keep in the fridge for a few days. The tart eats very well with a pesto mayonnaise sauce.

SERVES 6

25 g (1 oz) unsalted butter

2 onions, sliced

1 large red pepper, sliced

1 large green pepper, sliced

1 garlic clove, crushed

Salt and freshly ground black pepper

1 quantity Basic Tart Mix (see p. 188)

2 courgettes, sliced

1–2 tablespoons olive oil

4–5 plum or salad tomatoes, sliced

6 × 10 cm (4 in) or 1 × 25 cm (10 in) Puff
Pastry cases, baked blind
(see p. 393)

FOR THE SAUCE

1 tablespoon Pesto Sauce (see p. 374)

150 ml (5 fl oz) Mayonnaise (see p. 380)

Pre-heat the oven to 200°C/400°F/gas 6.

Melt the butter in a pan and add the onions, peppers and garlic. Season with salt and pepper and cook for 4–5 minutes over a moderate heat until the vegetables begin to soften. Add the basic tart mix and warm through gently until the mix thickens; this will take 15–20 minutes. Do not allow the mix to boil.

Fry the courgette slices in a hot frying-pan in a little olive oil for 20–30 seconds, giving the courgettes some colour. Spoon the filling into the tartlet case or cases, then decorate the top of the flans with slices of courgettes and tomato, making two alternating lines of each. Cook in the pre-heated oven for 15–20 minutes for individual tarts or 30–35 minutes for one flan until it sets to the touch. If the mix has been kept chilled it will take an extra 8–10 to minutes to cook.

Mix the pesto with the mayonnaise and check the seasoning with salt and pepper. Spoon the mixture on to the centre of the plates or bowls and sit the tart on top. Finish with a trickle of olive oil.

NOTE

The quantity of pesto to mayonnaise is only a guideline – more pesto can be added for a stronger taste. Shop-bought pesto and mayonnaise can be used.

Wild Mushroom Tart

Wild mushrooms are becoming increasingly readily available in our grocers and supermarkets. The variety also seems to be growing. Oyster mushrooms, ceps, trompettes de la mort and chanterelles can all be used in this tart, as a mixture or just using one type.

If you can't find fresh wild mushrooms, you should have no problems locating some dried mild mushrooms. These just have to be soaked in cold water until they soften, then you can use them as the fresh ones. Keep the soaking water, sieve it to remove any impurities, then boil it until reduced. This reduced liquor will increase the wild mushroom flavours.

The tart eats very well with a green salad and a dressing made with olive oil and chopped black olives and chives.

SERVES 6

100–150 g (4–6 oz) open-cup or flat
   mushrooms, sliced
175 g (6 oz) fresh wild mushrooms or
   100 g (4 oz) dried wild mushrooms
25 g (1 oz) unsalted butter
2 tablespoons olive oil

2 large onions, sliced
1 small garlic clove
1 quantity Basic Tart Mix (see p. 188)
6 × 10 cm (4 in) or 1 × 25 (10 in) Puff
   Pastry cases, blind baked
   (see p. 393)

Pre-heat the oven to 200°C/400°F/gas 6.

Fresh wild mushrooms must be washed and cleaned. If you are using oyster mushrooms, these can be torn by hand into strips. Any large mushrooms should be trimmed and sliced. If you are using dried mushrooms, soak them in water until soft, about 30 minutes, then drain.

Melt the butter with 1 tablespoon of olive oil in a large pan. Add the onions and cook for a few minutes, without colouring. Add the garlic and mushrooms. Increase the heat and stir for a few minutes. If some liquor has been formed during the cooking of the mushrooms with the onions, drain off this excess liquid to a separate pan and boil until reduced.

Add the mushroom and onion mix to the basic tart mix, with any reduced liquor. Warm and thicken the tart mix for 15–20 minutes over a low heat, without overheating or boiling. Spoon the mix into the pastry rings and finish in the pre-heated oven for 20 minutes for individual tarts or 30–35 minutes for one flan. Once cooked and just set, brush with the remaining olive oil and serve.

Parsley, Shallot and Onion Tart with Tomato and Mustard Seed Salad

Continental flatleaf parsley has more flavour than ordinary parsley. It looks similar to fresh coriander. If you can't find any, just use ordinary parsley. You can make one tart or six individual ones.

SERVES 6

6 × 10 cm (4 in) or 1 × 25 cm (10 in)
  **Puff Pastry cases, blind baked
  (see p. 393)**
1 large bunch of flatleaf parsley
1 tablespoon olive oil
25 g (1 oz) unsalted butter
3 large onions, sliced
225 g (8 oz) shallots, sliced
1 garlic clove, crushed

1 quantity **Basic Tart Mix (see p. 188)**
Salt and freshly ground white pepper

FOR THE SALAD
6 ripe plum or salad tomatoes
1 teaspoon grain mustard or to taste
4 tablespoons **Basic Vinaigrette**
  (see p. 379)
1 teaspoon snipped fresh chives

Pre-heat the oven to 200°C/400°F/gas 6.

Pick the flatleaf parsley from the stalks and blanch in boiling, salted water for 45 seconds. Drain and refresh with cold water. Squeeze out any excess water from the parsley and lightly chop.

To cook the onions and shallots, warm the olive oil and butter until the butter begins to bubble. Add the onions, shallots and garlic and cook over a moderate heat without colouring, until softened. Remove from the heat and allow to cool. Once cooled, mix with the chopped parsley and the basic tart mix. Season with salt and pepper. Warm the tart mix through gently, until thickened.

Spoon the tart mix into the pastry cases and bake in the pre-heated oven for 30–35 minutes for one flan or 15–20 minutes for individual tarts.

To make the salad, eye the tomatoes and cut into eight pieces. Season with salt and pepper. Add the mustard to the vinaigrette then add the snipped chives. Mix the dressing with the salad and serve with the warm tarts.

Ratatouille Tart with Crispy Aubergine and Tomato Dressing

We all like ratatouille; it has that Mediterranean theme and is packed with different flavours. Well I've taken all these flavours and put them into a tart case bound with my basic tart mix. One of the most exciting tastes in this dish is the aubergines. They eat like home-made aubergine crisps.

SERVES 6

3 tablespoons olive oil

25 g (1 oz) unsalted butter

2 onions, sliced

1 garlic clove, crushed

Salt and freshly ground black pepper

1 large red pepper, seeded and thinly sliced

1 large green pepper, seeded and thinly sliced

1 quantity Basic Tart Mix (see p. 188)

2 courgettes

6 × 10 cm (4 in) on 1 × 25 cm (10 in) Puff Pastry cases, blind baked (see p. 393)

1 large aubergine

100 g (4 oz) plain flour

1 teaspoon cayenne pepper

Oil, for deep-frying

1 quantity Tomato Dressing (see p. 380)

Pre-heat the oven to 200°C/400°F/gas 6.

Heat a large pan and add 1 tablespoon of oil and the butter. When the butter starts to bubble, add the onions and crushed garlic, season with salt and pepper and cook for a few minutes until softened. Remove the onions from the pan and add a dash more olive oil to the pan. Allow the oil to heat, then fry the peppers, seasoned, until lightly coloured. Return the onions to the pan, add the basic tart mix and thicken on the stove for about 15–20 minutes over a low heat. Do not allow to boil.

Split the courgettes lengthways and cut into thin slices. Quickly shallow-fry in a little oil in a hot pan until golden; about 1–2 minutes. Add these to the mix.

Spoon the mixture into the flan cases and finish in the pre-heated oven for 15–20 minutes for individual tarts or 30–35 minutes for one flan. The tart should only be set to the touch. If the mix has been chilled, it will take a further 8–10 minutes to cook.

Split the aubergine lengthways, then cut across into thin slices. Mix the flour and cayenne pepper with a pinch of salt. Dust the aubergine with the flour mixture, then deep-fry in hot oil until golden and crispy. Place the tart in the centre of a plate and spoon some tomato dressing around. Sit the aubergine crisps on top of the tart and serve.

Basic Crumble Mix

This recipe really couldn't be simpler. It's just two ingredients held together with butter and, of course, seasoned with salt and pepper. The nicest thing about it is that it lends itself to so many flavour combinations: from parsley and lemon to horseradish or mustard and herbs. If you are using additional flavours, add them before stirring in the shallot butter. All of these flavours work equally well with fish, meat or vegetarian dishes.

It's best to use sliced bread that is 24 hours old, as this will firm the bread slightly and prevent the crumbs from becoming doughy.

SERVES 4
6–8 slices of white bread
25–50 g (^{1}/2 oz) unsalted butter, melted

2 large shallots or ^{1}/2 onion, finely chopped
Salt and freshly ground black pepper

Remove and discard the crusts from the bread and cut into quarters. The quickest way to turn these slices into crumbs is to blitz in a food processor. If you don't have a food processor, simply push the slices through a metal sieve.

Melt the butter with the chopped shallots and bring to the simmer. Remove from the heat and leave to cool.

Gradually spoon some of the shallot butter into the crumbs, mixing all the time. The mix will be ready when it holds once pressed together, but it should still stay free-flowing.

Use the crumble as directed in the following recipes.

Spinach and Horseradish Crumble

This crumble recipe has the sharp tang of horseradish, which goes so well with the buttered spinach. I've used this with lots of dishes, especially roast meats, grilled herrings or salmon.

SERVES 4
1 quantity Basic Crumble Mix (see above)
2 tablespoons horseradish sauce
25–50 g (1–2 oz) unsalted butter

900 g (2 lb) fresh spinach, washed and picked
Salt and freshly ground white pepper
Freshly grated nutmeg (optional)

Follow the recipe for the basic crumble, only using a maximum of 25 g (1 oz) of butter. Mix the horseradish sauce with the crumble mix and taste, adding a little more if you like a stronger taste.

Cook the spinach at the last moment for the maximum taste, and cook it quickly. Heat a large, shallow pan and add the butter. As soon as the butter is bubbling, add the spinach, increasing the heat. Stir lightly with a wooden spoon to ensure even cooking. The leaves will immediately start to break down and will be cooked within 1–2 minutes. Season with salt, pepper and nutmeg, if using. If the spinach has produced a lot of liquor, drain it into a small pan and boil to reduce, then return it to the spinach. Spoon the spinach into a buttered flameproof vegetable dish and cover with the horseradish crumble mix. Finish under the grill until golden brown.

VARIATIONS

Herbs can be added to the crumbs: parsley, tarragon, thyme or sage will all work well.

You can reserve the spinach liquor and blitz in a little butter with a hand blender to create a spinach butter sauce. This works well with grilled herrings.

It is best to make this dish at the last minute, but there is an alternative. Plunge the spinach into boiling, salted water for about 1–2 minutes until just tender, then drain and refresh in ice-cold water. Squeeze any excess water from the spinach, add a knob of softened butter and season with salt, pepper and nutmeg. Spoon into a flameproof, microwave vegetable dish and cover with the crumble mix. Before serving, re-heat the whole dish in the microwave, then colour and crisp under the grill.

Leek and Mustard Crumble on Cheesy Mashed Potatoes

This recipe can be adapted to so many dishes, plus it's a complete vegetarian meal. You can even make it without the cheesy mashed potatoes to eat with simple meat or fish dishes.

SERVES 4–6

100 g (4 oz) unsalted butter

2 onions, sliced

150 ml (5 fl oz) Vegetable Stock (see p. 400)

450–675 g (1–1 1/2 lb) leeks, split and sliced

2 teaspoons chopped fresh parsley

2 teaspoons chopped fresh tarragon

1 quantity Basic Crumble Mix (see p. 193)

2 teaspoons grain mustard

450–675 g (1–1 1/2 lb) Mashed Potatoes (see p. 230)

100–225 g (4–8 oz) Cheddar, grated

Salt and freshly ground white pepper

Pre-heat the oven to 200°C/400°F/gas 6.

Melt 25 g (1 oz) of butter in a pan. When the butter begins to bubble, add the sliced onions and cook for a few minutes over a medium heat, until slightly softened. Add the stock and bring to the boil. Add the leeks, return to the boil and cook for 30 seconds. Strain off the leeks and onions, keeping the stock. Boil the stock until reduced by half, to increase its flavour.

To finish the crumble mix, add the chopped parsley and tarragon and then the grain mustard to taste.

Warm the mashed potatoes with 100 g (4 oz) of the grated Cheddar until melted. I prefer the cheese flavour to be stronger, so continue to stir in the cheese until you have the flavour you want. Check for seasoning with salt and pepper.

Spoon the mashed potatoes into a large vegetable dish. Warm the onions and leeks in a teaspoon of the vegetable liquor, then spoon over the potatoes, and finish with the mustard grain crumble mix. Finish in the pre-heated oven or under a hot grill for about to 10 minutes, until the crumble is golden and crunchy.

To make the sauce, re-heat the reduced vegetable liquor and vigorously whisk in the remaining butter to give an almost creamy consistency. If you have an electric hand blender, just blitz the liquor and butter together; this will really bind the sauce. Season with salt and pepper and serve with the crumble.

VARIATIONS

Try different cheeses instead of the Cheddar; a smoked cheese tastes good.

The filling can also be left to cool and chilled and either re-heated through in the oven or microwaved.

Parsnip Crumble

If you want to make this in individual portions. divide the parsnips between four or six 10 cm (4 in) buttered flan rings, pushing them in so they almost mould together.

SERVES 4–6
900 g (2 lb) parsnips
2 tablespoons unsalted butter or
    cooking fat
Salt and freshly ground black pepper

1 quantity Basic Crumble Mix
    (see p. 193)
1 teaspoon chopped fresh thyme
1 teaspoon chopped fresh rosemary

Pre-heat the oven to 220°C/425°F/gas 7.

Peel and split the parsnips lengthways into quarters, and cut out the woody centres. To roast the parsnips, pre-heat a roasting tray on top of the stove with a little butter or cooking fat. Add the parsnips and colour until golden brown. Season with salt and pepper. Roast in the pre-heated oven for 15–20 minutes, turning occasionally for even colour and cooking. For this particular dish, the parsnips need to be slightly overcooked to help shape them into the moulds and also give the centre a purée texture while the outside remains crispy.

To make the crumble, add the herbs to the crumbs before moulding with the shallot/onion butter. Spoon the crumble over the top of the parsnips in a vegetable dish or individual rings and finish in the hot oven or under a hot grill until golden and crunchy.

Roast Parsnip and Chestnut Crumble on Bubble and Squeak

This dish makes a great alternative vegetarian Christmas lunch that includes all those familiar traditional flavours. It can be eaten on its own, or you can use this recipe as your total accompaniment to roast turkey. It can also be made at any time of the year (perhaps leaving out the chestnuts).

You can buy cooked chestnuts in tins or frozen. If you are using fresh chestnuts in shell, you will need about 225g (8oz). Pre-heat the grill. Pierce the chestnuts once with a knife, then grill for about 15 minutes until the skins split. Leave to cool. then peel and chop roughly.

This dish eats very well with cranberry sauce, especially my recipe flavoured with orange and port (see p. 371).

I like to make this in individual moulds but if you don't have them, don't worry. It works just as well and looks really tasty in a large vegetable dish. Just make the bubble and squeak in the traditional way in a large frying-pan, colouring on both sides, and then spooning into the vegetable dish in the same way.

If you have decided to make this in advance and have chilled it before finishing with the crumble, then it's best to re-heat in the oven for 30 minutes before adding the crumble. Return the dish to the oven or grill until it turns golden brown.

SERVES 4

FOR THE PARSNIPS
15 g ($1/2$ oz) unsalted butter
2 tablespoons cooking oil
1.1 kg ($2^1/2$ lb) peeled parsnips. split
   into quarters lengthways and cored
Salt and freshly ground black pepper
1 tablespoon clear honey (optional)

FOR THE BUBBLE AND SQUEAK
1 quantity Bubble and Squeak Mix (see
   p. 237), made with 675 g ($1^1/2$ lb)
   Brussel Sprouts (other quantities
   the same)

FOR THE CRUMBLE
25 g (1 oz) unsalted butter
1 large onion, finely chopped
100–175 g (4–6 oz) cooked chestnuts,
   chopped (optional)
2 tablespoons chopped fresh parsley
2 tablespoons chopped fresh sage
1 tablespoon chopped fresh thyme
175 g (6 oz) fresh white breadcrumbs
Watercress sprigs, to garnish
1 quantity Vegetable Butter Sauce
   (see p. 372) to serve

Pre-heat the oven to 200°C/400°F/gas 6 and grease a baking sheet.

Heat the butter and oil in a roasting pan on top of the stove, add the parsnips and fry on a medium heat, turning the parsnips until golden. Season with salt and pepper, then transfer to the pre-heated oven and roast for 15–20 minutes. The parsnips will now be deep golden brown and crispy; but almost overcooked and soft inside. While still hot, lightly toss in the honey, if using.

If you wish to make these into individual crumbles, grease four to six 10 cm (4 in) pastry cutters and divide the mix between them. Heat the remaining butter in a frying-pan and place the squeaks, still in the cutters, in the pan. Fry until golden brown underneath; this will take 4–5 minutes. Once ready, place the moulds on the greased baking sheet, cooked-side down. Spoon the cooked parsnips on top of the bubble and squeak, lightly pressing down. You can leave the recipe to cool then chill at this stage and finish before serving.

To make the crumble (almost a Christmas stuffing), heat the butter in a small pan and cook the onion over a medium heat for 2–3 minutes. In a large bowl, mix the chestnuts, if using, chopped herbs and crumbs and season with salt and pepper. Add the onion and butter and mix together.

Sprinkle the crumble mix on top of the warm bubble and squeak and parsnips and place in the pre-heated oven for 10–12 minutes (double the time if it has been chilled). The dish should now be hot all the way through and can be finished under a hot grill until golden and crunchy. Remove the rings, arrange the bubble and squeak on plates, garnish with watercress and serve with the vegetable butter sauce.

Chard Potato Cake with Stilton Rarebit

Chard is an interesting vegetable, one that is picked like spinach but without throwing the stalks away. It can also be braised or pan-fried as a vegetable, having the consistency of a soft celery. The leaves are like a spinach with a slightly coarser texture and are best cooked in boiling, salted water for a minute until tender. They can then be finished in butter and seasoned with salt and pepper. Chard can be finished in the same way as most spinach dishes, however, it doesn't hold its colour quite as well. If it is hard to find, substitute spinach for this dish.

The Stilton rarebit is a variation of my classic Welsh rarebit, and you can make that by simply using all Cheddar. The strength of flavour of the Stilton is up to you; use 100 g (4 oz) of Stilton and 225 g (8 oz) of Cheddar if you prefer a milder taste. This mix will make quite a large quantity of finished rarebit; you won't need it all for the recipe. It can be used for many dishes or simply grilled on toast for a snack. The mix also freezes very well for use later.

MAKES about 450 g (1 lb) rarebit to serve 4

FOR THE STILTON RAREBIT
225 g (8 oz) Stilton, chopped
100 g (4 oz) Cheddar, grated
75 ml (3 fl oz) milk

25 g (1 oz) plain flour
25 g (1 oz) fresh white breadcrumbs
1/2 tablespoon English mustard powder
1–2 shakes of Worcestershire sauce
1 egg
1 egg yolk

FOR THE POTATO CAKE
2 large cooked jacket potatoes, about
    450 g (1 lb)
50 g (2 oz) unsalted butter
Salt and freshly ground black pepper

Freshly ground nutmeg
675 g (1^1/$_2$ lb) chard, picked, blanched
    and refreshed
50 g (2 oz) walnuts, chopped (optional)
175 g (6 oz) Stilton Rarebit

Butter four 7.5 cm (3 in) flan rings for individual portions or a flameproof vegetable dish. To make the rarebit, put the Stilton and Cheddar into a pan and add the milk. Slowly melt over a low heat, making sure it does not boil as this will separate the cheese. Once the mix begins to bubble mildly, add the flour, breadcrumbs and mustard and cook for a few minutes, stirring over a low heat until the mixture comes away from the sides of the pan and begins to form a ball shape. Add the Worcestershire sauce and leave to cool.

When cold, place the mixture in a food processor, turn on the motor and slowly add the egg and egg yolk. If you don't have a food processor or mixer, then just beat vigorously with a spoon. When the eggs are mixed in, chill for a few hours.

Pre-heat the grill.

Halve the jacket potatoes and fork the potato into a bowl. Add half the butter and season with salt, pepper and a pinch of nutmeg. Spoon the mix into the buttered rings or vegetable dish.

Blanch the chard in boiling, salted water for I minute and refresh in iced water, squeezing out any excess. (Chard can be prepared in advance and refrigerated.) Heat the chard in the remaining butter and season with salt and pepper. Add the chopped walnuts, if using. Sit the chard on top of the potatoes. Mould the Stilton rarebit to cover the chard. Finish under a hot grill until the rarebit is golden.

VARIATIONS

The potato and chard can be moulded and allowed to cool and then be chilled. When needed, simply microwave until warm, then cover with the rarebit before finishing under the grill.

As a starter, these can be served in the potato skins. Simply spoon the creamy potatoes back into the skins, top with chard and finish with glazed rarebit.

Chard also works well blanched in boiling water, then sautéed with sliced mushrooms and walnuts. Finish the dish with chopped Stilton cheese added at the last moment and, if you want it to be very rich, simply add 2–3 tablespoons of double cream.

Mushroom Pancake Gâteau

This is a great vegetarian dish that can be served with equal success as a starter or main course. The recipe came to me from a chef in New York. His name is Jean-Georges Vongerichten, probably the most famous chef in the United States. I've eaten his food many times (he has restaurants in New York and London) and each time I get a new inspiration.

This is basically savoury pancakes that are layered with a mushroom stuffing, a duxelle. Wild mushrooms can also be used in the filling but, if they're available, I prefer just to use them in the finished sauce. This can be a simple mushroom sauce with the shallots and herb, or become a chunky sauce with the addition of wild mushrooms. The selection of wild mushrooms is really up to you: you can use oyster mushrooms or a mix of chanterelles, ceps, trompettes de la mort and girolles. If wild mushrooms are unavailable, then just use some button mushrooms.

This gâteau keeps very well and can be cut and warmed in the microwave.

SERVES 4–6

FOR THE PANCAKES
100 g (4 oz) plain flour
Salt and freshly ground black pepper
1 egg
300 ml (10 fl oz) milk
25 g (1 oz) unsalted butter, melted
2 teaspoons chopped fresh parsley
Oil, for frying

FOR THE MUSHROOM FILLING
900 g (2 lb) cup mushrooms
A knob of unsalted butter
2 large onions, finely chopped
1 large garlic clove, crushed
A pinch of chopped fresh thyme
225 g (8 oz) button mushrooms, sliced
   (optional)
Salt and freshly ground black pepper

FOR THE MUSHROOM SAUCE
1 large shallot, finely chopped
8–12 tablespoons reserved mushroom
   stock
100–175 g (4–6 oz) mixed wild
   mushrooms or button mushrooms,
   chopped
50 g (2 oz) unsalted butter
1 teaspoon chopped fresh flatleaf
   parsley
Salt and freshly ground black pepper
2 tablespoons chopped chestnuts
   (optional)
A squeeze of fresh lemon juice

To make the pancakes, sift the flour and season with salt and pepper. Add the egg with three-quarters of the milk and whisk in. Add the melted butter. Once mixed, check the consistency of the mix; it should barely coat the back of a spoon. If it appears to be a little too thick, then add the remaining milk and finish by adding the chopped parsley.

Heat a 20 cm (8 in) pancake pan or frying-pan and brush with oil. Add a ladle of pancake mix, tilting the pan so that it is totally covered in a thin layer of batter. Cook over a medium heat for about 30 seconds until golden. Turn the pancake over and cook for a further 20–30 seconds. Remove the pancake from the pan and place it on a square of greaseproof paper. Repeat the same process until all the mix has been used. For the gâteau recipe you will need 8–9 pancakes. This recipe may well give you 8–10, depending on the size of the pan used.

To make the filling, mince or blitz the cup mushrooms in a food processor or liquidizer, then place them in a pan and bring to a simmer. The mushrooms will create a lot of water. Leave them over a medium heat for about 20 minutes so that the liquid is reduced, to intensify the flavour while the mushrooms are cooking. Half-way through the cooking time, strain off 8–12 tablespoons of the mushroom water. This is a natural mushroom stock that will be used to make the finished sauce for the dish. Allow 1–2 tablespoons of stock per portion of sauce. Continue to cook the mushrooms.

While the mushrooms are cooking, melt the butter in a pan and add the chopped onions with the garlic and thyme. These need to be cooked for a few minutes until the onions are soft and translucent. The sliced button mushrooms are an optional extra. I like to use them to give another bite to the dish. To cook just add to the onions and cook for a further 4–5 minutes. Mix the reduced mushroom mixture with the onions and season with salt and pepper.

To assemble the gâteau, spread the mushroom filling 2–3 mm (1/8 in) thick on to a pancake and then sit another pancake on top and repeat the process until at least 6 layers of mushroom have been spread. I prefer to have 8 layers of mushroom between 9 pancakes. This gives you a better height and look to the dish.

To make the sauce, place the shallot in a pan with the reserved mushroom stock, bring to a simmer and cook for 1 minute. Add the wild or button mushrooms and continue to cook for a few minutes. Now add the butter and stir in to give a slightly creamy finish. Add the parsley and season with salt and pepper. Stir in the chopped chestnuts, if using. Add a few drops of lemon juice and taste. You will find this has lifted all the other flavours.

The gâteau can now be cut into wedges like a cake. Sit a wedge of hot gâteau on a plate and spoon the wild mushroom sauce on top.

Mushroom Tart

This must be the only the only tart recipe without pastry. The mushrooms themselves are, in fact, the pastry.

This is a great vegetarian main course. The mushrooms I am using are large flat ones that have a good 'meaty' (excuse the expression.) texture. These are then topped with tomatoes, braised onions and Swiss cheese, all helped along with garlic butter. You can sit these on top of pastry discs for extra texture, or just serve them on their own.

As for a dressing, well, there are plenty to choose from in this book and they'll all work well.

SERVES 4

4 large flat mushrooms, cleaned and
   stalks removed

4 large onions, sliced

2–3 tablespoons water

A pinch of demerara sugar (optional)

Salt and freshly ground black pepper

4 teaspoons Garlic Butter (see below)

4 plum or salad tomatoes, sliced and
   ends discarded

8 slices of Gruyère, or 100 g (4 oz)
   Cheddar, grated

FOR THE GARLIC BUTTER

50 g (2 oz) unsalted butter

1 large garlic clove, crushed

Freshly ground black pepper

1 teaspoon chopped fresh parsley
   (optional)

1 teaspoon very finely chopped shallot
   (optional)

Squeeze of lemon juice

TO SERVE

Tomato Dressing (see p. 380), Spicy
   Tomato Dressing (see p. 381),
   Watercress and Herb
   Dressing (see p. 381)

Mustard Dressing (see p. 382) or
   Hazelnut Dressing (see p. 382)

The first job is to cook the onions. These can be placed in a heavy-based pan with the water and cooked on a very low heat, with a lid on, until softened. Then remove the lid and cook very gently, reducing the natural sugars in the onions, stirring occasionally. This will cause the onions to caramelize. At this point, they only need to be a light golden colour, any more will be too strong for this dish. This will take 2–3 hours. The finishing can be brought on by 30 minutes by adding the demerara sugar; this will sweeten the onions and they will caramelize more quickly.

If the thought of waiting that long is too much (although I can promise you the finished taste is worth it) then simply pan-fry the onions for 6–7 minutes until golden. Now add the sugar and continue to cook for 2–3 minutes before seasoning with salt and pepper.

To make the garlic butter, soften the butter and mix in the garlic, pepper, parsley, lemon juice and shallot, if using. The butter is now ready and can be kept chilled.

Pre-heat the grill.

The mushrooms can now be cooked. Season with salt and pepper and top each mushroom centre with a knob of garlic butter. Cook the mushrooms under the pre-heated grill for 7–8 minutes until just tender. Sit the sliced tomatoes on top and continue to cook for another minute. Spoon the onions on to the tomatoes and cover with the cheese. These can now be browned under the grill until melted and lightly coloured. The tarts are now ready to eat with the dressing of your choice or simply on their own.

VARIATIONS

There are, of course, many other flavours that can be added. Some sliced leeks, spinach or both of these mixed in with the cooked onions work very well. Another garnish to use is the Crispy Spinach (p. 225), which gives a real contrast of textures.

You could also try using Parsley and Tarragon Butter (see p. 373) instead of the garlic butter.

Risottos

There are many different types of rice – from basmati to long-grain, wild and others – but, for risotto, the best rice to use is Arborio, which can be obtained from most supermarkets and delicatessens. Arborio is a region in Italy where this rice is produced and, of course, there are several varieties available; you will find that they all make good risotto. The best is a medium-grain which has an outer layer that disintegrates during cooking, producing the starch to give a good, creamy texture.

My original basic risotto recipes included 100–175 g (4–6 oz) of butter, which gives you a wonderful creamy rich texture, but can be quite expensive and too rich for some taste buds. So for these recipes I'm only suggesting 50 g (2 oz). This does make quite a difference to the fat content. If that amount still worries you then simply only add a small knob of butter at the very end, just to finish off the dish and give it a good shine. The other basic quantities remain the same: 225g (8oz) of Arborio rice (speciality risotto rice from northern Italy) and 1.2 litres (2 pints) of Vegetable, Chicken or Fish Stock (see p. 399 or 400). These will give you four main-course servings of risotto with a good creamy consistency.

Although the basic method of making risottos will always be the same, the actual flavours can be totally different. Those featured here are all vegetarian with their own textures and tastes.

Why not try a Tomato and Spinach Risotto Tart finished with Stilton Rarebit? Line Some 10 cm (4 in) tartlet moulds with thin Shortcrust Pastry (see p. 394), adding 25–50 g (l–2 oz) of freshly grated Parmesan to the pastry recipe. Bake these blind. Once the risotto is made, spoon it into the tartlets and top with Stilton Rarebit (see p. 197), making sure the pastry edges of the tart are completely covered. Finish under the grill until golden.

The risotto list could just go on and on. I do have a couple more ideas here for you to try, both using the basic risotto recipe.

The first one is a Sweet Pepper Risotto. All you need is to take 3–4 red peppers and cut them into a 1 cm (^{1}/2 in) dice or 5 mm (^{1}/4 in) strips and cook them with a chopped onion before adding the rice and hot stock and cooking in the normal way. This releases all the pepper juices, giving a rich flavour and colour to the dish. One or two finely diced chillies can also be added to fire up the finished taste. The vegetable stock can also be helped by adding one or two peppers to the basic vegetables. To finish the dish, stir in some freshly grated Parmesan, a knob of butter and an extra trickle of olive oil.

Another way of cooking this dish is to turn it into a Ratatouille Risotto. Just use a red and green pepper with the chopped onion and also add some sliced mushrooms. Once the risotto is cooked, finish it with cooked sliced courgettes, chopped tomato flesh and freshly grated Parmesan cheese. To lift the tomato base, use half Tomato Stock and half Vegetable Stock (see p. 400). This will give you a good tomato/ratatouille flavour.

For the ultimate finish, I use crispy deep-fried aubergine slices. These are just very thin half slices dusted in flour flavoured with cayenne pepper (2–3 tablespoons of flour to 1 teaspoon of cayenne). They are then deep-fried in hot fat until golden and crispy. Lightly salt and sit them on top of the ratatouille risotto.

One more risotto can be made by just taking half the recipe, i.e. 100 g (4 oz) of Arborio rice and 600 ml (1 pint) of vegetable stock. This is then mixed with an equal quantity of braised lentils cooked in vegetable stock with sherry vinegar (see p. 243). Once both have been mixed and loosened with more stock, I like to finish the dish with soured cream or crème fraîche. This replaces the usual butter and Parmesan. This creamy Lentil Risotto eats very well as a winter dish or can accompany several fish and meat dishes. Home-made herb and pork sausages would work very well or perhaps a good portion of roasted cod.

So there are a few more to try. I think that's the last of the risotto recipes, well, at least the rice-based ones.

Chestnut, Onion and Brussels Sprout Risotto Cake, with Brandy Herb Butter

The real feature of this dish is it is completely vegetarian but has a good Christmas feel and taste. It's also great for a complete Boxing Day meal using up all the Christmas leftovers.

You can make the risotto cakes well in advance and breadcrumb them ready for frying. Or you can just serve all your friends with a large bowl of Christmas risotto and a mixed salad. In the risotto, you can shred up some leftover cooked turkey, bacon rashers and chipolatas and add them to the finished dish, if you prefer. I like to finish it in the normal fashion with some grated Parmesan. I also chop up any leftover stuffing, fry it until crispy and sprinkle it over the top. Whichever version you choose, there's a festive sauce to accompany it, which eats brilliantly.

SERVES 4–6

FOR THE RISOTTO MIX
225 g (8 oz) Arborio rice
225 g (8 oz) Brussels sprouts, finely shredded
100 g (4 oz) unsalted butter
4 onions, finely chopped
1.2 litres (2 pints) hot Vegetable Stock (see p. 400)
2 tablespoons freshly grated Parmesan
Salt and freshly ground black pepper

50–75 g (2–3 oz) shelled chestnuts, chopped

FOR THE CAKES
3 tablespoons plain flour
2–3 eggs, beaten
225 g (8 oz) fresh white breadcrumbs
Oil, for deep-frying

FOR THE BRANDY HERB BUTTER
1 tablespoon chopped shallots
2 tablespoons brandy

300 ml (10 fl oz) Vegetable Stock
  (see p. 400)
25–50 g (1–2 oz) unsalted butter
1/2 teaspoon chopped fresh flatleaf
  parsley
Salt and freshly ground black pepper

(see p. 400)

TO GARNISH
About 20 fresh sage leaves
Flour, for dusting
A pinch of cayenne pepper

If the shredded sprouts are raw, cook them quickly in boiling water for approximately 1 minute, then drain.

To make the risotto, melt the butter in a large pan and add the chopped onions. Cook for a few minutes until softened, without colouring. Add the rice and continue to cook for a few minutes. As with all risottos, the stock must be hot before using. Add 1–2 ladlefuls at a time, stirring and allowing the stock to be absorbed before adding more. The cooking process will take 20–25 minutes, until the rice is tender with just a slight bite. It's now time to add the Parmesan cheese and season with salt and pepper. Mix in the sprouts and chestnuts. A drop more stock may be needed to loosen the mixture slightly. The risotto is now ready to serve as it is.

If you are going to make the cakes, then pour the risotto into a 25 × 15 cm (10 × 6 in) tray lined with cling film and spread, making sure the risotto is 2.5 cm (1 in) deep. Leave to cool, then chill to set firm. Once chilled and set, the risotto can be turned out; the cling film will make this very easy. Cut out the risotto with 7.5–10 cm (3–4 in) round cutters or simply cut into 7.5–10 cm (3–4 in) squares.

Lightly flour the risotto cakes, then pass through the beaten eggs and bread-crumbs. Repeat the process through the eggs and crumbs, tidying up the shapes with a palette knife. A criss-cross effect can be made on top with a knife. Heat the oil to 160°C/300°F. Deep-fry the cakes for about 6 minutes to heat and cook through. If you find them colouring too quickly, then simply pop them into a pre-heated oven to finish. The cakes can also be just shallow-fried in oil and butter.

To make the brandy herb butter, place the chopped shallot in a shallow pan and warm. Flambé with the brandy, then boil to reduce until almost dry. Add the vegetable stock and boil to reduce by two-thirds. Whisk in 25 g (1 oz) of the butter. If you'd prefer the sauce a little thicker and richer, then simply add more butter. Finish with the chopped herbs and season with salt and pepper.

As a garnish for the top of the cakes, I like to dust some sage leaves, about 4–5 per portion, with flour seasoned with cayenne pepper and deep-fry them until verycrispy.

To serve the dish, sit the cakes on to plates and spoon the sauce around. Sit the crispy sage leaves on top. The dish is now ready to eat.

VARIATIONS

If you are making round cakes, the remaining risotto left after being cut can be rolled into balls and also breadcrumbed for deep-frying. These are very good if rolled small and used as hot crispy canapés.

Tomato, Spinach and Parmesan Risotto

Sun-dried tomatoes give a rich finish to this dish. Sun-dried tomatoes are literally left out to dry in the sun. This dries out all the juices in the tomato flesh, concentrating the flavour. I only use a tablespoon to help flavour this dish along with the tomato stock and fresh diced tomato flesh.

You can buy sun-dried tomatoes completely dry or in oil. It's best to buy them in oil, which makes them ready to use and very tender. Also the oil can be used to help flavour the risotto. The tomatoes in oil are also sometimes flavoured with garlic and chilli. This helps add spice to the finished dish. Completely dry tomatoes will need to be placed in boiling water and left to stand for up to 1 hour to soften.

SERVES 4–6

225 g (8 oz) Arborio rice
600 ml (1 pint) Tomato Stock (see p. 400)
600 ml (1 pint) Vegetable Stock (see p. 400)
2 tablespoons olive oil
2 onions, finely chopped
225 g (8 oz) spinach, picked and washed
2–3 tomatoes, skinned and diced
1 tablespoon sun-dried tomatoes, finely diced (optional)
2–3 tablespoons freshly grated Parmesan
50 g (2 oz) unsalted butter
Salt and freshly ground black pepper
Freshly shaved Parmesan flakes

Preferably use a braising pan to make the risotto, as this gives space for the stock to cook the rice evenly. Warm the olive oil in the pan, add the onions and cook for a few minutes, without colouring, until tender. The two stocks should be mixed together in a separate pan and brought to simmering point. This is important as risotto can only be made with a hot stock. This breaks down the outside of the rice, creating a creamy texture. Also the stock is only added 1–2 ladlefuls at a time, and kept on the move with stirring, creating a constant braising.

Add the rice to the onions and continue to cook for a few minutes. Add a ladle of the stock (about 150 ml/5 fl oz) and cook and stir over a medium heat. Once the stock has been absorbed by the rice, add another ladle and continue to cook, repeating the same process until the rice becomes tender with the slightest bite left in. This will take about 20 minutes. Meanwhile, blanch the spinach in boiling water for a few seconds until just wilted, then drain and roughly chop.

Now it's time to finish the dish. Add the diced tomato flesh, sun-dried tomatoes, grated Parmesan and butter to the risotto. Once completely warmed through. add the spinach and check the consistency. You will probably find the mix to be too thick, due to the Parmesan absorbing the stock. Add more stock until a loose consistency is achieved. Season with salt and pepper. The risotto can now be served and finished with Parmesan flakes.

Another good finish for this risotto is a nut-brown vinaigrette. This is simply 25–50 g (1–2 oz) of butter cooked in a hot frying-pan until it begins to bubble and take on a nut-brown colour and flavour. At this point, and no further otherwise it will burn, pour into a bowl with 4–6 tablespoons of Basic Vinaigrette (see p. 379). Season with salt and pepper and spoon over the risotto. The nutty flavour works very well with the sweet, acidic tastes of the tomatoes.

Roast Winter Vegetable Risotto

This risotto has a great texture with plenty of the roasted winter vegetables giving flavours and, of course, colours to the dish. It's as basic as our other risotto dishes but leaves a totally different taste.

To finish this dish, I've made what I call a Roast Gravy Dressing. It certainly doesn't sound vegetarian, but it is. The gravy taste comes from the reduction of Madeira. When reduced, Madeira can give a sweet but almost 'meaty' rich flavour. Also, once the vegetables have been roasted and removed from the pan, the dressing can be used to remove any taste residues left in the pan. So this is a good example of how I don't like to waste any flavours.

The 'roasted' flavour can be increased if, when you make the vegetable stock, you first roast the vegetables. They need to be well coloured in the pan before adding any water. This will give a good nutty roast taste.

SERVES 6–8

225 g (8 oz) Arborio rice
1.2 litres (2 pints) Vegetable Stock
  (see p. 400)
2 tablespoons olive or vegetable oil
2 onions, finely chopped
2 carrots, cut into 1 cm ($^1/_2$ in) dice
2 small white turnips, peeled and cut
  into 1 cm ($^1/_2$ in) dice
$^1/_2$ swede, cut into 1 cm ($^1/_2$ in) dice
2 parsnips, cut into 1 cm ($^1/_2$ in) dice

75 g (3 oz) unsalted butter
2 tablespoons freshly grated Parmesan
Salt and freshly ground black pepper

FOR THE ROAST GRAVY DRESSING
120 ml (4 fl oz) Madeira
1 heaped teaspoon finely chopped
  shallots (optional)
6 tablespoons Basic Vinaigrette
  (see p. 379)

Pre-heat the oven to 200°C/400°F/Gas 6.

Bring the vegetable stock to a simmer. Heat the oil in a pan or braising pan and add the chopped onions. Cook for a few minutes without colour until the onions begin to soften. Add the rice and continue to cook for a few minutes. It's now time to start adding the hot vegetable stock, just 1–2 ladles at a time to break down the layers of the rice and create a classic risotto texture. For even cooking it's important to stir the rice as the stock is added.

While the risotto is being made, heat a frying-pan and add a knob of butter. The carrots can be the first to be fried as these will take the longest to cook. Fry the carrots until a good golden colour, almost burnt at the edges, is achieved. Once coloured, transfer to a roasting pan and continue to cook in the pre-heated oven. Repeat the frying process with the turnips and swede, then add them to the carrots. Now finish by frying the parsnips. All the vegetables mixed together will now take a maximum 15 minutes to cook in the oven. The carrots take the longest which is why we start with them first. Basically, the vegetables should have a roasted, tender taste.

All we need now is to finish with the dressing. Boil the Madeira, and shallots, if using, until reduced by half, then add to the vinaigrette. You should have about 150 ml (5 oz). Another method is, once the vegetables have been cooked in the roasting pan, to remove them, then pour the Madeira into the hot pan. This will almost immediately reduce in quantity and at the same time lift the flavours from the pan. Strain through a sieve into the dressing.

When the risotto is ready, you can add either all or just half the vegetables. You may also need to add a little more stock with the Parmesan, to maintain the creamy texture. Add the remaining butter and adjust the seasoning with salt and pepper. The risotto can now be divided between bowls. If only half the vegetables were added, then the rest can now be sprinkled on top to give a coarser and more colourful finish. Spoon the roast gravy dressing over the risotto and serve.

Wild Mushroom Risotto

Risotto is one of the most popular dishes in all of Italy. I find it exciting because it can take on so many combinations.

I've used wild mushrooms in the recipe but, if you find these hard to get, then just substitute more sliced button mushrooms. The dish will still be good to eat as a starter or a vegetarian main course.

SERVES 4–6

1.2 litres (2 pints) Vegetable Stock
   (see p. 400)
100 g (4 oz) unsalted butter
2 onions, finely chopped
1 garlic clove, crushed
100 g (4 oz) button mushrooms, sliced
100 g (4 oz) fresh oyster mushrooms
   (optional)
50 g (2 oz) mixed wild mushrooms
   (optional)
225 g (8 oz) Arborio rice
50 g (2 oz) Parmesan cheese
Salt and freshly ground white pepper

Firstly heat the vegetable stock and keep it warm. Melt the butter in a large pan and add the chopped onions and garlic. Allow this to cook for 2–3 minutes, without colouring. Add all the mushrooms and continue to cook and stir for a further 2–3 minutes. Next, add the rice and stir continually over a low heat for a few minutes, just softening the rice.

Over a medium heat, begin to add the hot stock, a ladle at a time, allowing the rice to absorb all the stock before adding any more. Just continue to add stock gradually and stir until the rice has softened, which should take about 15–20 minutes.

Grate three-quarters of the Parmesan and slice the remainder as thinly as possible into flakes, or use a potato peeler. When the rice is ready, season with salt and pepper and stir in the grated Parmesan. The finished dish should be light and creamy. Sprinkle the remaining Parmesan flakes, and serve.

VARIATION

If you are not vegetarian, this risotto is delicious made with Chicken Stock (see p. 399) and 50–75 g (2–3 oz) chopped bone marrow, added after the mushrooms have cooked for a little, before you add the rice. The bone marrow adds extra richness and taste.

Potato Ravioli with Mushroom and Stilton

These are ravioli with a difference: the 'pasta' is actually made with mashed potato. The mixture rolls as easily as pastry, and fries to a crisp golden brown. This works well as a main course or a starter and can be served as a vegetarian dish.

SERVES 4–6

FOR THE RAVIOLI
350 g (12 oz) Mashed Potatoes, made
   without cream or butter (see p. 230)
2 egg yolks
2 tablespoons olive oil
Salt and freshly ground white pepper
3 tablespoons plain flour

FOR THE FILLING AND SAUCE
1 onion, finely chopped
1 sprig of fresh thyme
2 garlic cloves, crushed
25 g (1 oz) unsalted butter
100 g (4 oz) button mushrooms,
   quartered

100 g (4 oz) mixed wild mushrooms, or
   225 g (8 oz) button mushrooms, if
   unavailable
300 ml (10 fl oz) dry white wine
150 ml (5 fl oz) Vegetable or Chicken
   Stock (see pp. 400 or 399)
150 ml (5 fl oz) double cream
100 g (4 oz) Stilton, grated or crumbled

TO COOK AND GARNISH
25 g (1 oz) unsalted butter
50 g (2 oz) mixed wild mushrooms or
   sliced button mushrooms
50 ml (2 fl oz) olive oil
Juice of 1/2 lemon
1/2 teaspoon chopped fresh parsley

To make the ravioli paste, while the mashed potatoes are still warm, add the egg yolks and olive oil, season with salt and pepper and fold in the flour. This will now have a pasta paste texture. Cover with cling film and keep warm.

To make the filling, cook the chopped onion, thyme and garlic in the butter for 5 minutes. Add the mushrooms and cook for a further 5 minutes. Add the white wine and boil to reduce by half. Add the chicken or vegetable stock and simmer for a further 5 minutes. Add the cream and continue to cook gently for a further 10 minutes. Season with salt and pepper and strain off three-quarters of the liquid, which will be the sauce. Leave to one side.

Warm the remainder of the filling and add the Stilton. Melt this into the mixture then spread it on to a tray to cool. When cool, place in the fridge for 10–15 minutes until set.

Divide the ravioli paste into four or six pieces and roll out into circles (about the same thickness as pastry) on a lightly floured board. Spoon the mushroom filling on to one half of each ravioli circle and fold the other half over, pressing down all round the edges. The ravioli can now be shaped with a round pastry cutter to make a neater semi-circle. If the ravioli are made a few hours before eating, sit them on a tray sprinkled liberally with semolina to prevent then sticking.

To cook, melt the butter in a frying-pan and fry the ravioli for 3–4 minutes on each side until golden. Remove them from the pan. While the ravioli are frying, sauté the sliced mushrooms in the butter and a teaspoon of the olive oil. Season with salt and pepper.

Warm the cream sauce and pour it into four serving bowls. Place the ravioli on the sauce and spoon the garnishing mushrooms on top. Mix the remaining garnish olive oil with the lemon juice, some salt, pepper and chopped parsley and spoon over the mushrooms.

Spinach Dumplings

These make a lovely vegetarian main course or a delicious starter. I also use them as a garnish for stews and soups. They can be served in many combinations: with spicy Tomato or Red Pepper Coulis (see p. 375), fresh herb butter or just plain melted butter – delicious.

SERVES 4

1 onion, finely chopped

50 g (2 oz) unsalted butter

550 g (1 1/4 lb) fresh spinach, stalks removed

Salt and freshly ground white pepper

225 g (8 oz) Mascarpone or full-fat soft cheese

225 g (8 oz) plain flour

1 egg

1 egg yolk

A pinch of freshly grated nutmeg

100 g (4 oz) Parmesan, grated

Sweat the chopped onion in the butter for a few minutes until translucent, then allow to cool. Wash the spinach well to remove any grit, then shake off any excess water. Blanch the spinach in boiling, salted water for about 30 seconds then refresh in iced water. Squeeze the spinach until all the liquid is removed then chop it finely. Mix together the spinach and onion, then fold in the soft cheese and flour. Lightly beat the egg and egg yolk together, then add them to the mixture and season with salt, pepper and nutmeg. Leave the mixture to rest for about 15 minutes, then mould it into dumplings using floured hands, allowing three to four per portion.

The dumplings can now be cooked in simmering, salted water for 10–15 minutes. While they are cooking, pre-heat the grill. Arrange the dumplings in a flameproof dish and cover with the grated Parmesan. Finish under the hot grill until the cheese is lightly browned.

Macaroni Cheese with Leeks and Onions

We all know macaroni cheese, it's a family classic. The simple version of this recipe can be used as a vegetarian dish, but I will give a non-vegetarian alternative which I think takes it to new heights. I serve this particular version with Boiled Bacon (see p. 174), as an alternative to the barley stew.

SERVES 4–6
50 g (2 oz) unsalted butter
3 onions, sliced
350 g (12 oz) leeks, shredded
350 g (12 oz) dried or fresh macaroni
Salt
2 tablespoons olive oil (optional)
100 g (4 oz) mature Cheddar, grated
1 teaspoon English mustard (optional)

FOR THE BÉCHAMEL SAUCE
50 g (2 oz) unsalted butter
150 g (2 oz) plain flour
750 ml (1¼ pints) milk
150 ml (5 fl oz) double cream

FOR THE REDUCTION (OPTIONAL)
1 carrot, chopped
1 onion, chopped
1 leek, chopped
2 celery sticks, chopped
25 g (1 oz) unsalted butter
1 small garlic clove, crushed
1 sprig of fresh thyme
300 ml (10 fl oz) dry white wine
600 ml (1 pint) Vegetable Stock (see p. 400) or Chicken Stock (see p. 399)

To make the reduction, cook all the chopped vegetables in butter with a lid on for 10 minutes with the garlic and thyme. Add the white wine and boil until reduced by two-thirds. Add the chicken stock and continue to boil until reduced by half. Keep to one side.

To start the sauce, melt the butter in a pan, stir in the flour and cook over a low heat for 10 minutes. Warm the milk in a separate pan and slowly pour it into the flour and butter, stirring all the time. When all the warm milk has been added, cook the sauce on a low heat for about 30 minutes, stirring occasionally. If you are making the simple version, just add the cream, warm through and use as described below. However, it's at this stage that you add the reduction, with all the vegetables still in it, if you have made it. Cook this for about 10 minutes to infuse all the flavours, add the double cream and bring to the simmer. Push the sauce through a sieve. You now have a quite runny, rich cream sauce ready for its garnish and macaroni.

To cook the garnish leeks and onions, melt the butter, add the sliced onions and cook for 2–3 minutes. Add the shredded leeks and cook on a high heat for a further 2–3 minutes, stirring frequently. Remove from the heat.

If you are using dried macaroni, follow the cooking instructions on the packet. If you have bought fresh macaroni, simply boil a pan of water with salt and 2 tablespoons of olive oil. Drop in the macaroni and cook for 4–5 minutes, until tender.

Drain the pasta and mix with the leeks and onions in a pan. Pour the hot cream sauce over and stir in. The cheese can now be added but do not allow to re-boil or this will separate the cheese. Add the mustard, if using, to lift the taste. Warm through gently then serve with the boiled bacon or spoon into a flameproof vegetable dish, cover with grated cheese and glaze under a hot grill before serving as a dish on its own.

Stuffed Tomatoes with Fried Leeks

Plum tomatoes come mostly either from Italy or the USA. When cooked, they have a better taste and texture than the ordinary salad tomato. They can be found in large supermarkets but, if you can't get them, just use the others. This recipe makes an attractive vegetarian main course or a tasty starter.

SERVES 4
6 large plum or salad tomatoes
Salt and freshly ground white pepper
Freshly grated nutmeg

FOR THE STUFFING
50 g (2 oz) unsalted butter
2 shallots, sliced
350 g (12 oz) fresh spinach, stalks removed
500 g (1 lb) Mashed Potato (see p. 230)

2 tablespoons olive oil
50 g (2 oz) Cheddar or Gruyère grated

FOR THE LEEK GARNISH
Vegetable oil, for deep-frying
2 leeks, cut into very thin 5–7.5 cm (2–3 in) strips
300 ml (10 fl oz) Lemon Butter Sauce (see p. 371, optional)

Remove the eyes from the tomatoes and slice them in half top to bottom. Scoop out and discard the seeds and juice. Season with salt and pepper.

To make the stuffing, melt the butter in a pan and cook the sliced shallots for a few minutes. Add the spinach and cook on a high heat for a further 2–3 minutes, until softened. Season with salt, pepper and nutmeg. Warm the mashed potatoes and work in the olive oil.

Pre-heat the grill to hot. Place the tomatoes under the hot grill for 30 seconds to 1 minute. Remove from the heat. Spoon the spinach mixture into the tomatoes and top with the mashed potatoes (the potatoes can be piped in through a piping bag and plain nozzle). Sprinkle them with grated Cheddar or Gruyère and place under the grill until golden brown.

Meanwhile, to prepare the leek garnish, make sure the leek strips are thoroughly dry then deep-fry them in hot oil for about 30 seconds until they have crisped and taken a slight golden colour. Remove from the fat, drain well on kitchen paper and season with salt.

When the tomatoes are ready, divide them between individual bowls or plates and spoon the leeks on top. Sprinkle with a little extra olive oil or serve with the lemon butter sauce.

Vegetarian Stir-fry

This really is tasty to eat as a starter or main course. It also works well with some other fish or meat dishes.

SERVES 4
2 onions, sliced
2 tablespoons olive oil
50 g (2 oz) unsalted butter
225 g (8 oz) beansprouts, blanched in
   boiling water
225 g (8 oz) cup mushrooms, sliced
450 g (1 lb) spinach, washed and torn

175 g (6 oz) cooked fine
   spaghetti/noodles
1 tablespoon clear honey
2 tablespoons Spicy Marinade (see
   p. 165)
Juice of 1 lime
Salt and freshly ground black pepper
6 spring onions, diagonally sliced

The first thing is to start to cook the onions in a wok with the oil and butter for a couple of minutes. Add the blanched beansprouts and sliced mushrooms and continue to cook over a moderate heat for 2 minutes. Add the spinach and cook for a minute, until just wilted. Add the cooked spaghetti or noodles and cook for a further 2 minutes. Add the honey, marinade and lime juice. Check for seasoning with salt and pepper, divide between four bowls and spoon over the liquor. Finish with the sliced spring onions.

Side Dishes and Grains

French Bean and Sesame Salad

The flavours of Seared Tuna with Garlic and Almond Cream (see p. 61) eaten with this salad are just knock-out.

SERVES 4
225–275 g (8–10 oz) French beans

FOR THE SESAME DRESSING
25 g (1 oz) sesame seeds

2 tablespoons sesame oil
2 tablespoons groundnut oil
1/2 teaspoon soy sauce
1/4 teaspoon fresh lemon juice
Salt and freshly ground black pepper

Cook the beans in boiling, salted water until just tender but still with a little bite. Drain, then refresh under cold running water.

To make the dressing, the sesame seeds need to be lightly toasted under a hot grill or in a dry pan until golden. Mix together the oils and blitz in a food processor or liquidizer with the toasted sesame seeds. The consistency we are looking for is like a pesto sauce, loose but reasonably thick. Add a few drops of soy sauce and a good squeeze of lemon juice. If the mix still seems to be too thick, then simply add more equal quantities of both oils. Season with salt and pepper and the dressing is made. To serve the salad, warm the cooked beans in the dressing, then divide on to plates.

Warm Thai Salad

The ingredients in the salad itself are really very simple. The Thai flavours are given to us from the dressing, which uses chillies, groundnut oil, oyster sauce and the kaffir lime leaves. The dressing can be served either warm or cold. However, I find that all the flavours really liven up when served warm. The dish eats very well as a side salad or as a starter.

Kaffir lime leaves are dark green in colour and have a shiny finish. These can be bought fresh or dried from Indian shops. If you happen to find fresh leaves, then make them first choice. Any you don't use can be treated like bay leaves: just hang them up to dry. These leaves are, in fact, used in the same way as bay leaves, to add their sharp citrus flavour to the dish.

Oyster sauce can be bought in bottles and is made from oysters cooked with soy sauce and a brine. The sauce is a good seasoning in dressings, soups and many other savoury dishes. It's a sauce that also doesn't have to be matched with fish; many Chinese pork dishes are flavoured with it.

SERVES 4

FOR THE SALAD
1 small iceberg lettuce, shredded
4–6 spring onions, thinly sliced
12 fresh basil leaves
12 fresh coriander leaves

FOR THE DRESSING
2 garlic cloves, sliced
2 tablespoons groundnut oil
2 kaffir lime leaves, finely shredded
1 red chilli, seeded and very thinly
   sliced
2–4 tablespoons oyster sauce
3 tablespoons water

Mix together the iceberg lettuce with the spring onions and herb leaves. Fry the garlic slices in the groundnut oil, add the lime leaves and chilli and warm for a few minutes. Mix together half the oyster sauce and the water and whisk into the oil. Taste and add more oyster sauce, if liked. You will have about 120 ml (4 fl oz) of dressing. This can now be strained through a sieve and poured warm over the salad. Mix and serve the salad immediately.

Raw Fennel Salad

Fennel is a vegetable that is not used enough. It has the most wonderful aniseed flavour and can be eaten raw or cooked. To eat raw fennel, slice it very thinly otherwise it will be tough. All it needs then is a good marinade or dressing in which it should be served chilled. Eating a good, cold fennel salad with dressing is so refreshing and works all your taste buds. This can be eaten as a side dish to go with fish, or on its own.

Cooked fennel has many uses in salads, fish and meat dishes, or as a vegetable. It can also be served just with a dressing or grilled or shallow-fried with sauces and spices. I like it with hot Griddled Scallops (see p. 48), Seared Peppered Salmon (see p. 62) or grilled fresh tuna, cooked on a barbecue or hot grill.

SERVES 4
2 fennel bulbs
7 tablespoons olive oil

Juice of 2 lemons
Salt and freshly ground white pepper

Trim the root and tops of the fennel and slice on a machine or cut very thinly with a sharp knife into rings. Mix together the olive oil and lemon juice and season with salt and pepper. Add to the fennel rings. The fennel will now taste crunchy with an acidic taste of lemon and rich olive oil.

VARIATION

It's also nice to turn this recipe into a full starter served with a tarragon mayonnaise. Just add chopped fresh tarragon and a few drops of tarragon vinegar to Mayonnaise (see p. 380). Spoon the sauce into a bowl and sit some salad leaves on top, finishing with the fennel.

New Potato Salad

Potatoes are a great British vegetable and there are so many ways in which to prepare it. The golden rules to follow for all vegetables are: buy them fresh, cook them simply and eat plenty of them!

Serves 4
900 g (2 lb) new potatoes
1 large onion, finely chopped
4–5 tablespoons Basic Vinaigrette
  (see p. 379)

Salt and freshly ground black pepper
300 ml (10 fl oz) Mayonnaise (see
  p. 380)

Boil the potatoes until cooked. While still hot, cut into quarters and place in a bowl. Add the onion and sprinkle with vinaigrette to taste. Season with salt and pepper. While the potatoes are cooling, they will absorb the vinaigrette, which will help the taste. When cold, bind with the mayonnaise to finish.

Fresh Peas

Fresh peas are lovely to eat, providing they are properly cooked. Remember, don't try to cook too many at once, and don't cover the pan.

Once the peas have been shelled, bring a large pan of salted water to the boil. Drop in the peas, return the water to the boil and boil for 15–20 minutes, keeping the water boiling all the time. If the peas are not tender by that time, just keep boiling until they are ready. Drain the peas, toss in butter and season with salt and pepper. Peas also eat well mixed with Glazed Carrots (see p. 227); this then becomes a Flemish-style dish. Of course, you could substitute frozen peas.

This is a classic French dish called petits pois à la française. It is almost braised peas with onions and lettuce, with the liquor thickened with a little flour. Well I've changed it slightly and this is what I do.

SERVES 4
50 g (2 oz) unsalted butter
2 onions, sliced
4 smoked streaky bacon rashers,
  rinded and cut into strips

50–85 ml (2–3 fl oz) Chicken Stock (see
  p. 399) or Vegetable Stock (see
  p. 400)
Salt and freshly ground black pepper
450 g (1 lb) peas, cooked

Melt 25 g (1 oz) of butter and cook the onions and bacon until slightly softened. Add the stock and bring to the boil. Add the remaining butter and season with salt and pepper. Quickly re-heat the peas for 30 seconds in a pan of boiling water, then drain. Toss the peas in the reduced bacon and onion liquor and serve.

Pea Pancakes

Here's a great alternative for peas – home-made pea pancakes. This recipe works with fresh or frozen peas and goes beautifully with so many dishes: meat, fish or vegetarian. The pancakes are simple to make and can be served as a vegetable or part of a main-course dish. For a vegetarian dish, they eat very well topped with florets of cauliflower and grated cheese, browned under the grill and served with Spicy Tomato Dressing (see p. 381). I also like to serve them with roast lamb. If you add 2 teaspoons of chopped fresh mint to the recipe, you're adding a herb that suits both flavours, the lamb and the peas.

SERVES 4

**225 g (8 oz) Fresh Peas (see p. 216),
   cooked, or frozen peas, thawed**
1 egg
1 egg yolk
3 tablespoons plain flour
3 tablespoons double cream
50 g (2 oz) unsalted butter
Salt and freshly ground black pepper
Oil or butter, for frying

Place the peas, egg yolk, flour and cream in a food processor or liquidizer and blitz to a smooth consistency. Heat a frying-pan and add the butter, allowing it to colour to nut-brown stage. Add the butter to the mix and season with salt and pepper. The mix is now ready to cook. Heat a frying-pan and add a trickle of oil or small knob of butter. The pancake mix can now be dropped in, a tablespoon at a time. This will spread slightly, giving you small pea pancakes; you'll probably have room to cook 3–4 together, depending on the size of your pan. Cook until golden, then turn over and brown the other side. You should have enough for 10 to 12 pancakes in all. You can make the pancakes larger, if you prefer, by using a small ladle instead of a spoon to measure the batter.

Cabbage

Cabbage has a history almost as long as the potato. Probably the most common variety in Britain is the Savoy. It arrived in Britain in the mid 1500s from the Netherlands, just as the potato was arriving in Europe. Before then we were eating a wild variety that apparently is still grown in Europe and northern Britain around the sea coasts. This was very different to the cabbages we now know. It was very bitter and consequently had a bad reputation. It took the Romans to develop the plant, taking away some of that bitter flavour but still only supplying the open-leafed kale variety and not the round ones of today. In the days of the bitter plant, it was eaten for medicinal purposes, apparently to be eaten with your drinks and prevent you from becoming drunk. It was the Dutch who mastered the cabbage as we know it; the titles Savoy and coleslaw both coming from Dutch names.

Over the years the cabbage has formed a very large family: green, Savoy, white, red, then we go on to spring greens, sea kale, curly kale, watercress, cauliflower, broccoli, and the list goes on adding many more relatives of one plant.

One of the beauties of cabbage is that it is an all-year-round vegetable that can stand up very well against cold and even icy conditions. It does, however, carry one or two problems. The first being that unsavoury smell of overcooked cabbage that lingers in the room. My school dinner days (25 and more years ago!) remind me of that. The cabbage had a dull, almost yellow colour with a bad odour to go with it. That's the second problem, understanding the cooking of cabbage so that we can eat it at its best.

I think the problem may have started hundreds of years ago when almost all foods were cooked by the slow braising method. This meant that the cabbage would be added to a stew or broth at the beginning of cooking and just continued to cook and cook. As with all cooking methods and recipes, the ideas were just passed on, and consequently we have continued the habit of overcooking it.

Cabbage, in fact, cooks to its best in just minutes, keeping all its natural tastes and colours and giving a really inviting nose rather than odour. You will find that I use cabbage in many recipes. When potatoes and cabbage arrived in Europe, Ireland was one of the biggest growers and eaters of both products. It just shows how good, simple dishes will never die and continue to be enjoyed for years.

I thought I would just give you one or two ideas of some cabbage dishes to be enjoyed.

The Dutch white cabbage eats at its best as sauerkraut or raw in coleslaw. The coleslaw idea can take on completely different tastes.

White cabbage must be shredded or grated very finely if being served raw. This prevents it from being too tough and bitter to eat. Instead of mixing it with carrots and mayonnaise, why not simply mix it with Thai Dressing (see p. 215) or Hazelnut Dressing (see p. 382)?

Sweet and sour cabbage can also be made by boiling 1 tablespoon of caster sugar with 4 tablespoons of white wine vinegar. Bring to the boil and pour over the finely shredded cabbage, season with salt and leave to cool.

Green and Savoy cabbages can also be finely shredded or grated and used in salads. It's important to serve them straight away, otherwise the acidity of vinegar or citrus fruit (lime works very well with ginger and cabbage) will discolour the leaves.

The golden rule whenever cooking any variety of green cabbage or, for that matter, any green vegetable, is to always cook in plenty of boiling, salted water without a lid. Bring the water to the boil, remove the lid and add the shredded cabbage. This will now only take 1–2 minutes to cook or until the water just begins to simmer again. Now the cabbage can be drained, re-seasoned with salt and pepper and have a knob of butter added, to finish. It's also important to serve the vegetable immediately.

Another alternative is to cook the cabbage in the same way, but then refresh in ice-cold water. Once cold, drain, then season and top with butter. This is now ready either to microwave or drop back into a hot pan to re-heat.

Cabbage can be cooked, again as soon as needed, by heating several tablespoons of water with a knob of butter, then adding the cabbage, stirring for a few minutes on fast heat until tender. This method can be helped along with other flavours. Sliced onions and strips of bacon can be tossed in butter before adding the raw or pre-cooked shredded cabbage. This gives you a good vegetable dish or can be used as an accompaniment for a fish or meat dish.

If cabbage has been very quickly blanched in boiling water, just taking out the rawness, it can be sautéd to an almost golden brown tinge in butter or perhaps a flavoured oil. Sesame oil works very well, with sesame seeds. Also, prawns and a squeeze of lemon work beautifully with that sesame flavour. Pieces of pork scratchings mixed with sautéd cabbage also go very well.

Stir-fry dishes using all types of flavours give you really tasty vegetarian starters, main courses or vegetable dishes. The cabbage must be shredded very finely, then added at the last moment when cooking with other ingredients. How about mushrooms, onions, sweet peppers, leeks, beansprouts, chillies, herbs, ginger, garlic, lemon, limes, tomatoes, the list could just go on and on. All are readily available, easy to cook and serve and go very well.

Here's one more idea: Winter Vegetable Cabbage Lasagne. It's great as a starter or main course. The 'pasta' is actually the cabbage. Cut the stalk from the leaves individually, then blanch the leaves in boiling water and refresh in iced water. Take a loose-bottomed 20 cm (8 in) cake tin and place 1–2 leaves on the base, to cover. Now you need the winter vegetables, using 4–5 varieties. I suggest carrots, swedes, turnips, parsnips and maybe beetroot. These can now be roasted or puréed or a bit of both. If roasted, make sure they are slightly overcooked and tender. Now simply place either a roasted or puréed vegetable on top of the cabbage, then place some more leaves on top. This process should now be repeated until all the vegetables have been used, finishing with more cabbage.

This dish can now be kept chilled. Once you want to serve it, simply push from the ring and cut into wedges. This can now be microwaved as portions. You don't have to serve them individually. If you wish to present it as a whole dish, then simply build it on a plate and microwave the whole thing. It does, however, cut a lot more easily if it has been chilled first. The individual wedges look very neat and colourful. If you have decided to use purées, make sure they are not too wet or this will prevent the lasagne from holding up so well.

This dish can be served with a dressing, or make a vegetable and herb butter sauce to go with it. Just reduce the vegetable stock with some finely chopped shallots or onions. Add chopped fresh sage and thyme with a squeeze of lemon juice. Now just whisk in a little butter to emulsify. Season with salt and pepper and serve.

So there are a few cabbage ideas to be working with. Eating at The Savoy is one thing, but cooking and eating it is something else.

Crispy Cabbage

This recipe demolishes the myth that cabbage is tasteless and soggy.

SERVES 4–6
1/2 Savoy cabbage
Oil, for deep-frying
Salt

Cut the cabbage half into three wedges, removing the core. It's important to use the outside leaves as well, as this will give you a good contrast in colours from deep green to light. The cabbage now needs to be cut into 2.5 cm (1 in) strips.

Heat the deep-frying oil to 180°C/350°F. It is very important to use a lid on the fryer or pan when frying cabbage. This is due to cabbage having a high water content. For the first few seconds of frying the cabbage will cause the hot fat to spit.

Add the cabbage to the pan and put on the lid. Once the crackling has stopped, the cabbage should be ready with just a little colouring around the edges. Drain off all excess fat on kitchen paper, then lightly salt.

Fried Cabbage, Celeriac, Carrots and Bacon

This dish eats very well as a vegetable, or is delicious with Confit of Duck (see p. 127 and 128). I prefer to cook it in rich duck fat for extra taste. If you find that's not available, use olive oil. The vegetables and bacon are cooked individually in the fat then combined to give four different tastes and textures which all go very well together.

SERVES 4
50 g (2 oz) duck fat or 3 tablespoons olive oil
225 g (8 oz) carrots, cut into thin strips
225 g (8 oz) celeriac, cut into 1 cm (1/2 in) dice
1 garlic clove, crushed
225 g (8 oz) smoked streaky bacon rashers, rinded and cut into 2.5 cm (1 in) pieces
225 g (8 oz) Savoy cabbage leaves, cut into 2.5 cm (1 in) squares
Salt and freshly ground black pepper

Pre-heat a frying-pan and add some of the fat or olive oil. Fry the carrot sticks for 5–6 minutes until tender. Remove them from the pan and add a little more fat or oil. Fry the diced celeriac and garlic for a further 5 minutes and remove from the pan. Fry the bacon next; this will only take about 2 minutes in the hot pan. Lastly add the cabbage and cook for 2–3 minutes. Mix them all together and season with salt and pepper. This dish can be made in advance and then all reheated, seasoned and fried together when needed.

Roast Tomatoes with Sea Salt and Basil

The best tomatoes to use for this recipe are plum tomatoes. These have a much better taste and hold up better when cooked. If you are using salad tomatoes, only cook for 5–6 minutes. This dish eats well as a vegetable or vegetarian main course, finished with chopped black olives, capers and Mozzarella or Parmesan browned under the grill. They also eat very well with grilled fish or meat, in particular, lamb.

SERVES 4

7 plum tomatoes, eyed and halved

4 tablespoons olive oil

1 garlic clove, halved

12 fresh basil leaves

1 teaspoon coarse sea salt

Freshly ground black pepper

Pre-heat the oven to 200°C/400°F/gas 6.

Heat 1 tablespoon of the olive oil in a roasting pan with the garlic pieces. Fry the tomatoes, seed-side down, until coloured. Add 6 leaves of the basil and the remaining olive oil. Turn the tomatoes and sprinkle with the salt and pepper. Cook in the pre-heated oven for 6–7 minutes.

Once cooked, remove 12 tomato halves and keep warm in a serving dish. Heat the remaining 2 tomato halves in the oil on top of the pan and mash with a fork. This dressing can now be pushed through a sieve, leaving you with a tomato and olive dressing. Tear the remaining 6 basil leaves in half and sprinkle on top of the 12 tomato halves. Finish by spooning the dressing over the tomatoes and serve.

Quick Sweet and Sour Onions

These eat really well as a vegetable or to serve with another dish. Grilled chicken breasts or wings are delicious with these sweet and sour onions, as is grilled or sautéd liver. But one of my favourites is roast turbot or halibut with the onions trickling over, giving that sweet and sour flavour to work with the bitter-sweetness of the fish.

SERVES 4–6

450 g (1 lb) button onions

25 g (1 oz) unsalted butter

25 g (1 oz) caster sugar

50 ml (2 fl oz) white wine vinegar

Salt and freshly ground black pepper

Blanch the onions in boiling water for 5 minutes. Drain off the water. Melt the butter in a frying-pan. Once bubbling, add the onions and cook over a medium heat until golden. Add the sugar and continue to cook for a further 1 minute. Now add the white wine vinegar and boil to reduce until almost dry. Alternatively, the sugar and vinegar can both be added at the same time to create a syrup with almost a sauce consistency. Season with salt and pepper and serve.

Braised Onions

These are a wonderful vegetable to go with your roast Sunday lunch. They will give you your gravy already made. With the caramel onion taste along with slices of roast beef and good crispy Yorkshire puddings, second helpings become a standard procedure.

SERVES 4–6

450 g (1 lb) small onions
A knob of unsalted butter
A pinch of sugar
150 ml (5 fl oz) Chicken Stock
(see p. 399)

5 tablespoons Veal or Beef *Jus*
(see p. 398) or bought alternative
(see p. 401)
Salt and freshly ground black
pepper

Pre-heat the oven to 200°C/400°F/gas 6.

Blanch the onions in boiling water for 2–3 minutes. This will take out the absolute rawness of the onion. Heat a braising pan and add the butter. Add the onions and colour on top of the stove for about 8 minutes, until completely coloured with almost burnt tinges. Add the pinch of sugar and chicken stock and bring to a simmer. The onions can now be cooked in the pre-heated oven for 10 minutes, without a lid, until they become tender.

Once cooked, boil the stock with the onions and reduce until thick and syrupy. This will create a sweet glaze around the onions. Add the *jus* or gravy and bring to a simmer. The braised onions are now ready to check for seasoning before serving.

Fried Onion Rings

Here's a quick recipe for fried onion rings. Slice the onions into thin rings and separate. Dip through milk, then seasoned flour. Fry in hot fat at 180–185°C/350–360°F until golden and crispy. Season with salt and serve.

Broccoli

Good, firm broccoli is a very attractive and tasty vegetable. Broccoli comes in various sizes and varieties. My favourite is calabrese. This is the broccoli that grows in individual florets with a thick stalk. These really keep their colour and are very tender to eat, needing very little cooking. There is also the purple sprouting broccoli, which I believe was the first to grow. These also become very tender when cooked but never quite keep that rich purple colour.

SERVES 6–8

900 g (2 lb) broccoli

Salt and freshly ground black pepper
A knob of butter

Boil some salted water in a deep pan. Trim the stalks of the broccoli florets; these can be kept and also boiled to be used as another vegetable dish. Once the water is boiling, drop in the florets, making sure the lid is left off. The florets will only take 2–5 minutes to become tender but still with a little bite, depending on the size of the florets. Once cooked, remove from the water and, if not using immediately, plunge into iced water to stop the cooking and retain their green colour. These can simply be re-heated by dropping once again into boiling water for 1 minute, or microwaving.

The broccoli can now be seasoned with salt and pepper, buttered and served.

VARIATIONS

Here are some ideas of how to serve broccoli once cooked: top with Stilton Rarebit (see p. 197) and finish under the grill; sprinkle with Parmesan and brown under the grill; fry in Garlic Butter (see p. 201); fry with flaked almonds; finish with Hollandaise Sauce (see p. 373); finish *à la française*, with bacon, onions and lettuce (see Fresh Peas p. 216).

Sautéd Jerusalem Artichokes

These vegetables are most famous for a creamed soup known as Palestine. The soup, when cooked and creamed, has a very distinctive artichoke flavour with a rich, smooth, velvety consistency. They are also served roasted or puréed. The vegetable itself has a knobbly shape, with a brown/green colouring, and the flesh inside is white. Once peeled and trimmed, they must be kept in water with a dash of lemon juice or cooked immediately, to keep that colour.

SERVES 4
900 g (2 lb) Jerusalem artichokes
50 g (2 oz) unsalted butter
Salt and freshly ground black pepper

TO SERVE
2 tablespoons flaked almonds, toasted
2 tablespoons chopped fresh parsley
A squeeze of lemon juice

Pre-heat the oven to 200°C/400°F/gas 6.

Peel the artichokes with a sharp knife. Once completely trimmed, split in half. The chokes can now be cut into 2–3 mm (1/8 in) slices.

Heat a frying-pan and add a knob of butter. Once the butter is bubbling, add a handful of the artichokes. It's best not to fry too many at once as this tends to reduce the heat of the pan and stew the artichokes. Fry and toss the chokes until golden brown, then season with salt and pepper and transfer to a roasting pan while you fry the remaining artichokes. Finish in the pre-heated oven for 2–3 minutes. Sprinkle with the almonds, parsley and lemon juice and serve.

Braised Artichoke Bottoms

There are so many things you can do with artichoke bottoms, from adding them to a mixed salad to stuffing and braising. This recipe will help you cook them, the rest is up to you.

SERVES 4

2 large globe artichokes
Juice of 1/2 lemon
1 shallot, chopped
1 carrot, chopped
1 celery stick, chopped
25 g (1 oz) unsalted butter

1 tablespoon olive oil
1 bay leaf
1 sprig of fresh thyme
6 black peppercorns
6 coriander seeds
4 tomatoes, chopped

Firstly remove the stalks from the artichokes and then cut around the base, removing the leaves. Now cut across about 4 cm (1¹/₂ in) from the base and cut off any excess stalk or green left on. The centre of the bottom will still be intact. Rub with lemon juice.

Sweat the chopped shallot, carrot and celery in the butter and olive oil for a few minutes, then add the bay leaf, thyme, peppercorns, coriander seeds and chopped tomatoes. Pour in just enough water to cover. Bring to a simmer and cook for 10 minutes. Add the artichoke bottoms and about 1 teaspoon of lemon juice and simmer for 20–30 minutes, until tender. When cooked and cooled, remove and discard the bristly centres. Cut each bottom in half, and each half into four or five slices. They are now ready to use.

Spinach with Cream and Garlic

This is a good vegetable dish to accompany a number of main courses, but it goes especially well with stews and braised dishes.

SERVES 4

450 g (1 lb) fresh spinach, stalks
    removed
50 g (2 oz) unsalted butter
1 onion, finely chopped

1 garlic clove, crushed
75 ml (3 fl oz) double cream
Salt and freshly ground white pepper
Freshly grated nutmeg

Make sure you have removed all the tough stalks from the spinach and washed the leaves at least once to remove any grit. Drain off any excess water and place in a hot pan with half the butter. Cook for 1–2 minutes on a high heat then remove from the heat and leave to cool. Cut the spinach three or four times to break it down.

In a separate pan, cook the chopped onions and garlic in the remaining butter for a few minutes until soft but not coloured. Add the cream and bring to the boil. Add the spinach and cook for 2 minutes. Season with salt, pepper and nutmeg and serve.

Spinach with Shallots, Garlic and Croûtons

Any spinach dish should always be cooked just two or three minutes before you are going to eat. This way you get the maximum taste and texture. In this recipe there are one or two things that can be done ahead of time – the trimming and washing of the spinach, making the croûtons, and the pre-cooking of the shallots and garlic.

SERVES 4

450 g (1 lb) fresh spinach, stalks removed

2 slices of crusty bread

Olive oil

Salt and freshly ground white pepper

2 shallots, sliced

1 small garlic, crushed

25 g (1 oz) unsalted butter

Freshly grated nutmeg

Make sure that all the central, tough stalks have been removed from the spinach leaves, and that it has been washed in cold water at least once to remove any grit. Drain well.

Dice the crusty bread into 5 mm–1 cm (^{1}/4–^{1}/2 in) squares. Fry in about 5 mm (^{1}/4 in) of olive oil in a hot frying-pan or roast in the oven until golden brown. Drain well on kitchen paper and then sprinkle with salt.

In a large pan, cook the sliced shallots and garlic in 1 tablespoon of olive oil and butter for a few minutes until soft. These can now be left in the pan ready to cook the spinach.

When ready to cook the spinach, re-heat the shallots and garlic until bubbling. Add the spinach and keep on a high heat, turning the spinach in the pan. The leaves will quickly soften and, after 2–3 minutes, will be cooked. Season with salt, pepper and nutmeg. The crispy croûtons can now be added or just sprinkled over in the serving dish.

Crispy Spinach

This is wonderful with the Tuna Carpaccio (see p. 58).

SERVES 6–8

225 g (8 oz) spinach leaves, washed and picked (large stalks removed)

Oil, for deep-frying

Salt

Cayenne pepper

Heat the oil to 150°C/300°F.

The spinach leaves should be carefully spun and well dried, removing all excess water from the leaves. Cut the spinach into thin strips. This can be either very fine (as for Chinese 'seaweed') or 5 mm (^{1}/4 in) thick. Deep-fry in small batches in the hot oil until crispy. This will only take between 30 seconds and 1 minute. Shake off excess fat, then season with a pinch of salt and cayenne pepper. The crispy spinach is now ready to serve.

Fried Spinach, Mushrooms and Beansprouts

This eats well on its own but is even better with the Seared Spicy Pork Belly (see p. 164).

SERVES 4
750–900 g (1¹/₂–2 lb) spinach
1–2 tablespoons olive oil
25 g (1 oz) unsalted butter
225 g (8 oz) cup mushrooms, sliced

225 g (8 oz) beansprouts, blanched in
hot water
Salt and freshly ground black pepper
Juice of 1 lime

First, remove the stalks from the spinach and tear the leaves carefully into small pieces. Wash the leaves and leave to dry.

Heat a wok or frying-pan and add the olive oil and butter. Add the mushrooms and toss for 30 seconds. Add the beansprouts and continue to cook for 2 minutes. Add the spinach and continue to stir for 30 seconds. Add the seasoning and lime juice and cook for about 30 seconds more, until the vegetables are just tender.

Roast Parsnips with Honey

Parsnips are a vegetable that is far too often ignored. When roasted, they're always crisp, sweet and tender and I find these parsnips eat particularly well with roast lamb.

SERVES 6
900 g (2 lb) parsnips, peeled and
quartered
2 tablespoons olive oil

50 g (2 oz) unsalted butter
2 tablespoons clear honey
Salt and freshly ground black pepper

Pre-heat the oven to 220°C/425°F/gas 7.

If the parsnips have slightly woody centres, cut these out before cooking.

Pre-heat a roasting tray on top of the stove and add the olive oil and butter. Fry the parsnips in the oil until golden brown on all sides then roast them in the pre-heated oven for 20 minutes, turning occasionally. Pour the honey over the parsnips and carefully turn them, making sure they have all been covered. Season and put back in the oven for 5 minutes. The parsnips will now be tender and sweet. Stir them in a serving dish and spoon some of the honey glaze from the pan over the top to finish.

Roast Celeriac

Probably one of my favourite vegetable dishes is roast parsnips, but celeriac makes a great alternative and welcome change.

SERVES 4–6

900 g (2 lb) celeriac

2 tablespoons beef dripping, lard or

vegetable oil

50 g (2 oz) unsalted butter

Salt and freshly ground white pepper

Pre-heat the oven to 200°C/400°F/gas 6.

Celeriac has very thick skin, which has to be cut off with a knife rather than peeled. Cut the flesh into large 4 cm (1$^{1}/_{2}$ in) pieces. This should be done just before cooking, to prevent them from discolouring.

Pre-heat a roasting tray on top of the stove and add the dripping or lard. Start to fry the celeriac, turning the pieces in the pan, until golden brown on all sides. When coloured, add the butter and roast in the pre-heated oven for 25–30 minutes, until the celeriac is tender and crispy. Season and serve.

That is the basic recipe. To add a bit more, during the last 5–10 minutes of roasting, some pieces of smoked bacon and/or some garlic, sage and thyme will lift the dish, giving lots of extra taste.

Glazed Carrots

Cooking carrots has become a very standard job. While they are a useful everyday vegetable, they are great to flavour so many things and I like cooking them this way to make them really tasty and exciting to eat.

SERVES 4

450 g (1 lb) carrots

A pinch of salt

Water

1 teaspoon caster sugar

25–50 g (1–2 oz) unsalted butter

Salt and freshly ground black pepper

The carrots can just be sliced into rings for this recipe, but I like to split them lengthways, twice if they are thick, then cut them at an angle into 1 cm ($^{1}/_{2}$ in) pieces. This gives more substance and texture to the vegetables. Place the carrots in a pan with a pinch of salt. Literally just cover, and only just, with water. Add the sugar and butter. Bring the water to the boil and then simmer until the carrots are just tender but still with a slight bite. The cooking time will be determined by how you have sliced them; 8–15 minutes. Drain the liquor into another pan and boil to reduce until 5–6 tablespoons are left. In the reduction process, the butter and sugar content will thicken the liquor, giving you a glaze. Add a little more butter if you want to thicken it a little more. Add the carrots to the pan and re-heat in the glaze. Check the seasoning and serve.

Braised Chicory

This can be used as a vegetable dish, or as part of a fish dish, particularly good with Mashed Potatoes (see p. 230) and Grilled Sea Bass (see p. 89).

SERVES 4

6 heads of Belgian chicory
25 g (1 oz) unsalted butter
3 tablespoons olive oil
2 shallots, sliced
1 sprig of fresh thyme

A few fresh basil leaves
A few white peppercorns
150 ml (5 fl oz) sweet white wine
600 ml (1 pint) Vegetable Stock
 (see p. 400) or Chicken Stock
 (see p. 399)

Split the chicory down the centre, giving you twelve pieces, three per portion. Pre-heat a frying-pan and add the butter. Fry the chicory pieces in the butter for about 3–4 minutes, until they have coloured on all sides.

In a separate pan, warm the olive oil, add the sliced shallots, herbs and peppercorns and cook for a few minutes. Add the white wine and boil to reduce until almost dry. Add the stock and boil to reduce by one-third. Sit the chicory in the stock, bring to the simmer and cook for 15–20 minutes, until the chicory is tender.

Remove the chicory from the cooking liquor and keep it warm. Taste the liquor; it may well need reducing a little more to increase in strength. When ready, push the liquor through a sieve and pour over the chicory. The dish is now ready.

Beetroot Fritters

These fritters eat very well with a classic accompaniment of just salt and vinegar, and also if just dipped in soured cream or yoghurt and chives. They make a good alternative vegetable dish or can be used as a vegetarian starter (using the right beer).

To cook beetroot, plunge it into boiling, salted water then return to the boil. The cooking time depends on age and size. Don't test them with a fork or they will bleed. Lift one out of the water after 30 minutes and try to pull back the skin with your thumb. If the skin comes off easily, the beetroot is cooked. If not, continue to test every 5–10 minutes. Once cooked, drain and leave to cool, then peel, cut in half and cut into 2 cm (3/4 in) wedges. You can serve them as they are, with some salad dressing or vinegar, sugar and a little water mixed together and poured over, or you can try this.

SERVES 4

450 g (1 lb) self-raising flour
Salt
300 ml (10 fl oz) lager

Oil, for deep-frying
12 beetroot wedges
Salt and freshly ground black pepper
Malt vinegar (optional)

Mix the flour and salt into the lager until you have a smooth, thick batter with almost a glue-like consistency. Pre-heat the oil in a deep frying-pan to 180°C/350°F. Season the beetroot wedges and dust with flour. Coat with batter. Drop into the hot fat and fry for a few minutes until crisp and golden. Remove and salt lightly. Sprinkle with vinegar before serving, if liked.

VARIATION

Parsnips also work well in this recipe. Peel and quarter the parsnips lengthways, cut the woody core from the centre and blanch the parsnips in boiling, salted water for 2–3 minutes. Drain, cool and pat dry. Lightly flour, coat with batter and cook in the same way, then salt lightly before serving.

Beetroot Bubble and Squeak

Bubble and squeak is traditionally made using potatoes, onions and Brussels sprouts, the name coming from the noise it makes while cooking. I get the occasional mad idea of what variations can be made to the dish – there's one that actually works. It goes well with venison, pheasant, pigeon or just about any game. It also eats well with most meats, making a roast leg of pork or lamb, for example, just that bit more interesting. Top it with spinach and a crumble mix to make a complete vegetarian dish.

SERVES 4
2 large onions, sliced
50 g (2 oz) unsalted butter
225 g (8 oz) beetroot, cooked and
 grated

175 g (6 oz) Mashed Potatoes
 (see p. 230), made without milk
 or cream
Salt and freshly ground white pepper
1 tablespoon plain flour

Cook the onions in half the butter for a few minutes until softened but not coloured. Leave to cool.

Mix the beetroot with the potatoes, add the onions and season with salt and pepper. Stir well. The mix will be a shocking pink colour. It can now be fried as one large cake (the classic bubble) or shaped into small cakes. Pre-heat a frying-pan. Dust the bubble cakes with a little flour and fry in the remaining butter over a medium heat for about 4–5 minutes, until golden brown on each side.

VARIATIONS

This can become a black pudding and beetroot cake by dicing and frying some black pudding and bacon (or pieces of sausage) and adding it to the mix before frying it. Serve it with a fried egg on top, and grilled tomatoes.

Try making potato and onion bubble, top it with slices of corned beef, then thick slices of tomato, season and dot with butter then pop under the grill. If you're feeling really mad, top the lot with slices of Cheddar and let it melt over the bubble.

Deep-fried Crispy Potato Skins

These really are good and something we only normally eat in steak house restaurants. Well, why not make your own – they are so good. All you need are the skins (with 2–3 mm/¹/₈ in of potato left on) of some baked potatoes, cut into strips. The skin strips will keep in the fridge to fry whenever you like. Just heat some oil in a deep pan to 180°C/350°F and add the skins. After a few minutes' deep-frying they will become golden and crispy. Drain and lightly salt before serving.

These eat very well with the Peppered Roast Beef (see p. 142) and a good mixed salad. You can also make a dip to go with the potato skins: take some soured cream and season to taste with fresh lemon juice, snipped fresh chives, salt and freshly ground black pepper.

Mashed Potatoes

I find Maris Piper are one of the best varieties for making mashed potatoes, one of my favourite vegetable dishes – then all you need to add is a little care.

SERVES 4–6

900 g (2 lb) jacket, floury potatoes, peeled and quartered
Salt and freshly ground white pepper
100 g (4 oz) unsalted butter
120 ml (4 fl oz) single cream or milk
Freshly grated nutmeg

Boil the potatoes in salted water until tender, about 20–25 minutes depending on size. Drain off all the water and replace the lid. Shake the pan vigorously which will start to break the potatoes. Add the butter and cream or milk a little at a time, while mashing the potatoes. Season with salt, pepper and nutmeg. The potatoes will be light, fluffy and creamy.

Spring Onion Potato Cakes

This is a basic recipe that can be developed to suit so many other dishes. I like to add diced, smoked bacon, which goes well with the spring onions, and I serve this with a grilled herring dish (see Herrings with Spring Onion and Bacon Potato Cakes, p. 113). It's also good to keep this a vegetarian dish, so why not just add grated cheese and onion and serve with a good tomato salad?

SERVES 4
25 g (1 oz) unsalted butter
1 large bunch of spring onions, finely
   diced
350 g (12 oz) Mashed Potatoes (see
   p. 230), made without cream or milk

2 tablespoons olive oil
2 egg yolks
Salt and freshly ground white pepper
3 tablespoons plain flour

Melt half the butter and fry the spring onions quickly. While the mashed potatoes are still warm, add the olive oil, egg yolks and spring onions and season with salt and pepper. Fold in the flour. The mix can now be divided into four discs about 1–2 cm ($1/2$–$3/4$ in) thick and pan-fried in the remaining butter and a little extra olive oil. The cakes will take about 3–4 minutes on either side.

It is always best to pan-fry the cakes as soon as the mix is ready. This will prevent it from becoming soggy. Once cooked, the cakes can be kept and chilled, then baked through in the oven when needed. However, to eat them at their best, eat as soon as cooked.

Fondant Potatoes

These are potatoes that traditionally are shaped into barrels and then braised in chicken stock until all the stock has reduced and been absorbed. The potato is then packed with flavour. Well, I'm not changing this recipe too much, except the potatoes don't need to be shaped, they are just peeled and halved.

SERVES 4
2 large baking potatoes, peeled and
   halved lengthways
600 ml (1 pint) Chicken Stock (see p.
   399) or Vegetable Stock (see p. 400)

Salt
25 g (1 oz) unsalted butter

Pre-heat the oven to 200°C/400°F/gas 6.

Sit the potatoes in a small, buttered baking tray or flameproof dish. Pour in the stock, filling just three-quarters up the sides of the potatoes. Brush the potatoes with butter and lightly season with salt. Bring the stock to the simmer on top of the stove, then transfer to the pre-heated oven for 30–40 minutes. During this time the potatoes will be absorbing the stock. If the stock becomes almost dry, simply check the potatoes with a knife; they may be ready. If not, just add a little more stock, about 5 mm ($1/4$ in) and continue to cook.

For the last 10 minutes of cooking time, brush the potatoes with butter to help give them a nice golden colour. They can also be finished under a hot grill.

Champ

I'm not quite sure if champ comes from Scotland or Ireland. I first experienced it in Northern Ireland, but have read in several books that it was first made in Scotland. It's one of those recipes that everybody believes their way is the only way to make it. Well, I'm not going to say that this is the way; I'll sit on the fence and just give you my version of champ.

The dish can be eaten on its own or just as a potato dish with boiled ham or bacon. I normally serve it with a boiled bacon collar (see p. 171), just spooned over with its cooking liquor and served with English mustard.

SERVES 4
150 ml (5 fl oz) milk
225 g (8 oz) spring onions, sliced
450–675 g (1–1 1/2 lb) Mashed Potatoes (see p. 230), made without cream or butter

Salt and freshly ground white pepper
A pinch of freshly grated nutmeg (optional)
100–175 g (4–6 oz) unsalted butter

Bring the milk to the simmer with the spring onions. Add this to the mashed potatoes and season with salt and pepper. I like to add a pinch of nutmeg. Add half the butter to give a creamier texture. Spoon the potatoes into a bowl and make well in the middle. The remaining butter can now be set in the centre. The champ is ready.

VARIATIONS
You can substitute chives, nettles, onions or even peas for the spring onions. You can also make red champ, with pieces of cooked beetroot added to the potatoes.

Celeriac and Potato Dauphinoise

This a French potato dish that has undergone one or two changes. The flavours are lovely and this eats well with most of the main courses.

SERVES 4
2 large onions, sliced
50 g (2 oz) unsalted butter
600 ml (1 pint) double cream
1 garlic clove, crushed

Salt and freshly ground black pepper
450 g (1 lb) potatoes, thinly sliced
1 large celeriac, peeled and thinly sliced

Pre-heat the oven to 180–190°C/350–375°F/gas 4–5.

Cook the onions in half of the butter for 2–3 minutes without colouring, then allow to cool. Bring the cream to the boil with the crushed garlic and remaining butter and season with salt and pepper. Arrange the onions, potatoes and celeriac in layers in a large ovenproof dish, making sure the potatoes are on the top and bottom. Overlap the top layer of potatoes to give a neater finish. Pour over the cream, making sure the potatoes are covered. Bake in the pre-heated oven for 45–60 minutes until the vegetables are tender and have absorbed the cream. Test the vegetables by piercing with a knife. Cover with foil if the potatoes are browning too quickly. Once cooked, finish, if necessary, under a hot grill for that golden colour.

VARIATIONS

For a creamier texture, sit the dish in a roasting tray filled with hot water to come three-quarters of the way up the dish, cover with foil and bake in the oven for 1–1¼ hours, finishing under the grill.

This dish eats well without the celeriac as a straightforward Dauphinoise Potato. I also like to run anchovy fillets through the centre of the potatoes, to add another taste.

Boulangère Potatoes

This is a classic potato dish with the potatoes simply sliced with onions and cooked in the oven in stock. It is a traditional French recipe that is served in restaurants all over Britain, traditionally with roast best ends or legs of lamb.

SERVES 4
25–50 g (1–2 oz) unsalted butter
2 onions, sliced
675 g (1½ lb) potatoes, thinly sliced

Salt and freshly ground white pepper
450 ml (15 fl oz) hot Chicken Stock
 (see p. 399) or Vegetable Stock
 (see p. 400)

Pre-heat the oven to 230°C/450°F/gas 8.

Melt a little of the butter and fry the onions until softened. Reserve some good round potato slices to arrange on the top of the dish, then mix the remainder with the cooked onions and season with salt and pepper. Place the mixture in an ovenproof vegetable dish and cover with the reserved potato slices, overlapping them across the top. Pour over the warm stock and dot with the remaining butter. Cook in the pre-heated oven for 20 minutes, until the potatoes begin to colour. Reduce the oven temperature to 200°C/400°F/gas 6 and cook for a further 40–50 minutes, pressing down the potatoes with a spatula occasionally for more even cooking. By the end of cooking, the potatoes will have absorbed the stock and should be golden and crispy on top. To finish, just sit the potatoes under the grill to achieve that extra rich colour.

VARIATIONS

There are a good many variations you can try. Add some strips of smoked bacon; sliced leeks; truffles (very nice – expensive, too); sliced celeriac; sage and thyme – or just use your imagination.

Chips and French Fries

Chips and French fries are readily available in all shapes and sizes. There are many good-quality frozen fries around, but I don't believe you can find any frozen chip that can beat good home-made fries. I use large jacket potatoes, which will cool after pre-cooking and become tender without losing their potato texture. For each portion, 1–1½ potatoes will be plenty. You really need a deep-fat fryer to make these and guarantee the right temperature. If you don't have one, they will have to be treated with even more care and attention to give you fluffy, tender, crisp potatoes.

SERVES 4–6

4–6 peeled jacket potatoes, about 1.5 kg (3 lb)

Salt

Oil, for deep-frying

Heat the oil in the deep-fat fryer or deep heavy-based pan to 95°C/200°F for blanching. For good large chips, trim the potatoes into rectangles. Now cut into 1 cm (½ in thick) slices, then cut again to give chips 1 cm (½ in) thick and 6–7.5 cm (2½–3 in) long. If you want French fries, then simply halve the thickness, making them 0.5 × 6–7.5 cm (¼ × 2½–3 in). The chips now need to be blanched in the pre-heated fat fryer. This is very important, to guarantee the chips will be totally cooked before serving.

Frying them at 95°C/200°F will cook them without colour. The large chips will take up to 10–15 minutes before becoming tender. The smaller fries will only need 6–8 minutes. Once cooked, check by piercing with a knife. When ready, remove from the oil and drain. The chips or fries can be left to cool on greaseproof paper and even chilled before finishing in the hot fryer.

To finish, pre-heat the oil in the fryer to 150°C/300°F. Once hot, place the chips in the fat. These will now take 2–3 minutes before becoming golden brown and crispy. Shake off any excess fat and sprinkle with salt before serving.

NOTE

Using a domestic fat-fryer, you may need to heat the oil to a temperature of 180°C/350°F to finish.

Soured New and Baked Potatoes

These potatoes dishes really excite me. They have such scope and variety, from a potato salad with a difference to an Indian curry side dish. The combination of flavours is unlimited, and I promise you if you don't usually like soured cream you certainly will in this recipe. This is not a strict ingredients recipe, the measurements are for guidelines. I'll give you the basic recipe for new potatoes, and you simply follow the same method for the baked potatoes.

SERVES 4
450 g (1 lb) new potatoes
2–3 tablespoons olive oil

Juice of 1 1/2–2 lemons
Salt and freshly ground black pepper
3–4 tablespoons soured cream

To make the soured new potatoes, the new potatoes should be cooked in boiling, salted water for 15–20 minutes until tender, then drained. While still hot, mash with a fork, not making them too fine. With the new potatoes, I prefer to leave the skin on. New potatoe skins hold a lot of flavour. If you prefer them skinned, then just peel once cooked.

Once the potatoes have been forked, add 2 tablespoons of the olive oil and the juice of 1 lemon. Season with salt and pepper. The oil and lemon will have loosened the potatoes slightly. If you feel they need more, then just continue to add until the mix has been softened and has quite a sharp flavour from the lemon. The potatoes up to this stage can be made in advance.

The soured cream should be added at the last minute just before serving. Warm through the potatoes, then lightly mix in 3 tablespoons of the soured cream, adding the rest if necessary. Do not overmix the potatoes; if you do, the creaminess will be lost and the mix will become almost chewy. Re-season with salt and pepper and serve.

SOURED BAKED POTATOES

This recipe is the same as the above, using four baking potatoes in place of the new potatoes. Baked potatoes will take approximately 1 hour to cook in a pre-heated oven at 200°C/400°F/gas 6. Once cooked, split them lengthways and fork out the insides, saving the skins to serve the potatoes in. Mix the potato flesh with the olive oil and lemon juice before adding the soured cream and seasoning with salt and pepper. Once creamed and seasoned, the potato can be spooned back into the skins before serving. I usually just spoon the filling into four skin halves, making them very full.

The remaining potato skins can now be quartered, giving you 4 strips per half potato. I bet you can guess what I'm going to do with these. Yes. Deep-fried Crispy Potato Skins (see p. 230).

VARIATIONS

If you're thinking of serving the soured baked potato in its skin, then top it with Gruyère or Cheddar cheese and melt under a hot grill before serving.

Both recipes for soured new and baked potatoes have room for different flavours – chives, tarragon, basil, parsley, pesto, limes, tomatoes can all be used.

Pommes Parmentier

One of the first potato dishes taught at catering college is pommes parmentier. This is a 1cm (1/2 in) diced potato that is shallow-fried in butter, then finished with chopped parsley – an attractive potato dish as well as good to eat. While at college you never think to ask how the dish got its name. As with many recipes, which are frequently named after people and places, this dish takes the name of the man who made the French public aware of the potato in the mid to late 1700s.

SERVES 4

675 g (1 1/2 lb) potatoes, peeled and cut into 1 cm (1/2 in) dice

2–3 tablespoons cooking oil

25–50 g (1–2 oz) unsalted butter

Salt

Chopped fresh parsley (optional)

Once the potatoes have been cut, wash them, then dry them in a cloth. It's best to fry them in stages; trying to cook them all at once will reduce the heat and also totally overcrowd the pan, giving you uneven colouring.

Simply heat a frying-pan and add a drop of the oil and a knob of butter. Add just enough potatoes to cover the pan and begin to shallow-fry (sauté) over a medium heat for 10–12 minutes, turning the potatoes for an even, all-round golden colour.

Once the potatoes are coloured, remove from the pan and transfer to a roasting tin. Repeat the same process until all are cooked. The potatoes should now all be tender and ready to serve. They can be placed in a hot oven to finish cooking or simply heat through. Season with salt and sprinkle with chopped parsley, if liked, before serving.

VARIATIONS

Pommes parmentier has many variations. Crushed garlic, crispy bacon or mixed herbs can be fried with the potatoes. I like to fry pieces of smoked bacon and onions, then mix them with the raw potato dice. This can now be placed in an ovenproof serving dish, having the potatoes just roughly sitting above the dish. Now pour in some Chicken Stock (see p. 399), filling three-quarters of the dish. Brush the potatoes with butter and bring to a simmer. These can now be baked in a pre-heated oven at 220°C/425°F/gas 7 for 30–40 minutes. During this time the potatoes will become golden brown and crispy on top, with moist fluffy potatoes underneath, having absorbed all the stock.

These are great to serve straight on the table at a dinner party or Sunday lunch. Here's an extra thought. Why not sprinkle grated cheese on top and melt under the grill? Then you have a variation for a supper dish.

Irish Potato Cakes

Here's a recipe for Irish potato cakes if you fancy giving them a try. They are perfect with Pork and Black Pudding Patties (see p. 167) and Apple and Mustard Seed Relish (see p. 388).

MAKES 8

450 g (1 lb) Mashed Potatoes (see
    p. 230), made not too wet and
    without cream or butter
100 g (4 oz) plain flour, plus extra for
    dusting

15 g ($^1/_2$ oz) unsalted butter, plus extra
    for frying
Salt and freshly ground black
    pepper

Pre-heat the oven to 200°C/400°F/gas 6.

Mix the potatoes with the flour and butter and season with salt and pepper. Divide into eight balls, and then pat into rounds 1 cm ($^1/_2$ in) thick. Lightly flour and pan-fry in butter until golden brown on both sides. It's also best to finish them in the pre-heated oven for 2–3 minutes. This will cook out the flour added to the mix.

VARIATIONS

Of course, these potato cakes can be used with many other dishes and can also have many other flavours added. Chopped bacon, onions, spring onions, herbs, chestnuts, pesto, mustard and I'm sure many more. It's really just a question of using the flavours that suit the dish they are to accompany.

Bubble and Squeak

Bubble and squeak is a strange name for a vegetable dish, but I believe it's so called because of the noises the vegetables make while being fried in the pan.

As you can see in the recipe, I have given one or two alternatives. This is because bubble and squeak can really be your own invention, and either mashed or cooked potatoes, sprouts or cabbage will do the trick. I prefer mashed potatoes as this gives me more of a cake consistency but, if you're using plain boiled potatoes, just peel them and cut into thick slices. The dish is usually made from leftovers so the sprouts or cabbage should be boiled or cooked. The sprouts can be sliced.

There are so many variations to a bubble and squeak. Half cabbage and half sprouts can be used, and any additions can be made: garlic, smoked bacon, leeks, herbs and so on. But as I've always said, 'Get the basics right first, then move on.'

SERVES 6–8

2 large onions, sliced
50 g (2 oz) unsalted butter

900 g (2 lb) potatoes, cooked or 750 g
    (1$^1/_2$ lb) leftover Mashed Potatoes (see
    p. 230), made without milk or cream

450 g (1 lb) brussels sprouts or green
 cabbage, cooked

Salt and freshly ground white pepper
50 g (2 oz) vegetable oil or dripping

Cook the sliced onions in half the butter until softened. Mix in the potatoes and sprouts or cabbage and season with salt and pepper. Pre-heat a small frying-pan and add the remaining butter and the oil or dripping. Fry the bubble mix for 6–8 minutes, pushing it down with a spatula to create a potato and vegetable cake. The pan should be kept hot, as this will create a crispy base. To turn over the bubble, cover the pan with a plate, invert the pan so the cake falls on to the plate, then slip it, uncooked-side down, back into the pan and repeat the cooking process. The bubble and squeak is now ready and can be cut into six or eight wedges before serving, or be left whole as a cake.

Colcannon

This is lovely as a totally vegetarian dish – perhaps with a poached egg on top – or a great accompaniment for Boiled Bacon (see p. 174) with a parsley sauce or Home-made Pork Sausages with Onion Gravy (see p. 170 and 367). You can use kale, or white or green cabbage.

SERVES 4
450 g (1 lb) potatoes, peeled
450 g (1 lb) kale or cabbage, shredded
2 small leeks or spring onion tops,
 chopped

150 g (5 oz) unsalted butter
Salt and freshly ground black
 pepper
A pinch of ground mace
150 ml (5 fl oz) milk or single cream

Boil the potatoes in salted water until cooked, about 20–25 minutes depending on size. Drain off all the water and replace the lid. Shake the pan vigorously which will start to break the potatoes, then mash them until light and fluffy. Blanch the shredded kale or cabbage in boiling water for 2–3 minutes, until softened but not coloured. Drain well. Fry the chopped leeks or spring onions tops in 25 g (1 oz) of the butter for a few minutes until softened, then add the cabbage and continue to cook for a few more minutes. Add the potatoes with the salt, pepper, ground mace and milk or cream. Melt the remaining butter and add it to the mix. Heat through, check for seasoning with salt and pepper, and serve.

Potato and Leek Gratin

This beautifully creamy, tasty potato dish goes very well with most of my main course dishes.

SERVES 4

450 g (1 lb) leeks
2 onions, sliced
25 g (1 oz) unsalted butter
600 ml (1 pint) double cream
**450 g (1 lb) potatoes, peeled and thinly
  sliced**

1 small garlic clove, crushed
**Salt and freshly ground white
  pepper**
Freshly grated nutmeg
**50 g (2 oz) Cheddar, grated
  (optional)**

Pre-heat the oven to 180°C/350°F/gas 4 and grease a shallow ovenproof gratin dish.

Cut the leeks diagonally into 5 mm (1/4 in) slices and blanch in boiling water for 30 seconds. Re... ...der cold water, drain again and pat dry.

...utter for 2–3 minutes, until softened.

...iced potatoes in a pan. Add the garlic and season with ...g to the boil then stir in the leeks and onions. Pour the ...a depth of 4 cm (1 1/2 in), covering with all the cream. ...filled with very hot water and bake in the pre-heated ...es are cooked through and golden brown on top. To ...ing, just pierce with a small vegetable knife. When it ...w they are cooked.

...hot water. As a finish you can top with the grated ...grill until golden brown.

Rice and Peas

This isn't quite as it sounds because the peas are, in fact, kidney beans. However, this is the traditional name for this Caribbean speciality that I have grown to love. It's a dish that can be eaten hot or cold and, once you've had one taste, you just can't stop eating.

It can go with so many dishes, whether they be dry spicy curries, fried chicken, fish kebabs or salads – all work very well. The flavour of the kidney beans works through the rice, making them very predominant. The whole dish is also enriched with the addition of coconut cream.

SERVES 6–8

350 g (12 oz) long-grain rice, washed
175 g (6 oz) kidney beans, soaked in
   water for a minimum 8 hours
About 1.2 litres (2 pints) water
75 g (3 oz) coconut cream (block), cut
   into pieces

2 onions, finely chopped
4 garlic cloves, crushed
^{1}/$_2$ teaspoon chopped fresh thyme
25 g (1 oz) unsalted butter
Salt and freshly ground black
   pepper
Water

Place the kidney beans in a pan and cover with the water. Bring to the boil, then turn down to a simmer. The beans will now settle in the pan. Now any impurities should be skimmed off. Now add all the other ingredients except the rice and coconut. The beans can now be left to simmer until they become tender, stirring occasionally. This will take 45–60 minutes. During this time the onions and other ingredients will have cooked to a purée and totally flavoured the beans.

Now it's time to add the block of coconut cream and cook for a few minutes until dissolved. Once dissolved, add the rice. There should still be sufficient water to cook the rice. Continue to simmer for 15–20 minutes, stirring occasionally. During this time, the rice will become tender and absorb the excess liquor. The rice will take on the flavour and a slightly pink colour from the kidney beans. Season with salt and pepper and serve.

Braised Rice

Using this recipe, you can make a simple braised rice or a spicy version flavoured with cloves, cinnamon and cardamom pods. Choose your stock to go with whatever dish you are serving.

SERVES 4–6

225 g (8 oz) basmati or patna rice,
   washed
1 tablespoon cooking oil
2 onions, finely chopped
Salt and freshly ground black pepper
450 ml (15 fl oz) Vegetable Stock (see
   p. 400), Chicken Stock (see p. 399),
   Fish Stock (see p. 399) or water
A knob of unsalted butter (optional)

FOR SPICY BRAISED RICE

2–3 cloves
$1/2$ cinnamon stick
1 garlic clove, crushed
5–6 cardamom pods
A few saffron strands (optional)
1 bay leaf

Pre-heat the oven to 200°C/400°F/gas 6.

Warm the cooking oil in a braising pan and add the chopped onion. If you are making the spicy version, then add all the other ingredients except the stock, otherwise just add the rice. Cook for a few minutes, until the onions have softened. Pour on the stock or water. Bring to a simmer, cover with greaseproof paper and a lid and place in the pre-heated oven. This should now be cooked for approximately 20–25 minutes, stirring occasionally to keep an even cooking. While the rice is cooking, check the stock. If the rice seems to be very dry, then simply add more stock or water to moisten. It is, however, important that the rice does absorb the stock and still have a very slight bite in texture. The rice when forked up will remain light and fluffy. If too much stock is used and the rice cooks too long it will become very heavy and stodgy. The maximum the rice will take is 30 minutes. Once cooked, season with salt and pepper and serve. A knob of butter can also be forked into the rice, to enrich the texture and taste.

The spicy rice should have the cinnamon, bay leaf and cloves removed before serving. To make this easier these can be tied in muslin before being added. The flavours will not spread quite so much but will still be detectable.

VARIATION

The rice eats very well if bound with the Soured Cream, Lime and Mint Yoghurt (see p. 385). Great as a vegetarian dish with grilled vegetables or spinach and toasted flaked almonds added to it.

Braised Nutty Rice

This dish has the same basic ingredients as the Braised Rice (see above) but also has plenty of extras that can be added. The addition of butter is what is going to give it the nutty taste. The butter will first be cooked to a nut-brown, bubbling stage before colouring the rice. I have only listed vegetable stock in this recipe because I prefer to keep this recipe vegetarian. If you prefer to use chicken or fish stock, you can use either.

SERVES 4–6

225 g (8 oz) basmati or patna rice,
 washed
75 g (3 oz) unsalted butter

1 onion, very finely chopped
450 ml (15 fl oz) Vegetable Stock
 (see p. 400)
Salt and freshly ground black pepper

Pre-heat the oven to 200°C/400°F/gas 6.

 Melt the butter in a braising pan and cook to a nut-brown stage. The butter at this stage will be bubbling and have a nutty colour and aroma. Add the rice immediately, before the butter becomes burnt. Now the rice should be cooked until it becomes a nut-brown colour. At this point, add the finely chopped onion and continue to cook for a few minutes. Now add the stock and bring to a simmer. Cover with greaseproof paper and a lid and cook in the oven for 20–25 minutes, until tender. During the cooking time, check the rice has sufficient stock. The rice should be cooked, absorbing the stock and still having a slight bite. The maximum time the rice will need to cook is 30 minutes. Once ready, season with salt and pepper and serve.

VARIATIONS

Extra flavours that can be added for a different taste and texture are: toasted chopped pine nuts; diced tomato flesh; chopped fresh coriander; a dash of Tabasco sauce. All these can be added together. I also like to beat 1–2 eggs and then add them at the last moment, to create a scrambled egg effect running through the braised rice.

Braised Lentils

Braised lentils can be used in so many dishes – fish or meat – and are perfect as an accompaniment to a main course or as a vegetable dish in their own right.

SERVES 4

50 g (2 oz) unsalted butter
1 carrot, finely diced
1 small onion, finely diced
2 celery sticks, finely diced
225 g (8 oz) lentils

1 piece of bacon trimming (optional)
900 ml (1 1/2 pints) Vegetable Stock
 (see p. 400) or Chicken Stock
 (see p. 399)
Salt and freshly ground black
 pepper

Pre-heat the oven to 200°C/400°F/gas 6.

 Melt the butter in a flameproof casserole and fry the finely diced vegetables for a few minutes. Add the lentils and bacon, if using, and fry for a further minute. Add about 600 ml (1 pint) of the stock, making sure the lentils are just covered with stock, and bring to a simmer. Cover with a lid and cook in the pre-heated oven for 30–40 minutes, stirring occasionally, until the lentils are tender. As the lentils cook, they will tenderize as they absorb the stock. You may need to add a little more stock during cooking.

You can serve the lentils straight away, or they can be cooled and chilled. They will keep in the fridge for two to three days and can be re-heated in a spoonful of stock or water with a knob of butter.

VARIATIONS

This recipe can also be made into lentil soup, by doubling the quantity of stock. Bacon is a good flavouring for lentils, so try adding a small dice or piece of bacon during cooking. If you've had a boiled bacon collar dish for lunch or dinner one day, then make sure that you keep all the stock it was cooked in and dice any leftover bacon. With some chopped vegetables, you'll have an almost instant lentil and bacon soup to put together.

Rich Sherry Lentils

Whether or not you are serving this with the Confit of Pork Belly (see p. 169), this dish is best served in a large soup plate or bowl. It tastes great with other rich meat dishes, too. Puy lentils are tiny green lentils which are available in most large supermarkets; there is no need to soak them before you start cooking.

SERVES 4
100–175 g (4–6 oz) Puy lentils
40 g (1¹/₂oz) unsalted butter
1 carrot, finely chopped
1 onion, finely chopped
2 celery sticks, finely chopped
1 small fennel bulb, finely chopped (optional)
2 tablespoons brandy

450–600 ml (15–20 fl oz) Chicken Stock (see p. 399) or Vegetable Stock (see p. 400)
2 tablespoons double cream (optional)
Salt and freshly ground black pepper
1 tablespoon sherry vinegar or more for a sharper taste
1 tablespoon chopped fresh flatleaf parsley

Pre-heat the oven to 200°C/400°F/gas 6 if you are cooking the dish in the oven.

Melt 15 g (¹/₂oz) of the butter and cook the chopped vegetables without colouring for 2 minutes. Add the lentils and brandy and boil to reduce until almost dry. Add 450 ml (15 fl oz) of the stock and bring to a simmer. Cover with a lid. The lentils can now be cooked on top of the stove or in the pre-heated oven for about 30 minutes, until they are tender. During the cooking time, you may need to add the remaining 150 ml (5 fl oz) of stock so that the finished lentils have a thick soup consistency.

To finish, add the remaining butter and the double cream, if using. Season with salt and pepper and add the sherry vinegar. The vinegar is added neat, without any reduction. It really lifts the flavour of the lentils. Finish with the chopped parsley and serve.

NOTE

Crème fraîche can be used in place of the double cream, to give a sharper taste.

Braised Split Peas

The classic dishes of Boiled Bacon (see p. 171 and 173) and Deep-fried Cod in Batter (see p. 93) go very well these braised peas. I also like to make Split Pea Fritters (see below) and serve them with Home-made Pork Sausages (see p. 170). This is similar technique to Braised Lentils (see p. 242).

SERVES 6–8

100 g (4 oz) carrots
2 celery sticks
2 onions
1 garlic clove, chopped
1 tablespoon olive oil

25 g (1 oz) unsalted butter
450 g (1 lb) dried split peas
About 900 ml (1¹/₂ pints) Vegetable
  Stock (see p. 400) or Chicken Stock
  (see p. 399)
Salt and freshly ground white pepper

Pre-heat the oven to 200°C/400°F/gas 6.

Cut the carrots, celery and onions into 5 mm (¹/₄ in) dice. Sweat with the garlic in the olive oil and butter for a few minutes in a flameproof casserole dish. Add the split peas and cook for 1–2 minutes, stirring. Cover with the stock and bring to the simmer. Cover and cook in the pre-heated oven for 20–25 minutes. The peas will need stirring during cooking, and, possibly, more stock will need to be added. After 30 minutes the peas should be ready, just starting to break and tender to eat. Season with salt and pepper before serving.

Split Pea Fritters

SERVES 4

100 g (4 oz) plain flour
A pinch of salt
1 egg
300 ml (10 fl oz) milk
1 tablespoon unsalted butter, melted

1 teaspoon chopped fresh parsley
8 tablespoons cold Braised Split Peas
  (see above)
Salt and freshly ground white
  pepper
2 tablespoons vegetable oil

Sieve the flour and salt into a bowl. Beat the egg with half the milk then fold the mixture into the flour. Gradually add more of the milk until the mixture is thick enough to coat the back of a spoon. Add the melted butter and chopped parsley.

The split peas must be cold. Slowly fold some of the batter into the peas until you have a thick pancake mix; not all the batter may be needed. Season with salt and pepper.

Heat a little oil in a 15 cm (6 in) pancake pan and pour in the batter to about 5 mm (¹/₄ in) thick. Fry until golden brown, then turn over in the pan and fry the other side. Keep warm while you make three more fritters.

Braised Butter Beans

Braised butter beans go well with many dishes, such as Confit of Duck (see p. 127).

SERVES 4

1 onion, chopped

2 smoked bacon rashers, rinded and
   cut into strips

1 tablespoon olive oil

1 tablespoon unsalted butter

1 garlic clove, crushed

8 fresh basil leaves, chopped

1 bay leaf

100 g (4 oz) dried butter beans

600–900 ml (1–1¹/₂ pints) Chicken Stock
   (see p. 399)

2 tomatoes, skinned, seeded and diced

Salt and freshly ground black pepper

TO SERVE

A few curly endive leaves

1 quantity Confit of Duck (Marinated
   Version, see p. 127)

2–3 tablespoons Basic Vinaigrette
   (see p. 379)

1 quantity Red Wine Sauce
   (see p. 368)

Pre-heat the oven to 180°C/350°F/gas 4.

Sweat the chopped onion and bacon in a flameproof dish in the olive oil and butter for a few minutes, then add the garlic, basil, bay leaf and butter beans. Cover with 600 ml (1 pint) of chicken stock and bring to the simmer. Cover and cook in the pre-heated oven for 1–1¹/₂ hours until the beans are tender; they may need a little more stock added during the cooking process.

When the beans are tender they will have created a thick sauce. Add the tomatoes, salt and pepper and spoon on to hot plates. Mix the curly endive with the vinaigrette and sit some on top of the beans. Finish with the hot, glazed duck confit and pour some red wine sauce around.

Braised Pearl Barley

Perfect with the Turkey Saltimbocca (see p. 132), and great with grilled meats.

SERVES 4

100 g (4 oz) pearl barley

1 large onion, finely chopped

15 g (¹/₂ oz) unsalted butter

600 ml (1 pint) Chicken Stock
   (see p. 399) or Vegetable Stock
   (see p. 400)

Salt and freshly ground black pepper

Pre-heat the oven to 200°C/400°F/gas 6.

In an ovenproof pan, soften the chopped onion in the butter. Add the pearl barley and cook for a further minute. Add the stock and bring to a simmer. Cover with a lid and transfer to the oven for about 30–40 minutes, stirring from time to time, until the barley becomes tender. Once cooked, remove from the oven. The barley can now be seasoned with salt and pepper and used immediately or left to cool and re-heated later in a pan or in the oven, with a little more stock or water.

Mustard Pearl Barley Risotto with Parsley Coulis

This dish will probably create a few raised eyebrows. After all, I've always stated that risotto can only be made with Arborio rice, and I still believe that.

It's unusual for me to use a cookery term that doesn't really apply. That's normally something that irritates me. So many chefs will put a navarin of lamb (a classic braised lamb dish) on the menu and, when you receive the dish, you find it's lamb fillet medallions with turned baby vegetables. A nice, well-presented dish but certainly not a navarin.

So do I have a better excuse? No, is the answer. I'm basically calling it a risotto because this dish is being finished in a similar way; extra stock and butter being added to give a creamy texture. Once you've tried it you'll know exactly what I mean: the tender, soft barley bound with the creamy stock is so good to eat. It also has, as for risotto, almost unlimited variations. Any of my risotto recipes will work so well with this recipe.

I like to serve this with main-course fish or meat dishes: this creamy risotto with either grilled fillet or chunks of salmon running through it are a delight to eat. Chicken is also a perfect meat to go with this, whether it be a plain roast accompanied by a large bowl of savoury thyme barley risotto, or chicken escalopes cooked on a barbecue, or simple chicken breasts. All work very well.

The basic recipe is made with vegetable stock, but fish and chicken stocks can be used; it really depends on what you are serving with the dish. The mustard I'm using is Dijon enhanced with the Mustard Dressing (see p. 382). Another good mustard to use is a grain mustard such as Meaux mustard.

This pearl barley dish also eats very well cold, loosened with Basic Vinaigrette (see p. 379). Many other flavours can be added: peas, tomatoes, spring onions, olives – endless combinations. If you want to serve the dish as a starter or side dish, you can halve the quantities.

The parsley coulis couldn't be more basic, with so few ingredients, but has so much flavour, with the strength of continental parsley coming through. It keeps very well chilled for a few days. It can also be served with many dishes: rice or barley risottos, pasta dishes and salad dressings.

SERVES 4–6

225 g (8 oz) pearl barley

1.2–1.5 litres (2–2^1/$_2$ pints) Vegetable Stock (see p. 400)

2 tablespoons olive oil

2 large onions, finely chopped

2 tablespoons Dijon mustard

50 g (2 oz) unsalted butter

4–6 tablespoons Mustard Dressing (see p. 382)

Salt and freshly ground black pepper

FOR THE PARSLEY COULIS

1 large bunch of fresh flatleaf parsley, about 40 g (1^1/$_2$ oz)

2 tablespoons ice-cold water

4 tablespoons olive oil

To make the coulis, very quickly blanch the parsley in boiling water and immediately refresh in cold water. Squeeze out the excess water and blitz in a liquidizer with the 2 tablespoons of ice-cold water. Slowly add the olive oil until totally blended in. Season the coulis with salt and pepper, then strain through a very fine sieve. This will leave you with a rich green parsley coulis with a coating consistency. This can now be kept in a bottle or bowl and chilled until needed. You will have about 150 ml (5 fl oz) of coulis.

Pre-heat the oven to 200°C/400°F/gas 6.

Warm the olive oil in an ovenproof braising pan and add the chopped onions. Cook over a medium heat, without colouring, until softened. Add the pearl barley and mustard and continue to cook for a few minutes. Add 900 ml (1½ pints) of the vegetable stock and bring to a simmer. Cover with greaseproof paper and a lid and cook in the pre-heated oven for 40–45 minutes, for a very soft, almost souffléd finish. After 20–25 minutes, check the barley. It may need another 300 ml (10 fl oz) of stock to finish the cooking.

Once tender, add the butter and the mustard dressing. You may find a little more mustard dressing or Dijon mustard is needed to give a stronger taste. Loosen the barley with more stock to give a creamy consistency. Adjust the seasoning with salt and pepper and serve in bowls, with the parsley coulis drizzled over the top.

Yorkshire Puddings

Served with roast beef, these must be the most famous of all our Great British dishes. A good basic Yorkshire pudding eats so well with a rich gravy, and these are perfect for that traditional lunch, served as individual puddings or larger puddings.

But why stop there? Yorkshire puddings can also have so many variations. The pudding mix itself can be flavoured with mustard, horseradish, fresh herbs and many other flavours. It really depends on what you want to serve them with. My favourite is a rich Onion Gravy (see p. 367). Another great classic is to make Toad in the Hole. This is, of course, sausages that have first been fried to give a golden brown colour and then baked in the Yorkshire batter. These can be made in one large tray or cooked in individual flan cases.

I also like to make the 'complete roast' as a starter in individual Yorkshire puddings. With this, I use sautéd or pan-fried potatoes, black pudding, pieces of sausage and peas. Sit all these in the moulds and just pour the batter over. Bake in a pre-heated oven at 200°C/400°F/gas 6 and, in 20–25 minutes' time, you have an almost complete meal. I like to serve these as a starter with a drop of the onion gravy.

Yorkshire puddings also eat very well with fish. For this I add the grated zest of 1 or 2 lemons to the batter, along with some roughly chopped parsley. Cook them in the normal way and then serve them with roast cod, turbot or salmon with Fish Gravy (see p. 98) and you have a real Alternative Great British Dish.

Another favourite of mine is to serve Yorkshire puddings with curry – does that sound odd? Well, they eat almost like a home-made naan bread, but with a lighter texture. All you need to do is add the grated zest of 2 limes and about 2 tablespoons of chopped fresh coriander; a pinch of curry powder can also be added to fire them up, perhaps make your own by mixing a pinch of turmeric with ground ginger, coriander and chilli. Once baked, serve them with Soured Cream, Lime and Mint Yoghurt (see p. 385). I can promise you they eat very well and create a lot of fun when you've cooked a home-made curry and rice for friends and then you bring a tray of Yorkshire puddings and sit them on the table. They certainly provide a good talking point. But just imagine when you break a piece of Yorkshire pudding, dip it into your curry and then spoon the soured cream on top – I told you it works.

But I still haven't finished with ideas for this recipe. Yorkshire puddings also eat very well as sweets. Golden syrup can be added to the mix to give a rich batter. Once cooked, trickle more syrup over and serve with fresh cream or Vanilla Ice-cream (see p. 252). Or sweeten the batter by adding 25 g (1 oz) of caster or icing sugar, bake as individual cooked puds and serve with fresh cream. Serve with poached pears and Rich Chocolate Sauce (see p. 336), or apples with honey or golden syrup. They also eat very well if baked to an almost burnt edge on top. Garnish with the fruit of your choice and dust heavily with icing sugar to give a bitter-sweet taste.

Here's one more idea: how about Yorkshire Pudding 'Suzette', finishing the dish as you would for Crêpes Suzette – with reduced orange juice with caramelized caster sugar, Grand Marnier and maybe even a touch of brandy? Warm fresh orange segments in the sauce, spoon it over the puddings and serve the dish with clotted cream.

So the next time you're having a dinner party tell your friends it's Yorkshire pudding for pudding.

MAKES 8 × 10 cm (4 in) PUDDINGS

225 g (8 oz) plain flour
A pinch of salt
3 eggs
1 egg white (optional)
300–450 ml (10–15 fl oz) milk
Oil, lard or dripping, for cooking

Pre-heat the oven to 220°C/425°F/gas 7. Oil eight 10 cm (4 in) moulds or larger moulds and pre-heat in the oven until almost smoking.

Sift the flour with the salt. Add the eggs and egg white, if using. The egg white gives extra lift to the batter. Whisk in 300 ml (10 fl oz) of milk. This will give you a thick batter which works very well. To check the consistency, simply lift a spoon in and out. The batter should hold and coat the back of the spoon. If it seems to have congealed, then simply add the remaining milk. The batter is now ready to cook. It can be made up to 24 hours in advance and will still rise.

Once the fat in the moulds is almost smoking, it's time to add the butter. Bake individual puddings in the pre-heated oven for 20–25 minutes and large ones for 40–45 minutes.

Buttered Spetzli with Leeks

What are spetzli? Well, really, they're just simple little dumplings. They can be served with stews and casseroles, or just as a vegetable dish, and they go particularly well with the Marinated Lamb Chumps on p. 151.

SERVES 4
350 g (12 oz) plain flour
4 eggs
1 egg yolk
2 tablespoons double cream or milk
Salt and freshly ground white pepper
Freshly grated nutmeg

TO SERVE
50 g (2 oz) unsalted butter
1 tablespoon olive oil
225 g (8 oz) leeks, finely shredded
   (optional)

Place the flour in a bowl and make a well in the centre. Add all the other spetzli ingredients and carefully mix in. When all is mixed together, beat with a wooden spoon to make the mixture a little lighter. It is ready when it comes away from the sides of the bowl.

To cook, fill a pan with salted water and bring to the boil. The spetzli can now be scraped into the water from a chopping board in small walnut-sized pieces. When these rise to the top, remove with a slotted spoon and refresh in cold water. It is best to cook them in batches of about ten or twelve.

To serve, drain the spetzli and dry them off. Melt the butter with the olive oil and fry the shredded leeks, if using, for a couple of minutes. Add the spetzli and warm through for a few minutes, then season with salt and pepper.

Puddings

ICE-CREAMS, SORBETS AND FROZEN DISHES

Ice-creams

These recipes could just go on and on – there are so many different ice-creams and sorbets. They all eat well as puddings on their own or as accompaniments for other dishes.

Most of these recipes are derivatives of a basic vanilla ice-cream. In the vanilla recipe, a vanilla pod is used. This gives the ice-cream a real vanilla taste and when split and scraped leaves a black speckled finish to the cream. This can be substituted by using a few drops of strong vanilla essence or if you keep some caster sugar in an airtight container with a vanilla pod the vanilla aroma and flavour will stay with the sugar.

In most of the other ice-cream recipes, I suggest that you leave out the vanilla. The quantity of ingredients given in the basic vanilla recipe can, of course, be halved and all the other recipes can follow suit.

Fruit-based ice-creams are best made with a Fruit Coulis (see p. 356) and then loosened with 150 ml (5 fl oz) of Stock Syrup (see p. 397) and creamed with 3 heaped tablespoons of crème fraîche. They're very quick and easy to make. All you have to do then is put them through the ice-cream machine.

If you don't have an ice-cream machine, the mix can be left in a bowl and placed in the freezer, making sure it is stirred every 10–15 minutes until set.

If you're in a real hurry, there are a few short-cuts you can try for any of the recipes. You can buy a good quality vanilla ice-cream and add the other flavours so it's almost home-made or replace the vanilla ice-cream base with tinned custard using 600 ml (1 pint) for the equivalent recipe; tinned custards work really well as a base for ice-creams. If it tastes a little too rich and thick, add some milk or single cream to loosen the flavour and texture. Crème fraîche is French fresh cream, and is now available in most supermarkets. It is cream that has been treated with a special culture which gives it a longer life and an almost sour taste. It works very well in ice-creams, giving a full body to the taste.

Crème Fraîche Ice-cream

Using crème fraîche in any ice-cream really lifts the taste of other flavours. But using it as a main flavouring gives a basic vanilla ice-cream a really good bite. For every 300 ml (10 fl oz) of Vanilla Ice-cream (see p. 252) you will need to add at least

150 ml (5 fl oz) of crème fraîche while the mixture is still liquid. This will give quite a strong taste. After that it's really up to you. If you want it stronger, simply start to add a spoonful at a time until you have the flavour you want. To make the flavour a little sharper, then also add 1 tablespoon of natural yoghurt to the mix.

The other alternative is to mix a tin of custard with 150ml (5 fl oz) of crème fraîche and you have instant ice-cream mix.

Vanilla Ice-cream

This is the base ice-cream, which you can vary in an infinite number of ways.

SERVES 4–8

300 ml (10 fl oz) double cream
300 ml (10 fl oz) milk
1 vanilla pod or a few drops of vanilla essence

6 egg yolks
175 g (6 oz) caster sugar

Mix together the cream and milk in a pan. Split the vanilla pod lengthways and scrape the insides into the milk and cream, then add the scraped pod. Bring to the boil.

Meanwhile, beat the egg yolks and sugar together until pale and light. This canbe done in a food mixer. Pour on the milk and cream, stirring all the time until well blended. Stir from time to time until the ice-cream mix has cooled. Remove the vanilla pod.

Once cooled, the mix is ready to be churned in the ice-cream maker. If you have made the full recipe, you'll need to churn it in two batches. Pour the mix into the machine and begin to turn. The ice-cream will take about 20–30 minutes and will have thickened and increased in volume. Don't leave the mix turning until completely frozen and set as this will be over-churned and slightly grainy in texture. Take out when thick and starting to freeze and then finish in the freezer. This will a lovely silky smooth texture.

If you don't have an ice-cream machine, simply turn the mixture into a freezer tray or bowl and freeze, turning regularly until set.

Liquorice Ripple Ice-cream

SERVES 4–8

Melt down 100 g (4 oz) of Pontefract liquorice cakes in a small pan with 150 ml (5 fl oz) of water, stirring occasionally until smooth. Leave to cool a little, then pour into one quantity of Vanilla Ice-cream (see above) at the last turn or two. This will give you white ice-cream with lines of black liquorice running through, perfect for serving with Black Treacle Pudding (see p. 327).

Soft Fruit Ice-cream

This is a simple recipe which uses a stock syrup (also used in sorbet-making).

SERVES 4–6
300 ml (10 fl oz) fruit purée (strawberry,
   raspberry, mango, etc.)
1–2 heaped tablespoons crème
   fraîche

FOR THE STOCK SYRUP
300 ml (10 fl oz) water
225 g (8 oz) caster sugar, flavoured
   with vanilla (see left)
1 tablespoon liquid glucose (optional)

To make the stock syrup, simply bring all the ingredients to the boil and cook for 2–3 minutes. This will leave you with a thick, sweet syrup. Leave until cold.

To make the fruit ice, mix the fruit purée with the cold stock syrup and add the crème fraîche. The mix is now ready to freeze, either in a machine or freezer, churning by hand every now and again.

VARIATION

The easy alternative is simply to take a tin of almost any fruit – peaches, pears, blackberries or whatever – and purée the contents in their own syrup. Add some icing sugar to increase the sweetness, then add 2–3 heaped tablespoons of crème fraîche. Now you have a quick and easy ice-cream, just churn it in the machine and it's ready.

Strawberry or Raspberry Ripple Ice-creams

These are lovely, home-made ripple ices that make a delicious pudding served in a Tuile Biscuit basket with fresh cream or Custard Sauce (see p. 337). The ice-cream has a wonderful flavour with the tartness of the raspberry or strawberry to excite your tastebuds. The quantities to follow are two-thirds ice-cream to one-third fruit, so whatever amount you want, if you follow these guidelines it will always work. This ice-cream also works very well in an Arctic Roll (see p. 267 and 268).

SERVES 4–8
450 ml (5 fl oz) Vanilla Ice-cream
   (see p. 252)

150 ml (5 fl oz) Raspberry or Strawberry
   Coulis (see p. 338)

Make the ice-cream, churn the mixture and place in a freezer container. Spoon the coulis on top and then lightly fold the coulis into the ice-cream. This will give you red streaks through the ice-cream. Set in the freezer.

Banana Ice-cream

Try this ice-cream with Chocolate Sauce (see p. 336) and warm pancakes (see p. 302).

SERVES 4–8
1 quantity Vanilla Ice-cream
  (see p. 252)
225 g (8 oz) peeled ripe bananas

A few drops of lemon juice
1–2 tablespoons banana liqueur
  (optional)

First you need to make the vanilla ice-cream base. Once made and still warm, peel and chop the bananas and toss them in the lemon juice to help them keep their colour. Then add them to the base. This can now be blitzed in a food processor and then pushed through a sieve. Stir in the liqueur, if using. The ice-cream can now be finished in an ice-cream machine, then frozen.

Toffee Ice-cream

Here's another use for my simple toffee mix (see p. 362).

SERVES 4–8
600 ml (1 pint) Vanilla Ice-cream (see
  p. 252)

1 × 400 g (14 oz) tin of toffee
  (see p. 362)

Follow the recipe for vanilla ice-cream, stirring in the toffee once you have made the custard. Turn the mix in an ice-cream machine.

Marmalade Ice-cream

This ice-cream is rich, tasty and wonderful. It goes really well with Steamed Orange Sponge (see p. 309) or Steamed Chocolate Sponge (see p. 319). It's best to buy a good-quality, coarse marmalade to give a strong orange taste.

SERVES 6–8
1 quantity Vanilla Ice-cream
  (see p. 252), made without the
  vanilla pod

1 × 350 g (12 oz) jar of coarse
  marmalade

Follow the recipe for vanilla ice-cream. Stir the boiled cream and milk into the egg yolks and sugar, then add the marmalade and then continue to follow the method.

Lemon Curd Ice-cream

This ice-cream is lovely and rich and eats beautifully as a pudding on its own or as an extra for a Steamed Lemon Sponge (see p. 331). The ice-cream also works very well if you substitute a jar of lemon curd for the fresh lemon curd.

SERVES 4–6
1 quantity Lemon Curd (see p. 363) or
   1 × 350 g (12 oz) jar of lemon curd

2 large tablespoons crème fraîche
1 large tablespoon natural
   yoghurt

Mix the cooled lemon curd with the crème fraîche and yoghurt and churn into ice-cream. It's as simple as that.

Maple Syrup and Pecan Nut Ice-cream

You need to make the base with less sugar so that the maple syrup does not make the ice-cream too rich.

SERVES 6–8
1 quantity Vanilla Ice-cream (see p.
   252), using only 75 g (3 oz) of caster
   sugar (vanilla pod optional)

300 g (11 oz) maple syrup
50–75 g (2–3 oz) pecan nuts,
   chopped

Follow the recipe and method of the vanilla ice-cream, using half the sugar quantity. This will allow the sweetness of the maple syrup to work without becoming over-rich. Once the vanilla base is made and cooled, add the maple syrup and begin to churn the ice-cream. The pecan nuts should only be added to the mix during the last few minutes of churning. If they are added too early, the nuts will break down and also discolour the cream.

Honey and Whisky Ice-cream

It is up to you how much whisky you like to add to this dessert – I use about two measures.

SERVES 4–8
1 quantity Vanilla Ice-cream
   (see p. 252) made without caster
   sugar (vanilla pod optional)

350 g (12 oz) jar of clear honey
Whisky to taste

This is really easy to make. Mix the honey with the egg yolks from the vanilla recipe and beat them together. Follow the method, adding the whisky to taste before turning.

Ovaltine Ice-cream

This is a very rich ice-cream that doesn't really need anything to go with it – perhaps a shortbread or Maple Syrup and Walnut Biscuit (p. 349) will be enough. I've also added some milk chocolate to enrich it even more, giving a fuller consistency to the finished dish. You will notice there is no sugar in this recipe. This is due to the sweetness of the Ovaltine and milk chocolate.

MAKES 900 ml (1¹/₂ pints)
300 ml (10 fl oz) milk
300 ml (10 fl oz) double cream
100 g (4 oz) Ovaltine powder

175 g (6 oz) milk chocolate, grated
6 egg yolks
2–3 measures Irish whiskey, 50–120 ml
   (2–4 fl oz) (optional)

Bring the milk and cream to the boil and whisk on to the Ovaltine. Add the milk chocolate and stir until melted. This mix can now be whisked on to the egg yolks and allowed to cool before finishing in the ice-cream machine. The Irish whiskey can be added before churning to give a richer flavour to the ice-cream.

I like to serve this ice-cream in a large mug with biscuits on the side, just as you would the drink.

Turkish Delight Ice-cream

This recipe is for a basic vanilla ice-cream, replacing the vanilla with rose-water to create that familiar Turkish Delight flavour. Of course, you're still going to need some diced Turkish Delight to finish the recipe and give the right texture to the dish. You can either make it (see p. 361) or buy some, dice it and add it at the last moment.

SERVES 4–8
300 ml (10 fl oz) milk
300 ml (10 fl oz) double cream
I–2 tablespoons rose-water

6 egg yolks
175 g (6 oz) caster sugar
175–225 g (6–8 oz) Turkish Delight
   (see p. 343) or bought

Mix together the milk and cream and flavour with the rose-water. It's best to add 1 tablespoon, then taste before adding more, to give you the full depth of flavour. Bring to the boil. While the cream mix is coming to the boil, beat together the egg yolks and sugar until pale. Pour the boiled cream on to the egg yolks and sugar, whisking until well blended. Leave to cool. Once cold, this can be churned in an ice-cream machine, or frozen in a freezer tray, whisking every 30 minutes or so until set.

Dice the Turkish Delight and add to the ice-cream at the last 2–3 turns. The Turkish Delight Ice-cream is now ready to freeze and eat.

This recipe works very well with Rich Chocolate Sauce (see p. 354) added, also at the end and not completely mixed in. This will give you a Turkish Delight and Chocolate Ripple Ice-cream. Or simply serve with warm or cold sauce poured over.

Tutti-frutti Ice-cream

This is a really fun ice-cream to make. I simply add a selection of glacé fruits, raisins, cherries and angelica to the vanilla ice-cream, keeping in the vanilla for extra flavour.

You can buy a mixed tub of glacé fruits, or buy them loose to choose your own. This really isn't important, although I'm amazed at the variety of fruits that can be bought crystallized; strawberries, melon, plums, damsons, greengages are just a few examples.

SERVES 4–8

1 quantity Vanilla Ice-cream (see p. 252)

175–225 g (6–8 oz) glacé fruits, including raisins and angelica

The fruits should first be cut into pieces. To maximize the taste, all the fruits can be added once the ice-cream mix is cold. They can then be churned with the mix, which will help flavour the complete custard.

VARIATION

This recipe also works very well mixed with Lemon Curd Ice-cream. Make some by mixing 1 × 350 g (12 oz) jar of lemon curd with 2 tablespoons of crème fraîche and 1 tablespoon of natural yoghurt. All you need to do now is add the fruits and churn into ice-cream. You will have about 400 ml (14 fl oz) of ice-cream.

Coconut Ice-cream

This ice-cream can take on loads of combinations. It can be coated in chocolate, almost like making your own 'taste of paradise', mixed with chopped pineapple, made into a Piña Colada pudding, or even served with Pineapple Fritters (see p. 299) and Chocolate Sauce (see p. 354). If you don't have a fresh coconut, just replace it with 50 g (2 oz) of unsweetened desiccated coconut.

SERVES 4–8

1/4 fresh coconut
175 ml (6 fl oz) double cream
250 ml (8 fl oz) milk

100 g (4 oz) caster sugar
5 egg yolks
200 ml (7 fl oz) coconut milk

Crack the coconut and peel off a quarter of the white coconut flesh. Chop the flesh finely and mix with the cream and milk. Bring to the boil. While the milk mix is coming to the boil, whisk the sugar and egg yolks together in a large bowl until pale and light. Pour over the boiling milk, then place the bowl over a pan of hot water and stir until thickened. Blitz in a blender until the coconut is shredded, then leave to cool. Add the coconut milk and churn in the ice-cream machine until beginning to freeze, then turn into a freezer container and freeze until firm.

If you don't have an ice-cream maker, pour the mix on to a tray and set in the freezer, turning from time to time until frozen.

Chocolate Ice-cream

This is a delicious ice-cream with lots of very adult alternatives.

SERVES 4–8

1 quantity Vanilla Ice-cream (see p. 252) made with 100 g (4 oz) caster sugar and without the vanilla pod

175 g (6 oz) good-quality plain chocolate, grated

Follow the vanilla base recipe using only 100 g (4 oz) of caster sugar. Once the milk and cream have been brought to the boil, pour on to the grated chocolate and stir. This will melt the chocolate. Taste before churning to check the chocolate flavour is strong enough. Continue with the basic recipe.

VARIATIONS

This ice-cream has many alternatives.

1 Add some rum to taste.
2 Add some Cointreau or Grand Marnier to taste.
3 Add 2–3 tablespoons of marmalade for chocolate and orange ice-cream (and maybe a little Cointreau too).
4 Add some broken Honeycomb (see p. 363) just at the end of churning.

White Chocolate Ice-cream

The same quantity of plain or milk chocolate can be used with this recipe to make the flavour of your choice.

SERVES 4–8

1 quantity Vanilla Ice-cream (see p. 252), made with 100 g (4 oz) caster sugar and without the vanilla pod

175–225 g (6–8 oz) white chocolate, grated

Follow the vanilla ice-cream recipe, using just 100 g (4 oz) of caster sugar. Once the milk and cream are at boiling point, add 175 g (6 oz) of the grated chocolate. This should now be tasted for strength. If more is needed, then add the remaining 50 g (2 oz) and continue as for the vanilla recipe.

VARIATIONS

This recipe also works very well with 50 g (2 oz) of desiccated coconut added at the same time, to give a rich white chocolate and coconut ice-cream. To make it even richer, serve it with the Chocolate Sabayon (see p. 340). With or without the coconut, this ice-cream also goes very well with the Chocolate Scotch Pancakes (see p. 316).

Another great chocolate ice-cream – whether it be dark, milk or white – is with Turkish Delight added. The Turkish Delight recipe (see p. 361) can be followed or simply buy some to dice and add to the mix at the end of the recipe.

This recipe can also be made into Chocolate Ripple Ice-cream by simply pouring in the Rich Chocolate Sauce (see p. 354) at the last turn or two. This will give you white chocolate creamy ice-cream with lines of dark chocolate running through.

To make Chocolate and Marshmallow Ice-cream, make the chocolate ice-cream with milk, plain or white chocolate. Cut some marshmallows into small pieces. To keep it separate, spoon some cold ice-cream mix on to the marshmallow. Churn the chocolate ice-cream, adding the marshmallow pieces at the end, not allowing the pieces to break down but instead keeping their texture mixed into the ice-cream. Once frozen and set, the chocolate ice-cream has small white toffee-like marshmallow pieces to make it even more exciting.

And here's just one more variation: add a few tablespoons of the Cherry Jam (see p. 341) to give a rich chocolate ice-cream with a cherry jam ripple.

Milk or Plain Chocolate Fruit and Nut Ice-cream

As it is one of my old favourite chocolate bars, it seemed a great idea to turn fruit and nut into an ice-cream. I've simply made a chocolate ice-cream using 175–225 g (6–8 oz) of plain or milk chocolate. The nuts are a mix of hazelnuts and almonds, both lightly toasted to improve and release more flavour.

SERVES 4–8

1 quantity Vanilla Ice-cream (see p. 252), made with 100 g (4 oz) caster sugar and without the vanilla pod
175–225 g (8 oz) milk or plain chocolate, grated

100 g (4 oz) raisins
Brandy (optional)
50 g (2 oz) hazelnuts, toasted and chopped
50 g (2 oz) almonds, toasted and chopped

**FOR THE STOCK SYRUP
(OPTIONAL)
100 g (4 oz) caster sugar**

**150 ml (5 fl oz) water
Brandy or liqueur
(optional)**

The raisins can be left as they are or soaked in just enough neat brandy to cover, or in a stock syrup made by boiling the sugar and water until thickened. The stock syrup can, of course, be flavoured to taste with brandy or another liqueur.

To make the ice-cream, follow the White Chocolate Ice-cream recipe (see p. 258). Once the milk and cream have come to the boil add the grated chocolate to melt. Now complete the recipe as for vanilla ice-cream (see p. 252). Towards the last 2–3 minutes, the raisins and nuts can be added. This obviously changes the texture and taste of the ice-cream. It will become even richer if topped with the Rich Chocolate Sauce (see p. 354).

Iced Chocolate Parfait

Sweet parfaits are like freezing a sweet sabayon. They take on a light ice-cream texture. The quantities here will fill a 25 cm (10 in) terrine mould, or you can use individual ramekins. The ingredients may look a little costly, but remember there are quite a lot of portions in a terrine – or you can simply make half the recipe. Serve the parfait as it is or with the Rich Chocolate Sauce (see p. 354), Orange Custard Sauce or Coffee Custard Sauce (see pp. 355–356). Of course, if you really want to finish this pudding with a little extra, then cover it with Chocolate Coating (see p. 280). This gives the parfait a lovely finish and another texture.

**SERVES 8
7 egg yolks
100 g (4 oz) caster sugar**

**175 g (6 oz) good-quality plain
chocolate
600 ml (1 pint) double cream**

Line a 25 cm (10 in) terrine with cling film.

Whisk the egg yolks and sugar in a bowl over warm water until thick and at least doubled in volume. Melt the chocolate in a bowl over a pan of hot water, then mix with the yolks and sugar. Pour on the double cream and whisk until a soft-peak stage is reached. The parfait is ready to freeze in the terrine or in individual moulds.

NOTE

The double cream can be whisked separately to soft peaks and then lightly folded with the chocolate mix.

Iced Cranachan Parfait

This is a Scottish recipe which is traditionally served at Hallowe'en, with soft red berries. It can also be made into an ice-cream by replacing the cream with Vanilla Ice-cream (see p. 252), but this is an iced terrine which eats well with a drizzle of honey, or Melba Sauce (see p. 361) and fresh raspberries.

This recipe is for a 25 cm (10 in) terrine mould, but you can halve the quantities and use four individual ramekins.

SERVES 4
225 g (8 oz) caster sugar
8 egg yolk
600 ml (1 pint) double cream

4 teaspoons clear honey
175–225 g (8 oz) oatmeal, toasted
Whisky, to taste (optional)
Clear honey, to serve

Whisk the egg yolks and sugar until pale and the mixture trails off the whisk in thick ribbons. (This is easier if you place the bowl over a pan of warm water.) Pour on the cream and continue to whisk (cold) until the cream begins to thicken. Fold in the honey, toasted oatmeal and whisky to taste. Pour into the terrine or individual moulds and freeze until firm.

The cranachan can now be sliced and served.

Christmas Pudding Parfait

This recipe has been designed to help you use up that half pudding we all have left after Christmas lunch – making it the perfect dish for New Year's Eve. As an extra advantage if you have guests, the pudding can, of course, be made a day or two in advance. The parfait can be made and moulded in a terrine mould or poured into individual ramekins – either looks really good. Serve the individual soufflés, or a couple of slices from the larger parfait on a plate. Dust around the outside with icing sugar and cinnamon and maybe decorate with a sprig of holly or some chocolate shavings to finish. You could even trickle a little maple syrup over the top – how does that sound? I'm also giving you a recipe for Rum or Cognac Sabayon, which goes very well with both versions. This needs to be made and served at the last minute.

SERVES 6–8
6 egg yolks
175 g (6 oz) caster sugar
350 g (12 oz) Christmas Pudding (see p. 328), chopped into small dice
450 ml (15 fl oz) double cream
4 egg whites

FOR THE RUM OR COGNAC SABAYON
2–3 egg yolks
50–75 g (2–3 oz) caster sugar
2–3 tablespoons rum or cognac

Line a 900 g (2 lb) terrine mould or loaf tin with greaseproof paper to make the parfait easier to turn out. Alternatively, tie a collar of greaseproof paper around the outside of eight 150 ml (5 fl oz) ramekin dishes with string or elastic bands.

To make the parfait, whisk together the egg yolks and sugar over a pan of warm water until the mix trails off the whisk in thick ribbons. Lightly whisk in the Christmas pudding, then leave to cool. Lightly whip the cream and fold into the cold Christmas pudding mix. Whisk the egg whites until they form stiff peaks, then fold into the mix. The parfait can now be poured into the prepared mould or ramekins and set in the freezer. The parfait will take a few hours to freeze.

To make the sabayon, mix all the ingredients together in a bowl sitting on a pan of hot water until the mix trails off the whisk in thick, light ribbons. The sabayon should almost hold a peak.

Now all you have to do is spoon some on to plates with the parfait, or serve it separately with the soufflés.

Christmas Pudding Ice-cream

This is a great Christmas pudding alternative to surprise your guests. It eats really well on its own or as an accompaniment to a tart or flan. The other great way to use this recipe is to make it from your leftover pudding, turning it into a new dish.

For this recipe I'm using a home-made custard as the base, but here is a quick and simple alternative: if you buy a 450 g (1 lb) Christmas pudding and just chop it all up, then stir it into two tins of ready-made custard you have an instant mix for Christmas Pudding Ice-cream. It can be as simple as that.

SERVES 4–8
450 g (1 lb) Christmas pudding

1.2 litres (2 pints) Custard Sauce
(see p. 355)

The Christmas pudding can be used straight from the packet. All you need to do is simply cut the pudding into slices and then into small rough dice. If you are using the leftovers from Christmas lunch, then just break it down into crumble pieces. Now all you have to do is stir in the custard and mix for a minute or two. Pour some of the mix into an ice-cream machine (making sure the Christmas pudding pieces are equally distributed) and allow to turn. Once the cream has started to thicken and cream, turn the ice-cream out and finish setting in the freezer. If you overturn the ice-cream it will break down the pudding and become darker and slightly bitter in taste. Repeat the same process for the remaining mix.

To re-create the pudding theme and shape, just set the ice-cream in a pudding basin and freeze. Once turned out, you have a Christmas pudding with a difference. I also like to pour maple syrup over the top to enrich it even more.

If you don't have an ice-cream maker, pour the mix on to a tray and set in the freezer, turning from time to time until frozen. The ice-cream doesn't quite have the full volume or texture but still tastes good.

Iced Neapolitan Parfait

Neapolitan Ice-cream was always a favourite of mine. Knowing that you had chocolate, strawberry and vanilla ice-creams all in one slice, it had to be a favourite. The recipes for all those flavoured ice-creams are featured on pp. 258, 253 and 252, so the classic ice-cream terrine can easily be made by following those. This recipe is going to give you a much lighter finish.

Sweet parfait use more or less the same ingredients as ice-creams – egg yolks, cream and flavouring – but instead of heating the cream or milk and adding it to the egg yolk mix, the eggs and sugar are whipped to a light sabayon before adding those flavourings (chocolate, strawberry, etc.) and then folding in the whipped cream.

This dish may also look hard work with three separate recipes, but each layer has to begin freezing before topping with the next layer, so really there's no choice, each has to be made individually. I like to make Neapolitan with the strawberry on top followed by the vanilla and then the chocolate so, if you are making this in a terrine mould or loaf tin, the strawberry will have to be made first. Then, when you turn out the parfait, the strawberry layer is sitting on the top.

SERVES 8–10

FOR THE STRAWBERRY PARFAIT
100 g (4 oz) strawberries, chopped
2 tablespoons strawberry jam
2 tablespoons water
2 egg yolks
25 g (1 oz) caster sugar
150 ml (5 fl oz) double cream

FOR THE VANILLA PARFAIT MIX
50 g (2 oz) caster sugar

2 egg yolks
1 vanilla pod or 2–3 drops of vanilla essence
150 ml (5 fl oz) double cream

FOR THE CHOCOLATE PARFAIT MIX
50 g (2 oz) plain chocolate
2 egg yolks
25 g (1 oz) caster sugar
150 ml (5 fl oz) double cream

Line a 1.2-litre (2-pint) terrine mould or loaf tin with cling film or greaseproof paper.

To make a strawberry coulis, mix the strawberry jam with the water and strawberries. Warm to break down the strawberries, then purée. Alternatively, you can simply purée 225 g (8 oz) of fresh, frozen or tinned strawberries with 2 teaspoons of icing sugar.

Whisk the egg yolks and sugar in a bowl over a pan of hot water until doubled in volume, then remove from the heat and whisk in the cold strawberry purée. This will immediately reduce the temperature. The cream can now be either whipped and folded in or added and re-whisked until the mix trails off the whisk in ribbons. The strawberry parfait mix can now be spooned into the terrine and set to freeze for at least 1 hour.

To make the vanilla parfait, cut and scrape the vanilla pod and mix with the sugar and egg yolks or add the essence to the sugar and egg yolks. Whisk in a bowl over a pan of hot water until doubled in volume, continue to whisk until cool, then whisk in the cream as for the strawberry recipe. Spoon into the terrine on top of the strawberry parfait and return to the freezer for at least a further 1 hour.

To make the chocolate parfait, whisk together the caster sugar and egg yolks in a bowl over a pan of warm water until at least doubled in volume. While whisking, the chocolate can be carefully melted in a separate bowl over a pan of hot water.

Once the sabayon is made, remove the pan from the warm water and whisk in the chocolate. This can now be either continually whisked by hand or machine, adding the double cream. This will cool the sabayon. Simply continue to whisk until the cream begins to thicken. Once the mix has reached a lightly whipped cream stage, it's ready to set and freeze in the terrine. Any excess mix can be frozen in ramekins, glasses or moulds.

Another method to finish the sabayon mix is to simply whip the cream separately, then fold in to the cooled sabayon. Pour into the terrine. To complete a total freezing of the parfait it's best left for a minimum 2–3 hours before serving.

Once set and frozen, the terrine can be turned out on to a small board (this may need to be lightly warmed under hot water) and the cling film or greaseproof removed. The presentation of the dish speaks for itself, a good slice showing the three very distinctive flavours doesn't need any help at all.

VARIATIONS

This parfait mix can be even lighter. Simply whisk the egg whites from the egg yolks in each recipe to a peak stage and fold into the mix after the cream has been added. The finished flavour will not be quite as rich, but the texture will be lighter.

For an instant strawberry coulis, simply purée 100–225 g (4–8 oz) of fresh, frozen or tinned strawberries with 2 teaspoons of icing sugar. Of course, to save all of that, some shops and supermarkets sell good-quality frozen purées that work very well. A few drops of strawberry liqueur also help. Of course, raspberries can also be used.

Lemon Curd and Prune Ripple Ice-cream

I like to serve this with my Steamed Lemon Sponge with Prunes (see p. 331). I have included my lemon curd recipe here, or you can use a basic jar of curd.

SERVES 4–8
225 g (8 oz) lemon curd (see p. 363)

**FOR THE PRUNE RIPPLE
ICE-CREAM**
4 tablespoons crème fraîche

2 tablespoons plain yoghurt
75 ml (3 fl oz) water
40 g (1¹/₂ oz) caster sugar
**75 g (3 oz) ready-to-eat prunes, stoned
and chopped**

Mix the lemon curd with the crème fraîche and yoghurt. This can now he placed in the ice-cream machine and churned, or frozen in a freezer tray, whisking regularly until it begins to set.

Boil the water with the caster sugar and add the chopped prunes. Simmer for 1–2 minutes, then blitz to a purée. Leave to cool and chill.

When the ice-cream is ready, slowly add the prune purée. This will only need a few turns to leave the purée running through. Return to the freezer to set.

Rice Pudding Ice-cream with Raspberry Jam Sauce

I love baked rice pudding. It was one of my favourites at home with the lovely skin on top. Creamed rice pudding is also one of my favourites, especially with raspberry jam spooned on top. Well, I thought I would come up with the opposite. Rice pudding ice-cream with warm jam sauce. It works really well and when you tell your guests they've got rice pudding and jam sauce, this will definitely surprise them. This ice-cream also works very well in a Rice Pudding Arctic Roll with Raspberry Coulis (see p. 268). Remember, you can always substitute the fresh vanilla base for a tin of custard to make the recipe quicker.

SERVES 4–8

FOR THE RICE PUDDING
600 ml (1 pint) milk
15 g (¹/₂ oz) unsalted butter
40 g (1¹/₂ oz) caster sugar
**50 g (2 oz) short-grain pudding
rice**

FOR THE ICE-CREAM
**600 ml (1 pint) Vanilla Ice-cream
(see p. 252), made with a pinch of
freshly grated nutmeg and without
the vanilla pod or vanilla essence**

FOR THE RASPBERRY JAM SAUCE
175 g (6 oz) raspberry jam
2–3 tablespoons water

Bring the milk, butter and sugar to the boil. Add the rice and bring to the simmer. Simmer and cook gently, stirring frequently, until the rice is over-cooked; this will take about 25–30 minutes. The rice has to be close to breaking/purée point to prevent it from becoming crunchy when made into ice-cream.

Once the rice pudding has cooled, mix with the vanilla base and churn in the ice-cream machine for 15–20 minutes until thickened and increased in volume. The rice pudding ice-cream can now be set in the freezer.

To make the sauce, just warm the jam and water together until they reach a thick sauce consistency. If the jam is still too thick, then add a little more water to correct the consistency. The sauce can also be pushed through a sieve to leave a smooth, clear jam sauce, ready to be poured over the creamy rich ice-cream.

Sorbets

Sorbets are also known as 'water ices'. They are good as a light pudding or to serve between courses as a palate cleanser. All you need is to mix equal quantities of stock syrup and fruit purée, exactly as the fruit ice-creams, but without the crème fraîche.

For example, 300 ml (10 fl oz) each of stock syrup and an apple purée mixed together and turned through an ice-cream maker will produce a simple sorbet. This, of course, can be improved by adding a squeeze of lemon juice to enrich the taste and some cider or calvados to make it even stronger.

All sorbets can be made and varied in this way. A raspberry sorbet can be really tasty with a little raspberry liqueur added in place of some of the stock syrup.

These sorbets can be used as a main item for puddings. How does a pear sorbet with chocolate sauce and fresh thick cream sound?

Fruit Sorbets

Sorbets are a light and refreshing alternative to ice-cream. They are good to have as a middle-course palate cleanser or as a dessert.

You can use any soft fruits you like – strawberries, raspberries, pineapple, mango, melon – and whichever stock syrup you prefer.

SERVES 4–8
225 g (8 oz) fruit
150 ml (3 fl oz) Stock Syrup (see p. 397)
Juice of 1/2 lemon

Simply mix the fruits with the syrup and blitz in a blender, then push through a sieve. You now have a fruit syrup. Add the lemon juice to this to help lift the flavours. Churn in an ice-cream machine for 20 minutes and freeze, or turn into a freezer tray and place in the freezer, stirring and turning every 20–30 minutes until frozen.

VARIATION

If you want to make an apple or pear sorbet double the quantity of fruit to get a full flavour and texture. Simply peel, core and chop the fruits, mix with the lemon juice and cook in the stock syrup until softened. Then blitz and push through a sieve and leave to cool before making into sorbet.

Chocolate Sorbet

You're going to love this recipe It's easy to make, rich in taste and also very refreshing.

SERVES 4
25 g (1 oz) cocoa
450 ml (15 fl oz) water

150 g (5 oz) good-quality plain
    chocolate
150 g (5 oz) caster sugar

Simmer the cocoa in the water for 5 minutes. While simmering, chop the chocolate. Pour the water and cocoa on to the chocolate and sugar and stir in. Once cool, churn in the ice-cream machine until thickened, then freeze.

Black Forest Arctic Roll

Black Forest gâteau is still a popular dessert. The flavours of chocolate, cherries and cream marry well – if the dessert is well made. With this dish I've taken all those flavours and turned them into a tasty and fun pudding. The sponge can also be used for a chocolate Swiss roll. You'll need a cylinder in which to freeze the ice-cream into shape. I use a piece of plastic piping from a hardware store, about 15 cm (6 in) long by 6 cm (2½ in) diameter. Wrap cling film securely round one end. The whole dish might sound a bit involved, but you can save time by using a ready-made ice-cream and tinned cherries if you like, so have a go.

SERVES 4–6

FOR THE CHOCOLATE SPONGE
3 eggs
75 g (3 oz) caster sugar
50 g (2 oz) plain flour
15 g (½ oz) cornflour
25 g (1 oz) cocoa

FOR THE ARCTIC ROLL
175–225 g (6–8 oz) fresh cherries or
    tinned cherries
50 ml (2 fl oz) Stock Syrup (see p. 397)
Kirsch (optional)
600 ml (1 pint) Vanilla Ice-cream
    prepared and churned (see p. 252)
3–4 tablespoons black cherry jam

Pre-heat the oven to 180°C/350°F/gas 4 and grease and line a Swiss roll tin.

Whisk the eggs and sugar together until pale and fluffy. Sift together the dry ingredients, then fold into the egg mix a little at a time. Spread the mix evenly in the prepared tin and bake in the pre-heated oven for 10–15 minutes. No colour is needed on this sponge, just set the mix. Allow to cool.

Stone the cherries and sit them in a pan with the syrup and a splash of kirsch, if using. Bring the cherries to the simmer and cook for 1–2 minutes. Leave to cool. Once cooled, mix half the cherries with the vanilla ice-cream. Stand the cylinder up making sure the base has been well cling filmed. Spoon the ice-cream into the cylinder and set in the freezer.

Sieve the liquid from the remaining cherries and bring the syrup to the boil with the cherry jam. The liquid will now be a lot thicker. Mix the cherries with the syrup.

Turn the chocolate sponge off the tray but leave it still attached to the lining paper. Brush the sponge with some cherry jam. Remove the cling film from one end of the ice-cream and pour hot water on to the cylinder to loosen and remove the ice-cream. Sit the ice-cream on the sponge and roll until the sponge meets, creating a cylinder and cutting off any excess. Roll the whole thing in cling film and freeze for 30 minutes.

To serve, remove from the freezer and take off the cling film before cutting into portions. Each plate can be garnished with a spoonful of the remaining cherries in syrup.

VARIATION

To add an extra garnish for a special occasion, simply shape some whipped cream and scrape a palette knife across some dark or milk chocolate to garnish with rolled pieces. Finish with sprigs of mint and lightly dust with icing sugar.

Rice Pudding Arctic Roll

This recipe is a variation on the Black Forest Arctic Roll (see p. 267). Simply make the rice pudding ice-cream and freeze in the plastic cylinder. Then you can create the Arctic roll with the Swiss roll sponge. Strawberry Ripple Ice-cream (see p. 253) also works. I'm going to serve it with some Raspberry Coulis (see p. 356).

SERVES 4–8

FOR THE SPONGE
3 eggs, separated
100 g (4 oz) caster sugar
75 g (3 oz) plain flour
25 g (1 oz) cornflour

FOR THE ARCTIC ROLL
Raspberry jam
Rice Pudding Ice-cream (see p. 265)
Raspberry Coulis (see p. 356)
Fresh raspberries (optional)
Double cream
1 sprig of fresh mint
Icing sugar, sifted

Pre-heat the oven to 180°C/350°F/gas 4 and butter and line a Swiss roll tin.

Whisk the egg yolks and 75 g (3 oz) of sugar together until thick and creamy. Whisk the egg whites with the remaining sugar to a firm meringue. Sift the plain flour and cornflour together, then lightly fold into the egg-yolk mix. Carefully fold in the egg white. Spread the mix into the prepared tray and cook in the pre-heated oven for 15–20 minutes. Remove from the oven and allow to cool.

Spread some raspberry jam on to the sponge, keeping the golden brown top for the outside. Remove the ice-cream from the cylinder by running the plastic under hot water for a few seconds. Sit the ice-cream on top of the sponge and roll around, cutting off any excess sponge. Roll in cling film and freeze for at least 30 minutes.

Once frozen, remove the cling film and cut into portions. Garnish each portion with Raspberry Coulis and fresh raspberries (optional). It's also nice served with thick fresh cream, a sprig of mint and lightly dusted with icing sugar.

Lemon Jelly

This is a simple home-made jelly. The lemon jelly goes very well with ice-cream. I like to serve either the Vanilla (see p. 252), Lemon Curd (see p. 265) or Crème Fraîche Ice-cream (see p. 251) with it. This is really a good, fun dessert to offer your guests at a dinner party – jelly and ice-cream.

The recipe also works well if the lemons are replaced or mixed with limes for a different flavour.

SERVES 4
600 ml (1 pint) water
275 g (10 oz) caster sugar

Finely grated zest and juice of
5 lemons
7–8 leaves of gelatine

Warm and dissolve the sugar in the water on the stove with the lemon juice and zest. Keep on the heat for 2–3 minutes. Remove from the stove. Soak the gelatine leaves in cold water until they become soft and jelly-like. Remove the gelatine and squeeze out any excess water. Stir the gelatine into the warm, sweet lemon water until dissolved. The sweet jelly water can now be left to cool, stirring occasionally. Once cooled, the jelly can be poured into a presentation bowl and left to set in the fridge.

Knickerbockerglory

This Knickerbockerglory can be made by the same method as the Chocolate and Toffee Bockerglory (see p. 271). Instead of using the chocolate sponge, sandwich the Swiss roll sponge (see p. 392) with raspberry jam and then cut into dice and place in the bottom of the glass. Spoon in some summer fruits mixed with a Fruit Coulis (see p. 356) Next is the ice-cream. I like to use two ice-creams, starting with some Vanilla (see p. 252), then adding more fruits before spooning in some Raspberry or Strawberry Ice-cream (see p. 253). Finish the bockerglory with some more fruits and then whipped cream, chocolate and mint (see p. 271).

It's awesome, good luck.

Chocolate and Toffee Bockerglory

This has to be the ultimate in sticky puddings. The combinations are unlimited and that's the beauty of cooking, there are no limits. So rather than give you a strict recipe, I'll just give you some ideas of how it can be put together. It's best to make it in tall glasses or deep bowls.

Remember to make this dish you don't have to go through the process of making every component. Most, if not all, of these can be found in most food stores, and you can vary the ingredients however you like. So if you want to have a try with no effort involved, use some Jamaican ginger cake diced up and mixed with chocolate or coffee sauce, top with some chocolate and vanilla ice-cream, more sauce and finish with almonds and chocolate.

To make chocolate shavings, take a bar of good, rich dark chocolate and turn it on its side, looking at the width of the bar. From top to bottom scrape along the chocolate with the edge of a palette knife. This will create shavings to sprinkle on top of your desserts.

SERVES AS MANY AS YOU NEED

Chocolate Fudge Cake (see p. 318), chocolate sponge or Jamaican ginger cake
Pecan Nut Sauce (see p. 319)
Chocolate Ice-cream (see p. 258)
Toffee Ice-cream (see p. 254)
Chocolate Sauce (see p. 354)
Double cream, whipped
Flaked almonds, toasted
Chocolate shavings
Sprigs of fresh mint, to decorate
Icing sugar, for sprinkling
Wafer biscuits, to serve

Dice the cake into 1 cm (½ in) pieces and mix them with some of the pecan nut sauce. Spoon the cake into the glasses. Next spoon some chocolate ice-cream on top and follow that with some toffee or vanilla ice-cream. Pour cold chocolate sauce on top. Cover with whipped cream and sprinkle over the toasted almonds and chocolate shavings. This pudding can now be served with a sprig of mint on top, a dusting of icing sugar, a long spoon and a biscuit. How does that sound?

Poached Peaches

Before poaching the peaches, they should be skinned. This is achieved by lightly scoring the peach skin all the way around the fruit with a sharp knife. Plunge the fruits into boiling water for a few seconds and then into cold water. This method is called blanching – very similar to skinning a tomato. The skin will now peel off.

These peaches eat very well as almost a pudding on their own or halved and used in a great Auguste Escoffier classic – Peach Melba (see p. 272).

SERVES 4
4–8 peaches, skinned
¹/₂ lemon
¹/₂ cinnamon stick (optional)

300 ml (10 fl oz) water
300 ml (10 fl oz) white wine
225 g (8 oz) caster sugar

Sit the skinned peaches into a pan with the lemon and cinnamon stick, if using. Pour the water and white wine on top and add the sugar. If you find this is not enough you can add either half or the same quantities again. Cover with some greaseproof paper and bring to the boil. Simmer the peaches for 4–5 minutes (3–4 minutes if they are very ripe and soft), then leave to cool in the syrup. The peaches are now ready and can be used straight away (even while still warm) or chilled. If you wish to keep them for some time then seal them in airtight jars.

When cooking the fruits if you have any problems keeping them submerged in the syrup, simply sit a plate on top to hold them in place.

Peach Melba

I like to serve Peach Melba in Tuile Baskets (see p. 348). It's simply vanilla ice-cream (see p. 252) topped with Poached Peaches (see above) and then finished with Melba Sauce (see p. 361). I also like to add whipped cream flavoured with fresh vanilla and sprinkled with toasted almonds, but this isn't essential. The Melba Sauce can be spooned on to the plate and the finished basket placed on top.

Poached Pears

This is an easy recipe to follow, using simple quantities of two parts water to one part sugar, for example, 600 ml (1 pint) of water to 225 g (8 oz) of caster sugar. The best pears to use are Williams, which have a good sweet taste and texture.

The pears can be used for many dishes like the Chocolate and Pear Brûlée (see p. 317). They can also be made into a French classic, Poires Belle Hélène, which is poached pears with Vanilla Ice-cream (see p. 252) and Chocolate Sauce (see p. 354). This dish eats and looks very good if served in a Tuile Biscuit basket (see p. 348). You could also use some poached pears in a knickerbockerglory glass layered with Vanilla Ice-cream (see p. 252), pecan nuts, chocolate sauce and finished with Toffee Cream (see p. 360). Now that is a rich pudding.

SERVES 6
6 pears
¹/₂ lemon
1 vanilla pod or cinnamon stick
   (optional)

1.2 litres (2 pints) water
450 g (1 lb) caster sugar

Peel the pears, then cut them in half. Remove the core with either a Parisienne scoop cutter or a sharp knife. Also remove the vein of stalk running from the centre to the top of the pear, by cutting diagonally either side of the vein. The pears can now be lightly rubbed with the lemon to prevent discoloration. Sit the pears in a pan with the lemon and vanilla or cinnamon if using, and cover with the water and caster sugar. Cover with greaseproof paper and bring to the boil. Simmer for a few minutes, then remove from the heat, leaving the pears to cool in the syrup.

The pears can now be kept chilled in the syrup with the lemon and vanilla or cinnamon in an airtight container until you want to use them.

Fresh Fruit Salad

Fresh fruit salad has endless combinations. It's basically prepared fruits all mixed together. The recipe here for fruit salad is just to give you an idea and a basic recipe to work from. Some fruits have a coarser texture and eat a lot better if just lightly softened in Stock Syrup (see p. 397). Or you can try using Poached Peaches (see p. 271) or Poached Pears (see p. 272).

Any soft red fruits should always be added just before serving, to prevent them colouring the other fruits.

One particular favourite of mine is summer-fruit salad, which is just poached blackberries, blueberries, redcurrants, blackcurrants, tayberries, strawberries and raspberries in a warm Stock Syrup. The flavours and colours together are fantastic.

And here's just one more extra flavour. Use scissors to cut some thin strips of mint leaves and add them to the syrup. You get a lovely sweet mint flavour with every bite.

Of course, the best accompaniment to fresh fruit salad is simply pouring cream or even home-made Vanilla Ice-cream (see p. 252).

SERVES 4

2 apples, peeled and cored
50–75 g (2–3 oz) fresh pineapple chunks
300 ml (10 fl oz) Stock Syrup (either recipe) (see p. 397)
2 plums, each cut into 8 segments
¹/₂ Ogen or Galia melon
1 large orange, segmented
2 kiwis, peeled and cut into 8 pieces each
12 strawberries or raspberries
1 banana, sliced

Cut the apples into 12 segments and mix them with the pineapple chunks. Bring the stock syrup to the boil and pour on to the apple and pineapple. While the syrup is still warm, add the plums. The mix should now be left to cool to room temperature.

Peel the mango, then cut it in half, removing the stone. Cut the mango into chunks. Repeat the same cutting process for the melon. Add the mango, melon, orange and kiwi to the other fruits in the syrup.

The fruit salad is now ready. The strawberries, raspberries and banana should not be added until the salad is about to be served.

Glazed Pear and Almond Zabaglione

This dish looks very simple and almost like a crème brûlée, but just think of all those textures and tastes. When you break through the sugar topping it's into the warm zabaglione then on to the cooked pears and finally the moist almond sponge. I've chosen Comice pears, because they have a good sweet taste and texture. Other varieties will work but may need more cooking and more sugar to taste. This dish comes in a very close second to the bread and butter pudding.

The Frangipane or almond paste or sponge recipe is wonderful for home-made Bakewell tart, Bakewell and apple tart, or prune, Armagnac and almond tart. Because of the large amount of ground almonds, it's very moist and keeps a lot longer than a traditional sponge.

SERVES 4–6

6 Comice pears

50 g (2 oz) icing sugar

1 tablespoon unsalted butter

1 quantity Frangipane (Almond Paste)
  (see p. 396)

FOR THE ZABAGLIONE

5 egg yolks

40 g (1½ oz) caster sugar

25 ml (1 fl oz) Poire William liqueur
  (Marsala or Calvados will both work)

25 ml (1 fl oz) dry white wine

Pre-heat the oven to 200°C/400°F/gas 6.

Grease and line a 20 cm (8 in) square baking tray. Spread the frangipane mix 1 cm (½ in) thick in the prepared baking tray. Bake in the pre-heated oven for 20–30 minutes, until firm and set. Allow to cool.

Meanwhile, prepare the pears. Peel and chop two of the pears and cook quickly in a pan with a tablespoon of icing sugar and the butter. These pears need to cook to a purée. When very soft, push them through a sieve. Peel and cut the remaining pears into 1 cm (½ in) dice. Bring the purée to the boil and add the diced pears. Cook for just 2–3 minutes on a high heat; then allow to cool slightly.

Cut the frangipane into rounds to fit four 9 cm (3½ in) soufflé moulds or one 23 cm (9 in) bowl. Spoon the warm pears on top.

To make the zabaglione, beat together the egg yolks and sugar until light in colour. Add the Poire William and white wine and whisk in a bowl over a pan of hot water until light, thick and frothy. This will take 5–10 minutes. The zabaglione should be thick enough to make soft peaks when the whisk is drawn from the mix. Spoon over the pears in the moulds or bowl.

Sieve the remaining icing sugar on top of each mould or on to the bowl. Place under a hot grill for a few minutes until golden brown. If you are very generous with the icing sugar, this will give a crunchy topping.

Plum and Almond Slice with Cognac Zabaglione

Instead of the round flan tin usually used for frangipane or Bakewell tart, here I'm using a rectangular 'ring' 20 × 10 × 4 cm (8 × 4 × 1 in) but, if you can't find one, use a 20 cm (8 in) flan ring. When a slice is cut you see the plums running through. It looks and eats really well, with the moist frangipane holding it all together. As for the cognac zabaglione, this is an optional extra that is so delicious with the flan. It just gives the whole dish a special edge. Just cream, clotted cream or custard can be served with this dish or, if you're feeling very greedy, why not have the lot?

SERVES 6–8

225 g (8 oz) Sweet Shortcrust Pastry (see p. 394)

4 tablespoons plum jam

10 plums, halved and stoned

Icing sugar, sifted

1/2 quantity Frangipane (Almond Paste) (see p. 397)

2–3 tablespoons water (optional)

Icing sugar, sifted (optional)

FOR THE ZABAGLIONE

4 egg yolks

40 g (1 1/2 oz) caster sugar

25 ml (1 fl oz) dry white wine

25 ml (1 fl oz) brandy or cognac

Grease and flour a 20 × 10 × 4 cm (8 × 4 × 1 1/2 in) cake tin or 20 cm (8 in) flan ring. Sit the mould on a greaseproof-papered baking tray.

Roll out the pastry and use to line the prepared tin. When lining, it's best to leave the excess pastry around the edges just folded over. This will prevent the pastry from shrinking in the mould and, once cooked, it can simply be trimmed with a knife. Spread half the plum jam in the pastry case. The remaining jam will be used to help glaze the finished dish. This can now be chilled while the plums are being prepared.

Pre-heat the oven to 180°C/350°F/gas 4.

Sit the plums, skin-side down, on a roasting tray and dust generously with icing sugar. Bake in the pre-heated oven for 4–6 minutes, until softened. The cooking time will really depend on the ripeness of the plums. Once softened, drain off any excess liquor, adding it to the remaining jam, and leave to cool. Once cold, sit 10 plum halves in the mould, skin-side up. These can now be covered with the frangipane, to 2–3 mm (1/8 in) from the top of the mould. The remaining plums will not be used until 10–15 minutes before the end of the cooking time. If they are put on now they will sink without trace during cooking.

The flan can now be cooked in the pre-heated oven. It will take approximately 1 1/4 hours to cook. After 45–50 minutes, sit the remaining plums on top and finish cooking.

The jam and liquor can now be warmed to glaze. A little water may also be needed to loosen the jam. To give the tart an even richer colour before glazing, sprinkle liberally with icing sugar and finish under the grill or with a gas gun. This will give you one or two burnt edges, creating a bitter-sweet top. Trim the excess pastry from the edges, then brush with the jam glaze. Once cooled slightly, remove the flan ring or mould. This pudding can be served warm or cold.

To make the zabaglione to accompany the pudding, beat together the eggs and sugar until light in colour. Add the white wine and cognac, sit the bowl over a pan of simmering water and whisk vigorously (an electric hand-mixer reduces the hard work) until light, thick and frothy. This will take at least 8–10 minutes. The zabaglione should be thick enough to form soft peaks when drawn back on itself.

To serve the dish, take a slice of the plum and almond cake, present on a plate and spoon some zabaglione on the side. I like to serve clotted cream as well and have the zabaglione just falling off the slice.

Cherry and Almond Tart with Pear Sorbet

In some ways, I suppose, this is similar to my Plum and Almond Slice (see p. 275). These, however, are individual tarts. They can, of course, be made in a 15–20 cm (6–8 in) flan ring, to give you a single cherry and almond tart but, when you make them individually and then shape some pear sorbet and sit it on top, the dish not only looks good but eats even better.

SERVES 4

225 g (8 oz) Shortcrust Pastry (see p. 394)

1 1/2 tablespoons Cherry Jam (see p. 359) or bought

225 g (8 oz) cherries, cooked as on p. 298, the cooking liquid boiled to reduce by half for a glaze

275 g (10 oz) Frangipane (see p. 396)

300 ml (10 fl oz) Custard Sauce (see p. 355)

1–2 measures Poire William liqueur, to taste (optional)

Pear Sorbet (see p. 267)

Pre-heat the oven to 180°C/350°F/gas 4. Lightly grease 4 × 10 cm (4 in) fluted, round, loose-bottomed moulds about 2.5 cm (1 in) deep.

Roll out the pastry and line the tart cases. Spread 2 teaspoons of cherry jam in each mould, and then divide half the cherries between the moulds, reserving a few. Fill the moulds with the frangipane, and then finish by sitting the reserved whole cherries on top. Cook in the pre-heated oven for 30–35 minutes, covering with foil or greaseproof paper at the end of cooking if they are browning too quickly. Once cooked, allow to cool to a warm temperature. These can now be glazed with the reduced cherry syrup.

Flavour the custard sauce with Poire William, if available. If Poire William is difficult to find, then simply use custard sauce.

The pudding can now be finished. Spoon some custard sauce on to a plate. Remove the tart from its mould and sit it in the centre. Shape the sorbet between two serving spoons and sit it on top.

NOTE

Tinned or griottine cherries (the latter being steeped in alcohol) can also be used.

Baked Orange Tart

This really is a simple pudding to make that certainly isn't short of taste. The flavour of the oranges, the bitter-rich taste of the zest, together with the sweetness of the juice working together give a lovely aroma as well as flavour. Of course, the total flavour of this dish can be changed by simply replacing the oranges with lemons or perhaps lemon and lime. For the cake crumbs, simply use a basic Vanilla Sponge (Genoise) (see p. 392) or Victoria Sponge (see p. 337), or use a bought cake.

MAKES 1 × 20 cm (8 in) TART
2 oranges
50 g (2 oz) caster sugar
50 g (2 oz) cake crumbs
25 g (1 oz) unsalted butter, diced
150 ml (5 fl oz) milk

2 eggs
1 × 20 cm (8 in) flan ring, lined with
175 g (6 oz) Shortcrust Pastry or
Sweet Shortcrust Pastry
(see p. 394)

Pre-heat the oven to 180°C/350°F/gas 4.

Finely grate the orange zest and mix the zest with the sugar until a yellow/orange colour is achieved. Add the cake crumbs and the butter. Warm the milk and pour over the crumb mix. Stir until the butter has melted.

Squeeze the juice from the oranges; you'll need 150 ml (5 fl oz). Separate the eggs, adding the yolks and orange juice to the mix. Whisk the egg whites to a soft peak, then gently fold into the mix. This can now be carefully spooned into the pastry case and baked in the oven for 30–35 minutes until set and light golden brown. Allow to relax for 20 minutes before serving warm, or leave until cold. To capture the rich orange flavour I like to eat it just warm, almost at room temperature, and of course with a spoonful of fresh cream.

Cappuccino Mousse

I always enjoy a cappuccino coffee – it's lovely with the frothy milk on top – so I thought, why not have a pudding to match? Chocolate and coffee go so well with each other, and the lightly whipped cream on top is a really good finish to the dish.

If you make your own biscuits it would be very nice to offer cappuccino mousse and biscuits for pudding. Why not try the Palmier Biscuits (see p. 345)?

SERVES 4

175 g (6 oz) plain chocolate
3 tablespoons strong black coffee
5 egg whites
50g (2 oz) caster sugar
2 egg yolks
150 ml (5 fl oz) double cream,
   whipped

Break 150 g (5 oz) of the chocolate into small pieces and melt with the coffee in a bowl over a pan of hot water. Beat the egg whites with the sugar to a meringue consistency, creating soft peaks. Fold the egg yolks into the melted chocolate, making sure it is not too hot, add one-third of the egg-white meringue and whisk into the chocolate. Carefully fold in the remaining egg whites and half of the whipped cream.

The mousse can now be spooned into glasses, ramekin dishes or one large bowl and placed in the fridge for 2–3 hours to set. The remaining cream can be piped or forked on top of the mousse. To finish the dish, just finely grate the remaining chocolate over the top. So now we have a cappuccino coffee pudding with extra chocolate taste.

Chocolate Sponge Cake with Cappuccino Mousse

If you would like to be more adventurous, here is a way to make the mousse even more exciting. The sponge adds a good texture to the mousse, but of course can be used with any mousse or other puddings.

SERVES 4

1 quantity Cappuccino Mousse
   (see above)
Rum or liqueur, to taste
4 sprigs of fresh mint, to decorate
1 quantity Coffee Sauce (see p. 356)
   or Clementine or Orange Sauce
   (see p. 354), to serve

FOR THE SPONGE

175 g (6 oz) plain chocolate
3 tablespoons strong black coffee
5 eggs, separated
100 g (4 oz) caster sugar
A pinch of salt

Pre-heat the oven to 180°C/350°F/gas 4 and line a 30 × 25 cm (12 × 10 in) baking tray and four 6 cm (2½ in) flan rings with greaseproof paper to come up 5–7 cm (2–3 in) round the sides.

To make the sponge, melt the chocolate with the coffee in a bowl over a pan of hot water. Leave to cool slightly. Beat the egg yolks until smooth and then add the caster sugar. Continue to beat until the mixture is pale and trails off the whisk in ribbons. In a separate bowl, beat the egg whites and salt until they form soft peaks.

Add the melted chocolate the egg-yolk mix then fold in the egg whites. Spread on to the lined baking tray to between 5 mm (¼ in) and 1 cm (½ in) thick. Bake in the pre-heated oven for 15 minutes. Remove from the oven and allow to cool.

Make the mousse but do not allow it to set. Cut out four rings from the sponge the same diameter as the flan rings, and place them in the bottom of the rings. The sponge can now be flavoured with a little rum or liqueur, if required. Spoon the mousse into the moulds on top of the sponge, chill and now leave to set.

When the mousses are set, lift off the flan rings and carefully take off the paper. Finish with the whipped cream and grated chocolate of the mousse recipe. Place the mousses on plates, decorate with a sprig of mint and serve with your chosen sauce.

Chocolate Mousse

This is a rich and light chocolate mousse which can be served in glasses or moulds. It can also be served between layers of Chocolate Sponge (see Sponge Base Without Flour, p. 392) in a terrine mould or round cake tin.

SERVES 8
150 g (5 oz) good-quality plain chocolate
275 g (10 oz) unsalted butter, diced
150 g (5 oz) cocoa

300 ml (10 fl oz) double cream
200 g (7 oz) caster sugar
6 eggs, separated

Chop the chocolate and melt it slowly in a bowl over a pan of hot water. Add the butter and let it melt in the warmth of the chocolate. Add the cocoa and whisk in until the mix is smooth. Whisk the double cream until it forms soft peaks, then reserve in the fridge. Whisk half the sugar with all the yolks until pale and fluffy. Whisk the remaining sugar and egg whites together until they form stiff peaks.

Fold the chocolate mix with the egg yolks and sugar, add the meringue mix and lastly fold in the cream. The mousse can now be set in glasses or moulds and needs half a day minimum to set.

Chocolate Terrine

This is the sort of pudding for a special dinner party. It's rich in texture and taste and eats like a chocolate dream. One of the big advantages of making this dish is that it freezes so well and doesn't spoil. So, if you've got a party coming up, make this now and just pop it in the freezer ready for the big day. The best size terrine mould to use is a Le Creuset 29 × 9 cm (11½ in × 3½ in). The terrine mould is lined with a chocolate sponge, filled with a chocolate mousse and then coated with more chocolate.

SERVES 12

FOR THE SPONGE
225 g (8 oz) caster sugar
5 eggs, separated
100 g (4 oz) cocoa

FOR THE MOUSSE
150 g (6 oz) good-quality plain
    chocolate
175 g (6 oz) unsalted butter
175 g (3 oz) cocoa

300 ml (10 fl oz) double cream
4 eggs, separated
175 g (6 oz) caster sugar

FOR THE CHOCOLATE COATING
120 ml (4 fl oz) milk
65 ml (2^1/2 fl oz) double cream
275 g (10 oz) good-quality plain
    chocolate, chopped
65 g (2^1/2 oz) unsalted butter,
    chopped

Pre-heat the oven to 160°C/325°F/gas 3 and butter and line a 40 × 30 cm (16 × 12 in) baking tray. Line a 29 × 9 cm (11^1/2 × 3^1/2 in) terrine with greaseproof paper or cling film.

To make the sponge, mix half the sugar with the egg yolks and whisk until pale and fluffy. Whisk the egg whites until they form soft peaks, then add the remaining sugar and continue to whisk to a stiff meringue. Fold the cocoa into the egg yolk mix, then whisk in a quarter of the meringue mix. Carefully and lightly fold in the remaining meringue. Spread the mix in the prepared tin. Bake in the pre-heated oven for about 20–30 minutes. Leave to cool.

To make the mousse, melt the chocolate with the butter in a bowl over a pan of warm water until it binds to a thick cream consistency. Add the cocoa and beat until completely smooth and cooled. Whisk the cream until it forms soft peaks, then chill. Whisk the egg yolks with half the sugar until white and fluffy. Fold into the chocolate mix. Whisk the egg whites with the remaining sugar to meringue stage, then fold into the chocolate mix. Now fold in the whipped cream.

Cut the cold sponge into four, making sure you measure from the mould, then line the base and sides, saving one piece for the top. Pour the chocolate mousse into the mould, then place the last piece of sponge on top. Chill for 2–3 hours, or freeze.

The chocolate coating finishes and really lifts the pudding. Bring the milk and cream to the boil, then pour on to the chocolate and butter. Stir until melted and blended. Cool until thick and at room temperature. To cover the terrine, remove from the fridge or freezer, spoon some on top and spread on until completely covered. Return to the fridge or freezer until set.

To finish, turn out the terrine on to a small board or tray then spoon over the remaining chocolate coating and spread evenly over the sponge. The terrine will, of course, no longer fit in the mould and so can be kept chilled or frozen on the tray or board. Once the coating has completely set, just cover with cling film.

The terrine will make at least 12 portions. However, the finished dish can be cut into four and then frozen so that it can be eaten whenever you like.

VARIATIONS

This pudding can be made a lot easier by simply sitting half the sponge in a lined flan case and then pouring the mousse on top and finishing with another layer of sponge. This can then be set in a fridge or freezer. Remove the flan ring and lining and finish with the chocolate coating. It will look like a rich chocolate cake but is in fact a rich chocolate mousse.

This chocolate pudding eats very well with either Orange Custard Sauce (see p. 355) or Coffee Custard Sauce (see p. 356).

Chocolate Fudge Cake

This is a recipe for the children to make for you with very little help. It's also a recipe for which all the ingredients are usually sitting in our cupboards. It's great to make for children's birthday parties or for children to present to their teachers.

MAKES 1 × 20 cm (8 in) cake
225 g (8 oz) plain or milk chocolate
100 g (4 oz) unsalted butter
25 g (1 oz) caster sugar
1 egg

Juice and finely grated zest of 1 orange
4 tablespoons brandy (for adult version only!)
225 g (8 oz) digestive biscuits, crushed

Line a 20 cm (8 in) loose-bottomed cake tin with greaseproof paper.

Gently melt the chocolate with the butter in a heavy-based pan. Beat the sugar with the egg and orange zest over a pan of warm water until the mixture trails off the whisk in thick ribbons. Pour the chocolate mix into the egg and stir well. Stir in the orange juice, brandy, if using, and the crushed digestive biscuits. Now just pour into the cake tin and leave to cool and chill overnight. Once set and cold just turn out, cut and serve.

NOTE

The sugar, egg and orange zest can be whisked by machine without using the pan of hot water. This is obviously a safer method for children.

White and Dark Chocolate Cream/Mousse

I wasn't quite sure what title to give this recipe. It's really a recipe from many years ago that was called Chocolate Marquise. It is a good chocolate recipe to try as it simply can't go wrong. Another plus is how well it works with plain, milk or white chocolate. It can also be used for so many different puddings, from a basic marquise terrine to cold mousse soufflés or good mixed chocolate slice.

SERVES 8–10

FOR THE CHOCOLATE SWISS ROLL SPONGE
100 g (4 oz) caster sugar
2 eggs, separated
25 g (1 oz) cocoa
25 g (1 oz) plain flour

FOR THE CHOCOLATE CREAM/MOUSSE
1 × 11 g sachet of gelatine
600 ml (1 pint) double cream
275 g (10 oz) chocolate (plain, milk or white)
50 ml (2 fl oz) water
2 tablespoons liquid glucose
2 egg yolks (optional)

Pre-heat the oven to 160°C/325°F/gas 3. Grease and lightly flour a 28 × 20 cm (11 × 8 in) Swiss roll tin for the sponge. If you are making a chocolate terrine, line a Le Creuset 25 cm (10 in) terrine mould or a 23 cm (9 in) loose-bottomed cake tin with greaseproof paper.

To make the sponge, whisk half of the caster sugar with the egg yolks until thick and pale. Whisk the egg whites to a soft-peak stage, add the remaining caster sugar and whisk to a stiff meringue. Sift the cocoa and flour on to the egg-yolk mix and fold in. Add a third of the meringue and whisk in. Carefully fold in the remaining meringue. Pour and spread the mix into the prepared tin about 1–2 cm (1/2–3/4 in) deep and bake for 20–25 minutes. Leave to cool.

To make the mousse, first soak the gelatine in cold water. Whip the cream to a soft peak. Break or grate the chocolate into small pieces. Bring the water and glucose to the boil and add the gelatine and chocolate. Remove from the heat and beat until the chocolate has become smooth. When cool, add the egg yolks, if using. The yolks simply enrich the flavour and give a silky texture. Fold in the whipped cream and the mix is ready to pour into the prepared mould. A slice of the sponge can be placed on top, cutting it to make it fit, so when you turn out the terrine the mousse is sitting on a sponge base.

VARIATIONS

The mousse mix could also be split in half using plain chocolate and white chocolate. If so, it's best to make them separately. Make the plain first so this can be setting in the fridge while you make and then pour in the white on top. This is also then topped with the sponge to finish.

The mix could even be split into three, starting with plain, then milk and finishing with white for a chocolate Neapolitan terrine.

I also like to use 15 cm (6 in) round or square flan cases or rings about 5–5.75 cm (2–3 in) deep. The sponge base can then be placed in the base and the mix poured on top. When making this variety, I normally make a dark and a white mousse. A slice of this dusted with cocoa or chocolate shavings eats very well.

Also, a sort of Black Forest dessert can be made this way. For this, I make a full recipe using only dark plain chocolate. Using a round flan or cake tin, line with sponge and sprinkle with kirsch syrup. This is made by boiling 75 ml (3 fl oz) of water with 50 g (2 oz) of caster sugar and 1–3 measures of kirsch or rum (to taste!). Now the sponge can be spread with a home-made (see p. 359) or bought cherry jam. The next stage is to cover the base with cherries. Griottine (steeped in alcohol) or tinned cherries can both be used. Fresh cherries also eat very well with this recipe. Take 225 g (8 oz) of fresh, stoned cherries, melt a knob of butter in a pan and, once sizzling, add the cherries with 25 g (1 oz) of caster or demerara sugar. These should now be cooked for a few minutes until tender. If you're going to use fresh cherries then a separate syrup will not be needed. Simply add a measure or two of kirsch or rum to the cherries at the last moment; this will create an instant syrup. These can now be spooned on to the sponge while still warm and then left to cool before topping with the dark chocolate mousse. This can now be simply finished with a dusting of cocoa or shavings of fresh chocolate.

This Black Forest variety can also be made into individual soufflés. Simply stick a strip of silicone or greaseproof paper around a ramekin dish, making sure it's at least 4 cm (1½ in) above the mould. Follow the method above, cutting 4–6 discs of chocolate sponge and placing them in the ramekins, then finishing them in the same fashion with syrup, jam, cherries and mousse to give cold Black Forest soufflé.

There are plenty of alternatives already, but that's not all – there are many more. Why not add chopped hazelnuts and raisins for a fruit and nut terrine? Or perhaps use blackcurrants instead of cherries or maybe all summer fruits set in a soufflé. Oranges also go very well on marmalade-spread sponge with a sprinkle of Cointreau or Grand Marnier.

With all these combinations – and I'm sure you'll think of more – it almost creates a headache! But remember, this also eats so well on its own, without the sponge: just set in a terrine mould or bowl and spoon or slice on to a plate and enjoy.

Chocolate Truffle Cake

The quantities of chocolate and cream in this recipe are quite frightening: it's really 450 g (1 lb) to 600 ml (1 pint), a lot of chocolate and cream. But remember there are always times when we want to spoil ourselves and indulge in rich foods. So if it's Christmas, Easter or perhaps a birthday, then this is the cake for you. This recipe will fill a 25 cm (10 in) cake tin at least 7.5 cm (3 in) deep. The recipe can be halved for a 15 cm (6 in) cake tin.

I'm using a Chocolate Vanilla Sponge (Genoise) (see p. 392) for the base. Once it's cooked and cooled, I'm cutting the sponge in half horizontally to give a round slice for the base of the cake. Any remaining sponge can be frozen and kept ready for the next time. I like to soak the base sponge with a rum syrup – it's optional, but tasty.

The chocolate topping recipe will give you enough to cover the top of the cake. If you want to cover the entire cake, you'll need to double the quantities.

MAKES 1 × 25 cm (10 in) CAKE
1 × 25 cm (10 in) Chocolate Vanilla
   Sponge (Genoise) (see p. 392), cut
   in half horizontally to give a 1 cm
   (1/2 in) thick slice (freeze any left)

FOR THE RUM SYRUP
85 ml (3 fl oz) water
50 g (2 oz) caster sugar
Rum to taste

FOR THE CAKE
450 g (1 lb) good-quality plain
   chocolate
600 ml (1 pint) double cream
4 egg yolks
50 g (2 oz) caster sugar

FOR THE CHOCOLATE TOPPING
100 g (4 oz) good-quality plain
   chocolate
50 ml (2 fl oz) double cream
25 g (1 oz) unsalted butter, softened

Place the chocolate sponge in the base of a 25 cm (10 in) loose-bottomed flan ring.

To make the rum syrup, boil the water with the sugar and add rum to taste. This can now be used to soak the sponge in the base. You will have about 120 ml (4 fl oz).

To make the cake, melt the chocolate with half the cream in a bowl over a pan of hot water. Whisk the egg yolks together until pale and fluffy. Whip the remaining cream to soft peaks. Once the chocolate has melted, remove from the heat and beat in the egg mixture. Fold in the whipped cream and pour the truffle mix into the cake tin on top of the sponge base. Leave to set, refrigerated, for 2–4 hours (overnight is best).

Once set, remove the cake from the tin and finish with the chocolate topping. Melt the chocolate with the double cream. Add the butter and remove from the heat. Leave to cool and thicken, then spread over the top of the sponge. To ensure a glossy finish, place each slice under the grill or glaze with a gas gun for a few seconds before serving.

Chocolate Flan

Chocolate puddings can be so heavy and over-rich, but this flan has a light filling with a crisp base, packed with chocolate taste. This flan has a wonderful mousse-like texture, which eats at its best with pouring cream.

SERVES 4–6
225 g (8 oz) Sweet Shortcrust Pastry
   (see p. 394)

FOR THE FILLING
3 eggs

1 egg yolk
100 g (4 oz) caster sugar
350 g (12 oz) plain chocolate
50 g (2 oz) unsalted butter
25 ml (1 fl oz) double cream
50 ml (2 fl oz) dark rum

Pre-heat the oven to 180°C/350°F/gas 4 and grease a 24 cm (9$\frac{1}{2}$ in) flan tin or flan ring on a baking sheet.

Make the pastry and allow to rest for 1 hour before using.

Roll out the pastry and use to line the flan tin or ring. Line the pastry with grease-proof paper, fill with baking beans and bake blind in the pre-heated oven for 20 minutes. Remove the beans and paper and leave to cool.

To make the filling, whisk the eggs, egg yolk and sugar together until light and doubled in volume. Melt the chocolate, butter, cream and rum together in a bowl over a pan of hot water. Carefully fold into the eggs until well blended. Pour this into the cooked pastry case and bake in the pre-heated oven for about 15 minutes until set. Leave the flan to cool and rest before taking off the flan ring. The flan is now ready to serve.

Caramel Cream Pots

These pots are almost like a caramel crème brûlée, without the sugar topping. Having the caramel mixed into the brûlée mix gives you a bitter-sweet taste all the way through. I like to serve this with home-made biscuits: the Maple Syrup and Walnut Biscuits (see p. 349) work well, giving a good nutty flavour and texture.

SERVES 8–10

FOR THE CARAMEL
150 ml (5 fl oz) water
225 g (8 oz) caster sugar

FOR THE CREAM
450 ml (15 fl oz) milk
900 ml (1$\frac{1}{2}$ pints) double cream
10 egg yolks

Pre-heat the oven to 160°C/325°F/gas 3.

To make the caramel, bring the water and sugar to the boil gently, using a pastry brush dipped in cold water to brush away any crystallization around the sides of the pan. Heat gently until the sugar has dissolved completely, then boil fast for 10–15 minutes until a good, dark golden colour has been reached. Remove from the heat.

Bring the milk and cream to the boil, then whisk into the hot caramel. Lightly whisk the egg yolks and pour the caramel mix on top. Strain the mix through a sieve. Pour the mix into 150 ml (5 fl oz) ramekin moulds (size 1) and stand the moulds in a roasting tin half-filled with warm water. Cook in the pre-heated oven for approximately 45–50 minutes, until just setting. Remove from the bath and leave to cool.

These can be served at room temperature, or chilled and then served as a cold cream.

Cheesecake Cream or Marmalade Cheesecake Cream

You can make this as a straightforward cream or include the marmalade. The quantity of marmalade you use is really up to you, but I find this quantity makes the cream really tasty. It will keep in the fridge for up to three days. The beauty of this dish is that you can simply sit this mix on to a classic biscuit base for a very good alternative cheesecake.

MAKES about 450 ml (15 fl oz)
100 g (4 oz) full-fat soft cream cheese
15 g (¹/₂ oz) caster sugar

100 g (4 oz) marmalade (optional)
150 ml (5 fl oz) double cream, lightly whipped

Beat together the cream cheese and sugar until the sugar has dissolved and creamed. Mix in the marmalade, if using. Once the marmalade has been completely mixed in, lightly fold in the whipped cream. Spoon the mix into a bowl and chill until set. Once set, the cream can be served as a separate dish from the bowl or spoon on to plates by curling with a warm tablespoon.

American Cheesecake

While making a television series in New York, we visited a restaurant, baker, coffee shop – it really was all of these and more rolled into one – in Brooklyn. It's called Junior's. Junior's has been there for many years and has a great reputation for most of its food; everything is made fresh on the premises. But one dish is voted every year the best in New York. Yes you've guessed it, it's American cheesecake.

I helped in the kitchen for a day and just couldn't believe how many they make daily and send all over the USA – literally thousands. It took me some time to squeeze this recipe from them, so please give it a try. At Junior's they serve it either natural or topped with strawberries, nuts and jam, the choice is yours. Try my recipe for Home-made Cherry Jam (see p. 359), which is not over-sweet and is lovely served with the cheesecake.

The sponge base used is a basic Vanilla Sponge (Genoise) (see p. 392); if you don't use all the sponge, any remaining slices can be frozen and kept for next time. Failing that, simply buy a vanilla sponge base and cut it to fit the base.

SERVES 6–8
25 cm (10 in) Vanilla Sponge (Genoise) (see p. 392) or ready-made vanilla

sponge base
225 g (8 oz) caster sugar
3 tablespoons cornflour

675 g (1¹/₂ lb) full-fat soft cream
   cheese
2 eggs

1 teaspoon vanilla essence
300 ml (10 fl oz) whipping
   cream

Pre-heat the oven to 180°C/350°F/gas 4. Butter a 25 cm (10 in) loose-bottomed cake tin.

Cut the sponge horizontally in to 1 cm (¹/₂ in) thick slices. Line the prepared cake tin with one slice of the sponge (the remaining slices can be frozen).

Mix together the sugar and cornflour, then beat in the cream cheese, making sure it's mixed to a creamy texture. Beat in the eggs and vanilla essence. Slowly pour on the cream, beating constantly to give a thick, creamy consistency. Pour the mix over the sponge base in the cake tin. Sit the tin in a baking tray filled with 2–3 mm (¹/₈ in) of warm water to help create steam during cooking. Place into the pre-heated oven and bake for 45–50 minutes until the top is golden.

Remove from the oven and leave to cool completely and set before removing from the cake tin. If you find that, after 50 minutes, the cheesecake has not become golden, then don't worry. Simply remove it from the oven and cool. It can be browned later under the grill or with a gas gun. Even without browning, it eats just as well.

Hazelnut and Orange Cake with Orange Anglaise and Mascarpone Caramel Cream

This is a very light cake. You'll notice there's no flour in the ingredients; the sponge is set by the egg yolks and whisked egg white. It's also best eaten at room temperature. This is because of the chocolate: if the cake is chilled, the chocolate sets and changes the texture, so keep this cake in an airtight container rather than putting it in the fridge.

The cake eats very well as a dessert with caramel mascarpone cream and an orange Anglaise sauce, so both of those recipes are included here. If all of that sounds a bit too rich for you, then simply eat the cake as it is – light and tasty.

This cake can be baked in a cake tin, but I prefer to cook it in a loaf tin. This gives you the same shape as the classic Jamaican Ginger Cake.

MAKES 2 × 900 g (2 lb) LOAF CAKES
150 g (5 oz) skinned hazelnuts, toasted
150 g (5 oz) good-quality plain
   chocolate, chopped

1 teaspoon finely grated lemon zest
2 teaspoons finely grated orange zest
6 eggs, separated
100 g (4 oz) caster sugar

FOR THE ORANGE ANGLAISE
Anglaise Sauce (see p. 355)
Grated zest of 2 oranges
1–2 measures Grand Marnier or
   Cointreau (optional)

**FOR THE MASCARPONE CARAMEL
CREAM**
250 g (9 oz) caster sugar
150 ml (5 fl oz) water
250 ml (8 fl oz) double cream
250 g (9 oz)

Pre-heat the oven to 180°C/350°F/gas 4. Grease and line 2 × 900 g (2 lb) loaf tins or 2 × 15–20 cm (6–8 in) cake tins.

To make the cake, place the hazelnuts, chocolate, lemon and orange zest in a food processor or liquidizer and blitz to a fine consistency. Whisk the egg yolks and half the sugar together until pale and the mix trails off the whisk in ribbons, then fold in the hazelnut and chocolate mix. Whisk the egg whites to a firm stage. Add the remaining sugar and continue to whisk to a thick meringue stage. This can now be folded in to the main mixture. This mix can now be poured into the loaf or cake tins and baked in the pre-heated oven for 25–30 minutes, until just firm in the centre. Once cooked, leave to cool and rest before turning out of the mould.

To make an orange Anglaise to go with the loaf, simply follow the Anglaise recipe on p. 355, swapping the vanilla for the orange zest and then cooking as for custard, removing the zest at the last moment. To lift the flavour even more, add the Grand Marnier or Cointreau.

To make the mascarpone caramel cream, bring the caster sugar and water to the boil and simmer gently until you have a dark amber caramel. Bring the cream to the boil and add to the caramel, whisking as you're adding. Return the mix to the heat and allow to simmer for a few minutes, then strain through a sieve if the mix is not completely smooth. Allow to cool and set. You will have about 450 ml (15 fl oz). Whisk the mascarpone to soften it, then add half the caramel cream (more can be added if you prefer a richer flavour). The mix can now be whisked and mixed until it almost forms peaks. This is now ready to use or can be kept chilled until needed.

To serve the pudding, sit a slice of cake on a plate and spoon some orange Anglaise around. The caramel mascarpone can now be shaped between two large serving spoons and placed on top of the sponge. The remaining caramel cream can now be warmed for the ultimate in richness and dribbled with a teaspoon across the pudding.

Christmas Rice Pudding with Honey and Rum Glacé Fruits

The glacé fruits can be of your choice. Most of the superstores sell mixed 350–450 g (12–16 oz) tubs, which hold some very interesting fruits – melon, pear, fig, mandarin, plum and pineapple, as well as the classic cherries and lemon.

The quantities of the ingredients list assume you will have guests – but you can easily halve the amounts if you wish to make less.

SERVES 10–12
225 g (8 oz) short-grain pudding rice
1.2 litres (2 pints) milk
100 g (4 oz) caster sugar
450 g (2 oz) unsalted butter
6 egg yolks
300 ml (10 fl oz) double cream
Icing sugar, sifted

FOR THE FRUITS AND SYRUP
150 ml (5 fl oz) water
25 g (1 oz) caster sugar
2 tablespoons rum, or more to taste
3 tablespoons honey
25 g (1 oz) sultanas
25 g (1 oz) raisins
225 g (8 oz) glacé fruits

Butter a 1.75-litre (3-pint) pudding basin or 10 individual 150 ml (5 fl oz) moulds. Place the rice in a pan and cover with cold water. Bring to the boil then refresh under cold water and drain. Boil 1 litre (1¾ pints) of the milk, half the sugar and the butter in a pan, then add the rice. Bring to a simmer and cook for 15–20 minutes, until tender and soft. Beat the egg yolks and remaining sugar together in a bowl. Boil the cream and remaining milk. Pour the milk on to the eggs and sugar, mixing all the time. Stir this custard into the hot rice and cook gently for another few minutes. The rice mix will now thicken. Pour into the prepared mould or moulds and leave to cool before setting in the fridge for 1–2 hours.

To prepare the sultanas, raisins and glacé fruits, boil the water and sugar together. Remove from the heat and add the rum and honey to taste. Cut the glacé fruits into halves or wedges and mix all the fruits, including the sultanas and raisins, with the warm syrup.

Turn out the pudding on to a large plate. This is easily achieved by sitting the bowl in warm water for a few seconds to release. Now simply spoon the fruits over and around the pudding and finish with a sprig of holly or mint and dust with icing sugar.

Crème Brûlée

I've never been quite sure if this originates from France or England, but I've always called it crème brûlée. It sounds a lot tastier than 'burnt cream'. This recipe is very similar to the Custard Sauce (see p. 355) but is cooked in a slightly different way and certainly has a different finish.

SERVES 6
8 egg yolks
50 g (2 oz) caster sugar
600 ml (1 pint) double cream

1 vanilla pod, split, or a few drops of
  good vanilla essence
Icing sugar

Pre-heat the oven to 180°/350°F/gas 4.

Mix the egg yolks and sugar together well in a bowl. Bring the cream to the boil with the vanilla pod, if using. Remove the vanilla pod and scrape the insides into the cream. Now whisk the cream into the egg yolks and sugar. Sit the bowl over a pan of hot water and heat until the custard begins to thicken, stirring all the time. It should the consistency of single cream. It is now ready for the next stage.

Divide the custard between six 7.5 cm (3 in) ramekins or moulds. Sit these in a roasting tin and add warm water until it comes three-quarters up the sides of the moulds. Finish in the pre-heated oven until just set, about 20–30 minutes. To test, remove one of the moulds from the water after 20 minutes and shake gently. There should still be slight movement in the centre of the custard. If it is still runny, put it back in the and check after another 5 minutes. Remove from the oven and allow to cool. I prefer to eat these at room temperature, so I do not put them in the fridge.

To finish the *brûlée*, when set, sprinkle them liberally with icing sugar. If you have a blow torch, this is great for achieving a quick and even glaze. If not, then colour them under a pre-heated hot grill, having the moulds as close as possible to the heat. As the sugar is heating, it will bubble and start to colour. More sugar may need to be added and then continue to colour until deep golden brown. The *brûlées* are now ready to serve.

VARIATION

You can make chocolate *brûlées* by simply adding grated chocolate to the mix before putting it into the ramekins. About 100 g (4 oz) of good-quality plain chocolate should be enough for this recipe – but, of course, if you prefer it stronger, just add some more. The *brûlées* can be finished with icing sugar, but I think they are better when topped with chocolate shavings.

Pecan Pie

Probably the most popular of all American classic dishes, this is just like a nutty treacle tart – lovely tastes with a lovely texture.

SERVES 4
225 g (8 oz) Sweet Shortcrust Pastry
 (see p. 394)

FOR THE FILLING
4 eggs
175 g (6 oz) caster sugar

300 ml (10 fl oz) golden syrup
A pinch of salt
A few drops of vanilla essence
225 g (8 oz) pecan nuts

Pre-heat the oven to 180°C/350°F/gas 4 and grease a 20 cm (8 in) flan tin or flan ring on a baking sheet.

Roll out the pastry and use to line the flan tin or ring. Line the pastry with grease-proof paper, fill with baking beans and bake blind in the pre-heated oven for 15–20 minutes. Remove to the beans and paper and leave cool. Increase the oven temperature to 200°C/400°F/gas 6.

To make the filling, beat the eggs lightly in a bowl, then add the sugar, syrup, salt and vanilla essence. Stir in the pecan nuts. Pour the mixture into the cooked flan case and bake in the pre-heated oven for 10 minutes. Reduce the oven temperature to 180°C/350°F/gas 4 again and bake for a further 35 minutes until set. You may need to cover the tart with foil to prevent any burning. Allow the pie to cool, then serve with clotted cream.

Gypsy Tart

This is a recipe I had been searching for for years. It's a pudding I remember from school days and it was my favourite. When I found somebody who knew the dish and was given the recipe I couldn't believe how simple it is – and it still tastes great.

SERVES 6
225 g (8 oz) Shortcrust Pastry
  (see p. 394)

1 × 400 g (14 oz) tin of evaporated
  milk
350 g (12 oz) dark muscovado sugar

Pre-heat the oven to 200°C/400°F/gas 6.

Roll out the pastry and use to line a 25 cm (10 in) flan ring. Line with greaseproof paper and baking beans and bake in the pre-heated oven for 15–20 minutes, until cooked. Leave to cool.

Whisk the evaporated milk and sugar together for 10–15 minutes, until light fluffy. The mix should be coffee coloured. Pour the mix into the pastry case and bake in the oven for 10 minutes. The gypsy tart will now have a slightly sticky surface but will not set completely until it has been left to cool. Serve cold. I told you this was easy.

Semolina Tart

We've all eaten semolina pudding with jam, which probably often tasted like glue. This semolina recipe is very different and finishes with a texture similar to a baked cheesecake, with a slightly different taste.

SERVES 4
225 g (8 oz) Sweet Shortcrust pastry
  (see p. 394)

FOR THE FILLING
1.2 litres (2 pints) milk
100 ml (3¹/₂ fl oz) double cream

200 g (7 oz) caster sugar
50 g (2 oz) unsalted butter
175 g (6 oz) polenta
50 g (2 oz) semolina

Grated zest and juice of 1 lemon
A pinch of salt
100 g (4 oz) sultanas, soaked in 50 ml
   (2 fl oz) dark rum

Pre-heat the oven to 180°C/350°F/gas 4 and grease a 20 cm (8 in) flan tin or flan ring on a baking sheet.

Roll out the pastry and use to line the flan tin or ring. Line the pastry with grease-proof paper, fill with baking beans and bake blind in the pre-heated oven for 20 minutes. Remove the beans and paper, trim round the top of the ring and leave to cool.

To make the filling, mix the milk, cream, sugar and butter in a pan and bring to the boil. Gradually whisk in the polenta and semolina, lemon zest and juice and salt, being careful to avoid any lumps. Transfer to a bowl and sit the bowl over a pan of hot water. Cook the mix for 20 minutes, stirring frequently, until the mix is very thick. Stir in the sultanas and rum. If the mix is too thick and slightly stodgy then simply thin down with a little more milk or cream. Pour the mix into the flan case, cover with buttered greaseproof paper to prevent a skin forming and leave to cool. The flan should not be turned out until completely set.

This eats very well on its own or with cream. As an alternative, some apple wedges cooked in butter and sugar can be placed on top, sprinkled with icing sugar and glazed under a hot grill.

Glazed Lemon Tart

This tart has become a classic amongst chefs. It eats very well on its own, but I also like to eat it with warm cherries. These can be made by stoning 450 g (1 lb) of fresh cherries and cooking them in 50 g (2 oz) of unsalted butter and 50 g (2 oz) caster sugar for about 6–8 minutes. You can also add a measure of kirsch to help the flavour. The cherries will have created their own syrup in the pan. Now simply spoon them on to the plate with a wedge of tart and serve with cream.

SERVES 8
225 g (8 oz) Sweet Shortcrust Pastry
   (see p. 394)
Finely grated zest of 1 lemon

FOR THE FILLING AND TOPPING
8 eggs
350 g (12 oz) caster sugar
300 ml (10 fl oz) double cream
4 lemons, juice from all, finely grated
   zest from 2
Icing sugar

Make the pastry for the flan case, adding the grated lemon zest to the flour and icing sugar. Chill for 20–30 minutes.

Pre-heat the oven to 180°C/350°F/gas 4 and grease a 24 cm (9½ in) flan tin or flan ring on a baking sheet. (A 20 cm/8 in ring will also work.)

Roll out the pastry and use to line the flan tin or ring. Line the pastry with greaseproof paper, fill with baking beans and bake blind in the pre-heated oven for 15–20 minutes. Remove the beans and paper and leave to cool. Reduce the oven temperature to 150°C/300°F/gas 2.

To make the filling, mix the eggs and caster sugar together until smooth, then pour on the cream and mix in the lemon juice and zest. Pour into the cooked flan case and bake in the pre-heated oven for 30–40 minutes, until the tart is just set. Remove from the oven and allow to cool.

The tart is now ready to serve, but it's nice to finish it with a golden glaze. To do this, simply sprinkle each portion with icing sugar and colour briefly under a hot grill.

Lemon Puffs Pudding

This pudding is really a combination of two of my favourite recipes: a glazed lemon tart with a puff pastry Palmier Biscuit. I'm sure you can imagine just how well these work together. The crisp but light puff pastry is mixed with the soft delicate lemon 'mousse' that has a sharp bite behind it. Use a home-made puff pastry or simply buy a block of frozen. The Palmier Biscuits can also be made from any puff pastry trimmings you may have frozen.

SERVES 8

FOR THE BISCUITS
Icing sugar, sifted
16 Palmier Biscuits (see p. 345),
    made with 225 g (8 oz) Puff Pastry
    (see p. 393) or bought puff
    pastry

FOR THE LEMON PUFF FILLING
8 eggs
350 g (12 oz) caster sugar
300 ml (10 fl oz) double cream
Juice of 4 lemons
Finely grated zest of 2 lemons

TO SERVE
Icing sugar
Pouring cream

Pre-heat the oven to 220°C/425°F/gas 7. Lightly grease and dampen a baking sheet.

Roll out and bake the biscuits as described on p. 358. For a darker, caramel-crisp finish, dust with more icing sugar and place under the grill or use a gas gun. These biscuits are now ready to use or will keep for 24 hours in an airtight container.

Reduce the oven temperature to 150°C/300°F/gas 2. Grease and base-line a 20 cm (8 in) loose-bottomed flan ring or eight 6 cm (2½ in) tins.

To make the lemon filling, mix the eggs and caster sugar together until smooth, then add the cream, lemon juice and zest. This mix can now be poured into the tin or tins and should be 2.5–4 cm (1–1^1/2 in) deep. Bake in the pre-heated oven for 45–50 minutes until the filling has just set. The small tins will only take 20–25 minutes. Remove from the oven and leave to cool. To make the mix slightly firmer and easier to use, chill for 30 minutes before cutting.

To finish the puddings, use a warm knife to release the filling mix from the edge of the case(s). For the small cases, dip very quickly in hot water to release the greaseproofed base. It's best to sit one of the palmier biscuits on top of the mould and turn the case upside-down. This will immediately sit the filling on the biscuit. Remove the greaseproof and then sit another palmier on top to complete the dish.

If using a large tin, then simply turn out on to a large tray or, if loose-bottomed, simply push out. Now the filling can be cut out with a 6–7.5 cm (2^1/2–3 in) ring and carefully lifted on to a biscuit using a spatula or fish slice. The filling is very delicate and will need careful handling. You can then assemble the biscuits. Obviously, when using a tray, you will be left with some trimmings. I always find it best just to eat and enjoy them. To serve, I simply sit the lemon puffs on the plate, dust around with icing sugar and serve with pouring cream.

NOTE

The lemon 'mousse' trimmings can be whisked with some pouring cream and then set in glasses for an extra pudding.

VARIATION

If you want an extra garnish, then cook some thin strips of lemon zest in a stock syrup. This can be made by boiling 150 ml (5 fl oz) of water with 100 g (4 oz) of caster sugar until a syrup is formed. Serve with the lemon puffs.

Lemon Posset

This must be the easiest pudding ever to prepare and cook, which is why I've included it in the book.

SERVES 6
900 ml (1^1/2 pints) double cream

250 g (9 oz) caster sugar
Juice of 3 lemons

Boil the cream and sugar together in a pan and cook for 2–3 minutes. Add the lemon juice and mix in well. Leave to cool slightly then pour into six glasses and leave to set in the fridge. The pudding is now ready. It is nice to pour a little more liquid cream on top before serving.

Sherry Trifle

Trifle, over the years, has taken on many variations. The word itself comes from an old term, 'trifling', which meant layering different sponges, fruits and jellies and finishing with a sabayon rather than a custard. Of course, most home-made trifles still have all those ingredients, even sometimes blancmange too but, as with most other things, I like good old-fashioned simplicity, and this recipe has plenty of taste and texture without all the extras.

The custard below can be used on its own for this pudding, but I like to go halves with Custard Sauce/Crème Anglaise (see p. 355), to give a richer and fresher taste. (I don't use all Anglaise because it wouldn't set.)

SERVES 4

FOR THE SPONGE
3 eggs
75 g (3 oz) caster sugar
75 g (3 oz) plain flour
40 g (1^1/$_2$ oz) unsalted butter, melted

FOR THE SYRUP
225 g (8 oz) caster sugar
300 ml (10 fl oz) water
4–5 tablespoons sweet sherry

FOR THE CUSTARD SAUCE
600 ml (1 pint) milk
50 g (2 oz) custard powder
50 g (2 oz) caster sugar

FOR THE FILLING AND TOPPING
Raspberry jam, to cover the sponge
300 ml (10 fl oz) double cream,
    whipped
100 g (4 oz) plain chocolate, grated

Pre-heat the oven to 200°c/400°F/gas 6 and grease and line a 20 cm (8 in) flan tin or flan ring and baking sheet.

To make the sponge, whisk the eggs and sugar in a bowl over a pan of hot water until the mixture has doubled in bulk and is light and creamy. Very gently fold in the flour and melted butter. Pour the mix into the lined flan tin or ring and bake in the pre-heated oven for 30 minutes. Turn out and allow to cool.

To make the syrup, boil the sugar and water together for about 2 minutes to a syrup, then add sherry to taste – more than above if you like the taste.

To make the custard sauce, mix some of the milk with the custard powder in a pan. Bring the remaining milk to the boil in another pan. Pour this on to the custard powder, whisking all the time. Return to the heat and bring back to the boil. While stirring, the sauce will thicken. Add the sugar, cover with buttered greaseproof paper and allow to cool.

Split the sponge in half horizontally and spread jam on both pieces. Place one half in a bowl and soak with half the sherry syrup. Sit the other sponge on top and again soak with sherry syrup. Pour the custard on top and allow to set in the fridge. When set, spoon the whipped cream on top and sprinkle with grated chocolate.

You can also make individual trifles in 10 cm (4 in) soufflé dishes. Bake little sponges to fit, or cut to fit, and assemble in exactly the same way.

Summer Pudding

I've listed quantities and varieties of fruits below but, of course, the beauty of this dish is that the choice of red berries is entirely your own, so use what is easily available. I have found that these fruits work well together. You need about 1.4 kg (3 lb) of soft fruit altogether. If there is a lot of the fruit mix left over, it can be kept for a few days and served as it is with ice-cream or cream – or make some more puddings.

SERVES 8–10
2 punnets of raspberries
2 punnets of strawberries
1 punnet of tayberries or loganberries
1 punnet of blackberries
1 punnet of redcurrants
1 punnet of blackcurrants
1 punnet of blueberries
2 tablespoons crème de framboise
    liqueur
1 loaf white bread, thinly sliced

FOR THE RASPBERRY PURÉE
450 g (1 lb) fresh or frozen raspberries
50 g (2 oz) icing sugar

FOR THE SUGAR SYRUP
600 ml (1 pint) water
350 g (12 oz) caster sugar

TO SERVE
Clotted or whipped cream

Lightly butter a 1.5-litre (2½-pint) basin or eight 150 ml (5 fl oz) moulds.

Trim and wash all the fruits and leave to drain.

To make the raspberry purée, simply blitz the berries and sugar together in a blender, then push through a sieve.

To make the sugar syrup, simply boil the water and sugar together for a few minutes to a clear syrup. Leave to cool.

Mix half of the raspberry purée with the sugar syrup and bring to the simmer. Add the fruits and the crème de framboise to the sauce, then remove from the heat and leave to rest. The fruits should have all softened but will still have kept their shape. When cool, pour some of the syrup into a separate bowl.

Remove the crusts from the bread and cut each slice into three. Dip these in the reserved raspberry syrup and line the basin or moulds with the soaked bread, overlapping slightly with each slice. When the basin or all the moulds are lined, fill with the fruits and a little of the sauce and cover with more bread. Cover with a plate, press down with a weight and leave in the fridge for a few hours.

Mix the remaining raspberry purée with a little of the remaining pudding juices until you have a sauce consistency. Turn out the summer puddings on to plates or divide the large one into wedges, and spoon the finished raspberry sauce over them. Garnish with some of the remaining fruit mix, raspberry purée and either clotted or whipped cream.

Cooking Fruits: Cherries, Plums, Greengages, Gooseberries and Damsons

All these fruits eat very well with different dishes. This recipe is really for cherries and plums, both of which are featured in the book, but also for the less frequently used fruits, gooseberries, greengages and damsons. Cherries and, in fact, all of these fruits, once stoned, can be cooked in a knob of butter with sugar. The fruits will create their own liquor/syrup and are then ready to use. For every 450 g (1 lb) of fruit you will need only 25 g (1 oz) of butter to 50–100 g (2–4 oz) of caster sugar, depending on the ripeness of the fruit. So there's one basic recipe already. Here are a couple more alternatives.

MAKES ABOUT 600 g (1¼ lb)

450 g (1 lb) cherries, gooseberries or damsons, washed and stoned

4 tablespoons water

100 g (4 oz) caster sugar

All the ingredients can be placed in a pan and brought to the boil. Remove from the stove and allow the fruits to cool in the liquor. These can now be kept in their own liquor and chilled, or the liquor can be used to soak sponges or boiled until reduced by half and used as a glaze to finish flans and tarts.

VARIATION

A liqueur can be substituted for half the water; for example, try 2 tablespoons of kirsch and 2 tablespoons of water when cooking cherries.

COOKING PLUMS, DAMSONS AND GREENGAGES

This method is best for fruits being used in fruit tarts and sponges; they keep their shape but also become very tender. All you need to do is halve and stone the fruits and place on a baking sheet, skin-side down. Sprinkle liberally with icing sugar and cook in a pre-heated oven 200°C/400°F/gas 6 for 4–6 minutes. The sugar will dissolve and sweeten the fruits as they soften. As the fruits cook on the baking tray, a little natural syrup will be created. It's best to save this and use it for a glaze.

These fruits will also work in the first recipe, but will not hold up so well when mixed with water. In fact they will purée very quickly which, of course, is fine if you're making a coulis or purée.

Pineapple Fritters

This recipe uses the same cider batter I use for Apple Fritters (see p. 304). That's the beauty of cooking, so many flavours help each other. With these I like to serve Coconut Ice-cream (see p. 257) and Rum Custard Sauce (see p. 355). It's almost like eating a hot Piña Colada cocktail. The fritters also eat well with clotted cream and Chocolate Sauce (see p. 354). If you don't fancy either of these serving ideas, just pour over fresh cream.

SERVES 4
1 small, ripe pineapple
300 ml (10 fl oz) sweet cider
100 g (4 oz) plain flour plus a little
   extra for coating

25 g (1 oz) caster sugar
Vegetable oil, for deep-frying

Cut the outside skin from the pineapple, then split it into quarters. Remove the central core from all four pieces. Each quarter can now be cut into three, leaving you with twelve large chunks.

To make the batter, mix together the cider, flour and sugar. Heat the oil to about 180°C/350°F. Lightly flour the pineapple chunks, then dip them into the batter and deep-fry for about 5 minutes until crispy and golden. You may need to do this in batches.

Pineapple and Almond Tart

This tart eats really well sitting on a Rich Chocolate Sauce (see p. 354) and topped with Coconut Ice-cream (see p. 257). All those flavours work so well with pineapple. The pineapple should be fresh and ripe. This will be a deep yellow colour with a moist sweet taste. If you find the pineapple to be firm and opaque in colour, the fruit will need to be poached in some Stock Syrup (see p. 397) until tender. This dish can also be made using a good-quality tinned pineapple. You can make this pudding with lots of different fruits, from apple and blackberry to raspberry, pear or peach. All these fruits work with different ice-creams and sauces.

SERVES 6–8
225 g (8 oz) Shortcrust Pastry
   (see p. 394)
1/2 fresh pineapple, peeled

2 tablespoons pineapple jam (optional)
1 quantity Frangipane (Almond Paste)
   (see p. 396)
Icing sugar, sifted

Pre-heat the oven to 190°C/375°F/gas 5 and grease a 25 cm (10 in) flan ring.

Roll out the pastry, use to line the flan ring and leave to rest in the fridge. Cut the pineapple into 2 cm (3/4 in) cubes. For extra pineapple taste, spread some pineapple jam on to the pastry base first before spooning in the almond paste and smoothing over.

Push the pineapple cubes into the almond paste. During the cooking of this tart the almond paste will become liquid and flood the tart case. As the paste cooks it will develop a moist sponge texture. Bake the tart in the pre-heated oven. The tart will take 45–60 minutes. The almond paste will rise slightly.

To give an extra finish and glaze to the tart, sprinkle liberally with icing sugar and glaze under the grill.

NOTE

For a different finish to the dish, liberally scatter diced fresh pineapple over the top of the tart 10 minutes before it is completely cooked and return it to the oven. The tart can still be finished with the icing sugar glazed under the grill.

Pear and Hazelnut 'Pasties'

The last time I called a dish a pasty (it was a lamb dish), I was inundated with letters telling me I didn't have a clue what a real pasty is! Well, after being shown several times since, I certainly do now. So please don't send me any more letters over this recipe. This is what I call using artistic licence.

All I'm really doing is taking the pasty shape and turning it into a pudding. The pastry I'm using is puff rather than a short/puff/crumbly pastry that's normally used. The frangipane made with ground hazelnuts rather than almonds immediately gives you a new flavour. Of course, almond frangipane can also be used. One of the advantages of this dish is that it can be made well in advance before being baked.

One of my joys of cooking is the number of variations each recipe can have. This recipe can be made with almost any fruit: apples, plums and cherries are just a few examples. I still have this run of 'Black Forest' ideas, so how about using Chocolate Frangipane (see p. 396), mixing in some chocolate chips and topping the frangipane with poached cherries and cherry jam on the base. So there's a fun idea: Hot Black Forest Pasties served with Chocolate Sabayon (see p. 358) and clotted cream.

SERVES 4

FOR THE PEARS
4 small pears, peeled, halved and
    cored
1/2 lemon
1 vanilla pod (optional)
1 cinnamon stick (optional)
600 ml (1 pint) water
22 g (8 oz) caster sugar

FOR THE PASTIES
350–450 g (12–16 oz) Puff Pastry
    (see p. 393) or bought puff pastry
175 g (6 oz) Frangipane (Almond Paste)
    (see p. 396, about 1/2 quantity),
    made with ground hazelnuts instead
    of almonds

OPTIONAL EXTRAS, TO SERVE
Rich Chocolate Sauce (see p. 354),
    Chocolate Sabayon (see p. 358),
    Custard Sauce (see p. 355) or
    Chocolate Custard (see p. 356)

Pre-heat the oven to 200°C/400°F/gas 6.

Rub the pear halves with the lemon, then place in a pan with the remaining lemon juice, the vanilla pod and cinnamon stick if using, the water and sugar. Cover with greaseproof paper and bring to the boil. Allow to simmer for a few minutes, then remove from the heat. Leave the pears to cool in the syrup to allow them to finish cooking.

The next stage is to roll out the puff pastry into four 20 cm (8 in) diameter circles. If using chocolate chips, add them to the hazelnut frangipane. Also, if it's plum, cherry or any red fruit you are going to use in this pasty, I always spoon some jam of the fruit flavour on the pastry before sitting the frangipane on top. Cherry jam can also be used with this pear recipe.

Divide the hazelnut frangipane between the pastry circles, spreading it on one half only and also leaving a 1–2 cm (½–¾ in) border to seal the pasty. The pears can now be placed on top, allowing two halves per portion. These should be placed core-side down, leaving a good domed top to fold the pastry over.

Beat the egg and brush around the border. The pastry can now be folded over and sealed. To shape the edge, twist as for a classic pasty, or mark with a fork, or perhaps cut to give a fluted finish. Brush the pasties with the remaining beaten egg, to give them a shiny finish. These can now be chilled to rest for 10 minutes before cooking. If you are making them in advance – and you can even make them the day before – do not glaze them until you are ready to cook.

Bake the pasties in the pre-heated oven for 20–25 minutes. If they seem to be colouring too quickly, then simply cover lightly with foil or greaseproof paper and continue to cook. They're now ready to eat. Serve with pouring or clotted cream.

VARIATION

The pasties will also work very well with tinned pear halves. Of course they don't have quite the same strength or taste as fresh pears, but they still eat well.

Apple Pies

This recipe can be used as individual pies or, of course, as one large one. I really don't mind either but it is nice to have your own personal apple pie. I like to place a disc of sponge in the base of the pies. This collects any apple juices and prevents the pastry from becoming soggy on the base. It also gives you a tasty sponge once cooked. You can use the Victoria sponge (see p. 337) or buy one from any supermarket.

This method and recipe could also have many other combinations: raisins and currants can be added, or you can make apple and cherry, blackberry or black-currant pies.

SERVES 4

350 g (12 oz) Shortcrust Pastry
(see p. 394)

1/2 Victoria Sponge (see p. 337)
(optional)

FOR THE FILLING

350–450 g (12–16 oz) Bramley cooking
apples, peeled, cored and cut into
1 cm (1/2 in) dice

Juice and grated zest of 1/2 lemon

1/2 teaspoon grated orange zest

1/2 teaspoon ground cinnamon

2 tablespoons demerara sugar

FOR THE GLAZE

2 tablespoons apricot jam, sieved

4 tablespoons water

Pre-heat the oven to 200°C/400°F/gas 6. Grease and flour four 9 cm (3½ in) loose-bottomed flan rings or tartlet tins or a 15 cm (6 in) mould.

Roll out half the pastry, cut into four strips and use to line the inside of the rings, making sure it's slightly higher than the ring to fold some over. Cut the remaining pastry into eight discs, four for the base and four for the lids. The bases can now be placed in the moulds. Cut the sponge into 5 mm (1/4 in) thick discs and place on top of the bases.

Mix together all the filling ingredients, then pack the filling into the moulds, making sure the moulds are absolutely full and brimming. This is basically because, during cooking, the apples will break down in texture and reduce in quantity. Brush the pastry edge with water and sit the lids on top. Trim off all excess pastry. The pies are now ready to cook. Cook in the pre-heated oven for 20–30 minutes for individual moulds and 40–45 minutes for one large pie. Once cooked and golden brown, allow to rest for 10–15 minutes before removing the mould.

To give an overall shiny glaze, bring the jam and water to a simmer, adding a little more water if the glaze is too thick, then brush over the complete pie. These are now ready to eat and go well with custard, clotted cream or ice-cream.

Apple Pancakes

I'm using apples for these filled pancakes, but pears or any other fruit can be used. There are also a few other additions you can make, some of which I list below.

SERVES 4

1 quantity Sweet Pancakes
(see p. 395)

6 ripe apples

50 g (2 oz) unsalted butter

50 g (2 oz) icing sugar

Peel, core and chop two of the apples and cook in half the butter and sugar until puréed. Peel and quarter the remaining apples then cut each quarter into four or five slices. Melt remaining butter and toss the apple slices in this for a few minutes until just softening. Add the apple purée and bring to the simmer. The filling is now ready.

Allowing three pancakes per portion, divide the purée between the pancakes and either fold them in half or in quarters. Sit them in bowls and sprinkle with the remaining icing sugar. They can now be glazed under a hot grill to give a crispy topping. You can serve them with clotted or double cream, but here are a few ideas of how to enhance all the flavours.

1 When making the purée, some calvados or reduced sweet cider can be added.
2 Serve the pancakes with home-made Apple Sorbet (see p. 267) or Vanilla Ice-cream (see p. 252).
3 Add calvados or reduced cider to some Custard Sauce/Crème Anglaise (see p. 355) to serve as a sauce.
4 For the ultimate dessert, serve a calvados Anglaise and Apple Sorbet with the pancakes.

Griddled Honey Apples with Toffee Cream

This must be the easiest and quickest apple pudding there is so, if you're ever stuck and time is running out, have a go. It's great to eat with the toffee cream but also works really well with just pouring cream or Vanilla Ice-cream (see p. 252).

To speed up the glazing of the top, I use a gas gun, which works really well to caramelize sugar.

SERVES 2
3 apples, peeled and cored
15 g (1oz) unsalted butter
4 teaspoons clear honey

2–3 tablespoons icing sugar sifted
Toffee Cream (see p. 360) to serve
2 sprigs of fresh mint (optional)

Slice the apples across through the middle to give six thick apple rings in total. Warm a frying-pan and add the butter. Sit the apples, middle-side down, in the pan and fry until the apples become a rich brown with tinges of burnt around the edges to give a bitter-sweet apple taste. Turn the apples and continue to cook over a medium heat for 1–2 minutes (or you can place them in a medium oven for 1–2 minutes, until the apples become just tender).

Spoon the honey on top of the apples. Spoon the icing sugar into a teastrainer and sprinkle well over the top. Finish under a hot grill until the sugar becomes crispy. To increase the crunchy topping, just sprinkle more icing sugar on top and re-glaze.

To serve the apples, Sit three pieces on each plate and serve with thick toffee cream and a sprig of mint.

Apple Tart with its own Sorbet

This recipe gives you a tart that is hot, thin and crisp and, if you can't imagine the sorbet melting all over it, you're just going to have to try it. For a variation, try flavouring the sorbet with calvados or replacing the water with cider.

SERVES 4

FOR THE TART
225 g (8 oz) Puff Pastry (see p. 393) or
   bought
50 g (2 oz) unsalted butter
8 Granny Smith apples
4 teaspoons caster sugar

4 tablespoons apricot jam
2 tablespoons water

FOR THE SORBET
225 g (8 oz) caster sugar
300 ml (10 fl oz) water
10 Granny Smith apples, peeled, cored
   and chopped

Grease one large or two smaller oven trays.

To make the tart bases, roll out the puff pastry as thinly as possible and leave to rest in the fridge. Cut the pastry into four 20 cm (8 in) circles, each forming one portion. Lay the tart bases on the oven trays and return to the fridge.

The next step is to make the sorbet. Dissolve the sugar in the water over a low heat then bring to the boil and boil for a few minutes to make a syrup. Add the apples and simmer gently for about 10–15 minutes, until they start to purée. When ready, push them through a sieve and wait for the mix to cool. This can now be made into a sorbet by freezing in an ice-cream maker or in the freezer; you'll have to whisk it every 15–20 minutes until frozen if not using an ice-cream a maker.

Pre-heat the oven to 230°C/450°F/gas 8.

To make the tarts, peel, core and quarter the apples. Slice the apple quarters into three or four pieces, and start to overlap them on the pastry discs all the way round, until each circle of pastry is totally covered. Chop the butter and divide between the tarts. Sprinkle each one with caster sugar and bake in the pre-heated oven for about 15 minutes, until the pastry is crisp and the apples have started to colour.

Boil the apricot jam with the water and brush on to the tarts to give a glazed finish. The apple tarts are now ready to serve. The sorbet may be shaped between two spoons to make a quenelle shape or simply served separately in a bowl.

Apple Fritters with Apricot Sauce and Vanilla Ice-cream

If it's a hot pudding you're after, this must be one of the easiest. So many other fruits can be used – bananas, apricots, pears – but I find apples go so well with the ice-cream and apricot sauce.

SERVES 4

1 quantity Vanilla Ice-cream (see
    p. 252)

FOR THE APRICOT SAUCE
225 g (8 oz) caster sugar
300 ml (10 fl oz) water
350 g (12 oz) fresh apricots, stoned and
    quartered
2 tablespoons apricot jam (optional)

FOR THE FRITTERS
300 ml (10 fl oz) sweet cider
100 g (4 oz) plain flour, plus a little
    extra for coating
25 g (1 oz) caster sugar
4 Granny Smith apples, peeled and
    cored
Vegetable oil, for deep-frying
1 sprig of fresh mint (optional)

To make the apricot sauce, dissolve the sugar in the water over a low heat then bring to the boil and boil for a few minutes to make a syrup. Cook the apricots in the syrup and jam for about 10 minutes until they have puréed. Push through a sieve and keep warm.

To make the fritter batter, mix the cider, flour and sugar together. Cut each of the apples into five wedges and lightly flour each piece. Dip them in the batter and deep-fry in hot oil for about minutes until golden and crispy. Drain well.

To serve, lay the fritters on a plate and pour the apricot sauce next to them. Serve a large spoonful of vanilla ice-cream with each portion. For extra colour, decorate with a sprig of mint.

Apple and Raisin and Honey and Rhubarb Brûlées

Crème brûlée is one of those puddings that we all enjoy but don't make often enough (if ever) at home. It's basically just a fresh custard mix in ramekins, cooked in a water bath in the oven. The beauty of making these and serving them is that you really don't need to worry about presentation; they always speak for themselves.

SERVES 8

FOR THE APPLE AND RAISIN
BRÛLÉE
50 g (2 oz) raisins
8 egg yolks
50 g (2 oz) caster sugar
1/4 quantity Simple Stock Syrup
    (see p. 397)
600 ml (1 pint) double cream
1 vanilla pod or a few drops of vanilla
    essence

TO GARNISH
2 Golden Delicious or Granny Smith
    apples
Icing sugar

FOR THE HONEY AND RHUBARB
BRÛLÉE
50 g (2 oz) clear honey
225 g (8 oz) rhubarb
25 g (1 oz) caster or demerara sugar
Icing sugar (optional)
A knob of butter

The apple and raisin recipe needs to be started with a few hours' notice, giving the raisins time to soften. You will need eight 150 ml (5 fl oz) ramekins.

Pre-heat the oven to 180°C/350°F/gas 4.

Make the stock syrup and bring it to the boil. This is now going to be used both for the raisins and apples. Take 2–3 tablespoons of the syrup and add the calvados or brandy, if using. Add the raisins to the syrup, bring them to a simmer, then leave to stand for 2 hours. This will soften them giving a more tender texture.

Now make the *crème brûlée* mix. Mix together the egg yolks and sugar. Bring the cream to the boil with the vanilla pod or essence. Once boiled, remove the vanilla pod, if using, and split and scrape the insides into the cream. Now whisk the cream into the egg yolks and sugar.

Place the raisins in the ramekins. You now have two methods of finishing. The mix can be simply divided between the ramekins and the ramekins placed in a roasting tin filled with hot water to come three-quarters up the sides. Cook in the pre-heated oven for about 30 minutes until almost set.

Another method, which can give the *brûlées* a slightly lighter and creamier finish, is to sit the bowl with the mix over a pan of hot water and keep stirring until the custard begins to thicken. This can now be finished as above, cooking for only about 15–20 minutes.

To test, remove one of the moulds from the water after 20 minutes and shake gently. There should still be slight movement in the centre of the custard. If it is still runny, put it back in the oven and check after another 5 minutes. Once ready, remove from the oven and water bath and allow to cool to room temperature. This is the temperature and consistency that I believe is the best to eat them at. *Brûlées* can be chilled, which will obviously give you a firmer texture.

While the *brûlées* are cooking and cooling, the apples can be prepared. It will take a quarter of an apple per portion. These should be peeled, quartered and then the core removed from each piece. Now slice the quarters thinly lengthways. Bring the remaining stock syrup to the boil and add the slices. As soon as it returns to the boil, remove the pan from the heat and allow to cool. The slices can now be taken from the stock and lightly dried before overlapping and covering the *brûlées*.

Pre-heat the grill.

Now it's time for the crispy sugar topping. Dust the apples heavily with icing sugar. The moulds can now be placed under a grill until the sugar begins to caramelize. To give a fine but crisp finish, the same process will need to be repeated at least once or twice more. For a more controlled glaze, a gas gun can be used. The *brûlées* are now ready and eats so well, as you cut through the crispy apples, through the thick vanilla custard and then find the rich raisins.

For the honey and rhubarb version, there's very little change to the basic recipe. Simply replace the caster sugar with 50 g (2 oz) of honey. The mix can now be cooked in ramekins as for the basic recipe. All you need now is the rhubarb topping.

Peel the rhubarb and cut into 1 cm (1/2 in) pieces. Melt the butter and, once bubbling, add the diced rhubarb with the caster or demerara sugar. The rhubarb, once slightly simmering, will only take 12 minutes before becoming tender. Turn the fruit carefully for even cooking and to avoid breaking it up.

Once cooked, the rhubarb can be placed immediately on top of the *brûlées*, with some of its own syrup and served. Or allow to cool, then spoon on top, heavily dust with icing sugar and finish under the grill or with a gas gun, as for the apple recipe.

Apricot and Almond Tart

For this recipe I'm using a large 28 cm (11 in) diameter × 4 (1½ in) deep flan ring, which really does make a large pudding. The recipe can easily be cut down by half and a smaller 18 cm (7 in) flan can be used. You can use whichever stock syrup you prefer for this recipe.

The flan eats well hot or cold and goes well with clotted cream, custard or ice-cream and is a great alternative for Christmas when served with Christmas Pudding Ice-cream (see p. 262).

SERVES 6–8

20 dried, ready-soaked stoned apricots

300 ml (10 fl oz) Stock Syrup
  (see p. 397)

225 g (8 oz) Shortcrust Pastry
  (see p. 394)

4 tablespoons apricot jam

1 quantity Frangipane (Almond Paste)
  (see p. 396)

Icing sugar, sifted

Pre-heat the oven to 190°C/375°F/gas 5. Butter and lightly flour a 28 cm (11 in) flan ring.

Split the apricots through the middle, leaving circular discs of fruit. Warm the stock syrup with the fruits and then leave to cool. These can be prepared and chilled days in advance or left until the last minute and drained off before using. The stock will still keep in the fridge. This process softens the apricots even more and leaves them tender.

Roll out the pastry and use to line the flan case. Heat the jam and reduce by half. Spread the jam over the pastry base, then place 20 apricot pieces evenly over the jam. Spoon over the almond paste, leaving a smooth finish on top, and filling to about three-quarters of the way up to allow for it to rise during cooking. Bake in the pre-heated oven for 45 minutes.

Remove from the oven and arrange the remaining apricots on top in a circular pattern. (If you put them on before cooking, they sink into the almond paste as it warms and loosens.) Return to the oven for a further 10–20 minutes, until golden brown and just firming to the touch.

Sprinkle the flan liberally with icing sugar and glaze under a hot grill, allowing the sugar to caramelize and almost burn in places for a bitter-sweet taste.

Steamed Apricot Sponge with Apricot Sauce

This recipe has many alternatives – you can use dried or tinned apricots, or even apricot jam. This, of course, makes it quite a rich pudding that is packed with flavour.

When buying dried apricots it's best to select 'ready-to-eat' or no-soak ones that are available in almost all supermarkets. They still have about 25 per cent moisture left in them, which leaves them soft and almost toffee-like to eat straight from the packet. Also for this recipe choose the apricots which are still orange in colour. The texture of this dish is lovely to eat. You have good soft apricots on top of a light fluffy sponge with the rich sauce. The best accompaniment is simply clotted cream and apricot sauce.

SERVES 4–6
12–16 ready-to-eat dried apricots
1 × 425 g (15 oz) tin of halved apricots in syrup

1 quantity Steamed Sponge Pudding mix (see p. 329)
1 tablespoon apricot jam
Icing sugar, sifted

It's best to start this recipe either in the morning or day before to achieve the best flavour from the apricots. To give them more moisture and flavour they should be soaked in some syrup, and with this recipe you don't even have to make it. Just open the tinned apricots and pour off and keep the syrup. Warm the syrup and add the dried apricots. Leave them to stand for a few hours. The apricots should be a little softer and more juicy.

Grease and flour six 150 ml (5 fl oz) moulds or one 900 ml (1½ pint) mould.

You can now place three halves of apricot per portion, without syrup, in the bottom of the individual or large pudding moulds. If you have soaked some extra, then simply chop them up and mix into the basic sponge mix. Spoon the mix on top and steam as for the basic recipe (see p. 329).

To make the apricot sauce, blend the tinned apricots to a purée. Warm in a pan with the apricot jam, then add enough of the remaining syrup until you have a good sauce consistency. The sauce may taste a little sharp. To help this, just add some icing sugar a pinch at a time until you have the right sweetness. Push the sauce through a sieve and it is ready.

Once the sponge is cooked, turn out on to a plate and spoon the warm apricot sauce over.

Steamed Orange Sponge with Hot Orange Sauce and Marmalade Ice-cream

This pudding gives us three different orange flavours from bitter to sweet, and also three different textures. It has to be my favourite steamed sponge.

SERVES 4–6

100 g (4 oz) unsalted butter

150 g (5 oz) caster sugar

2 eggs

1 egg yolk

Finely grated zest of 1 orange

200 g (7 oz) self-raising flour

Juice of 2–3 oranges, boiled to reduce by two-thirds then cooled

FOR THE SAUCE

600 ml (1 pint) fresh orange juice

25–50 g (1–2 oz) caster sugar

1 teaspoon arrowroot or cornflour

1 tablespoon cold water

Marmalade Ice-cream to serve (see p. 254)

A few fresh mint sprigs

To make the sponge, cream the butter and sugar together. Mix the eggs and egg yolk together and beat into the butter and sugar mix. Add the orange zest and fold in the flour. Add the orange juice, making sure it is cold.

Line six 150 ml (5 fl oz) moulds or one 900 ml (1½ pint) mould with butter and flour. Spoon in the sponge mix to fill three-quarters of the way up the mould and cover with buttered paper or tin foil. Steam individual puddings for about 35–40 minutes or larger puddings for 1¼–1½ hours.

Meanwhile, make the orange sauce. Boil the orange juice until reduced by half, then add the sugar to taste (start with a tablespoon and add until you have the sweetness you want). Mix the arrowroot or cornflour with the water then whisk a few drops at a time into the simmering juice until you have a good sauce/coating consistency. Allow to cook for 3–4 minutes.

Once the pudding is cooked, just turn out and serve with a spoonful of marmalade ice-cream, some hot orange sauce and a sprig of mint.

VARIATIONS

This is a recipe for a basic orange sauce. To change the flavour, some grated zest can be added or a little Cointreau, Grand Marnier or brandy to lift the taste.

Banana and Toffee Cream Pancakes

Here's a great alternative for Shrove Tuesday. Of course, the pancakes can also be used in many other puddings, especially when served with ice-creams. How does warm pancakes with vanilla ice-cream and hot jam sauce sound?

SERVES 4–6

¹/₂ quantity Sweet Pancakes batter (see p. 395)

4 bananas

1 quantity Toffee Cream (see p. 360)

Maple syrup (optional)

Icing sugar, sifted

A few sprigs of fresh mint

Pre-heat a 25 cm (10 in) pancake pan and trickle some vegetable oil into the pan, making sure the oil has very lightly covered the pan. Add a thin layer of pancake mix to the pan. Cook for 15–20 seconds, until golden, then flip over and cook for a further 10–15 seconds on the other side. The pancake is now ready. Repeat the same process until all the mix is finished.

Peel the bananas and cut diagonally into thick slices. Sit the pancake on the plate and fold in half, keeping the semi-circular side facing you. Overlap the banana slices on one quarter of the pancake and spoon some toffee cream on top. Fold the other half of the cake over the cream, leaving a triangular-shaped pudding on the plate. Sprinkle with maple syrup, if using, and dust icing sugar around the plate. Garnish with a sprig of mint.

VARIATIONS

Try dusting the sliced bananas with icing sugar and glazing them under the grill until the sugar has caramelized, then use them in the pancakes.

Blackberry Jam Tart

I used to love jam tarts as a child: just sweet pastry tartlet moulds filled with jam. I thought they were really delicious. Well, this recipe is for a jam tart with a difference. I have always felt that a jam tart needed another texture, so read on and you'll see exactly what I mean.

For this recipe I'm going to use four individual tartlet cases, but a 28 cm (11 in) flan case will be fine. If you use a large flan case, the pastry can be left raw before adding the almond mix then all baked at the same time, in which case it will need 1–1¹/₄ hours.

The jam tart eats well just with thick or clotted cream. I also like to serve home-made Custard Sauce (see p. 355), either cold or warm, or sometimes flavoured with calvados.

SERVES 4–6
175–225 g (6–8 oz) Puff Pastry (see
   p. 393)
175 g (6 oz) unsalted butter
175 g (6 oz) caster sugar

175 g (6 oz) ground almonds
40 g (1¹/₂ oz) plain flour
3 eggs, size 2
225 g (8 oz) Blackberry Jam
   (see p. 364)

Pre-heat the oven to 180°C/350°F/gas 4.

Roll out the pastry thinly and line the flan cases, leaving any excess pastry hang-ing over the edge of the rings. This will prevent the pastry from shrinking back into the mould during baking. Leave to rest for 20 minutes. Line the pastry with grease-proof paper and fill with baking beans or rice and bake in the pre-heated oven for 15–20 minutes, until the pastry is cooked and set. Remove the paper and beans and cut off any excess pastry hanging over the flan cases. To do this, simply take a sharp knife, position it at the top of the tart ring and cut all the pastry away. By cutting this way the pastry will be neatly flush with the tart case.

You can, of course, make the filling in a food mixer or processor. Beat the butter and sugar together until well creamed. Fold in the almonds and flour. Beat in one egg at a time, making sure they are well mixed in. Spoon the almond filling into the flan case, leaving it about 2 mm (¹/₈ in) from the top. (If you find you have some mix left over, then simply chill it and it will keep for up to one week.) Bake the tarts in the pre-heated oven, allowing 30–35 minutes for the small tarts or 45–60 minutes for a large flan case. When cooked, the tarts will be firm to the touch and a knife inserted in the centre will come out almost clean.

Once cooked, the almond sponge mix should have risen slightly. This can simply be sliced off the top to expose the sponge. While the tart is still warm, spoon some of the jam over the tarts until just covered. Return to the oven for 1–2 minutes, by which time the jam will be making its way through the sponge. To serve, simply remove the flan case and eat either hot or cold.

VARIATIONS

We all know what a great combination blackberry and apple is. If you really want to make this different, simply add some grated apple to the almond mix, or place poached apples or pears in the pastry cases before spooning on the mix. This gives you different textures as well as tastes.

Greengage and Lime Sponge Pie

Greengage is a fruit we just don't see enough of. The greengage is a member of the plum family and probably more sweet and perfumed than basic plums. With this recipe they can be used completely raw, if very ripe. If the only ones you can find are under-ripe and firm, then it's best to soften them through in the oven with icing sugar before using – I'll explain this in the recipe.

These fruits in France are known as the reine-claude, named after France's first queen. So the next time you're in France and have ordered a Tarte Reine-Claude you now know you'll be eating a greengage tart or pie. This recipe gives you a combination of all these elements: it's in pastry, so there's the tart connection; and it's also set in a sponge, so there's the pie or gateau connection.

MAKES 1 × 20 cm (8 in) PIE
175–225 g (6–8 oz) Sweet Shortcrust
    Pastry (see p. 394)
400 g (14 oz) fresh greengages, halved
    and stoned
Icing sugar (optional)
2–3 tablespoons greengage jam or lime
    marmalade

FOR THE VICTORIA SPONGE
50 g (2 oz) unsalted butter
50 g (2 oz) caster sugar
1 egg

50 g (2 oz) plain flour (or use
    self-raising for a lighter finish)
Grated zest and juice of 1 lime

TO GLAZE AND FINISH
1 tablespoon greengage jam or lime
    marmalade (optional)
2 tablespoons water (optional)
Icing sugar, for dusting (optional)

Pre-heat the oven to 200°C/400°F/gas 6. Grease a 20 cm (8 in) flan ring.

Line the flan ring with the pastry, leaving any excess pastry over the edge of the ring. Line with greaseproof paper and baking beans or rice. Cook in the pre-heated oven for 20 minutes. The greaseproof paper and beans or rice can now be removed and excess pastry trimmed off.

If the greengages are very ripe then these are ready to use. If they feel firm and under-ripe, then sit them on a baking tray, skin-side down, and dust generously with icing sugar. These can now be cooked and softened in the pre-heated oven for 4–6 minutes.

To make the sponge, cream together the butter and sugar. Beat the egg and then add it slowly to the butter mix. Fold in the flour with the zest of lime. The lime juice can now be added to finish the mix.

Reduce the oven temperature to 180°C/350°F/gas 4. To make the pie, spoon the greengage jam or lime marmalade into the pastry and spread over the base. The sponge mix can now be spread into the case. Sit the greengages skin-side up on top of the sponge mix. This can now be baked in the pre-heated oven for 35–40 minutes. As the pie is cooking, the sponge will rise around the fruit. Once cooked, remove from the oven and leave for 10 minutes before serving. This dish eats very well warm or cold.

For an extra glaze finish, heat the jam or marmalade with the water and brush over. For a simple rustic finish, dust round the edges with icing sugar and serve.

This recipe has so much scope. It can be made with plums, cherries, raspberries, damsons, apricots, more or less any fruit. All you need to do is use the right jam or marmalade to go with it.

Steamed Victoria Plum Pudding

A lemon sponge was the first of my steamed puddings, and I still think it can never be repeated. But here's one that comes very close. It is best served with a warm Custard Sauce (see p. 355).

SERVES 6
225 g (8 oz) caster sugar
300 ml (10 fl oz) water
750 g (1 1/2 lb) Victoria plums, stoned
   and chopped

FOR THE SPONGE
100 g (4 oz) unsalted butter
150 g (5 oz) caster sugar
1 vanilla pod, split
2 eggs
1 egg yolk
200 g (7 oz) self-raising flour
Finely grated zest and juice of
   1/2 lemon

Grease six 150 ml (5 fl oz) moulds or one 900 ml (1 1/2 pint) basin with butter.

Dissolve the sugar in the water then bring to the boil and boil for a few minutes to make a syrup. Add the plums and cook gently for about 8–10 minutes to a lumpy, marmalade consistency.

To make the sponge, mix the butter and sugar together until almost white, then add the insides of the vanilla pod and beat in the eggs and egg yolk. Fold in the flour, lemon juice and zest. Spoon some of the plums and their syrup into the bottom of the moulds or basin. Cover with the sponge mix to come three-quarters up the sides. Cover with buttered foil and place in a steamer or a pan half-full of hot water. The small puddings will only need 40 minutes in the hot steamer, the large pudding will need 1–1 1/2 hours.

When cooked, turn the puddings out on to a plate or plates and spoon some of the hot Victoria plum syrup over each portion. The dish is now ready to serve and will eat well with either fresh cream or Custard Sauce.

Jaffa Cake Pudding

There are three stages to this recipe: the sponge base, the orange jelly and the chocolate topping. It's important to make the jelly first. This can be made a few hours ahead of time, or up to 24 hours in advance. The jelly itself will keep for up to a week, chilled, and also freezes well. Yorkshire pudding moulds make good individual jelly discs to sit in the sponge. If you use bought fresh orange juice, add the grated zest from 3 large oranges for extra flavour. The sponge recipe is a basic vanilla sponge with the addition of orange zest. To make it even easier, you can make it as one large pudding using one of those sponge base flan cases that are sold in most super- markets. Add some orange syrup, place one large disc of jelly in the middle and finish with the chocolate ganache spread.

I can promise you these eat so well. You might not be able to dunk them in your tea but, when you've finished one, you'll be looking for another.

SERVES 6–8

FOR THE JELLY
1 × 11 g sachet of powdered gelatine
300 ml (10 fl oz) fresh orange juice
    (approximately 4–5 oranges)
Finely grated zest from all oranges
    used
75 g (3 oz) caster sugar

FOR THE SPONGE BASE
3 eggs
75 g (3 oz) caster sugar
75 g (3 oz) plain flour
Finely grated zest of 1 orange
40 g (1^{1}/2 oz) unsalted butter, melted

FOR THE ORANGE SYRUP
Grated zest and juice of 1 orange
2 tablespoons water
50 g (2 oz) caster sugar

FOR THE GANACHE
300 ml (10 fl oz) double cream
2 tablespoons Cointreau or Grand
    Marnier (optional)
250 g (9 oz) good-quality plain
    chocolate
Finely grated zest of 1 orange
2 egg yolks
25 g (1 oz) caster sugar

FOR THE SHINY TOPPING
100 g (4 oz) good-quality plain
    chocolate
120 ml (4 fl oz) double cream
25 g (1 oz) unsalted butter, softened

For this recipe I am making individual portions using small, round 9 cm (3^{1}/2 in) moulds 2.5 cm (1 in) deep, buttered and floured. One large 'Jaffa' can be made instead, in which case you will need a 20 cm (8 in) cake tin or flan mould. For the jelly; line a cake tin, baking tray or Yorkshire pudding moulds with cling film. The base should also be lined with greaseproof or silicone paper.

To make the jelly, dissolve the gelatine in a little hot water. Boil the orange juice with the zest and caster sugar. Simmer for 2 minutes, then remove from the heat and add the gelatine. The syrup jelly can now be strained through a sieve. This will remove the zest, preventing the syrup from becoming over bitter and strong. Now it's best to test a tablespoon of the mix on a saucer and chill. If the jelly has set well once cold, then the mix is ready. If it seems to be a little too soft, then add a little more dissolved gelatine. Pour the jelly into the lined cake tin or tray so that it is 1 cm (1/2 in) thick. Set the jelly in the fridge. When set, cut out 6–8 × 6 cm (2^{1}/2 in) discs of jelly. Freeze any left over to use another time.

Pre-heat the oven to 190°C/375°F/gas 5. To make the sponge, whisk the eggs and sugar together in a bowl over a pan of hot water until light, creamy and at least doubled in volume. Remove from the heat and continue to whisk until cold. Gently fold in the flour, orange zest and melted butter. The mix can now be poured into the moulds so that they are three-quarters full and baked in the pre-heated oven for 15–20 minutes. If you are using one large mould, then cook for 25–30 minutes. Once cooked, leave to cool.

Now a central disc can be cut out to make space for the jelly. To do this take a 6 cm (2½ in) diameter cutter and press into the sponge 1 cm (½ in) deep, leaving a 5 mm (¼ in) border and a 5 mm (½ in) thick base or, if you are making a large one, cut out a disc of sponge 2 cm (¾ in) deep, leaving a 1 cm (½ in) border and base. You will now find that the sponge simply lifts out, leaving you that space. In both cases, do not cut through the base.

As an added extra and something that will really lift the texture and flavour of the sponge, I like to make a rich orange syrup to soak the sponge bases. Mix the orange zest and juice, water and sugar in a pan. Bring to a simmer and cook for 1–2 minutes to a rich orange syrup. Now pour 1 tablespoon of syrup into each sponge base. The discs of orange jelly can now be placed in the sponge base.

Now it's time to make the chocolate ganache filling. Melt together half the cream, the Cointreau or Grand Marnier, chocolate and orange zest. Whisk the egg yolks and sugar together until the mixture trails off the whisk in ribbons. Lightly whip the remaining cream. Mix the egg and sugar mix with the melted chocolate mix, then gently fold in the whipped cream. The mix can now be left to cool, stirring occasionally until it has reached piping consistency. The chocolate ganache can now be piped or spooned on top of the jelly sponge, making sure you have a 1 cm (½ in) topping. This can now be rippled with a palette knife for that 'Jaffa' finish.

To give the ultimate 'Jaffa' effect, here is a recipe for a shiny topping.

Melt the chocolate with the cream, add the softened butter and spoon a thin layer on top of the puddings. The puddings are now finished and can be chilled. They eat at their best at room temperature. This prevents the chocolate from becoming over-set.

To serve, remove the puddings from the moulds and for a real shiny finish place them under the grill for a few seconds or fire with a gas gun.

NOTE

The orange jelly can also be made by quartering 3 oranges and poaching them in 150–300 ml (5–10 fl oz) of stock syrup for 1 hour. Liquidize the orange with the syrup and push the mixture through a sieve, giving you a totally fresh orange taste. Then just add the gelatine and set before using.

VARIATIONS

When making the ganache, you can leave out the egg yolk and sugar mixture and simply fold the whipped cream into the melted mix.

I also like to serve on Orange Anglaise Sauce with this dish. Simply follow the basic Crème Anglaise recipe (see p. 355), omitting the vanilla and adding the zest from 2 oranges to every 600 ml (1 pint) of milk or cream used. Once made, Cointreau, Grand Marnier or brandy can be added.

For a quick 'Anglaise', simply add one of the liqueurs to some tinned custard. If none of these takes your fancy, serve pouring cream. It eats just as well.

Any ganache left over can be rolled into small balls and then rolled in cocoa powder for home-made *petit four* chocolates.

Chocolate Scotch Pancakes

These are really easy to make and cook. If you're not sure about the chocolate (after all, there are plenty of chocolate puds in this book) the cocoa can simply be replaced with 50 g (2 oz) of self-raising flour. The beauty of sweet scotch pancakes is how much scope you have with them, from afternoon teas to a full dessert. The choice is yours. A good warm Coffee Custard Sauce (see p. 356) can be served with them, or perhaps some clotted cream.

SERVES 6
175 g (6 oz) self-raising flour
50 g (2 oz) cocoa
25 g (1 oz) unsalted butter
150 ml (5 fl oz) milk

2 eggs
100 g (4 oz) caster sugar
A pinch of salt
Butter or oil, for frying

Sift together the flour and cocoa. Melt the butter and whisk into the milk with the eggs, sugar and pinch of salt. You now have 750 ml (1¼ pints) of chocolate scotch pancake batter.

To cook the pancakes, heat a thick-bottomed pan or griddle and brush with butter or oil. The batter can now be spooned, using a tablespoon, into the pan allowing one spoon per pancake. These will only take approximately 2–3 minutes before they are ready for turning over. To help the timing for turning, small bubbles will appear on the surface. This tells you they are ready to turn. Once turned, cook for 2 more minutes before removing from the pan. In a large pan, 4–6 pancakes can be cooked at the same time. To keep them warm while you are cooking the rest of the batter, simply wrap in a warm tea towel. You should have about 18 in all. The pancakes are now ready to eat.

VARIATION

For a dessert, I like to slice bananas and totally cover each pancake. These can now be heavily dusted with icing sugar and then caramelized under a grill or with a gas gun. You now have crunchy bananas on top of chocolate pancakes. Finish them with clotted cream and they are a treat.

Chocolate and Pear Brûlées

Chocolate and pears are a classic combination; the flavours work so well together. The texture of the brûlée has an almost chocolate-toffee consistency which can become more toffee-ish if you use extra chocolate.

I like to eat crème brûlées at room temperature so the consistency is similar to egg custard. However this pudding can also be eaten chilled.

SERVES 4
8 egg yolks
50 g (2 oz) caster sugar
600 ml (1 pint) double cream
100 g (4 oz) or more good-quality plain chocolate, grated

4–6 Poached Pear halves (see p. 272)
  or tinned pear halves
100 g (4 oz) icing sugar. sifted

Pre-heat the oven to 160–180°C/325–350°F/gas 3–4.

Beat the egg yolks and sugar together in a bowl. Bring the cream to the boil and whisk it into the egg yolk mix. Sit the bowl over a pan of hot water and heat until the custard thickens, stirring all the time; it should have the consistency of double cream. Add the grated chocolate and stir until melted. Taste the mix. If the chocolate flavour is not strong enough, simply keep adding, stirring and tasting until you have the right flavour. Divide the chocolate custard between individual ramekins and sit them in a roasting tray. Fill the tray with hot water to come three-quarters up the sides of the moulds. Finish in the oven for 20–30 minutes until the mix thickens and sets. Check the *brûlées* by removing a ramekin from the tray and shaking gently. The *brûlée* should be only slightly runny in the centre. If the mix is too liquid, return to the oven and check after a further 5 minutes. Once cooked, remove from the oven and tray and allow to cool to room temperature.

To finish the dish, cut the pears lengthways into slices and arrange overlapping on top of each pudding. Sprinkle liberally with icing sugar and glaze under a hot grill until you have a golden crisp sugar topping. To achieve a good glaze the icing sugar may have to be applied two or three times.

VARIATIONS
It's also possible to slice a quarter of a pear per pudding, then dice the remaining fruit and place it in the bottom of the ramekins before adding the *brûlée*.

Chocolate and Prune Soufflé Cake

This recipe gives you a rich chocolate pudding with the rich prunes to help moisten and provide extra flavour. I usually cook these in individual moulds, but a 15–20 cm (6–8 in) cake tin or flan mould can be used. If so, cook the pudding for

35–40 minutes instead of 20 minutes. The pudding rises and has an almost soufflé consistency when warm but, once cold, becomes a sunken soufflé, giving it an even more puddingy texture. The cakes are light to eat and can be served as puddings or cakes. As a pudding, I like to serve them with thick whipped or clotted cream or perhaps a Custard Sauce (see p.355).

SERVES 8
8–10 prunes, stoned and cut into strips
1 tablespoon brandy
225 g (8 oz) dark plain chocolate
100 g (4 oz) unsalted butter

4 eggs, separated
100 g (4 oz) caster sugar

TO SERVE
Whipped or clotted cream or Custard Sauce (see p. 355)

Pre-heat the oven to 180°C/350°F/gas 4.

You will need individual, loose-bottomed 9 cm (3½ in) cake tins 2.5 cm (1 in) deep, lightly dusted with flour and base-lined with greaseproof paper.

Before using the prunes, soak them in the brandy until plump and soft.

Melt the chocolate and butter together in a bowl over a pan of warm water, not allowing the water to boil or come into contact with the bowl. Once melted, remove the bowl from the pan and allow to cool to room temperature.

Whisk together the egg yolks and sugar until the mixture is pale and has thickened so that it trails off the whisk in thick ribbons. Fold the egg yolk mix into the chocolate, making sure both are at room temperature. Whisk the egg whites until they form soft peaks, then carefully fold them into the chocolate mix. Divide the mix between the moulds and add the prunes. Bake in the pre-heated oven for approximately 20 minutes, until the cakes have risen like soufflés. Once removed from the oven, they will take on a sunken soufflé look. Leave in the tins for 5 minutes, then carefully remove and serve as a cake or pudding. Accompany with custard sauce, cream or both. You can also garnish the plates with a dusting of icing sugar or cocoa.

Chocolate Fudge Cake with Pecan Nut Sauce

This pudding is rich, sticky and very tasty. You won't be able to eat it too often but every now and again it's a wonderful treat. This makes quite a large cake but it is worth the effort. It keeps brilliantly for days in the fridge and can be simply microwaved a portion at a time or as a whole pudding. To serve the pudding just pour the pecan sauce over each slice.

SERVES 8
6 eggs

350 g (12 oz) caster sugar
A few drops vanilla essence

225 g (8 oz) good-quality plain
   chocolate
225 g (8 oz) unsalted butter
100 g (4 oz) ground almonds
150 g (5 oz) fresh white breadcrumbs

FOR THE PECAN NUT SAUCE
175 g (6 oz) soft brown sugar
100 g (4 oz) unsalted butter
85 ml (3 fl oz) double cream
25–50 g (1–2 oz) pecan nuts, chopped

Pre-heat the oven to 180°C/350°F/ gas 4 and grease a 20 × 25 cm (8 × 10 in) baking tray. The baking tray needs to be at least 2.5 cm (1 in) deep for the cake to achieve the right texture.

Whisk together the eggs, sugar and vanilla essence until the mixture forms stiff peaks (sabayon stage). Melt the chocolate with the butter in a bowl over warm water. Pour on to the egg and sugar mixture and then fold in the ground almonds and bread-crumbs. The mix will be very loose, almost liquid. Pour the mix into the prepared baking tray and bake in the pre-heated oven for 50–60 minutes. The texture of the pudding should be cooked but almost stodgy and moist. The pudding should be left to rest for 10 minutes before serving.

To make the sauce, place the sugar, butter and cream in a saucepan and bring to the boil. Simmer the sauce until the sugar has dissolved. Stir in the pecan nuts. The sauce is now ready.

Steamed Chocolate Sponge

Along with steamed jam sponge, this has to be a children's favourite. In fact, I think it's a favourite for everyone. One of the pleasures of cooking is never allowing recipes to be over-strict. This pudding can have so many different textures and tastes added, from walnuts and almonds to dates and orange zest – and many more.

There are two or three sauces which go very well with this pudding. Try Chocolate Sauce (see p. 354), Coffee Custard Sauce (see p. 356) or Pecan Nut Sauce (see above). They're all very rich but very tasty.

SERVES 4–6
1 quantity Steamed Sponge Pudding
   mix (see p. 329), omitting 50 g (2 oz)
   of the self-raising flour

50 g (2 oz) cocoa
50–100 g (2–4 oz) good-quality plain
   chocolate, grated

Simply follow the basic sponge recipe mixing the cocoa with remaining self-raising flour. Stir the grated chocolate into the mix to lift the flavour and texture.

To cook this pudding, only steam for 35 minutes if using individual moulds or for 1½ hours in a large mould. This leaves it slightly softer in the centre. Turn out and serve with the sauce of your choice. I also like to finish the dish with either grated chocolate or chocolate shavings.

Soufflés

I think we are all a little afraid of serving a soufflé or, for that matter, even having a go at one at home. But they are not so difficult; there are a few golden rules we must all stick to for success: clean whisks and bowls, the soufflé dishes well buttered and sugared, and the oven temperatures right.

The classic sweet soufflé is made from a pastry cream, which is what I'm going to give you here, but I also have a quick and simple alternative. It doesn't have quite the same depth and texture but still eats very well and can be turned into a soufflé so quickly.

First we'll start with the traditional recipe. This one is going to be for a lemon soufflé. There are many other flavours that can be made using the same recipe, so this is not a recipe just for lemon.

SERVES 4–6

FOR THE PASTRY CREAM BASE
300 ml (10 fl oz) milk
1 vanilla pod or a few drops of vanilla
  essence (optional)
50 g (2 oz) caster sugar
40 g (1 oz) plain flour
2 egg yolks
Finely grated zest of 1–2 lemons, limes
  or oranges (optional)
Icing sugar for dusting

FOR THE SOUFFLÉS
8 tablespoons Pastry Cream
  (see Pastry Cream Base,
  previous column)
Juice of 2 lemons
2 egg yolks (optional)
8 egg whites
25 g (1 oz) caster sugar
Butter and caster sugar, for lining the
  moulds

To make the pastry cream, bring the milk to the boil with the vanilla pod or essence, if using. Mix the caster sugar, flour and egg yolks together to a paste. If you are making this base for lemon, lime or orange soufflés, then add the finely grated zest of 1 or 2 fruits to the mix to increase the basic flavour. Remove the vanilla pod from the milk and pour the milk on to the flour mix, whisking as you pour. This mix must now be brought back to boiling point and cooked for 1–2 minutes, stirring. Transfer to a bowl and cover with cling film to prevent any skin forming. Cool at room temperature. You will have 400 g (14 oz).

Pre-heat the oven to 220°C/425°F/gas 7. You will need four size-2 soufflé dishes or six size-1 ramekins. The dishes should first be well buttered and then caster sugar should be added and rolled around the dish until it is well and completely coated.

Mix the 8 tablespoons of pastry cream with the lemon juice and the extra egg yolks, if using. These are optional but will give you an extra-rich base. Whisk the egg whites to soft peaks and then add the caster sugar. Continue to whisk until slightly thicker. Add a quarter of the egg whites to the soufflé mix and whisk in until completely bound. The remaining whisked whites must now be very carefully folded in. Divide the soufflé mix between the soufflé dishes, smoothing the top with a palette knife. It is best now carefully to release the mix from the edge of the soufflé dish with the point of a knife. Place the soufflés on the bottom shelf of the oven for 12–15 minutes, to prevent the tops from becoming over coloured. Once well risen and cooked, remove from the oven and dust with icing sugar before serving.

These can now be served as they are or with a sauce. To make a lemon sauce simply follow the recipe suggestion from the Custard Sauce (see p. 355). Another alternative, or even both, is to serve the hot soufflé with iced lemon sorbet.

So there's the recipe for a completely home-made soufflé. Now for the quick and easy option. It will make the same quantity as before.

QUICK LEMON SOUFFLÉ	**2 egg yolks (optional)**
200 ml (7 fl oz) tinned custard sauce	**6 egg whites**
Juice of 2 lemons	**50 g (2 oz) caster sugar**

Simply follow the previous method of putting this together, using 8 tablespoons of the tinned custard sauce. The advantage is not having to make the pastry cream. Release the mix from the edge of the soufflé dishes with the point of a knife. Cook the soufflés on the bottom shelf of the oven at the same temperature. I find that these take no more than 12–13 minutes to cook.

Loosen the remaining custard with some milk or single cream to a better sauce consistency, and flavour with lemon juice. You may also like to sweeten it with caster sugar.

VARIATIONS

Probably one of the most classic of all is Grand Marnier Soufflé. This recipe will work replacing the lemon juice with strongly reduced orange juice mixed with Grand Marnier and perhaps some finely grated orange zest. You can serve the soufflé with a rich Grand Marnier Sauce. Make this by first boiling 100 g (4 oz) sugar in 150 ml (5 fl oz) water to give a stock syrup. Roughly chop a whole orange (including pith and peel) and place in a pan with 150 ml (5 fl oz) orange juice, the stock syrup and 2–3 measures Grand Marnier. Simmer for 30 minutes until completely tender. Blitz in a liquidizer and push through a fine sieve. The sauce should have a coating consistency. If it is a little too thin, thicken with 1–2 teaspoons of arrowroot.

Manchester Pudding (Queen of Puddings)

This is a really sweet pudding, the one you want to eat plenty of but always regret afterwards. Here are two recipes which both work very well. The one using bread-

crumbs is the more traditional, but the sponge and jam one is also delicious. The beauty of using sponge is that you can use up your Madeira cake when it's past its best.

SERVES 4–6

RECIPE 1
600 ml (1 pint) milk
Grated zest of 1 lemon
50 g (2 oz) unsalted butter
50 g (2 oz) caster sugar

100 g (4 oz) fresh white breadcrumbs
6 egg yolks
4 tablespoons raspberry jam

FOR THE MERINGUE
4 egg whites
225 g (8 oz) caster sugar

Pre-heat the oven to 180°C/350°F/gas 4 and prepare six 7.5 cm (3 in) soufflé dishes or one 1.75 litre (3 pint) soufflé dish.

Bring the milk and lemon rind to the boil in a pan, then remove from the heat and leave to stand for 15 minutes. Remove the zest and add the butter and sugar. Bring back to the simmer and remove from the heat. Stir in the breadcrumbs and allow to cool slightly. Beat the egg yolks and add to the mix. Pour it into the soufflé dish or dishes and stand them in a roasting tray filled three-quarters full of hot water. Bake in the pre-heated oven for 30–40 minutes, until set. When the puddings have just set remove from the oven and the water bath and leave to rest for 10 minutes.

Increase the oven temperature to 230°C/450°F/gas 8. Divide the jam between the tops of the puddings. To make the meringue, whisk the egg whites with the sugar until they form firm peaks. Pipe or spoon the meringue over the top of the puddings and return them to the hot oven or place under a pre-heated grill, for about 6–8 minutes until golden brown. The queen of puddings is now ready to serve.

RECIPE 2
1/2 baked Vanilla Sponge (see p. 392)
Raspberry jam
4 eggs
75 g (3 oz) caster sugar
300 ml (10 fl oz) milk

300 ml (10 fl oz) double cream
1 vanilla pod, split (optional)

FOR THE MERINGUE
4 egg whites
225 g (8 oz) caster sugar

Pre-heat the oven to 160°C/325°F/gas 3 and prepare six 7.5 cm (3 in) soufflé dishes or one 1.75 litre (3 pint) soufflé dish.

Split the sponge into three layers and sandwich together again with the raspberry jam. Cut into 1 cm (1/2 in) squares and divide between the soufflé dishes or arrange in the base of the large dish.

Whisk the eggs and sugar together and add the milk, cream and the scraped out insides of the vanilla pod, if using. Strain through a sieve and pour on top of the sponge sandwich. Sit the moulds in a roasting tray three-quarters filled with hot water and cook in the pre-heated oven for 30–40 minutes until the custard has just set. Remove from the oven and the water bath and leave to rest.

Increase the oven temperature to 230°C/450°F/gas 8.

To make the meringues, whisk the egg whites with the sugar until they form firm peaks. Pipe or spoon the meringue over the top of the puddings and return them to the hot oven for about 8 minutes until golden brown.

Rhubarb Rice Pudding

This is a delicious pudding which combines a traditional rice pudding with the slightly sharp taste of the rhubarb.

SERVES 6
450 g (1 lb) rhubarb
25 g (1 oz) unsalted butter
100 g (4 oz) caster sugar

1 quantity Rice Pudding mixture
  (see below)
75 g (3 oz) icing sugar

Pre-heat the oven to 180°C/350°F/gas 4.

Lightly peel the rhubarb and cut into 2.5 cm (1 in) pieces. Melt the butter in a pan and cook the rhubarb and caster sugar over a high heat for about 4–5 minutes until soft, stirring frequently. The rhubarb should now be tasted to see if it is sweet enough. Allow the mixture to drain through a sieve, keeping any syrup comes through. Spoon the rhubarb into six 9 cm (3¹/₂ in) soufflé dishes, only filling them about one-third deep.

Make the rice pudding mix as described in the previous recipe, then add the reserved syrup to the rice pudding mixture and use this to cover the rhubarb. Stand the moulds in a baking tray three-quarters filled with hot water and bake in the pre-heated oven for about 20–30 minutes, until set.

Remove the moulds from the water bath, sprinkle liberally with the icing sugar and glaze under a hot grill. Unlike the caramel rice pudding, this can be served hot and left in the moulds.

Caramel Rice Pudding

This recipe shows how a simple pudding can become a great dessert.

SERVES 6

FOR THE CARAMEL
225 g (8 oz) caster sugar
300 ml (10 fl oz) water

FOR THE PUDDING
225 g (8 oz) short-grain rice
1.2 litres (2 pints) milk
100 g (4 oz) caster sugar
50 g (2 oz) unsalted butter
8 egg yolks
300 ml (10 fl oz) double cream

Pre-heat the oven to 180°C/350°F/gas 4.

Prepare the caramel for the moulds first. Dissolve the sugar in three-quarters of the water, bring to the boil then boil for a few minutes without shaking the pan until the caramel is golden brown. Add the remaining water and re-boil. The caramel is now ready and can be divided between six 9 cm (3^1/$_2$ in) soufflé dishes. Leave to set.

To make the pudding, place the rice in cold water to cover, bring to the boil drain, refresh under cold water and drain again. Boil 1 litre (1^3/$_4$ pints) of the milk, half the sugar and the butter in a large pan and add the rice. Bring to the simmer and cook for about 8–10 minutes, until tender. Beat the egg yolks and remaining sugar together in a bowl. Boil the cream with the remaining milk. Pour the milk on to the yolks, stirring all the time. Mix this with the rice, then pour carefully into the caramel-lined moulds. Stand the moulds in a baking tray three-quarters filled with hot water and bake in the pre-heated oven for about 20–30 minutes, until set. When set, remove from the water bath and leave to cool.

The puddings must now be chilled until firm and totally set. Release from the dishes with a warm knife and turn out. The rice puddings will hold together with the custard, and the caramel will pour over the top.

Bread and Butter Pudding

Bread and butter pudding has become one of our great classics. It was always a good way of using up stale bread with milk, sugar and eggs, but this would often result in a firm and tasteless pud, which left it with a bad name. This recipe will give you quite a different dish. I'm using just egg yolks and half milk and double cream; it is, obviously, a little more expensive to make but, once you've tried it, you'll never want to make it any other way.

SERVES 6–8

12 medium slices white bread
50 g (2 oz) unsalted butter, softened
8 egg yolks
175 g (6 oz) caster sugar
1 vanilla pod or a few drops of vanilla
   essence

300 ml (10 fl oz) milk
300 ml (10 fl oz) double cream
25 g (1 oz) sultanas
25 g (1 oz) raisins

TO FINISH
Caster sugar

Grease a 1.7-litre (3-pint) pudding basin with butter.

Firstly, remove the crusts and butter the bread. Whisk the egg yolks and caster sugar together in a bowl. Split the vanilla pod and place in a pan with the milk and cream. Bring the milk and cream to the simmer, then sieve on to the egg yolks, stirring all the time. You now have the custard.

Arrange the bread in layers in the prepared basin, sprinkling the sultanas and raisins in between layers. Finish with a final layer of bread without any fruit on top as this tends to burn. The warm egg mixture may now be poured over the bread and cooked straightaway, but I prefer to pour the custard over the pudding then leave it to soak into the bread for 20 minutes before cooking. This allows the bread to take on a new texture and have the flavours all the way through.

Pre-heat the oven to 180°C/350°F/gas 4.

Once the bread has been soaked, place the dish in a roasting tray three-quarters filled with warm water and place in the pre-heated oven. Cook for about 20–30 minutes in the pre-heated oven until the pudding begins to set. Because we are using only egg yolks, the mixture cooks like a fresh custard and only thickens; it should not become too firm.

When ready, remove from the water bath, sprinkle liberally with caster sugar to cover, and glaze under the grill on medium heat. The sugar should dissolve and caramelize and you may find that the corners of the bread start to burn a little. This helps the flavours, though, giving a bitter-sweet taste, and certainly looks good. The bread and butter pudding is now ready to serve and when you take that first spoonful and place it in a bowl you will see the custard just seeping from the dish – it's delicious.

Walnut and Maple Syrup Sponge

Sweet suet sponges have a thicker and denser texture, so I always think they need stronger tastes. The syrup helps the taste, the walnuts help the texture.

SERVES 6

175 g (6 oz) self-raising flour
75 g (3 oz) dried shredded suet
75 g (3 oz) caster sugar
1 egg

1 egg yolk
About 2 tablespoons milk
175 g (6 oz) shelled walnuts, chopped
8 tablespoons maple syrup

Grease a 900 ml (1 pint) or six 150 ml (5 fl oz) pudding basin(s) with butter.

Mix the flour, suet and sugar together. Beat the egg with the egg yolk then mix it to the dry ingredients. Add a little milk to give the mixture a pudding consistency when the mix just drops from the spoon. Add half the walnuts and half the maple syrup. Pour into the prepared pudding basin, cover and cook in a hot steamer or a pan half-filled with hot water for 1$1/4$–1$1/2$ hours.

Warm the remaining walnuts in the maple syrup. Turn out the puddings on to one large or several individual plates, spoon the syrup and nuts over and serve with cream or custard.

Toffee and Banana Crumble

We've all had apple, rhubarb or apricot crumbles, but this one is almost a banana and toffee pie, which makes it a crumble with a difference.

SERVES 4

1 × 200 g (7 oz) tin of condensed milk
225 g (8 oz) Puff Pastry (see p. 393) or
  bought puff pastry

225 g (8 oz) plain flour
100 g (4 oz) unsalted butter
100 g (4 oz) caster sugar
3 bananas

To make the toffee, place the unopened tin of condensed milk in a pan of water and boil for 3 hours, topping up with boiling water as necessary. Leave the tin to cool, and the toffee is ready.

Pre-heat the oven to 180°C/350°F/gas 4 and dampen a 25 cm (10 in) flan tin or individual flan rings on a baking sheet.

While the tin is boiling, roll out the pastry and use to line the flan tin or rings. Line the pastry with greaseproof paper, fill with baking beans and bake blind in the pre-heated oven for 15 minutes. Remove the beans and paper and leave to cool. Increase the oven temperature to 220°C/425°F/ gas 7.

To make the crumble, rub the flour and butter together until the mix is like fine crumbs, then add the sugar. Chop the bananas and spoon into the flan cases. Top with the toffee from the tin and sprinkle with the crumble. Bake in the pre-heated oven for about 15–20 minutes, until the crumble is golden brown. The pudding is ready to serve, and will eat very well with fresh cream or custard, or even both.

Sticky Toffee Pudding

This is a good old English pudding which is made all over the country. I think this recipe originated with Francis Coulson of Sharrow Bay in Ullswater, and it works better than any of the other recipes I have tried. The best dates to use are Medjool, which come from India; they are plump and meaty, with almost a treacle taste.

SERVES 4

175 g (6 oz) dates, stoned and chopped
300 ml (10 fl oz) water
1 teaspoon bicarbonate of soda
50 g (2 oz) unsalted butter
175 g (6 oz) caster sugar
2 eggs, beaten

175 g (6 oz) self-raising flour
1 teaspoon vanilla essence

FOR THE SAUCE

300 ml (10 fl oz) double cream
50 g (2 oz) demerara sugar
2 teaspoons black treacle

Pre-heat the oven to 180°C/350°F/gas 4 and grease a 28 × 18 cm (11 × 7 in) baking tin.

Boil the dates in the water for about 5 minutes until soft, then add the bicarbonate of soda. Cream the butter and sugar together until light and fluffy, then add the eggs and beat well. Mix in the dates, flour and vanilla essence then pour into the greased baking tin and cook in the pre-heated oven for about 30–40 minutes until just firm to he touch.

To make the sauce, simply place all the ingredients in a pan over a low heat and stir together until blended, then bring to the boil, Some of this can be poured over the sponge and finished under the grill, or it can be kept totally separate and ladled over the sponge when portioned. Good, fresh, thick cream is just right for this pudding.

Black Treacle Pudding

This recipe comes from Northern Ireland and is actually made with black treacle, unlike what we usually call a treacle pudding which is, in fact, a golden syrup sponge. That is lovely, too, but now you have the recipe for the real thing. For an even stronger taste, use the soft brown sugar instead of caster sugar.

I like to eat this with pouring cream and Custard Sauce (see p. 355) but, if you feel like being really rich, then try the Rum Sabayon (see p. 358) to go with it (perhaps with the cream and custard as well), or even with the Liquorice Ripple Ice-cream (p. 252).

SERVES 4–6

225 g (8 oz) self-raising flour
A pinch of salt
2 teaspoon ground mixed spice
100 g (4 oz) unsalted butter
6 tablespoons black treacle (optional)
50 g (2 oz) caster sugar or soft brown
    sugar

$^1/_2$ teaspoon bicarbonate of soda
6 tablespoons milk
2 eggs
2 tablespoons golden syrup, warmed
    (optional)

Butter and flour a 1.2-litre (2-pint) pudding basin. Sift together the flour, salt and mixed spice. Work in the butter to a breadcrumb texture. Warm the treacle with the sugar. Mix the bicarbonate of soda with the milk and eggs. Add both to the dry ingredients, then fill the prepared basin with the mixture. Cover with foil, loosely, on the top to allow the pudding to rise, and place the basin in a pan filled with water to come half-way up the basin. Bring the water to the boil, cover and steam for $1^1/_2$–2 hours, topping up with more water as necessary. The sponge is now ready to turn out. To make it really shine, spoon some more treacle or golden syrup on top. Now that is a rich pudding.

Treacle Tart

This is a very quick and easy recipe. It has, like so many other recipes, many alternatives. Half a teaspoon of ground ginger works very well, so does the addition of a little grated orange zest, or you can enrich the whole recipe with the addition of a few tablespoons of double cream and one or two eggs. You can eat it on its own or with clotted or pouring cream.

SERVES 4

**1 quantity Sweet Shortcrust Pastry
(see p. 394)**
50 g (2 oz) unsalted butter
10 tablespoons golden syrup

225 g (8 oz) fresh breadcrumbs
**Finely grated zest and juice of
1 lemon**

Pre-heat the oven to 200°C/400°F/gas 6.

Roll out the pastry and use to line a 23 cm (9 in) flan ring. Cover with greaseproof paper and baking beans or rice and bake in the pre-heated oven for 10–15 minutes until set. Remove the paper and beans. Reduce the oven temperature to 180°C/350°F/gas 4.

Melt the butter and syrup together. Add the breadcrumbs and lemon juice and zest. Pour the mix into the pastry case and bake in the oven for 20 minutes. If the treacle filling is bubbling, then remove from the oven. If it is not quite at that stage, cook for a further 5–10 minutes. When the treacle is at the bubbling/sizzling stage, remove the tart from the oven and allow to settle. The tart can be eaten warm or cold.

Christmas Pudding

I always plan my Christmas puddings well ahead of time. They are usually made by August, giving them time to mature and improve the flavour. I like to make several, as it's always a very nice gift to give: a good home-made Christmas pudding.

This pudding mix can also be kept chilled for a week before cooking. This gives the raw ingredients time to work their tastes together. It should at the least have 24 hours before cooking.

**MAKES 3 × 1.2-litre (2-pint)
PUDDINGS**
225 g (8 oz) plain flour
1 teaspoon baking powder
225 g (8 oz) fresh white breadcrumbs
225 g (8 oz) shredded dried suet
100 g (4 oz) ground almonds
550 g (1 1/4 lb) dark muscovado sugar
1 teaspoon ground mixed spice

1/2 teaspoon freshly grated nutmeg
1/2 teaspoon cinnamon
175 g (6 oz) stoned prunes
175 g (6 oz) carrots
**750 g (1 1/2 lb) mixed currants, sultanas
and raisins**
50 g (2 oz) chopped mixed peel
2 apples, peeled, cored and chopped
Juice and grated zest of 1 orange

Juice and grated zest of 1 lemon

5 eggs

4 measures rum

4 tablespoons black treacle

4 tablespoons golden syrup

300 ml (10 fl oz) stout

Sift the flour with the baking powder. Add the breadcrumbs, suet, ground almonds, muscovado sugar and spices. The prunes and carrots should be minced together through a medium mincer and then added to the mix together with the currants, sultanas, raisins, mixed peel, apples and lemon and orange zest. Beat the eggs and add to the mix with the orange and lemon juice, rum, treacle, golden syrup and stout. The pudding ingredients can now be totally mixed together; you should have about 3 kg (7 lb) in weight. This mix should have a loose consistency; if it feels too dry then simply add a little more stout. Cover and keep in a cool place for 24 hours to a week; if it's still bland, add more spices and rum.

Butter and lightly flour 900 g (2 lb) pudding basins. Fill three-quarters full with the mix and top with a circle of lightly greased greaseproof paper. The pudding basins can now be covered with parchment paper, leaving a fold in the paper. These should now be steamed for 4 hours, topping up with boiling water as necessary.

Once cooked, leave to cool before chilling, or store in a cool, dark place. The puddings will simply mature, becoming more tasty as the time goes on. If they take up too much space in your fridge, keep them well sealed in a cool place.

To serve the puddings on The Day, they will need to be steamed for a minimum I hour to bring them back to a tender pudding texture.

Steamed Sponge Pudding

These puddings are real homely classics – just the sort of pudding to finish your meal, especially for a Sunday lunch. Steamed sponges seem to be playing a big part in The Great British Revival. In fact, steamed lemon sponge was one of the, if not the, first pudding that I made. The sponge can be so light and fluffy to eat and will take on so many other flavours, many of which I am featuring here.

To make it a lot easier to turn out the puddings, use plastic moulds which hold up very well to steaming, and when lightly pressed the sponge should fall out easily. You can use 150 ml (5 fl oz) individual moulds or a 900 ml (1½ pint) mould.

SERVES 4–6

100 g (4 oz) unsalted butter

150 g (5 oz) caster sugar

2 eggs

1 egg yolk

200 g (7 oz) self-raising flour

1–2 drops of milk, if needed

Lightly butter and flour four 150 ml (5 fl oz) moulds or one 900 ml (1 pint) pudding basin. Beat the butter and sugar together until almost white in colour and the sugar has dissolved. This is easily achieved in an electric mixer. It does, however, take a little while to cream to this stage. Beat in one egg at a time, making sure after each egg is added that the mix is beaten until completely mixed and fluffy again. Once both eggs have been added, continue with the same process for the egg yolk. Most recipes will tell you now to fold in the flour slowly and carefully. Well, I want you to do almost the opposite. Add the flour and beat until all the flour has completely creamed into the mix but do not over-work. Add the milk if needed.

Spoon in the mixture, filling each mould one three-quarters full. Cover the moulds with lightly buttered squares of tin foil, just lightly folding the foil over the rims so the sponge can rise and push up the foil during cooking. Steam the sponges over boiling water, allowing 35–40 minutes for individual puddings or $1\frac{1}{4}$–$1\frac{1}{2}$ hours for the larger mould. Top up the boiling water as necessary during cooking.

VARIATION

Golden syrup sponge is always a favourite – just add a generous spoon of syrup to the sponge mixture, sit some more in the base of each mould and then steam. Pour a little more syrup on top before serving.

Steamed Lemon and Rhubarb Sponge

Using the redcurrant jelly with the rhubarb is an optional extra that helps enrich the liquor and juices from the sugared rhubarb. If eaten cold, the mixture will almost set to jam. The beauty of the recipe is that so many other flavours work with it. A little ginger may be added, or you can use other fruits such as blackberries or blueberries. The rhubarb recipe can also be cooked a little more and then puréed and turned into a sorbet or ice-cream.

You can make individual puddings or one large one. The flavours of the rhubarb and lemon work really well together, and you can serve the dessert with pouring cream, Lemon Custard Sauce (see p. 355) or even Vanilla Ice-cream (see p. 252).

SERVES 4–6
450 g (1 lb) fresh rhubarb
25 g (1 oz) unsalted butter
225 g (8 oz) caster sugar

1 tablespoon redcurrant jelly
  (optional)
1 quantity Steamed Lemon Sponge
  Pudding Mix (see p. 332)

Peel any coarse skin from the rhubarb stalks; young, tender rhubarb will not need to be peeled. Cut the rhubarb into 2 cm (¾ in) pieces. Melt the butter in a pan until it begins to bubble. Add the rhubarb and stir gently for 1–2 minutes. Add the sugar and bring to the simmer. As the rhubarb is warming it will also be cooking. When it becomes tender, after about 4–5 minutes depending on size and ripeness, remove from the heat. Stir in the redcurrant jelly, if using. Allow the rhubarb mix to cool.

Butter and flour one large mould or individual moulds. Spoon 4–5 tablespoons of the rhubarb into the large mould or 1 tablespoon into the individual moulds, cover with the lemon sponge mix and finish and cook in the usual way (see p. 329).

When the sponges are cooked, re-heat the remaining rhubarb. Turn out the puddings and spoon some more fruit over the top.

Steamed Lemon Sponge with Lemon Curd Ice-cream and Lemon Custard Sauce

This sponge eats beautifully with lemon curd ice-cream and lemon custard sauce. If you feel this is all bit too strong, simply serve the pudding with one or the other and some whipped or pouring double cream.

SERVES 4–6

1 quantity Steamed Sponge Pudding Mix (see p. 329)

Finely grated zest of 1 lemon

Juice of 1 lemon

A little milk

Lemon Curd Ice-cream (see p. 255)

Lemon Custard Sauce (see p. 355)

Add the lemon zest to the butter and sugar mixture in the basic sponge method, then continue to make the sponge until the flour has been added and mixed. Fold in the lemon juice and a little milk, if necessary. Because the zest was in at the beginning the flavour will become more powerful and strong. The sponges can now be steamed in the usual way (see p. 329).

Steamed Lemon Sponge with Prunes, Damson or Tutti-frutti

Lemon must be one of the most versatile flavours we have. It lends itself to such variety of dishes, whether they be sweet or savoury. It also makes us think about menu compilation; starting off with a plate of smoked salmon, which is normally served with lemon, then following with chicken with lemon and parsley and finishing with one of these sponges, wouldn't really be a good idea. But I have found that using any of these three flavours with a lemon sponge, rather than just a basic vanilla recipe, really lifts all their tastes. First I'll give you the lemon sponge, followed by the alternatives.

**MAKES 1 × 900 ml (2-pint) SPONGE
OR 4 × 150 ml (5 fl oz) SPONGES**

FOR THE SPONGE
100 g (4 oz) unsalted butter
150 g (5 oz) caster sugar
Finely grated zest and juice of I lemon
2 eggs
1 egg yolk
200 g (7 oz) self-raising flour
1–2 drops of milk (optional)

FOR THE PRUNE PUDDING
About 12 stoned, ready-to-eat prunes
A little Stock Syrup (see p. 397)
(optional)

FOR THE DAMSON PUDDING
About 8 ripe damsons, stoned and
halved

FOR THE DAMSON COULIS
175 g (6 oz) stoned damsons, each cut
into 4
40 g (1 1/2 oz) caster sugar
50 ml (2 fl oz) water

FOR THE TUTTI-FRUTTI PUDDING
225 g (8 oz) mixed crystallized fruits
and raisins, such as glacé cherries,
strawberries, melon, orange, lemon,
angelica and raisins, chopped

FOR THE HONEY STOCK SYRUP
40 g (1 1/2 oz) caster sugar
5 tablespoons water
1 tablespoon honey or golden syrup

Butter and flour a 900 ml (2-pint) mould or four 150 ml (5 fl oz) moulds. Beat together the butter and sugar with the lemon zest until almost white and the sugar has dissolved. This is easily achieved in an electric mixer. It does take a little while for the sugar to dissolve. Beat in 1 egg at a time, making sure that, after each egg, is added the mix is beaten until mixed and fluffy again. Once both eggs have been added, repeat the same process with the egg yolk. Fold the flour into the mix well, then add the lemon juice and milk, if needed, to give a dropping consistency. So that's the basic mix made. Here are the alternatives to go with it.

For the prune pudding, use stoned, ready-to-eat prunes as these are already tender. They can be made even softer by soaking in warm stock syrup. If you are going to soak them for the base of the moulds, do not allow them to become too wet as this will loosen the sponge mix and prevent the base from cooking. Just place two or three stoned prunes in each the individual moulds before spooning the mix on top. As the pudding begins to cook the mix will soften the prunes. The prunes can also be cut into small dice and simply added to the pudding mix.

For the damson pudding, I take 1 1/2–2 ripe damsons per portion, stoned and halved, and sit them in the bottom of the moulds before adding the sponge mix. To finish and enrich the dish, I like to serve stewed damsons (by cooking for 2–3 minutes) or coulis over the top, or both. Put all the coulis ingredients into a pan and bring to a simmer. Then cook for 5 minutes and push through a sieve. This eats very well with custard and fresh cream.

The tutti-frutti pudding simply needs 100–175 g (4–6 oz) of the glacé and crystallized fruits bound into the lemon sponge mix before being steamed. The remaining fruits can be warmed in a honey stock syrup made by heating and dissolving the caster sugar with the water and honey or golden syrup. Trickle the fruits and syrup on top of the sponge and serve with Vanilla Ice-cream (see p. 252).

For any of the puddings, steam individual puddings for 40 minutes or a large pudding for 1½ hours, topping up with boiling water as necessary. Turn out the puddings and serve with the sauces or creams of your choice.

VARIATIONS

To lift the flavour of the prune sponge, I like to serve it with Lemon Curd and Prune Ripple Ice-cream (see p. 265), along with a Lemon Custard Sauce (see p. 355). If you wish just to see the custard, it's best to dice two or more prunes per pudding and add them to the sponge mix. This will obviously give you a much stronger prune flavour.

The same quantity of fruits and raisins used in the tutti-frutti pudding can be added to Frangipane (Almond Paste) (see p. 396) and cooked in tartlets as for the Cherry and Almond Tart (see p. 276).

Spotted Dick

Spotted Dick was always one of those puddings I would look forward to at school. The moist dough with currants or raisins topped with loads of custard (usually lumpy) was a treat. Like most of my recipes, this has so many variations. I always like the grated zest of 1 lemon added to the mix; this really helps lift all the other flavours. So how about exchanging or adding to that the grated zest of a lime or orange? If it's orange you're going to use, then add chopped hazelnuts – the orange and nut flavours work so well together – or add some chocolate chips to the orange mix, another classic combination. The dish can be served with thick cream or custard and also eats very well drizzled with honey or golden syrup.

SERVES 6–8

300 g (11 oz) plain flour
10 g (¼ oz) baking powder
150 g (5 oz) shredded dried suet
75 g (3 oz) caster sugar

100 g (4 oz) currants
Finely grated zest of 1 lemon
About 150 ml (5 fl oz) milk

Mix together all the dry ingredients with the currants and lemon zest. Add enough milk to give you a binding/dropping consistency. Roll the mix with a rolling pin or by hand into a 15 cm (6 in) cylinder about 5 cm (2 in) in diameter. Either lightly dust a tea towel with flour or butter some greaseproof paper and wrap around the cylinder, leaving enough space for the sponge to rise. Tie the towel or paper at both ends. This can now be placed in hot steamer and cooked for about 1 hour. Once cooked, remove the towel or paper and the pudding is ready to serve. Cut it into slices at least 2.5 cm (1 in) thick to keep a good texture.

The quantity of grated lemon zest can be doubled to give a strong lemon taste. This pudding can then be served with the Lemon Custard Sauce (see p. 355).

Steamed golden syrup sponge log is also very good. Simply omit the sugar and milk and replace with 5–6 tablespoons of golden syrup. The richness of this pudding eats so well, especially with clotted cream.

In the introduction I mentioned adding orange zest and chocolate chips. This works very well, but if you want to make it even richer then replace 50 g (2 oz) of the flour with cocoa. This will give you a Chocolate and Orange Spotted Dick.

Another favourite is adding chopped Medjool dates and dried figs, about 50–75 g (2–3 oz) of each works very well, with 2–3 tablespoons of honey. This gives you a steamed suet fig roll. If you don't want to put the honey in the mix, then simply trickle some over every slice or add some to taste to the Custard Sauce (see p. 355).

So there are some ideas of how to turn a Spotted Dick pudding into something completely different – and still as good to eat.

Cloutie Dumpling

I ate this recipe for pudding when I visited Alan Craigie at the Creel Restaurant in the Orkneys. It was delicious. What did surprise me was that I had also eaten it that morning with my cooked breakfast. Now that's what I call variety.

Cloutie dumpling is a Scottish speciality. Cloutie comes from the word 'clout' meaning cloth, which is what the dumpling is wrapped in before boiling. I would describe it as a light Christmas dumpling. For me, it ate best as a pudding with lots of thick cream.

If you have any left over, just cut it into slices and shallow fry in butter for breakfast the next day.

SERVES 4–6

175 g (6 oz) self-raising flour	1 teaspoon bicarbonate of soda
175 g (6 oz) brown breadcrumbs	A good pinch of ground ginger
175 g (6 oz) shredded dried suet	A good pinch of freshly grated nutmeg
100 g (4 oz) currants	A good pinch of ground cinnamon
175 g (6 oz) raisins	100 g (4 oz) soft dark brown sugar
175 g (6 oz) sultanas	2 tablespoons golden syrup or treacle
	250 ml (8 fl oz) milk

Simply mix all the ingredients together. Boil a large cloth then dust with flour. Place the mix in the cloth, then pull the cloth around, making a ball shape. Boil in water for 2–2½ hours, topping up as necessary, then unwrap, slice and serve with cream.

Cakes and Baking

Irish Chocolate Coffee Cake

This recipe was given to me a close friend, Gabrielle, who produced one of my television series, Rhodes Around Britain. *We often have different ideas about cooking and filming but one thing is for sure, we both want the same results, and with this dish she won. It eats and keeps beautifully, especially when flavoured with good Irish whiskey.*

MAKES 1 × 20 cm (8 in) cake

175 g (6 oz) good-quality plain chocolate

4–6 tablespoons strong black coffee

2–4 tablespoons Irish whiskey

75 g (3 oz) caster sugar

100 g (4 oz) unsalted butter, at room temperature

3 eggs. separated

A pinch of salt

50 g (2 oz) ground almonds

A few drops of almond essence

50 g (2 oz) plain flour, sifted

FOR THE ICING

100 g (4 oz) good-quality plain chocolate

2 tablespoons whiskey or strong coffee

100 g (4 oz) unsalted butter

Pre-heat the oven to 180°C/350°F/gas 4. Butter and flour a 20 cm (8 in) cake dish.

Melt the chocolate, coffee and whiskey in a bowl over a pan of simmering water, then cool to room temperature. Reserve a tablespoon of sugar, then cream together the remaining sugar with the butter until you have a pale yellow, fluffy mixture. Beat in the egg yolks until well blended. Whisk the egg whites and salt until soft peaks form. Sprinkle on the tablespoon of caster sugar and beat until stiff peaks form. With a rubber spatula. blend the melted chocolate into the butter and sugar mixture, then stir in the ground almonds and essence. Fold in a quarter of the egg whites, sift in a quarter of the flour, then continue folding and sifting alternately until everything is blended. Turn the mixture into the prepared cake dish, pushing the mixture up to the rim with the spatula. Bake in middle of the pre-heated oven for about 25–30 minutes. The cake is done when it has puffed, and a skewer pushed into the middle comes out clean. Allow the cake to cool. It must be thoroughly cold to be iced.

To make the icing, melt the chocolate and whiskey or coffee in a bowl over a pan of simmering water until you have a smooth cream. Remove the bowl from the heat and beat in the butter a tablespoon at a time. Stand the bowl over cold water and beat until the chocolate mixture is cool and of spreading consistency. Spread it over the cake and serve with Cheesecake Cream (see p. 360).

Gingerbread Cake

This gingerbread can be served as a warm pudding or simply as a cold cake. I like to use it as both, and find that it eats really well with Clementine or Orange Sauce (see p. 354) and clotted cream.

SERVES 4
225 g (8 oz) self-raising flour
3/4 tablespoon ground ginger
A pinch of salt
100 g (4 oz) demerara sugar

100 g (4 oz) unsalted butter
100 g (4 oz) treacle
175 g (6 oz) golden syrup
1 egg
150 ml (5 fl oz) milk

Pre-heat the oven to 180°C/350°F/gas 4 and grease and line a 900 g (2 lb) loaf tin.

Mix together the flour, ginger and salt in a bowl. Warm the sugar, butter, treacle and golden syrup together in a pan. Beat the egg into the milk, then mix all the ingredients in the bowl. The gingerbread is made. Pour the mixture into the lined tin and spread evenly. Simply bake in the pre-heated oven for 45 minutes–1 hour. Remove from the tin and leave to stand for a few minutes before serving warm, or just leave to cool.

Victoria Sponge

This is a basic sponge mix that can be used in so many puddings. I'm using a Victoria Sponge recipe with the addition of lime in the Greengage and Lime Sponge Pie (see p. 311).

I thought it would be a good idea to include this recipe because it's easy and quick to make. So, if you're really stuck for time, make this recipe and join the sponges with whipped double cream and jam. There you have a real English cake: fresh cream Victoria Sponge.

MAKES 1 × 18 cm (7 in) sponge
  sandwich
175 g (6 oz) unsalted butter
175 g (6 oz) caster sugar

1 scraped fresh vanilla pod
  (optional)
3 eggs, beaten
175 g (6 oz) self-raising flour

Pre-heat the oven to 190°C /375°F/gas 5 and grease and flour two 18 cm (7 in) sandwich tins.

Beat together the butter, caster sugar and fresh vanilla, if using, to a creamy consistency. Slowly mix in the eggs until all is accepted. Fold in the flour. Pour into the prepared tins and bake in the oven for 20–25 minutes until well risen and golden and spring back when pressed with a finger. Turn out and leave to cool on wire racks.

VARIATIONS

Other flavours can be added to give a different taste: the finely grated zest of 1–2 lemons and/or 1 orange can be added for a citrus flavour; 25 g (1 oz) of the flour can be replaced with 25 g (1 oz) of cocoa for chocolate sponges.

Carrot Cake

Carrot cake is a rich, moist cake that is packed with flavours. I like just to eat it as it is, but many bought carrot cakes are finished with a lemon or orange butter cream. So with this recipe I'm going to give you a recipe for a flavoured butter cream to top the cake with, giving you a choice.

MAKES 2 x 900 g (2 lb) loaf cakes
300 ml (10 fl oz) sunflower oil
225 g (8 oz) soft brown sugar
4 eggs
175 g (6 oz) golden syrup
350 g (12 oz) self-raising flour
2 teaspoons ground cinnamon
2 teaspoons crushed cloves
1 teaspoon ground ginger
1 teaspoon bicarbonate of soda

225 g (8 oz) carrots, grated
50 g (2 oz) desiccated coconut
1 tablespoon chopped walnuts
   (optional)

FOR THE BUTTER CREAM
Finely grated zest and juice of 1 lemon
   or orange
100 g (4 oz) unsalted butter
100 g (4 oz) icing sugar, sifted

Pre-heat the oven to 180°C/350°F/gas 4. Butter two 900 g (2 lb) loaf tins.

Process or whisk together the oil, sugar, eggs and golden syrup. Beat in the flour, spices and bicarbonate of soda. Add the carrots, coconut and the chopped walnuts, if using. Pour the mix into the prepared tins and bake in the pre-heated oven for 40 minutes. To test, stick a skewer into the middle of a cake at an angle. If it comes out clean, the cake is cooked. If not, return it to the oven for another 5 minutes, then test again. Once cooked, leave to rest for 10 minutes before turning out of the tins. The cake is now ready to eat.

To make the butter cream, place the orange or lemon zest and juice in a pan and bring to the boil. Boil until reduced by three-quarters. This process will only take 1–2 minutes. Leave to cool.

Beat the butter until pale and creamy. Add the icing sugar and the orange or lemon reduction. Beat the mix well to spread the citrus flavour. Once the carrot cakes are cold this can be spread on top. You will have about 225 g (8 oz) of butter cream.

Rich Stout Cake

This is a chocolate cake with a difference. It's a basic chocolate cake recipe with the addition of rich stout which makes a very deep, rich cake, not only with the flavour of stout but also the colour to go with it. Guinness works very well in this recipe. The combination of the soft brown sugar and stout gives you fuller texture and taste. Also 100–225 g (4–8 oz) of plain chocolate can be grated into the mix to give an even stronger taste. It's very good to eat as a cake, or for real chocoholics, you could warm a slice in the microwave and serve it with a Rich Chocolate Sauce (see p. 354).

MAKES 1 × 20–25 cm (8–10 in) cake
225 g (8 oz) unsalted butter
350 g (12 oz) soft brown sugar
4 eggs, beaten
225 g (8 oz) plain flour

1/2 teaspoon baking powder
2 teaspoons bicarbonate of soda
400 ml (14 fl oz) stout (Guinness)
100 g (4 oz) cocoa

Pre-heat the oven to 180°C/350°F/gas 4 and butter a 20–25 cm (8–10 in) deep cake tin.

Cream together the butter with the soft brown sugar. Gradually add the beaten eggs. Sift together the flour, baking powder and bicarbonate of soda. Mix the stout with the cocoa powder. Now add the flour and stout mixes alternately to the butter and eggs until completely and evenly bound. You will find the consistency to be quite soft.

Spoon into the prepared tin and bake in the oven for 1–1¼ hours until set. You may need to cover with a piece of brown paper after an hour to prevent it browning too much. Allow to cool before removing from the tin. The stout cake is now ready – cheers.

VARIATIONS

Pouring a glass of stout always leaves you with a lovely finish on the top. You can do exactly the same with this cake. Melt 100–175 g (4–6 oz) of grated white chocolate with 100–175 g (4–6 oz) of butter and 1–2 measures of Irish whiskey until just softened, then leave to cool. You now have a rich white chocolate icing to spread on top of the cake.

To make a glass of Stout Cake Pudding, simply blitz some of the cake to a crumb stage and spoon into 300 ml (1/2 pint) glasses, leaving 1–2 cm (1/2–3/4 in) clear at the top. Soak the sponge crumbs in a flavoured syrup or perhaps add freshly grated chocolate or even fruits or raisins. Finish the dish with Irish Whiskey Sabayon (see p. 357) and pour on top. This, as you can imagine, looks just like a real half pint of thick creamy stout and tastes just as good.

Whole Orange
and Almond Cake

I like to visit local schools, fêtes and jumble sales. The reason for going is to find the cakes that are always on offer. This recipe reminds me of those sorts of cakes: often quite simple but absolutely packed with flavour. This one is certainly both. It's made with whole oranges, which give it a good, sharp taste and make it very moist to eat, either as a cake or as a pudding served with Marmalade Cheesecake Cream (see p. 286). The quantities are quite large, but using three oranges gives a stronger finished taste. You could ask: why not just cut the recipe down to a third using just one orange? Well, I promise you the flavour is not as full and good. Also, this cake freezes so well for up to a month, so it will save you having to make one the next time you fancy a slice.

MAKES 3 × 900 g (2 lb) cakes
3 whole oranges
350 g (12 oz) ground almonds
350 g (12 oz) caster sugar
1/2 teaspoon baking powder
9 size-3 eggs

Pre-heat the oven to 180°C/350°F/gas 4. Grease three 900 g (2 lb) loaf tins. To cook the oranges, cover with cold water and bring to a simmer. Simmer the oranges for 1 hour until completely cooked. Remove from the water and cut into quarters. Drain well. Remove pips, then blitz all the orange (including pith and zest) to a purée in a food processor. Leave to cool.

To make the sponge, mix together the almonds, sugar and baking powder. Whisk the eggs until the mixture trails off the whisk in thick ribbons. Fold in the almond and sugar mixture, then add the orange purée. Pour the cake mix into the prepared tins, only filling about two-thirds full and using about 1.2 litres (2 pints) in each tin. Bake for about 40–45 minutes. The cake should be firm to the touch and, if pierced with a knife, should leave the knife clean. The cake is now cooked and can be left to cool before turning out. If the cake has sunk in the centre once cooled, this will have no effect on the finished result – the cake will still be lovely to eat. The cake will keep for several days in an airtight tin.

VARIATIONS

The recipe will also work well using 4 lemons instead of the 3 oranges, or perhaps using a combination of lemons and limes.

Banana and Pecan Nut Bread

This can be served as an afternoon teacake; or it eats very well with clotted cream and warm Chocolate Sauce (see p. 354), as a pudding.

MAKES 1 × 450 g (2 lb) loaf
3 large ripe bananas
225 g (8 oz) self-raising flour
A pinch of salt
175 g (6 oz) caster sugar
100 g (4 oz) unsalted butter, softened
2 eggs
2 tablespoons golden syrup
50 g (2 oz) pecan nuts

Pre-heat the oven to 160°C/325°F/gas 3 and grease a 450 g (2 lb) loaf tin.

Peel and mash the bananas in a bowl then add the remaining ingredients and beat vigorously for a minute to make sure they are well combined. Spoon the mixture into the loaf tin and spread it to the sides. Sprinkle the top with the pecan nuts and bake in the pre-heated oven for 1¼ hours until well risen and firm to the touch. Leave the loaf to rest for 10–15 minutes in the tin and then turn on to a cooling rack and leave to rest and become cold or just serve warm as a pudding.

Beremeal Bannocks

A recipe from my Scottish friend, this traditionally uses beremeal, which is an ancient northern barley. If you can't get hold of it, use oatmeal or wholemeal flour. I had a go at making these while staying in Scotland. They are easy and fun to make and eat superbly.

SERVES 4–6

100 g (4 oz) plain flour
1 teaspoon salt
2 heaped teaspoons bicarbonate of soda
1 heaped teaspoons cream of tartar
350 g (12 oz) beremeal or oatmeal
50 g (2 oz) unsalted butter
300–600 ml (½–1 pint) buttermilk

Sift the flour with the salt, bicarbonate of soda and cream of tartar. Add the beremeal or oatmeal. Rub in the butter, then gradually add the buttermilk, mixing to form a soft dough. You may not need all the buttermilk; it will depend on the meal you are using.

Warm a frying-pan or griddle. Shape the mix with a rolling pin or push and shape it by hand into a circle 3 cm (1¼ in) deep; or you might find it easier to shape it into smaller loaves. Cook the bannocks directly on the griddle or in the pan over a medium heat for 2–3 minutes each side. Serve at once.

Griddled Scones

These are great to eat at Sunday teatime with butter, jam and cream. They take no time to make and very little to cook, and we all seem to have these ingredients sitting in our cupboards. This recipe will give you about 20 scones – of course, you can halve the recipe, but I'm sure you'll eat 20. The other plus is the great variety of scones you can make by adding other flavours. I like to make them with the finely grated zest of lemon, but orange or lime can also be used. Chopped apple can be added, with a pinch of cinnamon, or you can even make them Christmassy with glacé fruits.

They can also be eaten as a pudding with fresh fruits and creamy sabayons. Just imagine lightly warmed raspberries tossed in butter and sugar sitting on the scones with a sweet White Wine Sabayon (see p. 357) or griddled strawberries that have thick whipped cream spooned over the top. What do you think? Delicious, I hope. And one last tip – eat them as quickly as possible.

MAKES 20 scones

450 g (1 lb) self-raising flour, plus extra
for dusting

A pinch of salt

50 g (2 oz) unsalted butter, plus extra
for frying

50 g (2 oz) lard

175 g (6 oz) currants or sultanas

Grated zest of 1 lemon

100 g (4 oz) caster sugar

2 eggs

2–4 tablespoons milk

Sift and mix the flour with the salt, then rub in the butter and lard. Fold in the currants or sultanas, lemon zest and sugar. Make a well in the centre and add the eggs and milk, mixing in the flour to form a soft dough. The dough can now be rolled out to 1 cm (1/2 in) thick and cut into 6 cm (2 1/2 in) rounds, or moulded by hand into 1 cm (1/2 in) thick individual scones.

Heat a frying-pan or griddle and cook over a medium heat in a little butter for 4–5 minutes on each side until golden brown. The scones are now ready to eat.

VARIATION

The scones eat very well with Griddled Strawberries. These are simply strawberries cooked on a grill plate, giving a slightly bitter, burnt tinge that is then balanced with a dusting of icing sugar. I like to eat these with crème fraîche.

For a richer scone, use 100 g (4 oz) unsalted butter instead of 50 g (2 oz) lard.

Oatmeal and Parmesan Biscuits

These biscuits eat very well with cheese. I like to cut them no bigger than 2.5 cm (1 in). This makes them just the right size for cheese bites. Herbs can also be added to this recipe, a teaspoon of chopped parsley, sage or both work very well.

MAKES ABOUT 40 large or 80
small biscuits

275 g (10 oz) plain flour

A pinch of baking powder

25 g (1 oz) oatmeal

50 g (2 oz) porridge oats

A good pinch of salt

5 tablespoons freshly grated
Parmesan

100 g (4 oz) unsalted butter

1 egg

5 tablespoons milk

Pre-heat the oven to 200°C/400°F/gas 6 and grease a baking tray or line it with silicone paper.

Work together all the dry ingredients, using 1 tablespoon of Parmesan, with the butter. Beat the egg into the milk and mix with the rest of the dough. Roll out the dough thinly and cut with a 2.5–5 cm (1–2 in) cutter. Lay the discs on the baking tray. Sprinkle each biscuit with a little more Parmesan. Bake in the oven for about 10 minutes until golden brown. Leave to cool and the biscuits are ready to serve.

Breakfast Muesli

This is a recipe I couldn't resist. It really is good just with cold milk for breakfast, or it can be mixed with chocolate to make a biscuit to be eaten with ice-cream and Custard Sauce (see p. 355) as a pudding.

MAKES 1 kg (2¹/₄ lb)
350 g (12 oz) jumbo oats
100 g (4 oz) sunflower seeds
100 g (4 oz) wheatgerm
75 g (3 oz) demerara sugar
75 ml (3 fl oz) olive oil
100 g (4 oz) clear honey

40 g (1¹/₂ oz) dried apple, coarsely chopped
40 g (1¹/₂ oz) dried apricots, coarsely chopped
75 g (3 oz) flaked almonds, toasted
75 g (3 oz) All-Bran (optional)
100 g (4 oz) raisins

Pre-heat the oven to 180°C/350°F/gas 4.

Place the first six ingredients in a small roasting tray, mix together, then cook in the pre-heated oven, stirring regularly, for 15–20 minutes until golden brown. Remove from the oven and leave to cool, stirring all the time.

When cold, stir in the remaining ingredients. Mix them together well, then store in an airtight container. The muesli is now ready to use. This will keep for up to two weeks.

Soda Bread

This is a recipe I tried in Ireland – another easy recipe with great results. The first time I ate soda bread, it was filled with bacon and fried egg with a big mug of tea for breakfast – it was lovely. So if you want to have a go at making your own bread for your next 'full Irish/English', follow this recipe.

If you can find traditional Irish self-raising soda bread flour, all you need to add is the salt and buttermilk, but this recipe will work just as well.

SERVES 4
350 g (12 oz) plain flour
1 level tablespoon bicarbonate of soda

A good pinch of salt
300 ml (10 fl oz) buttermilk

Pre-heat the oven to 190°C/375°F/gas 5.

Sift the flour, bicarbonate of soda and salt together and make a well in the centre. Poor in the buttermilk and mix gently to form a dough. Knead until smooth without overworking. Lightly dust the work surface with flour and roll out the dough to a circle about 2 cm (³/₄ in) thick. Cut the circle into quarters. Place on a baking sheet and bake in the pre-heated oven for 30–40 minutes until golden brown and hollow-sounding when tapped.

To cool and keep crispy, stand the bread on a wire rack. If you prefer a softer bread, wrap in a cloth to cool.

VARIATIONS

You can cook the bread on a griddle or frying-pan. Heat the pan over a moderate heat. To test the temperature, sprinkle a little flour on the pan; it should turn slightly off-white. Sit the bread into the pan and cook for 12–15 minutes on each side.

Raisin Focaccia

This recipe is really a basic focaccia bread with the addition of raisins that have been previously soaked in brandy. Focaccia is an olive bread that can be sweetened or eaten savoury. This recipe can have the raisins left out and simply be finished with sea salt or fresh herbs or both. I like to serve this as toast made on an open grill or barbecue with a pâté or maybe sautéd foie gras (that's a real treat).

It really does make a good and interesting alternative to serve this with a pâté as a starter with home-made chutney. The sweet flavour of raisins that have been soaked in brandy takes away the raw alcohol flavour and, in fact, the brandy just lifts the raisin taste.

For this recipe I am using fresh yeast, but soaked dried yeast can be used, simply making up the quantity required. It's worth making two loaves as the bread freezes so well.

The first thing to do is soak the raisins. I like to make sure plenty are added, so that every slice has enough to capture the flavour. You don't have to soak them; or you can choose other liqueurs or spirits. Calvados works very well with the addition of grated apple to the recipe, or grated orange zest and Grand Marnier. The loaf can then be sliced, dusted with icing sugar and grilled to be used as a base for a pudding: perhaps hot crispy orange focaccia served with home-made orange ice-cream or chocolate mousse. Here's the recipe, before I get carried away with more ideas.

MAKES 2 × 675 g (1¹/₂ lb) loaves

FOR THE RAISINS
225 g (8 oz) raisins
250 ml (8 fl oz) brandy or liqueur

FOR STAGE 1
2 teaspoons fresh yeast
2 tablespoons caster sugar
200 ml (7 fl oz) lukewarm water
2 eggs

200 g (7 oz) strong plain flour, plus extra for kneading

FOR STAGE 2
425 g (15 oz) strong plain flour
2 teaspoons salt
50 g (2 oz) unsalted butter, softened
1¹/₂–2 tablespoons olive oil
Beaten egg, to glaze

Pour enough brandy or liqueur over the raisins just to cover them. These should now be left to soak for 24 hours. To speed up the process, put both ingredients into a pan and bring to a simmer. Once up to a simmer, remove from the heat and allow to cool before using. This will swell the raisins and help them take on the brandy.

For stage 1, bind together the yeast and sugar. Mix with the water and eggs. Add the mix to the flour and beat to a smooth batter. Cover the bowl with cling film and leave the batter to ferment for about 30 minutes.

The second stage is best done with an electric mixer, but you can work by hand. Place the batter in the mixing bowl and add the flour and salt from stage 2. Mix for 3 minutes on a low speed or 6 minutes by hand. Now add the butter and olive oil and mix for a further 4 minutes on medium speed or 8 minutes by hand. Now it's time to add the soaked raisins (including any excess brandy) and simply mix for a further 1 minute or 5 minutes by hand. Now the mix is complete and should be covered and left to prove in a warm place for 30–40 minutes.

Once proved, knock the mix back by hand and either separate into greased loaf tins or roll into oval shapes (cooking as free loaves), then re-prove for another 30–40 minutes.

Pre-heat the oven to 200°C/400°F/gas 6.

Bake the loaves in the pre-heated oven for 20 minutes. Brush with beaten egg and return to the oven for a further 5 minutes or so to give a shiny glazed finish. The bread can now be left to cool before serving. You can finish by serving with Home-made Cherry Jam (p. 359).

Palmier Biscuits

When using puff pastry for different recipes there are always some trimmings left over, which quite often just get thrown away. Well, here is a way of using them all up and making great biscuits to serve with Cappuccino Mousse (see p. 277), Vanilla Ice-cream (see p. 252), sorbets (see p. 266) or petits fours. You could even freeze the trimmings for later use.

Puff pastry trimmings, rolled together
Icing sugar

Pre-heat the oven to 220°C/425°F/gas 7 and dampen a baking sheet.

Sprinkle icing sugar liberally on to the work surface and give the pastry one more double turn with the sugar. Rest in the fridge for 15 minutes.

Once chilled, sprinkle more sugar on to the surface and roll out the pastry to 3 mm (1/8 in) thick. Trim the edges. If this makes a large square, cut the pastry in half and fold the top edge to the middle of the square and the bottom to the middle as well, without overlapping them. Rest in the fridge or freezer for 20 minutes until set.

When set, cut each folded strip into pieces about 5 mm (1/4 in) thick, lay them flat on the work surface, dust with more icing sugar and flatten lightly with a rolling pin. Lay them on the baking sheet and cook in the pre-heated oven for about 5 minutes. Turn them over on the tray and cook for a further 5 minutes until golden and crisp. Leave to cool on a wire rack. The biscuits will keep in an airtight container for 24 hours, but are best eaten on the same day.

Crunchy Chocolate Muesli Biscuits

MAKES ABOUT 30 biscuits
225 g (8 oz) plain or milk chocolate
1/2 quantity Breakfast Muesli (see p. 343)

Melt the chocolate in a bowl over a pan of hot water. Remove from the heat and leave to cool for a few minutes. Stir in enough muesli so that the mixture will be just held together by the chocolate.

To make sweets, spoon the mixture into small paper cases, or just on to a tray. Cool, then chill until set.

To make biscuits, the mix can be spread on to a tray lined with waxed paper. When set, it can be cut into fingers. Alternatively, spread the warm melted chocolate on to waxed paper, then sprinkle the muesli liberally over the top. Set this in the fridge, and the resulting biscuits could almost be called 'country florentines'. When set, it can be cut into rounds or fingers and served with home-made ice-creams.

Gingerbread Biscuits

These biscuits taste delicious if you add some chopped pecan nuts or dates – or both. If you are using dates or nuts, simply stir them in with the evaporated milk.

MAKES ABOUT 20
225 g (8 oz) plain flour
1/4 teaspoon salt
2 teaspoons bicarbonate of soda
1 heaped teaspoon ground ginger

1/2 teaspoon cinnamon
50 g (2 oz) unsalted butter
100 g (4 oz) soft brown sugar
100 g (4 oz) golden syrup
1 tablespoon evaporated milk

Pre-heat the oven to 180–200°C/350–400°F/gas 4–6 and grease two baking sheets.

Sift together the flour, salt, soda and spices. Heat the butter, sugar and syrup until dissolved. Leave to cool. Once cooled, mix into the dry ingredients with the evaporated milk to make a dough. Chill for 30 minutes.

Roll out the biscuit dough to about 5 mm (¼ in) thick and cut into fingers, circles or even gingerbread men. Place on the baking sheets, allowing a little space to spread. Bake in the pre-heated oven for 10–15 minutes.

Chocolate Brownies

Here are two alternative chocolate brownie recipes. The first is very rich and tasty and can be used as petits fours or as a biscuit to go with ice-cream. Remember, when melting butter or chocolate, don't let it heat above room temperature.

SERVES 4
300 g (10 oz) caster sugar
4 eggs
225 g (8 oz) unsalted butter
75 g (3 oz) cocoa
75 g (3 oz) plain flour

225 g (8 oz) good-quality plain chocolate
100 g (4 oz) hazel or pecan nuts, chopped
100 g (4 oz) white chocolate, cut into 1 cm (½ in) chunks

Pre-heat the oven to 180–200°C/350–400°F/gas 4–6 and lightly grease a 20 cm (8 in) tin.

Beat together the sugar and eggs, making sure the sugar has completely dissolved. Melt the butter and whisk into the eggs. Sieve together the cocoa and flour and add to the butter and egg mix. Melt the chocolate in a bowl over a pan of warm water, then stir in. Add the chopped nuts and white chocolate. Turn the mix into the prepared tin and bake in the pre-heated oven for 30–40 minutes. Leave to cool, then cut into wedges or squares.

Quick Chocolate 'Brownies'

This recipe is even simpler and quicker to make than the one above, and it also goes well with ice-creams.

SERVES 4
200 g (7 oz) unsalted butter
50 g (2 oz) caster sugar
1 teaspoon vanilla essence
50 g (2 oz) chopped dates (Medjools are best)

175 g (6 oz) plain flour
1 teaspoon of baking powder
50 g (2 oz) cornflakes, crushed
25 g (1 oz) cocoa

Pre-heat the oven to 180–200°C/350–400°F/gas 4–6 and grease a 20 cm (8 in) tin.

Cream the butter and sugar together. Add all the other ingredients. Spoon the mixture into the prepared tin and bake in the pre heated oven for 25–30 minutes.

Basic Tuile Biscuits

This is a very basic tuile biscuit recipe. They eat very well with ice-creams and make good baskets to sit the ice-cream in. This mix keeps for up to a week if chilled. You can also change the flavour by adding the finely grated zest of 1 lemon or 1 orange (or both) or a little desiccated coconut.

SERVES 4

120 g (4$\frac{1}{2}$ oz) unsalted butter
150 g (5 oz) icing sugar, sifted

3 egg whites
120 g (4$\frac{1}{2}$ oz) plain flour

Soften the butter and add the icing sugar, beating until white. Add the egg whites and fold in the flour. The mix is ready and should now be chilled to set.

Pre-heat the oven to 180°C/350°F/gas 4 and butter a baking sheet.

Spread the mix very thinly into 13 cm (5 in) discs. This can be made easy by cutting a 13 cm (5 in) circle from a thin plastic ice-cream tub lid, then just placing it on the tray and spreading the mix in, keeping level with the lid. Bake the tuiles in the pre-heated oven for 5–6 minutes, until totally golden brown. Remove from the tray while still hot and place over a tin can or mould to shape the basket.

VARIATIONS

If you wish to serve these as biscuits to go with your coffee or serve separately with ice-creams, then simply make 6 cm (2$\frac{1}{2}$ in) discs and bake them the same way. To shape them, take the centre roll from cling film or tin foil and cut it lengthways to give two semicircular halves. Sit the warm biscuits in the mould to set.

Brandy Snap Biscuits

Brandy snap biscuits are easy to make and can be made into various shapes and sizes. I like to serve them with sorbets and ice-creams. If you roll this mix into balls the size of a 2p piece and push them on to a buttered tray, the mix will spread to give you a disc big enough to place over or in a cup, to make a basket for your ice-creams. But always make sure that you keep a good distance between each one on the tray or you'll have just one large tray of brandy snap.

MAKES ABOUT 24

100 g (4 oz) unsalted butter
100 g (4 oz) caster sugar
100 g (4 oz) golden syrup

100 g (4 oz) plain flour
A pinch of ground ginger
A pinch of ground cinnamon

Place the butter, sugar and syrup in a pan and heat gently to dissolve. Remove from heat. Mix the flour with the ginger and cinnamon, then beat into the sugar mixture. Leave to cool.

Pre-heat the oven to 180°C/350°F/gas 4 and grease two baking sheets.

Roll the mixture into balls the size of a 2p piece and place well spaced out on the prepared trays. Bake in the pre-heated oven for 7–10 minutes until golden brown with a perforated texture. Leave to cool slightly for a minute before removing from the tray and moulding over a tea cup or round the handle of a wooden spoon. If the snaps cool before you can finish shaping them all, just pop them back in the oven to warm slightly.

Shortbread Biscuits

This recipe works best if piped on to a greased baking tray.

MAKES ABOUT 16
225 g (8 oz) unsalted butter
75 g (3 oz) caster sugar

450 g (1 lb) plain flour
15 g (¹/₂ oz) cornflour

Pre-heat the oven to 180°C/350°F/gas 4 and grease and line a baking sheet.

Cream together the butter and sugar until the sugar has dissolved into the fat. Sift the flour and cornflour together and work into the butter mix. Pipe the mix on to the baking sheet and bake in the pre-heated oven for 20 minutes until golden brown. Leave to cool on a wire rack. The biscuits eat very well when sprinkled with caster sugar.

VARIATIONS

Lightly roll the shortbread mix about 1–2 cm (¹/₂–³/₄ in) thick and 20 cm (8 in) in diameter and place it in a flan ring. Mark it into eight pieces and prick all over with a fork before cooking. It will take about 30–35 minutes.

Maple Syrup and Walnut Biscuits

These biscuits have a wonderful texture and nutty flavour. They eat well on their own or with dessert dishes such as the Caramel Cream Pots (see p. 285).

MAKES 40–50 biscuits
225 g (8 oz) unsalted butter, softened
75 g (3 oz) caster sugar
1 egg yolk

1 tablespoon maple syrup
250 g (9 oz) plain flour, plus extra for dusting
75 g (3 oz) walnuts, chopped

Cream together the butter and sugar. Add the egg yolk and maple syrup. Fold in the flour, binding to a dough. Add the chopped walnuts. Using a little more flour, mould the mixture and roll it into cylinder-shaped logs about 18 cm (7 in) long and 5 cm (2 in) diameter. Wrap in cling film and put in the fridge. The mix can now be left to chill and will last for several days in the fridge.

Pre-heat the oven to 180°C/350°F/gas 4.

To cook, simply cut the log into 5 mm (¼ in) round or oval slices and bake the biscuits on a greaseproof papered tray in the pre-heated oven for 10–12 minutes, until the biscuits become slightly golden around the edges. Once cooked, the biscuits can be either dusted with caster sugar or left as they are.

Hazelnut Meringue Biscuits

These biscuits eat very well with ice-creams. They are also very quick and easy to make. The mix is basically a meringue mix with the addition of flour, butter and hazelnuts. Once the biscuits have been piped on to the silicone paper, chopped hazelnuts or raisins/currants can be sprinkled on before cooking. Also, finely grated orange zest can be added to the mix before piping to give another flavour. All of these are optional extras, so here's the basic recipe.

MAKES ABOUT 24 biscuits
4 egg whites
100 g (4 oz) caster sugar

25 g (1 oz) plain flour, sifted
75 g (3 oz) ground hazelnuts
15 g (¹/₂ oz) unsalted butter, melted

Pre-heat the oven to 150°C/300°F/gas 2. Line a baking tray with silicone paper or lightly greased greaseproof paper.

Whisk the egg whites and sugar together until stiff. Gently fold in the flour. Add the ground hazelnuts and melted butter and mix carefully. This mix can now be piped on to silicone paper using a plain 1 cm (¹/₂ in) tube, into fingers approximately 7.5 cm (3 in) long. These can now be gently smoothed over and baked in the pre-heated oven for 30 minutes. Once cooked, leave to cool a little, carefully lift from the tray with a palette knife and leave to cool completely before storing in an airtight container.

Fruit Shortcake Biscuits

These biscuits have always been a favourite of mine, so I thought why not make some of my own? These can be used just as a basic biscuit or served with a pudding or ice-cream.

There are also many combinations with this recipe: for example, chocolate chips can be added for some delicious chocolate and fruit cookies. The mix can also be made into small or large biscuits and even into small petits fours. Of course, by leaving out the currants and zest you'll have just a good shortcake biscuit.

MAKES ABOUT 16 biscuits
50 g (2 oz) caster or icing sugar, sifted
100 g (4 oz) unsalted butter, diced
50 g (2 oz) currants

1 egg yolk (optional)
175 g (6oz) plain flour, sifted
Caster sugar or icing sugar, for
    dusting

If using caster sugar, beat it with the butter until soft and creamy. If using icing sugar, this can simply be creamed in by hand. The currants or any other flavour (such as the grated zest of a lemon or orange, see below) can now be added to the butter. An egg yolk can also be added to enrich the mix. If using, add the egg to the butter. Gently work in the flour. Any overworking will spoil the light crumbly texture. Shape the dough into a cylinder about 6 cm (2¹/2 in) in diameter and 9 cm (3¹/2 in) long, wrap in cling film and chill for 1 hour.

Pre-heat the oven to 200°C/400°F/gas 6. Lightly grease a baking sheet.

Cut the chilled dough into 15–20 discs about 2 mm thick, or roll out 2 mm thick and cut out with fluted rings. Lay the dough on the baking sheet and bake in the pre-heated oven for about 4 minutes until golden. If you are dusting with caster sugar, remove the biscuits from the oven after 4 minutes, sprinkle with caster sugar and cook for a further 1 minute. If you are using icing sugar, simply dust the cooked biscuits with icing sugar.

VARIATIONS

If you have creamed the mixture and it has become quite soft, it can be piped on to a greased baking tray with a fluted piping tube. These biscuits will obviously be thicker and fewer in quantity. They will take twice as long to cook. If it's small piped *petit four* biscuits, they will only need 5–6 minutes cooking time.

This recipe will also work with many other flavours. The finely grated zest of 1 lemon or orange (or even both) or lime added to this mix will give you lovely short-bread biscuits with rich citrus flavours.

I also like to make poppy seed biscuits. These can be made by toasting a table-spoon of poppy seeds to release their flavour and adding them to the flour when mixing the biscuits together.

Mincemeat Doughnuts

These have to be the easiest doughnuts you can possibly imagine. Whenever I've asked anybody whether they fancy making some home-made doughnuts, the reaction usually is, 'no thanks, I haven't got the yeast to make the dough'. Well, with this recipe you don't need yeast, but what you will have is the finished texture and taste. The important thing to remember is the thick white sliced bread must be fresh, to give a light spongy texture.

You can eat the doughnuts as they are, or leave them without the sugar and serve them as a pudding with ice-cream, clotted cream or maybe a Custard Sauce flavoured with rum (see p. 355). They make a great alternative to traditional Christmas pudding. When you come to using these as a dinner party pudding, it's great fun to tell your guests they're having a deep-fried sandwich for pudding. They'll love it – have a go.

SERVES 4
8 thick slices of white bread
50 g (2 oz) unsalted butter
100 g (4 oz) mincemeat
Oil, for deep-frying

100 g (4 oz) self-raising flour
25 g (1 oz) caster sugar
150 ml (5 fl oz) strong dry cider
Caster sugar or icing sugar, sifted

Butter the slices of bread and place four slices butter-side up on the work surface. Divide the mincemeat between the slices of bread, placing a spoonful into the centre of each slice. Top with the remaining slices, pushing the bread gently around the dome of mincemeat. Using a 7.5 cm (3 in) round cutter, cut sandwiches from the bread, giving domed discs.

Heat a deep pan of oil to 180°C/350°F.

To make the batter, mix the flour and sugar, then add the cider, whisking and adding until a thick batter is achieved. It's important you have a thick batter. All you do next is dip the mincemeat sandwiches into the batter and carefully place them in the hot fat, a few at a time so that the pan is not crowded. The doughnuts will cook on one side only, so, after 1–2 minutes, turn them over with a slotted spoon, making sure they are golden on the cooked side. Continue to cook for another minute or so until completely golden brown. Remove from the pan with a slotted spoon and drain on kitchen paper. Continue with the remaining doughnuts. Dust the doughnuts with caster or icing sugar and serve.

VARIATIONS

Of course, how could I forget the classic jam doughnut? Well, this recipe suits just about any flavour you want. Just follow the same method, first making a jam, marmalade, or lemon curd, apple, plum, raspberry, apricot – the flavours can just go on and on – the domed sandwich, and fry in the same way.

Sweet Sauces, Confectionery and Preserves

Clementine or Orange Sauce

This is a good sauce for ice-creams, sorbets, Gingerbread Cake (see p. 336), or even Cappuccino Mousse (see p. 277).

MAKES ABOUT 600 ml (1 pint)
2.25 kg (5 lb) clementines or oranges

15 g (1/2 oz) arrowroot
Icing sugar, to taste

Squeeze the juice from the clementines or oranges then push the juice through a sieve. This should leave you with at least 600 ml (1 pint) of juice. Bring to the boil and boil until reduced by half; in fact, whatever quantity of juice you have, always reduce it by half. Mix the arrowroot with a little water to soften it, then add it to the reduced juice a little at a time, stirring continuously until you have a sauce that will lightly coat the back of a spoon. Allow the sauce barely to simmer for 3–4 minutes. Remove from the heat and leave to cool.

When the sauce is cold, it should be a rich orange colour and have a full taste. If you feel it needs to be a little sweeter, just stir in some icing sugar.

Chocolate Sauce

This sauce goes very well with pear sorbet, banana ice-cream, Vanilla Ice-cream (see p. 252), or a steamed chocolate pudding.

MAKES ABOUT 350 ml (12 fl oz)
225 g (8 oz) plain chocolate
150 ml (5 fl oz) milk

75 ml (3 fl oz) double cream
40 g (1 1/2 oz) caster sugar

Melt the chocolate in a bowl over a pan of hot water. Do not allow it to get too hot or this will make it grainy. Boil the milk, double cream and sugar together and stir into the chocolate. Allow the mixture to cool, stirring occasionally. The sauce is now finished and ready to use.

To enrich the taste and consistency, 25 g (1 oz) of unsalted butter can be added while the sauce is still warm.

Rich Chocolate Sauce

Chocolate sauce is very easy to make. However, when using chocolate, it's important never to overheat it as this will leave you with a grainy texture. Instead, what we are after is a rich thick glossy sauce. Well, this must be the ultimate thick chocolate sauce. It's very rich and tasty. It can be thinned out with the addition of more cream or milk.

MAKES ABOUT 450 ml (15 fl oz)
225 g (8 oz) good-quality plain
   chocolate

250 ml (8 fl oz) double cream
25 g (1 oz) unsalted butter

Melt the chocolate with the cream in a bowl over a pan of hot water and once warm, add the butter. You now have a thick rich chocolate sauce. This is best eaten cold or just warm. Trying to serve this as a hot sauce will simply separate the butter.

Custard Sauce or *Crème Anglaise*

This recipe can act as a base for so many different flavours. You must only ever serve it warm, not boiled, as that would scramble the egg yolks in the cream mix. The fresh vanilla is optional and can be omitted when using other flavours. To have the flavour of vanilla always close at hand, keep a vanilla pod in your jar of caster sugar; the aroma from the pod will impregnate the sugar.

MAKES 750 ml (1¼ pints)
8 egg yolks
75 g (3 oz) caster sugar

1 vanilla pod, split (optional)
300 ml (10 fl oz) milk
300 ml (10 fl oz) double cream

Beat the egg yolks and sugar together in a bowl until well blended. Split and scrape the insides of the vanilla pod, if using, into the milk and cream and bring to the boil. Sit the bowl over a pan of hot water and whisk the cream into the egg mix. As the egg yolks warm, the cream will thicken to create a custard. Keep stirring until it coats the back of a spoon. Remove the bowl from the heat. The custard can now be served warm or stirred occasionally until it cools.

VARIATIONS

For Lemon Custard Sauce, add the pared zest of 2 lemons, not the pith, to the milk and cream when heating, then leave it in the mix throughout the cooking process. Once the custard has thickened, add the juice of a lemon and taste. If the lemon flavour is not strong enough, simply add more lemon juice to taste. Strain the custard through a sieve.

For Orange Custard Sauce, add the pared zest of 2 oranges to the milk and cream when heating, then cook as for the basic recipe. Orange juice will not be used in this recipe. To lift the flavour of the sauce, try adding a few drops of Cointreau or Grand Marnier.

For Rum Custard Sauce, add some rum to taste at the end of cooking the vanilla custard. A spoonful or two of coconut milk could also be added to the milk and cream to make a Rum and Coconut Custard Sauce.

Coffee Custard Sauce can be made by replacing the vanilla pod with 2 tea-spoons of freshly ground coffee and cooking as for the vanilla recipe. Once the coffee custard has completely cooled, just strain through a sieve to remove any excess granules.

Chocolate Custard

This is a must for chocolate fans – well, in fact, everybody. It eats so well with a steamed sponge, or you can even use this recipe to make a chocolate bread and butter pudding. Leave out the currants or raisins and replace them with cherries and what do you have? Black Forest bread and butter pudding. Just imagine finishing that with lots of grated chocolate melted over the top. So there you are, another recipe in this introduction – that's the fun of cooking, it's just non-stop with seemingly endless combinations.

If you do decide to have a go at the chocolate bread and butter pudding, then you will not need to cook the custard as I do in this recipe. Simply pour the custard mix over the bread and leave to soak for 20–30 minutes before cooking in a water bath in a pre-heated oven at 180°C/350°F/gas 4 for 20–30 minutes, until thickened and just set. If you're not keen on cherries, then simply spread orange marmalade on the bread and have a chocolate, orange bread and butter pudding.

MAKES 750 ml (1¹/₄ pints)
300 ml (10 fl oz) milk
300 ml (10 fl oz) double cream
50 g (2 oz) good-quality plain
   chocolate, grated (or 100 g/4 oz)
   for real chocolate lovers), grated

8 egg yolks
75 g (3 oz) caster sugar

Heat the milk and cream together, then pour a quarter over the grated chocolate. Once the chocolate has melted, add the remaining cream. Beat together the egg yolks and sugar and pour the warm chocolate cream over, stirring as it's poured. This can now be strained through a sieve and then cooked in a bowl over a pan of hot water until thickened, stirring all the time. The custard is now ready to serve. Or you can chill and set it to be used for a dark chocolate trifle.

Fruit Purées or Coulis

Fruit purées, or coulis, are used for many things, particularly bases for sorbets, as sweet sauces and as flavourings in mousses. The French term coulis literally means 'sieved' and this method is used for soft fruits such as strawberries, raspberries and blackcurrants. Because of the sharpness in the flavour, the fruits may need to be mixed with icing sugar. These quantities are good guidelines; you can vary them to suit the tartness of the fruit. They go very well with ice-creams and iced parfaits.

MAKES ABOUT 225 g (8 oz)
225 g (8 oz) soft fruit

50 g (2 oz) icing sugar, sifted
A few drops of lemon juice

Blitz the fruit and sugar together in a food processor, then push through a sieve. If the flavour is still too tart, simply add more icing sugar to taste. The consistency will be that of a thick sauce, which can be thinned down if needed with some Stock Syrup (see p. 397), or some more icing sugar blended with a little water. A few drops of lemon will help lift the flavour of the fruit.

Fruit Sauce

This recipe is very similar to a Fruit Purée or Coulis (see p. 356) but gives you more of a sauce consistency.

MAKES 750 ml (1¹/₄ pints)
450 g (1 lb) fruit, such as plums,
    raspberries, etc.

100 g (4 oz) caster sugar
150 ml (5 fl oz) water
Juice of 1 lemon

All the ingredients can be mixed together and brought to the simmer for a few minutes until the fruits become tender. If the fruit is very sharp, the sugar quantity can be doubled to 225 g (8 oz). Once tender, after about 6–8 minutes, the mix can now be blitzed and pushed through a sieve. Once cold, this coulis will have a good sauce consistency to use with many puddings.

Sabayon

Sabayons go particularly well with ice-creams or can be spooned over tarts or flans and then made into a golden brown glaze under the grill. This recipe is different from the original; you can add almost any flavours and tastes to suit the dessert of your choice.

MAKES 900 ml (1¹/₂ pints)
4 egg yolks
50 g (2 oz) caster sugar

6 tablespoons liqueur, such as
    Champagne, white wine, brandy,
    Irish whiskey, Marsala, fruit liqueurs
    (pear, apple, raspberry, etc.), coffee

All these flavours can be made using the same method, whisking together the yolks with the sugar and the flavour of your choice over a pan of simmering water, which will at least double the volume.

NOTE

The sabayon can also be made with an electric mixer. To help it along, simply warm the bowl first.

VARIATIONS

There are many other flavours that can be added to a sabayon. To this quantity, the grated zest of 1–2 lemons, oranges or limes can be added, replacing half the Champagne or white wine with the juice of the fruit. This will give you a very strong citrus fruit sabayon that will eat well with a steamed sponge or maybe ice-cream of the same flavour. Of course, all of the flavours can be mixed. A good home-made or bought raspberry ice-cream or sorbet with a lemon sabayon is delicious. Or perhaps chocolate ice-cream or steamed sponge with orange sabayon or a good white chocolate ice-cream with lime sabayon.

To add even more taste to these, three-quarters of the liquid, wine or flavouring can be replaced with lemon curd or good orange marmalade.

Reducing the sugar content to 25 g (1 oz) and adding 3–4 tablespoons of golden syrup with 1–2 tablespoons of water gives you an amazing golden syrup sabayon. Eating that spooned over a golden syrup steamed sponge instead or as well as custard is wonderful.

Another variation is to make an Irish whiskey sabayon to go with the Rich Stout Cake on p. 338 to make a unique Stout Cake Pudding (see Variation on p. 339).

Chocolate Sabayon – and Others

This is a rich sauce but much lighter than many basic chocolate sauces. The sabayon is very tasty and goes with so many dishes: the Pear and Hazlenut 'Pasties' (see p. 300) is a great example. It also eats well as a topping for home-made ice-cream or sorbet served in a glass. The other option is to treat the sabayons as zabaglione and serve any of the flavours with a home-made biscuit or two.

For the chocolate recipe, I am using some whole eggs to hold the mix together and prevent the quantity from breaking down. Adding the melted chocolate to a basic sabayon recipe will always reduce the volume. So the addition of whole eggs will obviously help hold the complete volume. I also like to add rum, coffee liqueur or Cointreau to the mix for extra flavour.

MAKES ABOUT 450 ml (15 fl oz)
2 egg yolks
2 eggs
50 g (2 oz) caster sugar

3–4 tablespoons chocolate liqueur,
  Cointreau, coffee or rum (or water)
100 g (4 oz) good-quality plain
  chocolate, melted

This can be made by two methods. Both need a pan of simmering water to help thicken the eggs and hold their volume.

The first method is to mix the egg yolks, whole eggs, sugar and liquid together and add the melted chocolate. This can now be whisked over the pan of water until at least doubled in volume.

The second method is to simply whisk the egg yolks, whole eggs, sugar and liquid over the pan to a sabayon stage (at least doubled), and then slowly pour in the melted chocolate while still whisking. After 1–2 minutes of continual whisking the warm sabayon is ready.

Both methods will give you the same result: a thick, light, chocolate, creamy sabayon.

The sabayon can be continually whisked until it reaches room temperature. If you do this, the sabayon will keep for a little longer, although if it gets too cold, the chocolate will become thicker and lose that lovely soft, light texture, so the sabayon is really at its best when made and served immediately.

NOTE

It is important that the bowl does not come into contact with the simmering water.

Home-made Cherry Jam or Sauce

This recipe is almost the same process as for the Home-made Blackberry Jam (see p. 346). This cooks and stays slightly softer, making it into a thick cherry sauce with all the texture left in the cherries. I like to add the finely grated zest of an orange to give a slightly bitter taste against the cherries. The recipe is lovely to eat as a jam or can be used to accompany many puddings: the American Cheesecake (see p. 286) is one and why not just spoon it over ice-cream?

If you intend to eat the jam within a month, simply allow the jam to cool a little then spoon into warmed jam jars, leave to cool, then chill. The sugar and pectin are both natural preservatives, so the jam will keep perfectly fresh.

If you want to store the jam for longer, you'll need to sterilize the jars, as described in the recipe for Home-made Blackberry Jam (see p. 364). Stored in a cool, dark place, in sterilized jars, the jam will last almost indefinitely until opened.

MAKES ABOUT 675 g (1¹/₂ lb)
900 g (2 lb) cherries, stoned
450 g (1 lb) sugar with pectin

Juice of 1 lemon or orange
Finely grated zest of 1 orange
(optional)

Warm and sterilize, if necessary, 2 or 3 jam jars. The glass should be warm before adding the hot jam, to prevent the jars from shattering.

Place the stoned cherries, sugar, citrus juice and zest, if using, in a preserving pan or large pan and bring to a simmer. Increase the heat to a rolling boil and skim off any impurities rising to the top. Keep the jam boiling for 4–5 minutes, then remove from the heat, again skimming any impurities. You will now have a rich, deep, red shiny jam with the cherries still holding some shape and texture. Leave the jam to cool slightly, then spoon it into the warm jars, seal and label.

Toffee Cream

The standard proportions for this recipe are one tin of Toffee to 450 ml (15 fl oz) of cream, but this makes a lot of cream, so it is best to make it in a smaller quantity.

SERVES 4
200 g (7 oz) Toffee (see p. 363)
250 ml (8 fl oz) double or single cream

Stir the toffee in a bowl to loosen. If you're looking for a thick pouring cream, then simply add all the cream and whisk in until well mixed (single cream works well for this). If you want a thick and light cream, then use double cream, just adding a quarter of the cream and whisking until thickened, then adding another quarter, and so on until everything is mixed. The toffee cream may still seem to be a little soft, so it's best to make this 1–2 hours before you need it and then chill it in the fridge. This will give the cream a totally new texture and, when spooned on to the plate, it will hold its shape.

Cheesecake Cream

I like to serve this cheesecake recipe just as a cream. Of course, it can be spread on to a digestive biscuit base and covered with a fruit topping, for a classic cheesecake. Using this recipe as a cream gives it many more options, from serving with summer fruits, poached fruits, chocolate cake (especially the one on p. 336) or even ice-cream and raspberry sauce. It also eats very well if flavoured with honey and a drop of Irish whiskey. The other bonus is that it's quick and easy to make. The following quantities can be halved to make less.

SERVES 6–8
50 g (2 oz) caster sugar
450 g (1 lb) full-fat soft cream cheese
600 ml (1 pint) double cream, lightly whipped

Beat the caster sugar into the cream cheese until the sugar has dissolved and creamed. Fold in the lightly whipped cream. It is important that the cream is only lightly whipped. This will prevent the cream from becoming over-beaten and separating when mixing with the cream cheese. Place the cheesecake in a suitable bowl or dish and set in the fridge for about an hour.

Once the cream has set, it can be served in the bowl or shaped between two spoons to serve on the plate.

VARIATIONS

Lots of other flavours can be added to this mix. One of my favourites is toffee. To make a toffee cream, simply add a tin of Toffee (see p. 362) to the cream cheese mix before folding in the whipped cream.

To make a chocolate version, melt 100–225 g (4–8 oz) of good-quality plain chocolate, only allowing the chocolate to reach room temperature. The cream cheese must also be at room temperature and not chilled, as this would set the cream when added. Simply mix the chocolate with the cream cheese and sugar, then fold in the whipped cream and set in the fridge. The 100 g (4 oz) is the minimum quantity of chocolate; your taste will determine the rest, but the more chocolate you add, the firmer the cream will be.

Melba Sauce

Melba sauce, of course, is the sauce that goes with Peach Melba (see p. 272). There are many ways of making this raspberry sauce. This particular recipe gives a good balance of fruitiness to sweetness, but if you want a really quick version then simply boil 225 g (8 oz) of raspberry jam with 5 tablespoons of water and then strain through a sieve; or mix 225 g (8 oz) of fresh raspberries with 100 g (4 oz) of icing sugar, push through a sieve and add a squeeze of lemon juice. Well, there are two recipes. Now here's mine.

SERVES 4　　　　　　　　　　　**150 g (5 oz) caster sugar**
225 g (8 oz) frozen raspberries, thawed　　**225 g (8 oz) raspberry jam**

Heat the raspberries with 50 g (2 oz) of the sugar until dissolved, then bring to the simmer. Push through a sieve to make a raspberry purée. Mix the purée with the remaining sugar and the jam and bring to the boil. Simmer for 3–4 minutes, then strain through a sieve. The sauce is ready and can be eaten hot or cold with many puddings.

Turkish Delight

Turkish Delight has become an annual treat for me. Every Christmas a box of it seems to come my way and, I have to admit, I eat the lot.

I have included a recipe for Turkish Delight Ice-cream (see p. 256) which, you can imagine, eats very well especially with a Rich Chocolate Sauce (see p. 354) or Chocolate Sabayon (see p. 358). It's really taking the famous chocolate bar idea and turning it into a fun pudding. You can make the ice-cream with a bought Turkish Delight but, if you fancy having a go yourself, here's the recipe.

This quantity of gelatine leaves will give you a softer texture than a bought version; 25 g (1 oz) of powdered gelatine or 8–9 leaves will match that texture. I personally prefer the softer sweet but it's really up to you. The red food colouring is optional but a pale pink colour works well in the ice-cream recipe.

MAKES ABOUT 675 g (1½ lb)
675 g (1½ lb) caster sugar
300 ml (10 fl oz) water
50 g (2 oz) glucose syrup
About 2 tablespoons rose-water

A few drops of red food colouring
  (optional)
100 g (4 oz) cornflour
2 × 11 g sachets of powdered gelatine
25 g (1 oz) icing sugar

Line a 20 cm (8 in) square tin or mould at least 2.5 cm (1 in) deep with cling film.

Boil together the caster sugar, water and glucose syrup with the rose-water and food colouring, if using. Once up to the boil, cook for 8–10 minutes. Add a drop of water to 75 g (3 oz) of the cornflour to loosen. Soften the gelatine in water according to the instructions on the packet.

Remove the boiling syrup from the stove and add the gelatine. Once dissolved, whisk in the cornflour, cook for 2–3 minutes, then pour into the prepared tin or mould to about 2.5 cm (1 in) deep. Allow to cool, then chill for 2–3 hours until completely set.

To finish, mix together the remaining cornflour with the icing sugar. Turn the mix out of the mould and with a warm wet knife, cut into cubes and roll through the icing sugar/cornflour to coat lightly. Now all you have to do is eat it.

Toffee

This really is amazing. When I show people the results, most just can't believe it. As you can see you don't need a lot of ingredients. The toffee is great for so many things: crumbles, creams, ice-creams and sauces.

MAKES 400 g (14 oz)
1 × 400 g (14 oz) tin of condensed milk

All you have to do is place the tin of condensed milk (totally unopened) in a pan and cover with cold water, making sure the tin is completely covered. Bring to the boil and continue to simmer for 3 hours (no less). Leave to cool down in the pan. The toffee is now made and can be kept chilled in the unopened can until the date runs out.

Honeycomb

Honeycomb is, of course, the filling in a Crunchie bar. This recipe could be used to make your own, but I like to break the honeycomb into pieces and add it to a chocolate ice-cream just at the end of churning. This gives you a lovely crunchy texture in the ice-cream. It's also wonderful just broken and sprinkled on top of an ice-cream pudding.

To make honeycomb you need to boil the sugar, so do take care as it reaches very high temperatures. You must always make sure that you have a very clean, large pan for this recipe and also a sugar thermometer will be needed.

SERVES 4–6

2 tablespoons water
225 g (8 oz) demerara sugar
225 g (8 oz) granulated sugar
50 g (2 oz) golden syrup
15 g (1/2 oz) unsalted butter
1 tablespoon bicarbonate of soda

Pour the water into a saucepan, add the sugars, golden syrup and butter. Bring the mix to the boil and continue to cook to a small crack temperature. This is 138–140°C/280–284°F. The sugar mix will have a rich golden colour. Add the bicarbonate of soda; this will lift the sugar and create a light airy texture. Pour the honeycomb mix into a greased 23 × 28 cm (9 × 11 in) tray and allow to set. Once cooled and set the honeycomb is ready and can be kept in an airtight container.

Praline

Another lovely ice-cream is made with praline, a toffee-type mixture of sugar and hazelnuts boiled together. Simply crush the praline pieces in a bowl and add to the vanilla ice-cream mix when it's ready to be churned or frozen. This will be very sweet so it's best to omit 50 g (2 oz) of caster sugar from the basic ice-cream recipe.

100 g (4 oz) shelled hazelnuts, chopped
100 g (4 oz) caster sugar

Place the nuts and sugar together in a pan and slowly cook until the sugar is golden brown. Pour the mixture on to a lightly oiled tray and leave until set and cold. The praline is now ready to break.

Lemon Curd

Lemon curd eats very well just on toast or teacakes. I like to use it for Lemon Curd Ice-cream (see p. 255) or as a sauce for steamed sponges.

This recipe is very rich, with a high butter content. If you prefer, you can cut the butter down to 100 g (4 oz) and also cut down by 1 egg yolk. The lemon curd will still work without being over-rich and will have a slightly more fluid consistency. There are two alternative methods.

If you want to keep the lemon curd for any length of time, store it in jam jars, well sealed, that have been sterilized as described in the recipe for Home-made Blackberry Jam (see below). However it will not last as long as jam does.

MAKES ABOUT 675 g (1½ lb)
225 g (8 oz) caster sugar
225 g (8 oz) unsalted butter

**Finely grated zest and juice of 3
lemons
5 egg yolks**

For method I, sit the sugar, butter, lemon juice and zest in a bowl and stir over a pan of simmering water. Once the butter has melted, beat vigorously until well combined. Beat in the egg yolks and continue to cook and stir for 15–20 minutes until the curd has thickened. Pour into a clean jar and cover with waxed paper or cling film. Once cooled, seal tightly and keep in the fridge. This should keep for at least two weeks.

For method 2, whisk the sugar and egg yolks together until light and creamy. Melt the butter with the lemon zest and juice and add to the mix. Cook, stirring, in a bowl over a pan of simmering water until thickened; this will also take about 15–20 minutes.

Home-made Blackberry Jam

In this recipe there are two alternatives for the quantity of sugar, but both work by the same method. The difference is quite simple. If equal amounts of sugar and fruit are used, more syrup is made from the sugar. Also, by using a preserving sugar containing pectin, the jam is guaranteed to set. By using half the sugar content, less syrup is made and so consequently a thicker more 'jammy' texture and not quite as sweet taste is the result. I prefer to make the jam with half of the sugar content to achieve a stronger natural taste of the fruits, although jam made in this way will only last for a maximum of two weeks.

This is a basic recipe which can be applied to most soft fruits such as raspberries, strawberries and cherries. However, sharp, firmer fruits, such as blackcurrants, will require more sugar to balance the acidity.

These berries obviously have seeds so if you prefer to make jam without them, simply strain through a sieve once.

If you intend to eat the jam within a week or two, simply allow the jam to cool, place in warmed jam jars, leave to cool, then chill. The sugar and pectin are both natural preservatives so the jam will keep perfectly fresh.

If you want to store the jams for longer, you'll need to sterilize them. Sterilize the jars first by covering them with cold water in a large pan, then bringing the water to the boil. Leave to boil for 10–15 minutes, then remove and dry. The glass should be warm before adding the hot jam to prevent the jar from shattering. Once the jars are filled, covered and sealed, you can sterilize them further by sitting the jars on a wire rack or cloth in a large pan and almost covering with water. Bring the water to the boil, then repeat the process. Store the jam in a cool, dark place, or chill it; it will last almost indefinitely.

MAKES ABOUT 900 g (2 lb)
900 g (2 lb) blackberries

450 g (1 lb) or 900 g (2 lb) sugar with pectin
Juice of 1 lemon

Carefully rinse the blackberries, making sure you do not damage the fruits. Warm the sugar in a large, heavy-based pan over a low heat; this will take 1–2 minutes. Add the fruits and the sugar will begin to dissolve. Once some liquid is forming, turn up the heat and bring to the boil, stirring gently. Stir in the lemon juice. As the mix is heating, some froth and impurities will begin to rise to the top. This froth should be skimmed off. Once boiling rapidly, continue to cook for about 6–7 minutes. The jam should have reached the temperature of 105°C/220°F. With the pectin in the sugar this will be at setting point. If you don't have a sugar thermometer, simply sit a spoonful of mix on a saucer and set in the fridge. Once cold and touched, the jam should have a jellied, wrinkled texture and is now ready to pour into the jars and cover with waxed paper. Allow to cool before closing the lids. The jam should be kept in a dark, cool place or chilled for extra life.

Quick Home-made Lemonade

This simple recipe goes well with the Maple Syrup and Walnut Biscuits (see p. 349), Griddled Scones (see p. 341) with summer fruits and cream, or any other home-made biscuits.

MAKES 600 ml (1 pint)
2 whole lemons (including pith and peel), chopped

4 tablespoons caster sugar
600 ml (1 pint) water

Blitz all the ingredients in a blender until the lemon is puréed and then push through a sieve. To serve, simply pour on ice.

Sauces, Dressings and Savoury Preserves

Onion Gravy

This wonderful gravy is perfect with your Yorkshire Puddings (see p. 247).

MAKES ABOUT 450–600 ml (15–20 fl oz)

4 large onions, finely chopped
2 tablespoons water

300–450 ml (10–15 fl oz) Veal or Beef *Jus* (see p. 398) or bought alternative (see p. 401)

To make the onion gravy, place the chopped onions in a pan with the water. They must now be cooked on a very low heat. This will slowly draw the natural sugar content from the onions and, together with their juices, the two will caramelize. This is a slow process, possibly taking up to 2 hours. It is very important that the onions do not burn as this will create a bitter taste. Once a golden caramel flavour has been achieved, add the *jus*. By adding just 300 ml (10 fl oz) you will have a thick onion marmalade. This eats very well just spooned into the cooked Yorkshire puddings. For a thinner sauce consistency, use 450 ml (15 fl oz) of *jus*.

For a quicker caramelizing method, cook the onions to a golden brown colour in a knob of butter. Add a teaspoon of demerara sugar and cook for 1–2 minutes. Taste the onions for sweetness. If you feel they need more, then repeat the same quantity until the flavour you are after is achieved. Now just add the *jus* and cook for 6–8 minutes before serving.

VARIATIONS

This fish gravy eats very well with fish. The gravy itself should be of a thin sauce consistency. It can be made by simply adding *jus* to the roasting pan once the fish is cooked and lifted from the pan, leaving all the juices to be mixed with the *jus*.

Another alternative is to buy fish bones and roast them in a pan with onion, celery, leek, bay leaf and a sprig of tarragon. Once coloured, add 1–2 glasses of white wine and boil to reduce by three-quarters. Add the 300–600 ml (10–20 fl oz) of gravy (not too thick) and cook for 20 minutes. The sauce can now be strained through a sieve and used as a sauce for roast fish.

This sauce can also be made into a fish *chasseur* by simply adding some cooked chopped onion or shallot, sliced mushrooms, diced tomato flesh and chopped tarragon.

Tomato and Onion Flavoured Gravy

This sauce has a delicious variety of flavours, and goes particularly well with lamb and chicken dishes.

MAKES 1.5 litres (2¹/2 pints)
4 onions, sliced
1–2 tablespoons water
8 tomatoes, chopped
1 garlic clove, crushed
1 small sprig of fresh rosemary

8 fresh basil leaves
300 ml (10 fl oz) Noilly Prat or white
vermouth
300 ml (10 fl oz) dry white wine
1.2 litres (2 pints) Veal *Jus* (see p. 398)
or bought alternative (see p. 401)

Cook the sliced onions with the water very slowly until they have naturally caramelized, stirring occasionally. This will take at least an hour. Add the tomatoes, garlic and herbs and continue to cook for 15–20 minutes, until the tomatoes are soft. Pour in the Noilly Prat or vermouth and the white wine and boil to reduce until almost dry. Add the *jus*, bring to the simmer and cook for 30 minutes. Blitz using a hand blender or liquidizer. This will thicken the sauce and help it take on lots more tastes. Pass through a sieve and serve.

Cranberry *Jus* or Gravy

The flavour of this sauce can be helped by taking a good handful of vegetable mirepoix (roughly chopped carrots, shallots or onions, celery and leeks) and cooking them with 2 bay leaves and a sprig of fresh thyme for a few minutes before adding the red wine. The sauce will then need to be sieved before adding the cranberry sauce.

SERVES 4–8
2 glasses of red wine
600 ml (1 pint) Veal *Jus* (see p. 398) or
bought alternative (see p. 401)

2 large tablespoons Cranberry Sauce
(see p. 371)

Boil the red wine until reduced by two-thirds. Add the veal *jus* or alternative and bring the sauce to the simmer. Add the cranberry sauce and continue to simmer gently for 10–15 minutes. Stir in the cranberry sauce until well blended.

VARIATIONS

To make a quick cranberry-flavoured sauce, just take 600 ml (1 pint) of *jus* alternative (see p. 401) and add 2 tablespoons of bought or home-made cranberry jelly. More can be added to adjust the taste to your liking.

Red Wine Sauce

This sauce tastes good with almost any meat – chicken, beef, pork, veal – and even eats well with baked fish.

MAKES ABOUT 1.2 litres (2 pints)
4 shallots, chopped
1 large carrot, chopped
2 celery sticks, chopped
25 g (1 oz) unsalted butter
1 garlic clove, crushed
1 bay leaf
1 sprig of fresh thyme

225 g (8 oz) beef skirt or trimmings
    from the butcher (optional)
1 tablespoon olive oil (optional)
1 bottle of red wine
1.2 litres (2 pints) Veal *Jus* (see p. 398)
    or bought alternative (see p. 401)
Salt and freshly ground white pepper

In a large pan, cook the chopped vegetables in a little butter with the garlic and herbs, allowing them to colour. In a frying-pan, fry the meat, if used, in the oil, colouring on all sides, then add the meat to the vegetables. Pour the red wine into the frying-pan to release any flavours from the trimmings. Scrape and stir, then pour the wine on to the meat and vegetables and boil to reduce until almost dry.

Add the veal *jus* and bring to the simmer, skim off any impurities, then simmer the sauce gently for 30 minutes. Pass through a sieve, squeezing all the juices from the vegetables and meat. Check for seasoning, and you now have a rich, glistening sauce.

Quick Red Wine Sauce

At work, I always make fresh stocks, gravies and sauces, but when you're at home it's not always possible. But there is always an alternative. Whenever making packet sauces it's best to add half again or even double the quantity of water given in the recipe to give a better consistency. Bonne Cuisine Madeira Wine Gravy is a good one to use. To make the sauce even simpler, you can leave out the shallots, bay leaf and peppercorns.

MAKES ABOUT 1.2 litres
    (2 pints)
600 ml (1 pint) red wine
2 shallots, sliced

1 bay leaf
A few black peppercorns
1 packet of instant gravy, made up
    with 900 ml (1 1/2 pints) water

To make this red wine sauce, bring the wine to the boil with the shallots, bay leaf and peppercorns, then boil until reduced by three-quarters, leaving about 150 ml (5 fl oz) of strong red wine. Add the gravy and cook for a few minutes. Strain before serving.

Curry Cream Sauce

This recipe will provide a slightly yellow, creamy curry sauce with just enough strength to flavour the Smoked Eel Kedgeree (see p. 53). Any leftover sauce can be kept in the fridge for a few days. It's good added to any curry. This recipe gives you a mild sauce; 1 1/2–2 tablespoons of curry powder can be used for a hotter finish.

MAKES ABOUT 600 ml (1 pint)
Knob of butter
1 large onion, finely chopped
2 garlic cloves, crushed
1 tablespoon ready-made Madras curry
  powder

300 ml (1/2 pint) *Chicken stock* (see
  p. 399) or *Vegetable stock* (see
  p. 400)
300 ml (1/2 pint) double cream
150 ml (1/4 pint) coconut milk
Squeeze of lime juice (optional)
Salt

Melt the knob of butter and add the chopped onion and garlic. Cook on a medium heat, without colouring, for 5–6 minutes. Add the curry powder and continue to cook for a further 6–8 minutes, stirring occasionally. Add the vegetable or chicken stock and bring to the simmer. Allow the sauce to cook on a fast simmer, reducing the stock by half. This will increase its total flavour. Add the double cream and return to the simmer. This can now be cooked for 10–15 minutes. Add the coconut milk, bring to the simmer and the sauce is ready. Season with salt, adding a squeeze of lime, if using, to lift the total taste. Once cooked, strain through a sieve for a smooth sauce.

VARIATION

To cut down the cream by half, simply simmer the stock, but do not reduce. Instead take 1 teaspoon of arrowroot and moisten with a tablespoon or two of the cream. Whisk the arrowroot into the stock and return to the simmer. It's best to use single cream here, as the sauce will be thickened from the arrowroot. Cook as per the recipe, finishing with the coconut milk and squeese of lime.

Plum Purée Sauce

This sauce has a wonderful, spicy plum flavour. Use it with a Duck Confit (see p. 127 or p. 128) or with Chinese dishes. It can simply be added to a basic jus to make a rich spicy sauce.

MAKES ABOUT 600–900 ml (1–1 1/2
  pints)
150 ml (5 fl oz) malt vinegar
50 g (2 oz) demerara sugar
1 shallot, chopped
450 g (1 lb) red plums, stoned and
  chopped
75 ml (2 1/2 fl oz) Madeira
75 ml (2 1/2 fl oz) port

Juice of 1/2 orange
Juice of 1/2 lemon
Juice of 1/2 lime
1 tablespoon redcurrant jelly
A pinch of five-spice powder
1 muslin bag containing 4 cloves,
  1/2 cinnamon stick, 2 star anise and
  a few coriander seeds

Boil the vinegar and sugar together then add the chopped shallot and plums and cook for 5 minutes. Add the muslin bag and the remaining ingredients and cook slowly for 1 hour. Remove the muslin bag and liquidize the sauce. Push through a sieve to make a purée. The sauce is now ready and can be kept in airtight jars in the fridge almost indefinitely.

Spicing Essence

I think this little trick comes from Escoffier's days; it is often used for spicing up a sauce or other dish. It was also occasionally used to mask the flavours of a meat that wasn't quite right. Well, I'm glad to say that I use it purely for enhancing flavours, and it works its magic particularly with Tomato or Red Pepper Coulis (see p. 375).

MAKES ABOUT 150 ml (5 fl oz)
50 g (2 oz) demerara sugar
150 ml (5 fl oz) malt vinegar

Simply dissolve the sugar in the vinegar then boil for a few minutes until reduced to a syrup. It is now ready to use, and only a few drops are needed to spice your sauces. After that, it can be kept in an airtight jar in the fridge for as long as you like.

Cranberry Sauce with Orange

Cranberries are not always available fresh, but the frozen ones are equally good for this recipe. The shallots and port add extra flavour to this sauce but it can be made just with the fruit, juice and sugar. If you don't include them, add a little more orange juice.

MAKES ABOUT 450 g (1 lb)
1 teaspoon chopped shallots (optional)
1 glass of port, about 50 ml (2 fl oz) (optional)
Juice of 2 oranges
450 g (1 lb) fresh or frozen cranberries
100 g (4 oz) caster sugar

Place the shallots and port, if using, in a pan and boil until reduced by half. Add the orange juice and again boil to reduce by half. Add the cranberries and sugar and simmer for 10–15 minutes, until the cranberries have softened. The sauce is now ready. It can be made up to 2 weeks in advance, kept chilled, then served hot or cold as needed. I use this sauce with the Turkey Saltimbocca (see p. 132).

Lemon Butter Sauce

This is one of the simplest sauces. It has a silky texture and perfectly complements cod and salmon dishes in particular.

SERVES 4–6
225 g (8 oz) unsalted butter
Juice of 1 lemon
50 ml (2 fl oz) Chicken Stock (see p. 399) or Vegetable Stock (see p. 400)
Salt and freshly ground white pepper

Chop the butter into 1 cm ($^1/_2$ in) pieces and put it into a pan with the lemon juice and stock. Bring to a simmer, whisking all the time. Do not allow the sauce to boil or the butter will separate. If it is too thick, add more stock. If you like a sharper taste, add more lemon juice. Season with salt and pepper and serve immediately. To give a creamier texture, simply blitz the sauce with an electric hand blender.

Vegetable Butter Sauce

This is a simple sauce that is easiest to make if you have an electric hand blender.

SERVES 4
150 ml (5 fl oz) reduced Vegetable Stock (see p. 400)

50–75 g (2–3 oz) unsalted butter, at room temperature
Salt and freshly ground white pepper

Pour the vegetable stock into a small pan and add 50 g (2 oz) of the butter. Bring to the simmer, whisking all the time. Season with salt and pepper. Whisk vigorously or use the hand blender and you should have a light creamy consistency. If the sauce seems a little too thin, then simply add the remaining butter and blend once more. The sauce is now ready.

Fennel Butter Sauce

This is a good sauce for fish. The aniseed flavour of fennel is helped by the addition of star anise in the cooking liquor. To increase the flavour for a fish dish, use some Fish Stock (see p. 399) in the reduction for the sauce. However, you'll find that fennel creates a good stock and, when reduced by three-quarters, should be strong enough on its own.

SERVES 4
2 fennel bulbs
900 ml (1$^1/_2$ pints) water
Juice of 1 lemon

1–2 star anise
Salt
50–75 g (2–3 oz) unsalted butter

Trim the root and top stalks from the fennel. Place in boiling water with the lemon juice, star anise and a pinch of salt. Return to the boil, cover the fennel with a butter paper or greaseproof and simmer until tender; this will take about 20–30 minutes. When ready, a sharp knife will just be able to reach the centre of the bulb.

Remove the fennel bulbs, then boil and reduce the cooking liquor down to about 150–300 ml (5–10 fl oz) to give a good, strong taste. Dice the fennel into 5 mm ($^1/_4$ in) pieces. The liquor can now be finished with the butter, just whisking it in to create a fennel butter sauce. Remove the star anise. Blitz the sauce with a hand blender to give a more creamy texture. Add the fennel and warm through. Check and adjust the seasoning.

VARIATIONS

Chopped chives, tarragon or mint could be added to this sauce at the last minute, to give it another flavour.

Parsley and Tarragon Butter

If you're looking for something to excite a grilled or pan-fried fish dish, then try cooking it with this butter, or placing a tablespoonful on top and just melting it under the grill. It's packed with flavour and works a treat. It also eats very well with pasta dishes. The butter will keep for 1–2 weeks in the fridge and almost indefinitely if frozen.

MAKES 350 g (12 oz)

2 tablespoons very finely chopped
   onions

About 3 tablespoons dry white wine

225 g (8 oz) unsalted butter

1 teaspoon Dijon mustard

2 heaped tablespoons chopped fresh
   parsley

1 1/2 heaped tablespoons chopped fresh
   tarragon

Freshly ground black pepper

Juice of 1 lemon

Place the chopped onions in a small pan and just cover with white wine. Boil to reduce until almost dry. Leave to cool. Soften the butter in a bowl, then add the mustard, parsley and tarragon. Season with a twist of pepper and the lemon juice. Mix in the now cold onions and the butter is made.

It's best to shape and roll the butter in cling film, giving you a cylinder shape. This can now be cut into rounds to garnish your fish, pasta or chicken dish.

Hollandaise Sauce

This is a quick way of making a French classic.

MAKES ABOUT 150 ml (5 fl oz)

100 g (4 oz) unsalted butter

1 egg yolk

1/2 tablespoon warm water

Squeeze of lemon juice

Salt and cayenne pepper or freshly
   ground white pepper

Melt the butter in a pan, then leave it to cool slightly so that it is just warm when added to the sauce; if it is too hot, the sauce will curdle. The butter will have separated, so you will only be adding the butter oil to the sauce. This is clarified butter.

Add the egg yolks to the water in a bowl and whisk over a pan of hot water until cooked and thickened. Remove from the heat and add the clarified butter, whisking until the sauce is thick. Add the lemon juice and season with salt and cayenne or white pepper.

Spicy Tomato Sauce

This sauce goes so well with seafood of all types. It's almost like eating a loose, spicy tomato chutney. Once made, it can be kept chilled for up to two weeks.

MAKES ABOUT 450 g (1 lb)
85 ml (3 fl oz) olive oil
3 shallots or 2 onions, finely chopped
2 garlic cloves, crushed
A few fresh basil, thyme and tarragon
   leaves

900 g (2 lb) tomatoes, skinned and
   seeded
2 tablespoons red wine vinegar
1 teaspoon caster sugar
Salt
2–3 drops of Tabasco sauce

Warm the olive oil in a pan and add the chopped shallots or onions, the garlic and herbs. It's best to have the herbs in sprigs as these can then be easily removed at the end of cooking. Allow the shallots and herbs to cook gently for 4–5 minutes until tender.

Cut the tomato flesh into 5 mm (1/4 in) dice and add to the shallots. Have the pan on a very low heat, just on a light simmer, and cook for about 45 minutes. The sauce may cook a little quicker or take a little longer – this will really depend on the water content of the tomatoes. After 45 minutes, add the wine vinegar and sugar and cook for a further 15 minutes. The tomatoes should have taken on an almost lumpy sauce texture; if the sauce is very thick, simply fold in a little more olive oil. Allow to cool until just warm, then season with salt and Tabasco.

Pesto Sauce

Pesto can be bought in supermarkets, but here is a simple version to make yourself.

SERVES 4
50 g (2 oz) pine nuts
150 ml (5 fl oz) olive oil
1 small garlic clove, crushed

1 large bunch of fresh basil (2 bunches
   will give you a richer taste)
Salt and freshly ground black
   pepper

Simply colour the nuts lightly in the olive oil, then allow to cool. Add the crushed garlic, basil and a pinch of salt and pepper and blend to a purée. This is now ready and can be kept for 2–3 days in the fridge.

NOTE

In this recipe I am not using Parmesan, which is normally found in pesto sauce. If you prefer the Parmesan version, simply add 25–50 g (1–2 oz) freshly grated cheese to the ingredients.

Worcestershire Sauce

I enjoy finding, trying and hopefully developing recipes like this. I looked through a lot of old cookery books to find this so that I could have a go at matching the famous bottle we all know and use. Well, it's not quite the same, and you can't really match that distinctive taste, but it's fun and interesting to make, especially when you have to wait a few weeks for the result.

The Worcestershire sauce recipe must be 160 years old. The recipe was found and given to the makers in India. They soon discovered how popular the sauce was and I don't think they ever looked back.

MAKES 900 ml (1½ pints)
600 ml (1 pint) malt vinegar
150 ml (5 fl oz) walnut or mushroom
    ketchup
2 tablespoons anchovy essence
2 shallots or 1 onion, finely chopped
3 tablespoons soy sauce

A pinch of cayenne
A pinch of ground cinnamon
1 garlic clove, crushed
A pinch of freshly grated nutmeg
A pinch of ground cardamom
A pinch of salt

There are a few ways of putting this recipe together.

The first is simply to mix all the ingredients and keep in an airtight bottle or container for 2–3 weeks, making sure the bottle is shaken every day.

Another way is to mix all the liquid ingredients with the onion and garlic, bring to the boil and simmer for 30 minutes before adding the spices and salt. Bottle and cool, make airtight and keep for two weeks, shaking every day.

The mix can also be made without the herbs, just mixing the liquids and onion. This will still need to be left and shaken every day for 2–3 weeks.

After the marinating period, strain the sauce before use.

Tomato Coulis

This is a very useful basic for all sorts of recipes.

MAKES ABOUT 900 ml (1½ pints)
1 large onion, chopped
2 celery sticks, chopped
1 large carrot, chopped
1 garlic clove, crushed
A few fresh basil or tarragon leaves or
    a pinch of dried tarragon
1 sprig of fresh thyme or a pinch of
    dried thyme
2 tablespoons olive oil

50 g (2 oz) unsalted butter
150 ml (5 fl oz) dry white wine
450 g (1 lb) tomatoes, chopped
300 ml (10 fl oz) Chicken Stock
    (see p. 399) or Vegetable Stock
    (see p. 400)
1 tablespoon tomato purée
Salt and freshly ground white pepper
A few drops of Spicing Essence
    (see p. 371) (optional)

Cook the chopped onion, celery and carrot with the garlic and herbs in the olive oil and butter for a few minutes until softened. Add the white wine and boil to reduce until almost dry. Add the tomatoes and cook for a few minutes, then add the stock and tomato purée, bring to the simmer, cover with a lid and continue to cook for 20 minutes. Liquidize the sauce, then push it through a sieve to give a smooth sauce consistency. If the sauce is a little thick, add more stock to reach the right consistency. Season to taste with salt and pepper. The coulis is now ready. To make the sauce more spicy, add a few drops of spicing essence at a time, if using, whisking and tasting until you have the flavour you want.

RED PEPPER COULIS

You can also use this recipe to make a red pepper coulis. Just replace 350 g (12 oz) of the tomatoes with an equal weight of seeded red peppers, then follow the same procedure.

Piccalilli Sauce

By the way, here's a great way of making piccalilli into a sauce.

The ingredients have been halved from the quantities needed to make Piccalilli (see p. 387) and this will still give you at least 1.2 litres (2 pints) of sauce.

It keeps very well in the fridge for up to a month and eats well as a salad dressing or mixed with mayonnaise as an alternative prawn or crab cocktail sauce. I also use it as a straight piccalilli sauce to go with smoked fish such as trout, mackerel or eel; and salad; or hot fish or shellfish kebabs.

MAKES **1.2 litres (2 pints)**
1 small or $^1/_2$ large cauliflower, cut into
   1 cm ($^1/_2$ in) pieces
1 large onion, cut into 1 cm ($^1/_2$ in) dice
50 g (2 oz) salt
300 ml (10 fl oz) white wine vinegar
150 ml (5 fl oz) malt vinegar

A pinch of chopped dried chilli
175 g (6 oz) caster sugar
25 g (1 oz) English mustard powder
15 g ($^1/_2$ oz) ground turmeric
2 tablespoons cornflour
$^1/_2$ cucumber, peeled, seeded and cut
   into rough 1 cm ($^1/_2$ in) dice

Mix the cauliflower with the onion and sprinkle with the salt, then leave in a sieve or colander to stand for 24 hours.

Boil the two vinegars together with the chilli, then leave to cool and stand for 20 minutes before draining and discarding the chillies. Mix the sugar with the remaining dry ingredients. Pour a quarter of the vinegars on to the dry ingredients and mix. Re-boil the remaining vinegar and pour and whisk on to the sugar mix. Bring back to a simmer and cook for 3 minutes.

Mix the salted cauliflower and onions with the cucumber and pour the hot sauce over the vegetables. Leave to cool. Once cool, blitz in a food processor or liquidizer until fine, then push through a sieve to leave you with a smooth, rich piccalilli sauce. Store in airtight jars.

NOTE
If you don't want the sauce, then just leave it as a pickle.

Home-made Tomato Ketchup

Tomato ketchup is a sauce we've all grown up with and will, I'm sure, continue to be popular for many years to come. For me there's one 'real' tomato ketchup and that's Heinz. However, you know me by now, I love to have a go at recipes, so this is a home-made version. If you use demerara rather than caster sugar, it will give a stronger taste. In the ingredients, a choice of three vinegars is listed. The first choice is, of course, cider, followed by white wine or the malt. One thing I'm definitely not trying to do is go into any sort of competition with that famous company but we should all try – at least once.

MAKES 600 ml (1 pint)
1 clove
1 bay leaf
1/2 teaspoon ground coriander
1/2 teaspoon ground cinnamon or 5mm (1/4 in) cinnamon stick
250 ml (8 fl oz) cider, white wine or malt vinegar
8 tablespoons demerara or caster sugar

1.5 kg (3 lb) net weight of ripe tomatoes after quartering and seeding
1/2 teaspoon sea salt
1/2 tablespoon English mustard powder
1 garlic clove, crushed
A dash of Tabasco sauce
1 tablespoon tomato purée

Tie the clove, bay leaf, coriander and cinnamon stick, if using, in a piece of muslin. Place the vinegar and sugar in a heavy-based pan and bring to a simmer. Add the tomatoes and all other ingredients and bring to the boil, stirring to prevent any sticking. Once up to the boil, reduce the temperature and simmer, stirring occasionally, for 40 minutes. Be careful the mix doesn't stick to the base of the pan. Discard the muslin bag, blitz in a food processor or liquidizer and then push the sauce through a sieve.

If you find the sauce to be loose and thin once cold, then simply re-boil and thicken with a little cornflour or arrowroot mixed to a paste with a little water, being careful not to make it too starchy. This will prevent the tomato water separating from the sauce.

Home-made Mint Sauce/Reduction

This is probably the easiest recipe in the book. The quantity here will probably last for at least three meals to go with lamb. Of course, whenever vinegar is being used it preserves, so just keep this in a jar chilled and it will last indefinitely. Apart from just using this as a straight mint sauce I use it as an enhancer for gravies and other sauces. If you are making a lamb stew, just a teaspoon of this will lift all the flavours. Or, as in the gravy for the loin of lamb (see p. 154), I've used 5 teaspoons to create a mint gravy flavour. So the next time you have roast lamb for lunch why not just make a rich mint gravy to go with it.

MAKES 120 ml (4 fl oz)
150 ml (5 fl oz) malt vinegar
1/2 bunch of fresh mint

1 1/2–2 heaped tablespoons demerara
  sugar

The mint for the sauce needn't be picked or chopped, just left as it is.

Pour the vinegar on to the mint in a small pan. Add the demerara sugar. Using 2 tablespoons will make the sauce sweeter, which some tastebuds prefer. Simply bring to the boil and cook for a few minutes until the sugar has dissolved. Leave to cool. Once cool, it's best to leave all the mint leaves in and simply bottle or jar. This will then increase the mint flavour. In time the mint will completely discolour; this is only due to the acidity of the vinegar.

To make into mint sauce, strain some of the vinegar through a tea strainer and add chopped fresh mint.

Rouille

MAKES ABOUT 300 ml
  (10 fl oz)
1 red pepper, seeded and chopped
1 small dried or fresh chilli pepper,
  seeded and chopped

2 garlic cloves, crushed
50 g (2 oz) fresh white breadcrumbs
1 egg yolk
Salt
150 ml (5 fl oz) extra virgin olive oil

Place the pepper and chilli in a food processor or liquidizer with the garlic, breadcrumbs, yolk and salt and blitz until smooth. With the motor still running, slowly add the olive oil as if making mayonnaise. When all the oil has been added, push the sauce through a sieve. It can be kept in the fridge for a couple of days without spoiling.

Basic Vinaigrette

This basic recipe is very convenient. Once made, it can sit in your fridge and be used at any time and for any dish you might fancy. The vinegar just gives a very slight sweetness to the taste.

MAKES 600 ml (1 pint)
300 ml (10 fl oz) extra-virgin olive oil
(French or Italian)
300 ml (10 fl oz) groundnut oil
25 ml (1 fl oz) balsamic vinegar
1 bunch of fresh basil
1/2 bunch of fresh tarragon

3–4 sprigs of fresh thyme
12 black peppercorns, lightly crushed
3 shallots, finely chopped
2 garlic cloves, crushed
1 bay leaf
1 teaspoon coarse sea salt

Warm the olive and groundnut oils together. Place all the remaining ingredients into a 750 ml (1 1/4 pint) bottle. Pour the oil into the bottle and close with a cork or screw top. For the best results, leave to marinate for a week, which will allow the flavours to enhance the oils. To help the dressing along, shake the bottle once a day. Taste for seasoning before use.

Red Wine Vinaigrette

This is a very basic recipe. Many herbs can be added to the bottle to help infuse more flavours. The best to use, unchopped, are basil, tarragon and thyme. When the dressing is to be used, just add some chopped fresh chives, basil, thyme or tarragon to finish the dressing.

MAKES ABOUT 600 ml (1 pint)
4 shallots or 1 large onion, finely chopped
2 garlic cloves, crushed
300 ml (10 fl oz) red wine

300 ml (10 fl oz) red wine vinegar
2 teaspoons Dijon mustard
600 ml (1 pint) olive oil
Salt and freshly ground black pepper

Mix the chopped shallots or onion with the garlic in a pan and add the red wine. Bring to the boil then reduce until almost dry. Add the red wine vinegar and boil to reduce by three-quarters. Remove the pan from the heat.

While the shallots are still warm, add the Dijon mustard and blend in with the olive oil. Season with salt and pepper. The dressing can now be left to cool and then bottled. Chilled, it keeps for two to four weeks.

Mayonnaise

This is another classic recipe, but so much nicer than bought mayonnaise. Use it with potatoes in a salad, or in all kinds of sandwiches.

MAKES ABOUT 600 ml (1 pint)
3 egg yolks
1 tablespoon malt, white wine or
  balsamic vinegar
A pinch of English or Dijon mustard

Salt and freshly ground white pepper
300 ml (10 fl oz) basic olive oil
1 teaspoon hot water
A few drops of lemon juice
  (optional)

Whisk the egg yolks, vinegar, mustard and seasonings together, then slowly add the olive oil, whisking continuously. When all the oil is added, finish with the water and correct the seasoning. A few drops of lemon juice can be added to enhance the taste.

Vierge Dressing

This dressing has a very different taste to the basic dressing, and lends itself best to fish dishes. I was first inspired to make it whilst staying at La Côte St Jacques in Joigny, France, in the mid 1980s. The restaurant now has three Michelin stars. The dressing was served with a red mullet dish, so now I've got one of my own which is very simple to make (see p. 107).

MAKES 600 ml (1 pint)
600 ml (1 pint) extra virgin olive oil
  (French or Italian)
15 g (^{1}/2 oz) coriander seeds, crushed
1 bunch of fresh tarragon

12 black peppercorns, crushed
4 shallots, chopped
2 garlic cloves, crushed
A pinch of sea salt

Warm the olive oil with the coriander seeds. Place the remaining ingredients into a 600 ml (1 pint) jar and pour the oil and coriander on top. Leave to marinate for 1 week, shaking the bottle daily.

Tomato Dressing or Sauce

Here's another recipe I picked up in New York. It's really tasty to eat and has so many uses. Fish or meat work well with it, so anything from grilled sea bass, pan-fried or deep-fried cod to sausages, pork chops, chicken, liver, or steaks, the dressing goes with all. This is a last-minute sauce that will not keep well if made too for in advance. If you haven't got the capers, then just leave them out, and if you don't have sherry vinegar just replace with half malt vinegar.

MAKES ABOUT 150 ml (5 fl oz)
2 tablespoons unsalted butter
1 tablespoon tomato ketchup
3 tablespoons sherry vinegar

1 tablespoon diced apple
1 tablespoon diced tomato, flesh only
1 tablespoon chopped capers
Freshly ground black pepper

Melt the butter to a golden nut-brown stage. Add all the other ingredients and bring to the boil. Add a twist of black pepper and serve.

VARIATIONS

Chopped fresh herbs can be added to the sauce: parsley, tarragon and basil will all work together or on their own.

Spicy Tomato Dressing

This is a really quick and easy dressing to make. I use this recipe for salad dressings and also sometimes to add to the Sweet Pepper and Chilli Relish (see p. 388). It's also a great dressing to mix with warm pasta as a vegetarian dish or to serve with grilled fish or meat. You will get the best flavour if you use half extra virgin olive oil and the other half a cheaper oil.

MAKES 500 ml (14 fl oz)
9 tablespoons tomato ketchup
120 ml (4 fl oz) white wine vinegar
3 tablespoons Worcestershire sauce

A few drops of Tabasco sauce
150 ml (5 fl oz) extra virgin olive oil
150 ml (5 fl oz) olive oil
Salt and freshly ground black pepper

Mix together the tomato ketchup, white wine vinegar, Worcestershire sauce and Tabasco sauce. Now gradually whisk in the olive oil, by hand or in a processor or liquidizer, until completely mixed. Taste and season with salt and pepper.

VARIATIONS

Extra garnishes can also be added to give a chunkier texture to the dressing. Finely chopped shallots, diced tomato flesh and chopped fresh basil or tarragon all work very well.

Watercress and Herb Dressing

This is really a variation of pesto sauce, made by the same method but with a different finished taste. It is used in the recipe for Grilled Sea Trout with Soured New Potatoes and Watercress Dressing (see p. 91).

MAKES ABOUT 600 ml (1 pint)
50 g (2 oz) pine nuts
150 ml (5 fl oz) olive oil (more can be
    added for a looser consistency)
1 large garlic clove, crushed
2 large bunches of watercress, about
    175 g (6 oz)

1 bunch of fresh chervil
1 bunch of fresh tarragon
1/2 bunch of fresh flatleaf parsley
1 bunch of fresh coriander
1 bunch of fresh basil
Salt and freshly ground black
    pepper

Heat the pine nuts in the olive oil until lightly coloured. Leave to cool. It's very important to keep an eye and always stir the pine nuts while they are cooking as they over-colour and burn easily. Once cold, blitz in a food processor or liquidizer with the garlic, watercress and all the herbs until fine. Season with salt and pepper. This recipe is a cross between a dressing and a paste, so the mix must be quite thick.

Mustard Dressing

This is a basic recipe for a simple dressing that I have used in many recipes. It's so versatile and has a creamy texture. If you have a favourite mustard – such as English, French or grain – then simply use the one of your choice.

MAKES 300 ml (10 fl oz)
4 teaspoons Dijon mustard
2 tablespoons white wine vinegar

8 tablespoons walnut oil
8 tablespoons groundnut oil
Salt and freshly ground black pepper

Whisk the mustard with the vinegar. Mix together the two oils and gradually add to the mustard, whisking all the time as you would if making mayonnaise. Once everything is thoroughly mixed, taste for seasoning with salt and pepper.

VARIATIONS
This can also be made into a herb dressing by adding a choice of chopped mixed fresh herbs, or perhaps just chopped fresh tarragon to give you a mustard and tarragon dressing that will go so well with fish or poultry.

The addition of 1–2 egg yolks mixed with the mustard and white wine vinegar will guarantee a creamy texture, almost like mayonnaise.

Hazelnut Dressing

This is a good dressing for basic salads or vegetarian dishes. It's full of flavour with the hazelnut taste sparked with the addition of shallots, leeks and, of course, the sherry vinegar. The strength of the vinegar you use will determine the quantity needed – use 2 tablespoons and add a little more if the flavour demands. The dressing goes well with the Mushroom Pancake Gâteau (see p. 199) as an alternative to the sauce given in the recipe.

MAKES 250 ml (8 fl oz)
4 tablespoons hazelnut oil
4 tablespoons groundnut oil
2–3 tablespoons sherry vinegar

3 teaspoons water
2 shallots, finely chopped
1 leek, finely chopped
Salt and freshly ground black pepper

Mix the oils and vinegar together and blitz in a food processor or liquidizer. Add the water and continue to blitz. Mix together the shallots and leek and add to the vinaigrette. Season with salt and pepper. The dressing is now ready to use.

NOTE

The leeks can be blanched very quickly in boiling water to give a richer taste and colour.

Poivre Vert Dressing

This recipe is an extra I wanted to include because it can have so many uses with many recipes, even though I haven't featured it specially anywhere in the book. It goes particularly well with the Peppered Roast Beef (see p. 142) along with a good mixed salad. Or just use it as a dressing for a mixed salad.

MAKES ABOUT 200 ml (7 fl oz)
4 large shallots or 1 onion, finely
    chopped
1 tablespoon green peppercorns,
    lightly crushed

4 tablespoons brandy
6–8 tablespoons Basic Vinaigrette
    (see p. 379) or Mustard Dressing
    (see p. 382)
Salt

Mix the shallots with the peppercorns in a small pan and add the brandy. Bring to the boil, then boil to reduce until almost dry. Add the basic vinaigrette or mustard dressing and season with salt if it's needed. This mix can now be used as a warm or cold dressing.

VARIATIONS

When you have some roast beef, pork or lamb left over from Sunday lunch and you're having it sliced for supper, then try this dressing with it. It lifts a basic dish and makes it very special.

Red Wine Dressing

This recipe is very similar to the Mustard Dressing (see p. 382). The difference is, of course, the vinegar. In this dressing, the wine vinegar is the predominant taste. It's best to use a good quality, thick, red wine vinegar, possibly aged. If you manage to find a Cabernet Sauvignon vinegar it really will be the best. Failing that, simply use a standard red wine vinegar; the dressing will still work but not have quite the strength. It may be a good idea to take a quantity of the vinegar and boil it to reduce it by half in order to strengthen the taste. Anyway, just like the Mustard Dressing, this can be used for many dishes and salads.

MAKES 175 ml (6 fl oz)

3 teaspoons Dijon mustard
3 tablespoons red wine vinegar
  (preferably Cabernet Sauvignon)

6 tablespoons walnut oil
6 tablespoons groundnut oil
Salt and freshly ground black
  pepper

Whisk together the mustard and red wine vinegar. Mix the two oils together and gradually whisk into the mustard and vinegar a drop at a time, as you do when making mayonnaise. Once the ingredients are well blended, season with salt and pepper. The dressing is now ready.

Brandade Dressing

This may look fairly complex, but in fact is very simple to make. This recipe will make a reasonable amount and will keep very well in the fridge. It's also absolutely delicious to eat with the Cod Brandade (see p. 73) or other salads.

MAKES ABOUT 600 ml (1 pint)

1 onion, finely chopped
1/2 teaspoon chopped fresh thyme
1/2 teaspoon chopped fresh rosemary
1/2 teaspoon chopped fresh basil
1/2 teaspoon chopped fresh parsley
1 garlic clove, crushed
50 g (2 oz) unsalted butter
500 ml (17 fl oz) olive oil
300 ml (10 fl oz) red wine
50 g (2 oz) shelled walnuts, chopped

50 g (2 oz) black olives, stoned and
  chopped
25 g (1 oz) anchovy fillets, drained and
  chopped
25 g (1 oz) capers, drained and
  chopped
1 fennel bulb, cooked (see p. 372), and
  cut into 6 mm (1/4 in) dice
8 tomatoes, skinned, seeded and diced
Salt and freshly ground white pepper

In a large pan, sweat the chopped onion, herbs and garlic in the butter and 3 table-spoons of olive oil for a few minutes. Add the red wine and boil to reduce until almost dry. Add the remaining olive oil and all the remaining ingredients except the tomatoes, bring to the simmer and simmer for a few minutes. Add the diced tomatoes, season with the salt and pepper and remove from the heat. The sauce is now ready.

Soured Cream, Lime and Mint Yoghurt

This recipe is an extra flavour that suits many different dishes. In this book it's used in Steamed Halibut on Spinach (see p. 99) and also the Grilled Calves' Liver Steak with Spiced Potatoes (see p. 176). It also works very well in a cucumber salad accompanying a curry or mixed into mashed or forked potatoes to go with grilled fish or perhaps roast lamb against its mint flavour. Of course, one of the beauties is just how easy it is to make.

MAKES 350 ml (12 fl oz)
150 ml (5 fl oz) soured cream
150 ml (5 fl oz) natural yoghurt

Juice of 1 lime
1 heaped teaspoon chopped fresh mint
Salt and freshly ground black pepper

Whisk all the ingredients together and season with salt and pepper. The flavour of mint will increase the longer it is kept. I told you it's easy.

Salsa Dressing

Salsa is a Mexican relish that has so many variations. It's really a fresh sweet and sour chutney, come sauce, come dressing. Another ingredient is chillies, so not only is it sweet and sour but hot, too. This recipe goes well with hot or cold fish, meats, chicken or you can even use it as a relish for a hamburger. The most classic version is Salsa Verde, a green chutney with garlic, parsley, mint, mustard, capers, green chillies, oil and vinegar. There are also red salsas and fruit salsas and more, but this we'll just call 'Salsa Dressing'.

SERVES 4
2 red onions, finely chopped
2 green peppers, seeded and diced
2 green chillies, seeded and finely
    diced

1 garlic clove, finely chopped
1 tablespoon olive oil
Juice of 1–2 limes
8 plum or salad tomatoes, skinned,
    seeded and diced
Salt

Mix together the diced red onions, green peppers, chillies and garlic. Add the olive oil and the juice of 1 lime. Add the tomato flesh and stir in well to slightly break down the tomato flesh. Adjust the seasoning with a good pinch of salt.

The salsa should have a good balance of flavours. More lime juice maybe needed to lift the other tastes. The salsa is now ready and can be kept in the fridge for a few days.

Grape Chutney

This chutney improves with time and is delicious to serve with the Chicken Liver Parfait (see p. 79).

MAKES ABOUT 1.5 kg (3 lb)
10 Granny Smith or Golden Delicious apples, peeled, cored and chopped
2 onions, finely chopped
300 ml (10 fl oz) good balsamic vinegar
300 ml (10 fl oz) drinkable brandy
2.25 kg (5 lb) seedless white grapes, picked and washed

350 g (12 oz) demerara sugar
A pinch of salt
2 teaspoons ground mixed spice
2 teaspoons ground cinnamon
1 teaspoon ground ginger

Simmer the apples, onions, balsamic vinegar and brandy together in a preserving pan for 30 minutes. Stir in the grapes, sugar, salt and spices and continue to simmer for 1 1/2–2 hours over a low heat until the mixture is thick and pulpy, stirring occasionally. Should the chutney still seem a little too liquid, boil on a high heat to allow the excess liquid to evaporate.

Let the chutney cool slightly then spoon into warm, sterilized (see p. 364) jars. Seal then label and store in a cool, dark place until needed.

Green Tomato Chutney

MAKES ABOUT 1.5 kg (3 lb)
2.25 kg (5 lb) green tomatoes, cut into 8
600 ml (1 pint) malt vinegar
5 large onions, finely chopped
225 g (8 oz) raisins

450 g (1 lb) sultanas
350 g (12 oz) demerara sugar
25 g (1 oz) salt
4 teaspoons mixed spice
4 teaspoons ground cinnamon
2 teaspoons ground ginger

Place the tomatoes in a preserving pan, add the vinegar and simmer over a low heat for 30 minutes. Add the onions, raisins and sultanas and continue to cook for a further 30 minutes. Add the sugar, salt and spices and simmer gently for 1 1/2–2 hours until thick, stirring occasionally. Leave to cool slightly, then spoon into warm, sterilized (see p. 364) jars.

Piccalilli

This has to be one of the easiest pickle recipes that I make. There are so many variations that you can try – different vegetables, mustards and vinegars. This pickle eats particularly well with oily fish such as mackerel and herrings; its acidity works against the oils and leaves a good, clean taste.

MAKES ABOUT 1.25 kg (3 lb)
1 cauliflower
3 large onions
8 large shallots, or 16 pickling onions
    if unavailable
Salt and freshly ground white pepper
1 cucumber

600 ml (1 pint) white wine vinegar
300 ml (10 fl oz) malt vinegar
1/4 teaspoon chopped dried chilli
350 g (12 oz) caster sugar
50 g (2 oz) English mustard powder
25 g (1 oz) ground turmeric
3 tablespoons cornflour

Cut the cauliflower into small florets. Peel and cut the onions and shallots into 1 cm (1/2 in) dice. Place in a bowl, sprinkle with 25 g (1 oz) of salt and leave to stand for 24 hours. Afterwards rinse in cold water and dry.

Peel and de-seed the cucumber and cut it into 1 cm (1/2 in) dice. Sprinkle with a little salt and leave to stand for 10–15 minutes. Rinse in cold water, then dry and add to the onions and cauliflower.

Boil the two vinegars together with the chilli and then leave to cool for 30 minutes. Strain through a sieve and discard the chilli.

Mix together the sugar and remaining dry ingredients in a bowl. When the vinegar is cool, mix a little of it with the dry ingredients. Bring the bulk of the vinegar back to the boil, pour into the sugar mixture, and whisk until it is all blended together. Bring this mixture back to the boil and cook for 3 minutes, then simply pour over the vegetables and mix well. Leave to cool. The piccalilli is now ready and can be put into sterilized (see p. 364) jars and refrigerated, or served at once. It will keep refrigerated for at least a month.

Plum Chutney

This chutney eats very well with hot or cold meats, especially roast duck with vegetables, as well as pâtés and terrines.

MAKES 2 × 600 ml (1 pint) kilner jars
900 g (2 lb) plums, stoned and
    quartered
900 g (2 lb) cooking apples, peeled,
    cored and roughly chopped
2 onions, sliced
2 garlic cloves, crushed

600 ml (1 pint) malt vinegar
175 g (6 oz) golden syrup
175 g (6 oz) demerara sugar
2 teaspoons salt
2 tablespoons pickling spices in a
    muslin bag

Simmer the plums, apples, onions and garlic in the malt vinegar for 20 minutes. Add the syrup, sugar, salt and the muslin bag of spices and continue to simmer for 1 1/2 hours, stirring occasionally. The mixture should be quite thick.

Should the chutney seem to be a little liquid, then taste the liquor and check for seasoning. It may taste perfectly seasoned. If this is the case then it cannot be reduced any further as it will become too strong. If there is still room for reduction, then increase the heat and cook for another 30 minutes or so until thicker. If the flavour is too strong to reduce further, simply pour off some of the excess liquor. This can then be mixed with a *jus* or gravy to make a rich plum sauce. Once cooked, store in the sterilized (see p. 364) jars and keep refrigerated.

Apple and Mustard Seed Relish

This recipe came from chatting with two of my chefs, Stuart and Wayne. We were looking for a relish that would eat well hot or cold with the Pork and Black Pudding Patties (see p. 167). Basically, we had left a patty to go cold and then tasted and realized it eats like a coarse pork pâté or terrine. Hence we needed a relish to go with it. Apples must be the most classic accompaniment to pork and mustard also works very well. The relish was born. And if you try the relish with the Pork and Black Pudding Patties and the Irish Potato Cakes (see p. 237), you'll have the perfect combination for a main course. This is one of the beauties of cooking, finding recipes almost by accident. We've since found that the relish eats well warm with the hot patties as well. So we have a double bonus. The relish keeps very well refrigerated for up to one month.

MAKES ABOUT 1 kg (2 lb)

8 dessert apples, peeled, cored and
   cut into 5 mm ($^1/_4$ in) dice
175 g (6 oz) caster sugar
200 ml (7 fl oz) white wine vinegar
3 tablespoons white mustard seeds,
   plunged in boiling water and soaked
   for 2 hours

Finely grated zest of $^1/_2$ lemon
2 onions, finely chopped
Salt and freshly ground black
   pepper

Place the sugar, vinegar, drained mustard seeds and lemon zest in a pan and bring to the boil, then boil until reduced by half. Add the chopped onions and simmer for 3–4 minutes until softened. Add the diced apple and cook for 4–5 minutes until soft but just holding its shape. Drain off the liquid, leaving the apples and onions to one side, then continue to boil and reduce by half again. Once reduced, remove from the heat and return the apple mix to the syrup. Season with salt and pepper and leave to cool. The relish is now ready to use or can be served warm.

Sweet Pepper and Chilli Relish

This dish is a variation of Piccalilli (see p. 386). It has most of the basic flavours but a few changes to give it quite a different taste.

I like to serve this relish with pork or chicken – its sort of sweet-and-sour flavour works well with either. One of the best pork dishes to serve it with is a Confit of Pork Belly (see p. 169). To go with this relish, I cook the belly in small starter portions and just serve the relish warm, with the confit sitting on top. The pork is so tender it can be carved with a spoon and eaten with the lovely flavour of sweet peppers.

**MAKES ABOUT 3 x 600 ml (1 pint)
kilner jars**
300 ml (10 fl oz) white wine vinegar
150 ml (5 fl oz) malt vinegar
A pinch of chopped dried chilli
4 red peppers
2 yellow peppers

2 fresh red chillies
2 large onions
225 g (8 oz) caster sugar
15 g (^{1}/2 oz) ground turmeric
25 g (1 oz) English mustard powder
2 tablespoons cornflour
2 tablespoons chilli oil

Boil the two vinegars with the chopped dried chilli. Leave to cool for 30 minutes. Strain through a sieve, discarding the chilli.

Cut the peppers in half lengthways and remove the core and seeds. Cut the pepper halves into 1 cm (^{1}/2 in) strips. The red chillies must also be halved and have all core and seeds removed. Now chop the chillies very finely. Once the chillies have been chopped, always remember to wash the chopping board and your hands well. This is because the strong chilli flavour will linger, and the oil will irritate your lips or eyes if you have any on your hands.

The onions should be halved and cut into 1 cm (^{1}/2 in) thick slices. Make sure the onions are broken down from thick pieces into individual strips. Mix the sugar with the dry ingredients and moisten with a little of the cold boiled vinegars. Boil the remaining vinegar and whisk on to the mix. Now return to the heat and bring to the boil and cook for 3 minutes. While this is cooking, warm the chilli oil in a frying-pan. Fry the peppers and onions very quickly in the hot pan, allowing them to colour around the edges. They must not be allowed to stew as this will make them soft. Add the chopped red chillies to the onions at the last moment.

Next, simply pour the hot thick sauce over the peppers, onions and chillies in a bowl and leave to cool. The relish is now ready and should be ladled into sterilized (see p. 364) jars and kept chilled for up to 1 month. This eats very well cold or served warm.

VARIATIONS

A basic salad dressing or olive oil can be added to loosen the sauce into a dressing. It also eats very well when mixed with Spicy Tomato Dressing (see p. 381) or for a quicker alternative just add 2–3 tablespoons of tomato ketchup to the recipe for a sweeter, richer taste.

Cucumber Pickle

This pickle goes very well with salads. It can be served with pork pies, corned beef or just cold meats. But I like to serve it with fish, in particular salmon. We've all heard of smoked salmon and cucumber sandwiches, a classic combination. This pickle eats very well with simple poached salmon, but I particularly like it with Seared Peppered Salmon (p. 62).

SERVES 4

4 cucumbers, peeled and seeded

1½ teaspoons salt

150 ml (5 fl oz) groundnut oil

1 teaspoon chilli oil

1 large garlic clove, crushed

1 fresh red chilli, finely chopped

2 tablespoons soy sauce

25 g (1 oz) caster sugar

2 tablespoons white wine vinegar

½ bunch of spring onions, thinly sliced

Grate the cucumbers on a basic cheese grater. Mix the salt with the cucumber, place in a colander and allow to drain for 20 minutes. This will take out any excess water.

Warm the groundnut and chilli oils with the crushed garlic and finely chopped red chilli for a few minutes. Add the soy sauce, sugar and white wine vinegar and bring to the simmer. Lightly dry off the cucumber. Mix the spring onions with the cucumber, then add the mixture to the simmering oil and increase the heat, stirring for 30 seconds. Remove from the heat and tip the pickle on to a deep tray or into a large cold saucepan to cool as quickly as possible. Place in an airtight sterilized (see p. 364) jar.

Basic
Recipes

Vanilla Sponge (Genoise)

This sponge can be used for many things: cakes, gâteaux, trifles or puddings. If you keep a couple of vanilla pods in an airtight jar with your caster sugar, you will have vanilla sugar ready whenever you need it.

MAKES 1 x 20 cm (8 in) sponge
1 vanilla pod, split lengthways and
   scraped
6 eggs

175 g (6 oz) caster sugar, flavoured
   with a vanilla pod
175 g (6 oz) plain flour, sifted
50 g (2 oz) unsalted butter, melted

Pre-heat the oven to 200°C/400°F/gas 6. Grease a 20 cm (8 in) round cake tin and dust with flour.

Add the vanilla seeds to the eggs and sugar in a bowl and whisk together over a pan of hot water. Continue to whisk until the mixture has doubled in volume and is light and creamy. Remove from the heat and continue to whisk until cold and thick. This is called the ribbon stage as the mixture will trail off the whisk in ribbons when you lift it out of the mixture. Lightly fold in the flour and melted butter. Gently pour the mix into the prepared tin and bake in the pre-heated oven for about 30 minutes. The easiest way to test is with a skewer, which will come out clean when the sponge is ready.

Allow to cool for 10 minutes in the tin, then turn out on to a wire rack.

VARIATION

To make a chocolate sponge, replace 25 g (1 oz) of the flour with 2 tablespoons of cocoa.

Sponge Base without Flour

Here's another recipe for a sponge base, this time without any flour. Instead it's got chocolate.

MAKES 1 × 28 × 20 cm (1 × 8 in)
   Swiss roll or 1 × 20 cm (8 in) cake
100 g (4 oz) good-quality plain
   chocolate
2 tablespoons coffee granules, mixed
   with 1 tablespoon water

3 eggs, separated
75 g (3 oz) caster sugar
A pinch of salt

Melt the chocolate with the coffee and then leave to cool. Beat the egg yolks, then add the sugar and beat until the mixture is pale and trails off the whisk in ribbons. Stir in the chocolate mix. Beat the egg whites and salt until they hold stiff peaks. Carefully fold the beaten whites into the rest of the mix and spread on the Swiss roll mould or cake tin. This can now be cooked in the pre-heated oven for 15–20 minutes.

NOTE
This sponge can be used as the base for the Chocolate Truffle Cake (see p. 283) or with the White and Dark Chocolate Cream/Mousse (see p. 281).

Quick Puff Pastry

We might think that puff pastry is a French invention, but the British were making rich butter pastes – flour mixed with butter, sugar, rose-water and spices, then interleaved with more butter – in the sixteenth century. It was given the name puff pastry in 1605, and was used mainly in the making of sweet tarts and the precursors of vol-au-vents.

Making puff pastry in the traditional way cannot really be beaten. This recipe, however, is a lot quicker and does bring you very close to it. The resultant pastry can be used in any recipe needing puff pastry. Any not used will freeze very well. It's very satisfying to make your own pastry, but you can resort to the chill cabinet of your supermarket if you are short of time.

MAKES 750 g (1¾ lb)
300 g (11 oz) butter, chilled
450 g (1 lb) plain flour

1 teaspoon salt
200–250 ml (7–8 fl oz) cold water

Cut the chilled butter into small cubes. Sieve the flour with the salt. Add the butter, gently working into the flour but not totally breaking down. Add the water, mixing to a pliable dough, still with pieces of butter showing.

Turn onto a floured surface and roll as for classic puff pastry, into a rectangle (approximately 45 × 15 cm/18 × 6 in). Fold in the right-hand one-third and then fold in the left-hand side on top. Leave to rest for 20 minutes. The pastry now needs to be rolled three times in the same fashion, resting it for 20 minutes between each turn.

The quick puff/flaky pastry is now ready to use.

To make pastry cases, butter and flour your chosen moulds. This quantity is more than enough to line a 25 cm (10in) ring or six 10 cm (4in) rings. Roll out the pastry thinly and line the moulds, leaving any excess turned over the sides of the rings. Sit the cases on a baking sheet and rest in the fridge for 10–15 minutes. Line with greaseproof paper and baking beans or rice. Bake in an oven at 200°C/ 400°F/gas 6 for 15–20 minutes, until the pastry is golden. Remove the paper and beans, then use a sharp knife to trim off any excess pastry around the tart cases, leaving the cases in the pastry rings.

VARIATION
A richer version of this pastry can be made with a higher butter content and with the addition of the juice from 1 lemon. Just follow the above recipe, only adding 175–225 ml (6–7½ fl oz) of water with the juice.

Shortcrust Pastry and Sweet Shortcrust Pastry

The first pastries in England were probably hot-water crust, but a variety was used over the years. Both of the pastries here share a basic method: the difference is the sugar. Use the unsweetened, obviously, in savoury tarts and flans; the sweetened in open fruit tarts and other sweet pastries. The latter pastry contains sugar, but is also differs in that I've added an extra egg yolk for a richer finish. You could use water instead, but I'm giving you the recipe with the maximum flavour. Either caster or icing sugar can be used, but I have found that icing sugar gives a richer, smoother consistency. The choice is yours.

SHORTCRUST PASTRY
MAKES 400 g (14 oz)
225 g (8 oz) plain flour
Pinch of salt
150 g (5 oz) cold butter, chopped

1 whole egg
25 ml (1 fl oz) water
4 tablespoons cold water

For the basic shortcrust pastry, sift the flour with the salt. Rub the flour and butter together to a crumble texture. Add the egg and water together and mix briefly to a smooth dough. Wrap in cling film and refrigerate for 30–60 minutes before rolling and using.

SWEET SHORTCRUST PASTRY
MAKES 400 g (1 lb)
225 g (8 oz) plain flour
Pinch of salt

150 g (5 oz) cold butter, chopped
75 g (3 oz) caster or icing sugar
1 egg yolk
1 whole egg

To make the sweet pastry, sift the flour with the salt. Quickly rub in the butter in a bowl or cold work surface until the mixture resembles crumbs. Stir the sugar into the flour mixture, then add the egg yolk and egg. Work everything together and refrigerate for 30–60 minutes before using.

VARIATION
For a different flavour, add the finely grated zest of 1 lemon to the flour mix for a lemon crust, or the seeds from a vanilla pod. You could even use both.

Pasta Dough

This pasta dough can be used for lasagne, fettucine, ravioli and many more pasta dishes. You can make it by hand or in a food processor. It also freezes very well.

MAKES 450 g (1 lb) to Serve 4
250 g (9 oz) fine semolina or plain flour
A pinch of salt

¹/₂ teaspoon olive oil
2 eggs
3 egg yolks

Mix the semolina or flour with the salt and olive oil and mix well for 1 minute. Add the eggs and egg yolks and stir well until it becomes a dough. Knead the dough for 1–3 minutes until it has a smooth texture. Wrap it in cling film and chill for 30 minutes to rest.

The pasta is now ready to use. It can be rolled, cut and cooked straight away, or cut and left to dry and used later. If dried, the pasta will always take a little longer to cook.

Sweet and Savoury Pancakes

It certainly doesn't have to be Pancake Day to make these pancakes, which can be made both savoury and sweet. Perhaps their most classic sweet use is the flambéed Crêpes Suzettes, great for a bit of show at your dinner party. Or, of course, you can use savoury ones in your main course Fillet of Venison Wellington (see p. 138).

SERVES 4
225 g (8 oz) plain flour
A pinch of salt
2 eggs
600 ml (1 pint) milk

50 g (2 oz) unsalted butter, melted
Vegetable oil
2 teaspoons chopped fresh parsley or
  herbs (optional), if making savoury
  pancakes

Sift the flour and salt into a bowl. Beat the eggs into the milk, then whisk into the flour. Add the melted butter and whisk into the mix, which can now be used for sweet pancakes. For savoury pancakes, add the chopped herbs.

To cook the pancakes, pre-heat a 20 cm (8 in) or 15 cm (6 in) frying-pan; I prefer to make smaller pancakes. Lightly oil the pan and pour in some of the mixture, making sure the pan has only a thin layer of mix. Cook for 10–15 seconds until brown, turn in the pan and cook for a further 10–15 seconds. The pancake is now cooked. Keep warm while you make the remainder. Three small pancakes or two large will be enough for one portion.

Pancakes can be filled with anything you like – fruit or ice-cream for the sweet, seafood or vegetables for the savoury. Pancakes that are to be filled can, of course, be prepared in advance and then simply microwaved for 1–2 minutes to heat them through.

Frangipane (Almond Paste)

Some recipes are absolute classics that can be used in so many dishes. Well, this is certainly one of them. One thing I have found with this recipe is just how versatile it is. It's the mix that's used in Bakewell Tart and I use it in a few recipes in this book: Plum and Almond Slice (see p. 275), Cherry and Almond Tart (see p. 276) and Pear and Hazelnut 'Pasties' (see p. 300). For smaller quantities, halve or quarter the recipe.

MAKES ABOUT 900 g (2 lb)
225 g (8 oz) unsalted butter
225 g (8 oz) caster sugar

175 g (6 oz) ground almonds
50 g (2 oz) plain flour
4 eggs

Cream together the butter and sugar until almost white. Mix together the ground almonds and flour. Add an egg at a time to the butter and sugar mixture, sprinkling in a handful of the almond and flour at the same time. This helps the butter and sugar cream to accept the eggs. Once all the eggs have been added, just continue to fold in the remaining almond and flour mix. The frangipane is now ready to use.

VARIATIONS

Here are some alternatives for many different dishes.

The first alternative is to replace the ground almonds with ground hazelnuts. The mix cooks and tastes just as moist but with a definite hazelnut flavour.

To lift this or the almond mix, chopped hazelnuts, almonds or walnuts can be added (about 50 g/2 oz to this recipe). This gives you a completely different texture. It's also good, sometimes, to add a mix of two or even all three nuts. The variations are just unlimited: raisins, currants or sultanas can also be added. I like to soak them in brandy or a liqueur before adding them to the mix for extra taste. This, of course, can become a fruit and nut Bakewell tart, pasty or flan using some of each.

As I have mentioned in the Pear and Hazelnut 'Pasties' recipe, chocolate chips can be used, giving yet another texture. Why not have a fruit, nut and chocolate chip tart topped with Chocolate Ganache (see p. 314)? Of course, the frangipane can be made into a chocolate almond/hazelnut frangipane quite simply by omitting 25 g (1 oz) of the flour and replacing it with 25 g (1 oz) of cocoa. Also, to make it even richer 25–50 g (1–2 oz) of freshly grated plain chocolate can be added.

So now you'll have a chocolate frangipane mix that can also have all of those other flavours added, the nuts, chocolate chips, currants, etc., or all together. That would make a very rich and tasty chocolate fruit and nut tart.

Another – yes, there are more – combination is to add the finely grated zest of 2 oranges to the chocolate frangipane mix and bake this in a tart case and then completely cover the top with orange segments. These can now be heavily dusted with icing sugar and glazed under the grill or with a gas gun for a *brûlée*-style topping. Whichever way you glaze the tart, cover the pastry edge with thin foil all the way round to prevent it from catching and burning.

The grated orange zest can also be used in the basic frangipane mix (orange and hazelnut works particularly well) so if you fancy having a go at this recipe why not spread the pastry base with orange marmalade first (that will go very well with the chocolate and orange mix) and then top with the orange mix and bake? This can now be finished with the Chocolate Ganache (p. 314), already mentioned, on top or with the *brûléed* orange segments and served with Chocolate Sabayon (see p. 358) or Rich Chocolate Sauce (see p. 354). Prunes or Medjool dates also go very well in a plain frangipane or with chocolate orange or lemon.

Now about the lemon, here's yet another combination. Use the finely grated zest of 2–3 lemons, and you can also add the juice of one lemon to the mix. The lemon will also work with the chocolate frangipane; it's surprising how well lemon goes with chocolate.

I feel that an almond or hazelnut lemon frangipane tart eats very well when completely topped with berries. Fresh raspberries, blackcurrants or summer fruits make a good topping and also a fruit jam or lemon curd can be spread in the pastry first for extra taste. Brush the fruits with a jam syrup (1 tablespoon of jam to 2 tablespoons of water, boiled together) or perhaps top the whole tart with a meringue or lemon-flavoured meringue and glaze in a hot oven. Also the fruits, raspberries for example, can be placed in the tart sitting on top of the jam or lemon curd and then topped with the sponge and baked. This gives you a nice surprise when you cut into the flan. Remember, all of these can be made into individual tarts. A nice chocolate frangipane tart filled with chopped nuts and raisins, topped with mint and chocolate chip sorbet. How does that sound?

I think that's enough combinations for now …

Stock Syrups

These syrups have many uses. They are a great base for sorbets, for poaching, and for steeping fruits. Any spirits or liqueurs can be added; even teabags or fresh tea can be added for sorbets or ice-creams. I'm going to give two recipes. The first is very basic and the second is almost a dish on its own and packed with flavour. (For ice-creams and sorbets, you can also use the stock syrup recipe on p. 253.). All keep almost indefinitely if chilled. The fruit stock syrup is good to use in a fresh fruit salad and can also have mint added to take on another flavour.

FOR SIMPLE STOCK SYRUP
600 ml (1 pint) water
350 g (12 oz) caster sugar

FOR FRUIT STOCK SYRUP
600 ml (1 pint) water

350 g (12 oz) caster sugar
Pared zest and juice of 2 lemons
Pared zest and juice of 2 oranges
1/2 cinnamon stick
1 vanilla pod

Whichever syrup you are making, bring all the ingredients to the simmer, stirring to dissolve the sugar, then remove from the heat and allow to cool and infuse.

If you prefer a thicker, sweeter syrup, add an extra 100 g (4 oz) of caster sugar. If you are making the fruit stock syrup, it's best to leave the syrup with all ingredients included until needed, and thenjust drain off.

Veal or Beef Stock or *Jus*

This stock does take a long time to make, but it really is worth making and so satis-fying. It will give you great sauces and, of course, will store well in the freezer. It is best started in the morning, which will allow the stock to cook throughout the day. Ask your butcher for a few beef or veal trimmings to make the stock. (For information on ready-made alternatives, see p. 401.)

MAKES ABOUT 5 litres (9 pints) stock or 900 ml (1½ pints) *jus*
3 onions, halved
2–3 tablespoons water
2.25 kg (5 lb) veal or beef bones
225 g (8 oz) veal or beef trimmings
225 g (8 oz) carrots, coarsely chopped
3 celery sticks, coarsely chopped
1 leek, chopped
3–4 tomatoes, chopped
1 garlic clove, halved
1 bay leaf
1 sprig of fresh thyme

Pre-heat the oven to 120°C/250°F/gas ½.

Lay the onion halves flat in a roasting tray with the water. Place in the pre-heated oven and allow to caramelize slowly until they have totally softened and coloured. This process will take 1–2 hours. The sugars in the onions will slowly cook and give a wonderful taste. Put the onions on one side.

Increase the oven temperature to 200°C/400°F/gas 6.

Place all the bones and trimmings in a roasting tray and roast for about 30 minutes until well coloured. Roast the chopped carrots and celery in another roasting tray for about 20 minutes until lightly coloured.

When ready, add the bones, trimmings and vegetables to the onions in a large stock pan along with the leek, tomatoes, garlic, bay leaf and thyme. Fill the pan with cold water – you'll need about 5 litres (9 pints). Bring the stock to a simmer and skim off any impurities. Allow to cook for 6–8 hours, and with this you will achieve the maximum taste.

When ready, drain and discard the bones and vegetables. This is now your veal stock and you can cool it and freeze it in convenient quantities.

Alternatively, you can make a *jus* from the stock. Allow the liquid to boil and reduce down to about 900 ml (1½ pints), skimming occasionally. The stock should be thick and of a sauce consistency. Make sure that you taste all the time during reduction. If the sauce tastes right but is not thick enough, thicken it lightly with cornflour mixed in water. (Of course, I do hope that won't be necessary.) You now have a veal *jus*, a classic sauce.

Chicken Stock

Chicken stock is one of our most important bases. It's used for most soups and many cream sauces. It's also very simple to make. I'm sure your local butcher will help you out with some chicken bones. If not, then cook a boiling fowl with vegetables in water and you will have a tasty stock and the bird to eat as well. You'll need a large stock pot, about 8.5-litre (15-pint) capacity, but if you don't have one you can easily reduce the quantities. (For information on ready-made alternatives, see p. 401.)

MAKES 2.25 litres (4 pints)
2 onions, chopped
2 celery sticks, chopped
2 leeks, chopped
25 g (1 oz) unsalted butter
1 garlic clove, crushed

1 bay leaf
1 sprig of fresh thyme
A few black peppercorns
1.8 kg (4 lb) chicken carcasses, chopped
3–4 litres (6 pints) water

In a large stock pot, lightly soften the vegetables in the butter without colouring. Add the garlic, bay leaf, thyme, peppercorns and chopped carcasses. Cover with the cold water and bring to a simmer, skimming all the time. Allow the stock to simmer for 2–3 hours. Strain through a sieve. The stock is now ready to use and will keep well chilled or frozen.

Fish Stock

To make a good fish stock, you'll need a friendly fishmonger. Turbot and sole bones produce the best stock, giving a good, full taste and clear jelly-like finish. The stock is good for poaching fish and for making fish soups and sauces. (For information on ready-made alternatives, see p. 401.)

MAKES ABOUT 2 litres (3 1/2 pints)
1 large onion, sliced
1 leek, sliced
2 celery sticks, sliced
50 g (2 oz) unsalted butter
A few fresh parsley stalks

1 bay leaf
6 black peppercorns
900 g (2 lb) turbot or sole bones, washed
300 ml (10 fl oz) dry white wine
2.25 litres (4 pints) water

Sweat the vegetables in the butter without colouring. Add the parsley stalks, bay leaf and peppercorns. Chop the fish bones, making sure there are no blood clots left on them. Add them to the vegetables and continue to cook for a few minutes. Add the wine and boil to reduce until almost dry. Add the water and bring to a simmer. Allow to simmer for 20 minutes, then strain through a sieve. The stock is now ready to use, or to store for a few days in the fridge.

Vegetable Stock

The joy of cooking is the endless variations that recipes can have and this one is no exception. I think this gives you a fuller vegetable flavour than a usual vegetable stock, helped by the acidity of the lemon and bite from the pink peppercorns. It can be made without the carrots to give you a whiter stock, but the carrots do tend to give a sweetness to the finished flavour. I like to use this stock for vegetarian risottos and other braised dishes.

MAKES 1.2 litres (2 pints)

225 g (8 oz) carrots (optional)
2 onions
4 celery sticks
2 leeks, white part only
1 fennel bulb
1–2 courgettes
1 bay leaf
1 sprig of fresh thyme
1 teaspoon coriander seeds
1 teaspoon pink peppercorns
1/2 lemon, sliced
1.5 litres (21/2 pints) water
A pinch of salt
Vegetable oil

All the vegetables should first be cut into 1 cm (1/2 in) dice.

Warm the vegetable oil in a pan, then add all the diced vegetables along with the herbs, coriander, peppercorns and lemon. Cook without colour for 8–10 minutes, allowing them to soften slightly. Add the water with a good pinch of salt and bring to a simmer. Once at simmering point, cook for 30 minutes without a lid. During this time the stock should have reduced, increasing the flavour and depth. The stock can now be strained through a sieve, leaving you with about 1.2 litres (2 pints). If you find there is more than this quantity, then simply boil to reduce. You can also reduce if you find that the flavour is not full enough.

Tomato Stock

This must be one of the easiest stocks to make – it doesn't even have any cooking time. I use this recipe for a vegetarian tomato and spinach risotto. The tomato stock on its own is very strong, due to the acidity of the tomatoes. I normally mix half tomato with half vegetable stock to gives you a good balance between the two.

For the best results and maximum quality, it's best to use overripe tomatoes. These can be bought from the local greengrocer at a very good price and also have a lot more flavour. I often have tomatoes sitting in my fridge for far too long, so this is a great way of using them up. You can just make some from a few tomatoes and freeze it until you have enough to make the risotto (see p. 205).

MAKES 450 ml (15 fl oz)
1.5–1.75 kg (3–4 lb) overripe tomatoes
600 ml (1 pint) Vegetable Stock (see p. 400)

Quarter the tomatoes and blitz in a food processor or liquidizer with the stock. Now just leave to drain in a sieve or muslin cloth. Do not push through a sieve or you will be left with a tomato coulis. It's only the water that we want to use. This is best left overnight in the fridge or in a cool place. In the morning, the natural waters will have completely drained off, giving you a good strong tomato stock.

NOTE

For totally natural tomato stock blitz them on their own and leave to drain in the sieve or cloth. This will give you pure tomato water that can be mixed with the vegetable stock.

Alternative Stocks and Sauces

Making fresh stocks at home is not always possible, so here are a few good commercial alternatives I have tried, which make some of my recipes a little easier.

FISH AND CHICKEN STOCKS

Alternatives to these can be found in the chill cabinet of most quality supermarkets. They are sold in plastic tubs each containing about 284 ml (9–10 fl oz). The beauty of these is they taste great, they have good colour and jelly texture, and they are sold as stocks ready to use. They really are the best I've found but, if you can't get hold of them, there are also some good quality stock cubes.

BEEF AND VEAL *JUS*

In the basic recipe, these start out as stocks and then for use in other recipes they are reduced to a sauce consistency. I've found a sauce which will cut out all of this, and is an instant *jus* to use as a base sauce in many of the recipes asking for veal or beef *jus*. Madeira Wine Gravy or White Wine Gravy are both made by Crosse & Blackwell in their Bonne Cuisine range, and should be available in just about every supermarket or good grocery shop. The Madeira flavour gives good body and, when made, it has a lovely glossy finish. My only advice is to mix them with 600 ml (1 pint) of water instead of 300 ml (10 fl oz). This way, when slow-braising or stewing, there's room for reduction and they won't become too thick.

VARIATIONS

Another sauce I found, also in the Bonne Cuisine range, is their Hollandaise Sauce. If you are unsure about making hollandaise, give this version a try; it's so easy.

There's only one other small suggestion. If you don't have any chillies, use the chilli sauce made by Maggi. It's sold in bottles and can be added slowly to taste.

As for dried pastas and ready-made pastry, all varieties can easily be found in local shops. If you're lucky enough to have a good delicatessen nearby, then perhaps buy your pasta there; it's often made on the premises.

Gremolata

Gremolata is an Italian recipe that is normally used to serve with a veal osso bucco. Basically it's a mix of crushed garlic, zest of lemon and chopped flatleaf parsley. This is then sprinkled over the finished dish.

With this recipe you can do exactly that, or just sprinkle it over a chicken noodle dish to give it some extra zing. However, I'm turning this into a gremolata butter. This keeps well chilled or frozen. It can be used to toss with new potatoes or vegetables, or to melt over grilled fish or meat. You can leave out the parsley, if you prefer, and simply add it to any finished dish. I also use the gremolata in a recipe with cod (see p. 96), worked into mashed potatoes.

MAKES ABOUT 250 g (9 oz)
2–3 garlic cloves, crushed
Juice and finely grated zest of 3 large
    lemons

225 g (8 oz) unsalted butter
Salt and freshly ground black pepper
1/2–1 bunch of fresh flatleaf parsley,
    chopped

Mix the crushed garlic with the chopped lemon zest and lemon juice either with a fork or in a food processor. Mix into the butter and season with salt and pepper. Add the parsley and stir well. The gremolata butter is now ready and the flavours work themselves into the butter.

Garam Masala

Garam Masala was a mixture of spices put together originally to 'spice' people up. This lifted the body and prepared you for a hard winter and work. It was quite a hot spice and helped set people's appetites in India for hot dishes. It has since become a very varied mixture of spices for different dishes, some hotter than others.

The spice mixture does not have to be used just in Indian curry dishes, it will liven up vegetarian risottos, pancakes, ratatouille, lentils and most tomato-based dishes, as well as cream and yoghurt sauces. This recipe is a combination that should suit all of these. Once made, keep in an airtight container and use when wanted. Of course, you can buy garam masala already made, but the aromatic smell and flavour when you've made it yourself is wonderful.

MAKES ABOUT 50 g (2 oz)
2 tablespoons coriander seeds
2 tablespoons cumin seeds
1 teaspoon cardamom seeds
1 cinnamon stick
2 bay leaves

1 tablespoon black peppercorns
2 teaspoons cloves
1/2 teaspoon freshly grated
  nutmeg
1/4 teaspoon ground mace
1/4 teaspoon ground ginger

Dry roast all the ingredients, except the nutmeg, mace and ginger, in a dry pan over a medium heat until they colour and become aromatic. Leave to cool, then add the remaining spices and grind to a powder in a coffee grinder or blender. Store in an airtight jar.

Bone Marrow Dumplings

These dumplings can be eaten as a savoury dish and go particularly well with pan-fried diced bacon, button onions and button mushrooms in a red wine sauce. They are used mostly as an accompaniment in beef stews and casseroles but I also use them with a grilled steak in red wine sauce. Just one good dumpling a portion is enough, and the beauty of using this recipe is that it keeps for three or four days if chilled. So if you want to lift just a simple, ordinary steak then have a go at this recipe.

SERVES 4
100 g (4 oz) fresh bone marrow
100 g (4 oz) white breadcrumbs
2 tablespoons double cream
3–4 egg yolks

1 heaped tablespoon chopped fresh
  parsley
A pinch of freshly grated nutmeg
Salt and freshly ground black pepper
Chicken Stock (see p. 399) or water

Break the bone marrow down in a food processor, then add the breadcrumbs. Add the cream and 3 yolks with the chopped parsley. Add the remaining yolk if necessary to make a stiff mixture. Season with nutmeg, salt and pepper and chill for 1 hour before cooking to help set the mix.

Bring a pan of stock or water to the boil. The mix can be either shaped into ovals between 2 tablespoons or simply rolled into balls and dropped into simmering stock. The dumplings should be ready in 10–15 minutes. You can then add them to a stew or braised dish.

VARIATION
Try using other herbs instead of the parsley; thyme or sage taste particularly good.

Index